村田雄介

Yusuke Murata

I remember back when *Eyeshield* first started serialization. I was 24 years old. The first editor said the series would continue for at least 30 volumes and that I would be about 30 years old by that time. My head spun and I fell into a deep depression. Now that I've reached my thirties and so has the series, when I look back at myself, I realize I didn't understand how happy and thankful I would be to have the readers support me for so many years.

稲垣理一郎

Riichiro Inagaki

When I went to an American NFL game for research, I could go down by the bench and watch the players from up close during the game. All of the players radiated an overwhelming ferocity, but one lineman was especially intimidating. I felt like I was looking at a dinosaur and thought, "If I ever had to fight this guy, I would die." That's how I got the idea for Gao.

Eyeshield 21 is the most exciting football manga to hit the scene. A collaborative effort between writer Riichiro Inagaki and artist Yusuke Murata, *Eyeshield 21* was originally serialized in Japan's *Weekly Shonen Jump*. An OAV created for Shueisha's Anime Tour is available in Japan, and the *Eyeshield 21* hit animated TV series debuted in spring 2005!

EYESHIELD 21
Vol. 31: And the Winner Is...
SHONEN JUMP ADVANCED Manga Edition

STORY BY RIICHIRO INAGAKI
ART BY YUSUKE MURATA

English Adaptation & Translation/John Werry, HC Language Solutions, Inc.
Touch-up Art & Lettering/James Gaubatz
Cover & Graphic Design/Sean Lee
Editor/Kit Fox

VP, Production/Alvin Lu
VP, Sales & Product Marketing/Gonzalo Ferreyra
VP, Creative/Linda Espinosa
Publisher/Hyoe Narita

EYESHIELD 21 © 2002 by Riichiro Inagaki, Yusuke Murata.
All rights reserved. First published in Japan in 2002 by SHUEISHA Inc., Tokyo. English
translation rights arranged by SHUEISHA Inc.

Printed in Canada

Published by VIZ Media, LLC
P.O. Box 77010
San Francisco, CA 94107

10 9 8 7 6 5 4 3 2 1
First printing, April 2010

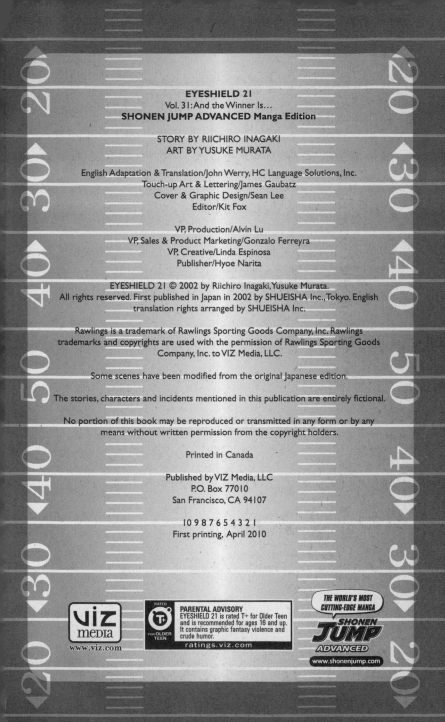

EYESHIELD 21

Vol. 31: And the Winner Is...

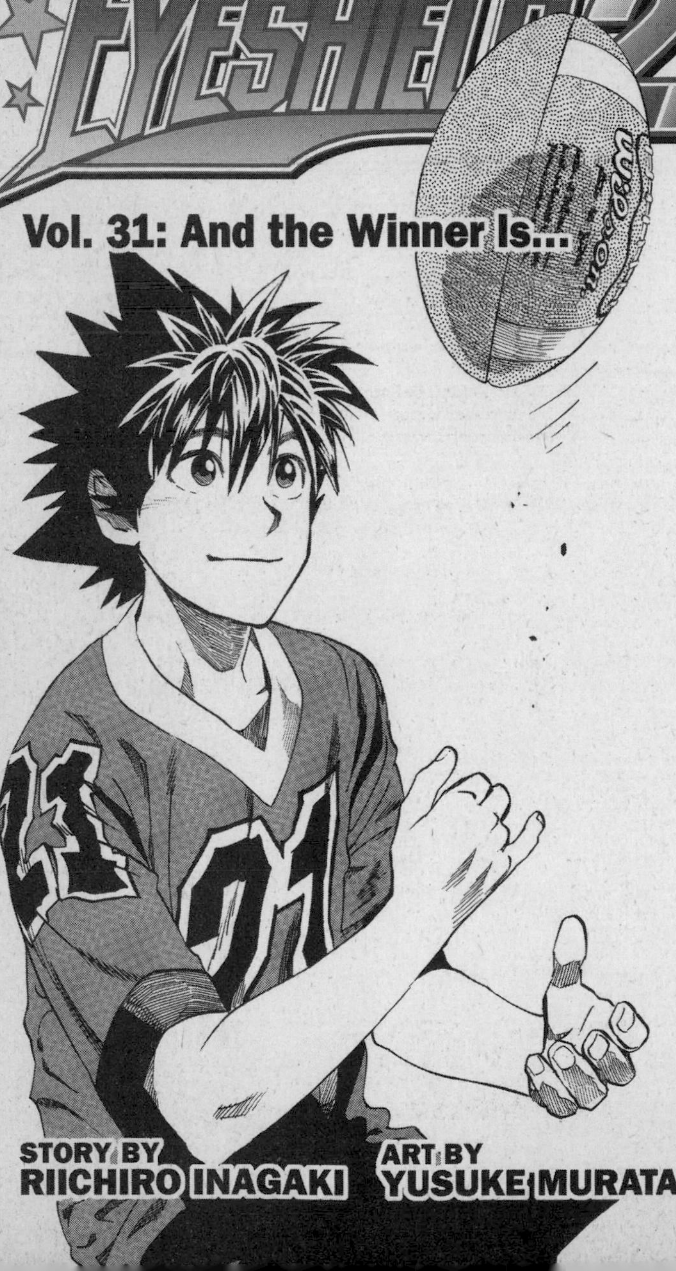

STORY BY
RIICHIRO INAGAKI

ART BY
YUSUKE MURATA

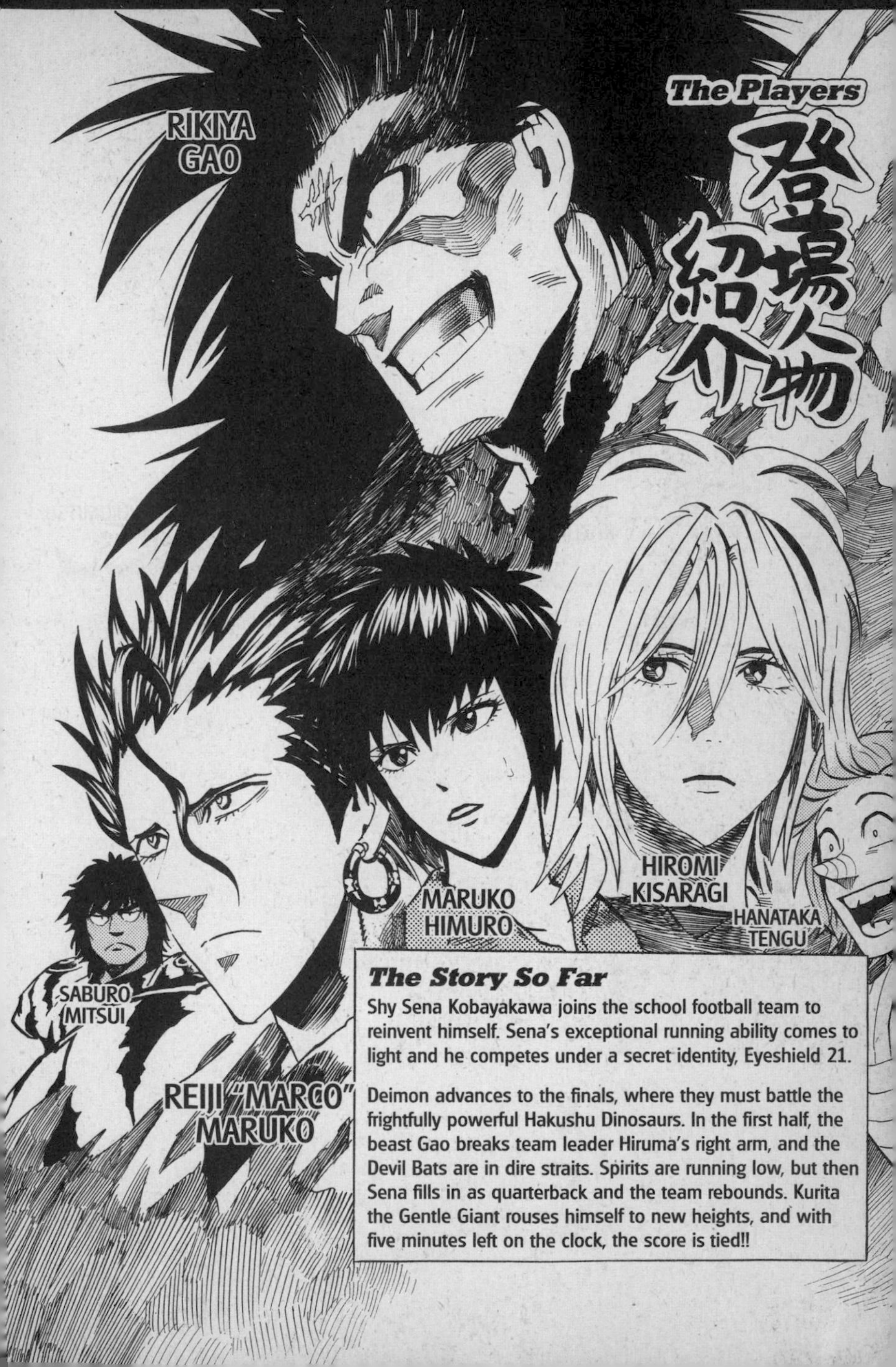
The Players
登場人物紹介
RIKIYA GAO
HANATAKA TENGU
HIROMI KISARAGI
MARUKO HIMURO
REIJI "MARCO" MARUKO
SABURO MITSUI

The Story So Far

Shy Sena Kobayakawa joins the school football team to reinvent himself. Sena's exceptional running ability comes to light and he competes under a secret identity, Eyeshield 21.

Deimon advances to the finals, where they must battle the frightfully powerful Hakushu Dinosaurs. In the first half, the beast Gao breaks team leader Hiruma's right arm, and the Devil Bats are in dire straits. Spirits are running low, but then Sena fills in as quarterback and the team rebounds. Kurita the Gentle Giant rouses himself to new heights, and with five minutes left on the clock, the score is tied!!

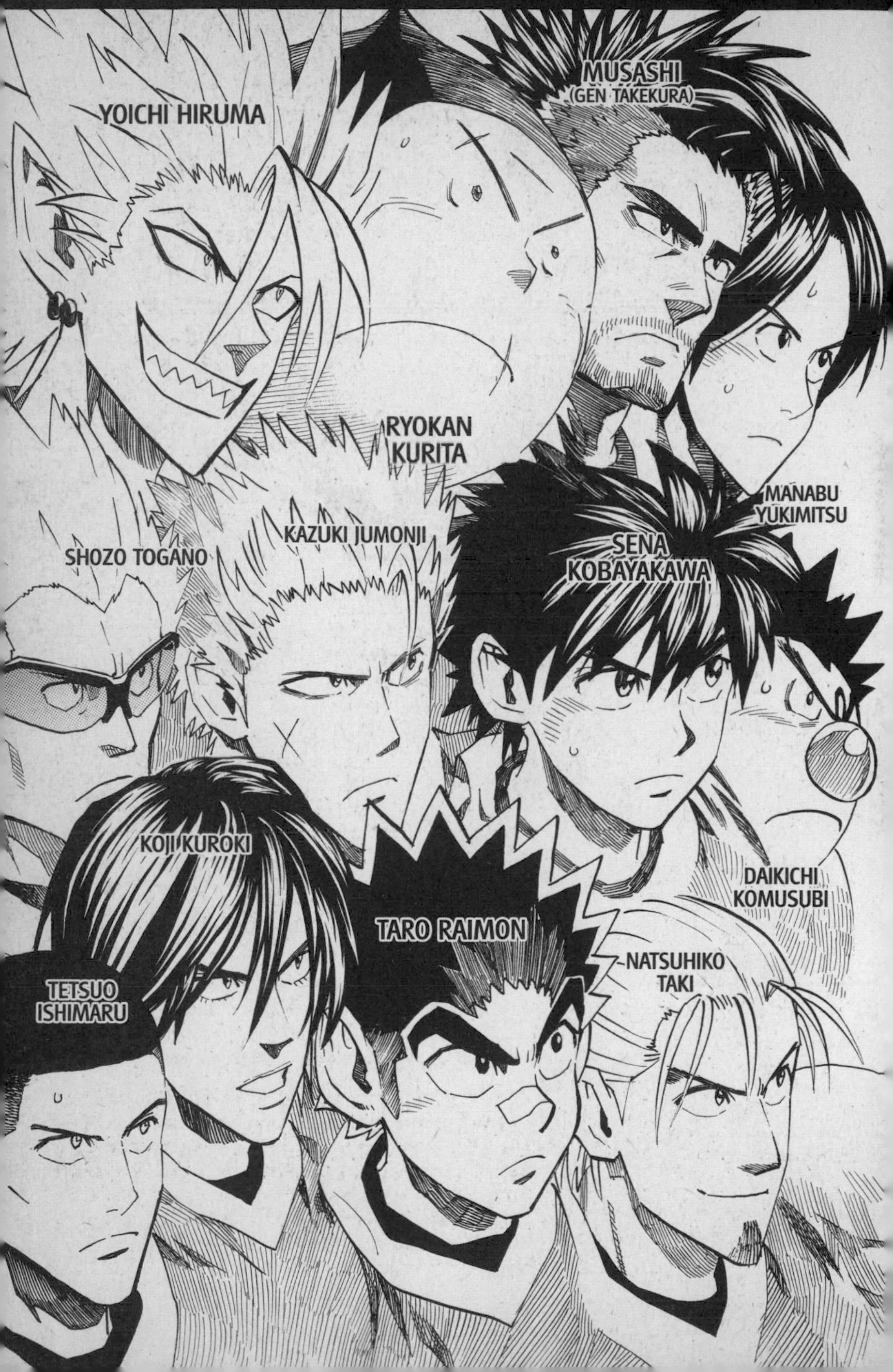
MUSASHI
(GEN TAKEKURA)
YOICHI HIRUMA
RYOKAN KURITA
MANABU YUKIMITSU
SENA KOBAYAKAWA
KAZUKI JUMONJI
SHOZO TOGANO
DAIKICHI KOMUSUBI
KOJI KUROKI
TARO RAIMON
NATSUHIKO TAKI
TETSUO ISHIMARU

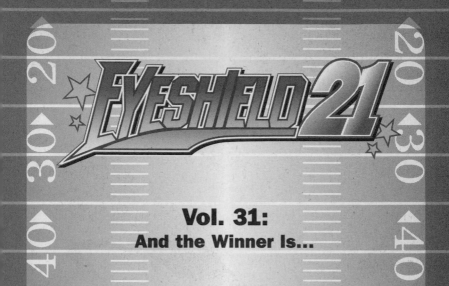

Vol. 31:
And the Winner Is...

CONTENTS

Chapter 269 The Strongest Guardian

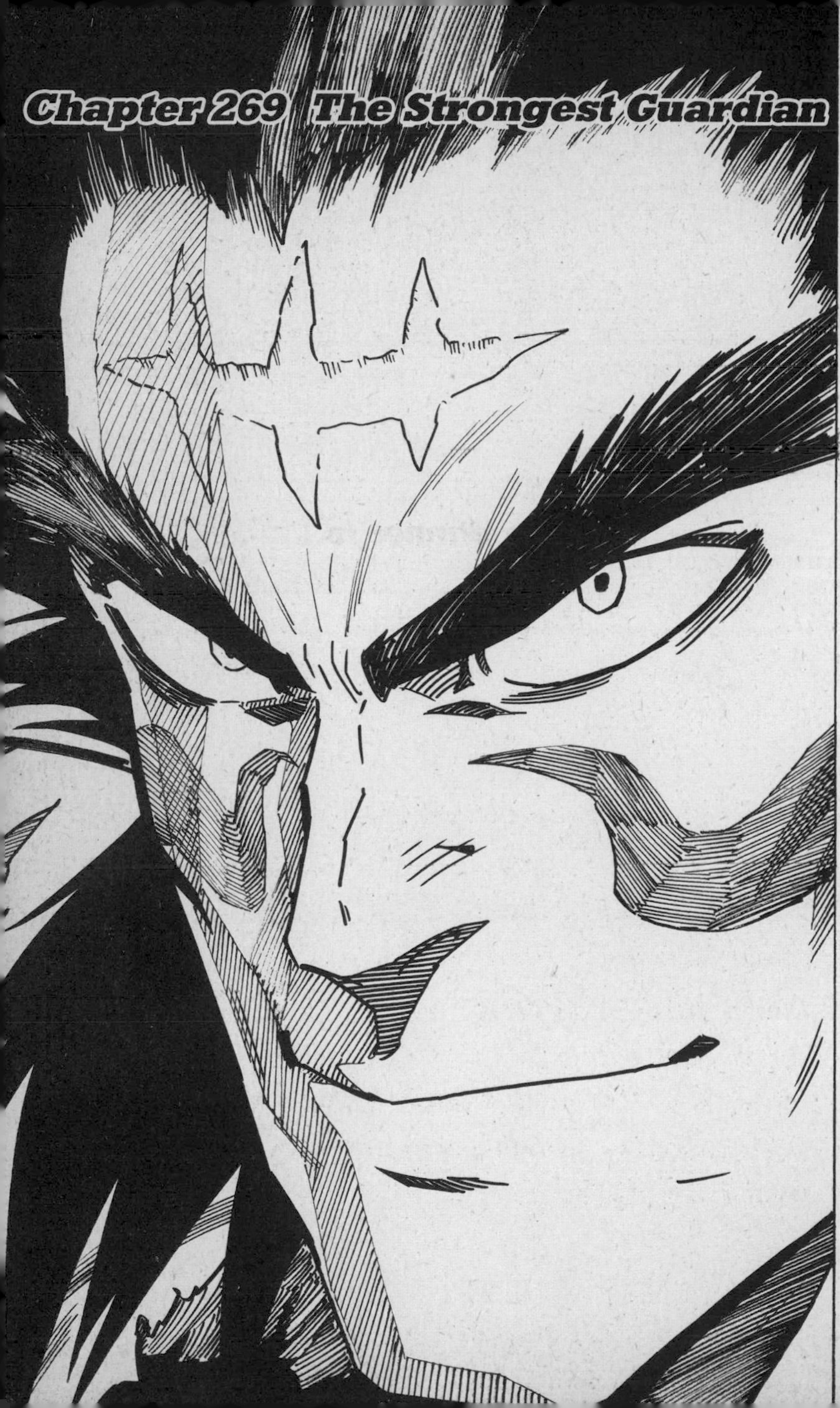

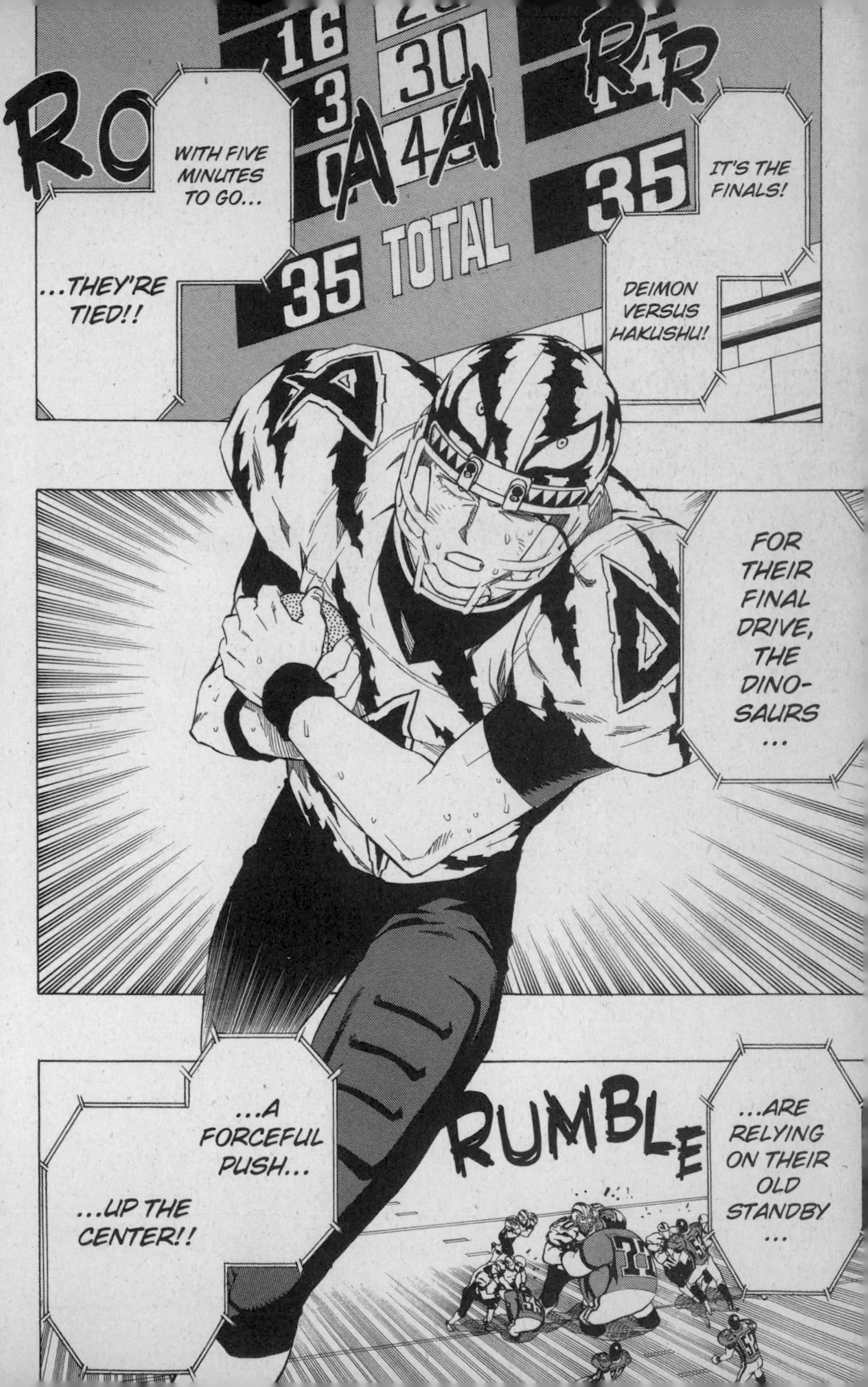
ROAAAR
IT'S THE FINALS!
DEIMON VERSUS HAKUSHU!
35 TOTAL 35
WITH FIVE MINUTES TO GO...
...THEY'RE TIED!!
FOR THEIR FINAL DRIVE, THE DINO-SAURS ...
...ARE RELYING ON THEIR OLD STANDBY ...
RUMBLE
...A FORCEFUL PUSH...
...UP THE CENTER!!

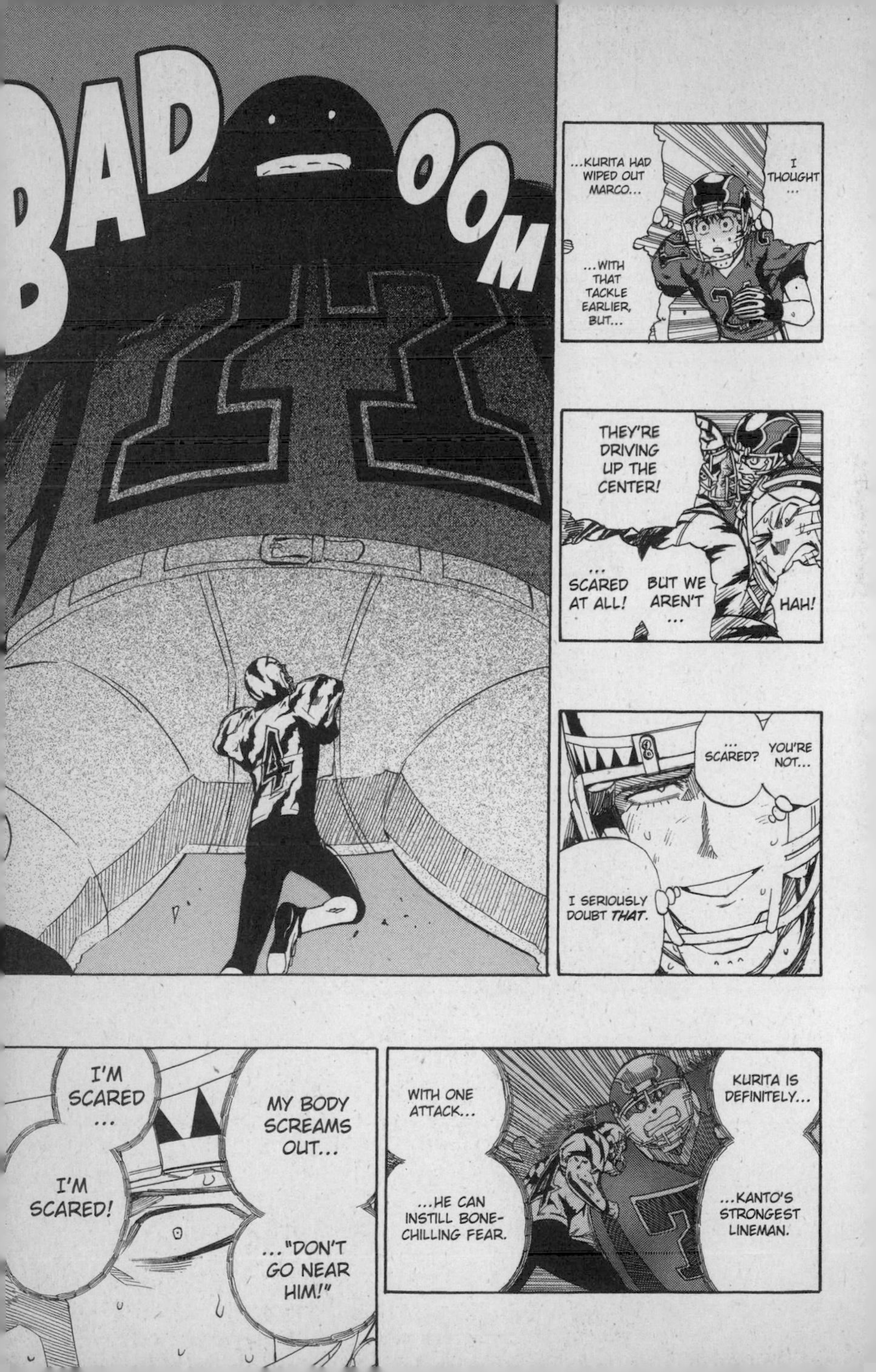
I THOUGHT...
...KURITA HAD WIPED OUT MARCO...
...WITH THAT TACKLE EARLIER, BUT...
THEY'RE DRIVING UP THE CENTER!
HAH!
BUT WE AREN'T...
...SCARED AT ALL!
YOU'RE NOT...
...SCARED?
I SERIOUSLY DOUBT *THAT*.
BAD-OOM
KURITA IS DEFINITELY...
...KANTO'S STRONGEST LINEMAN.
WITH ONE ATTACK...
...HE CAN INSTILL BONE-CHILLING FEAR.
MY BODY SCREAMS OUT...
..."DON'T GO NEAR HIM!"
I'M SCARED...
I'M SCARED!

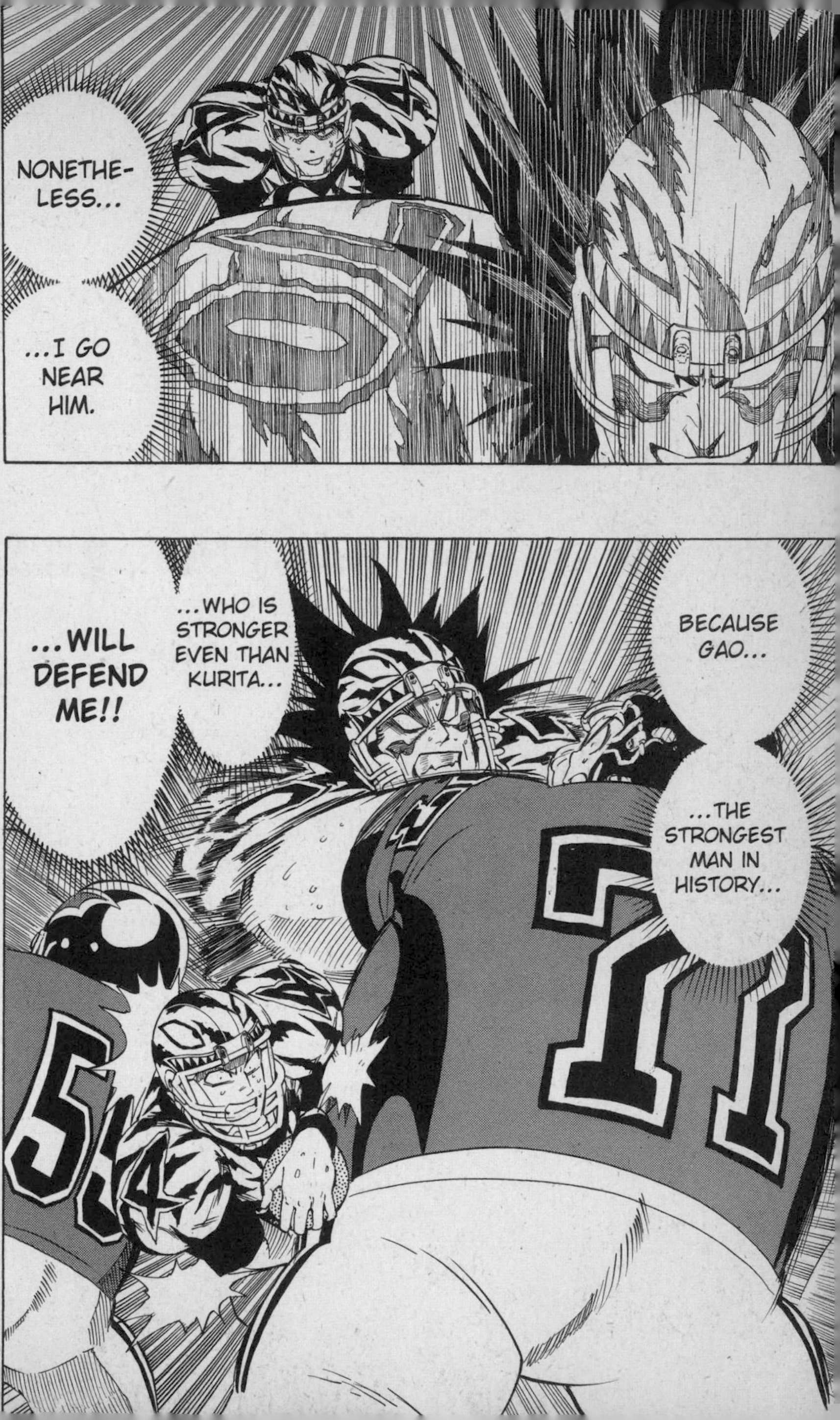
NONETHE-LESS...
...I GO NEAR HIM.
BECAUSE GAO...
...THE STRONGEST MAN IN HISTORY...
...WHO IS STRONGER EVEN THAN KURITA...
...WILL DEFEND ME!!

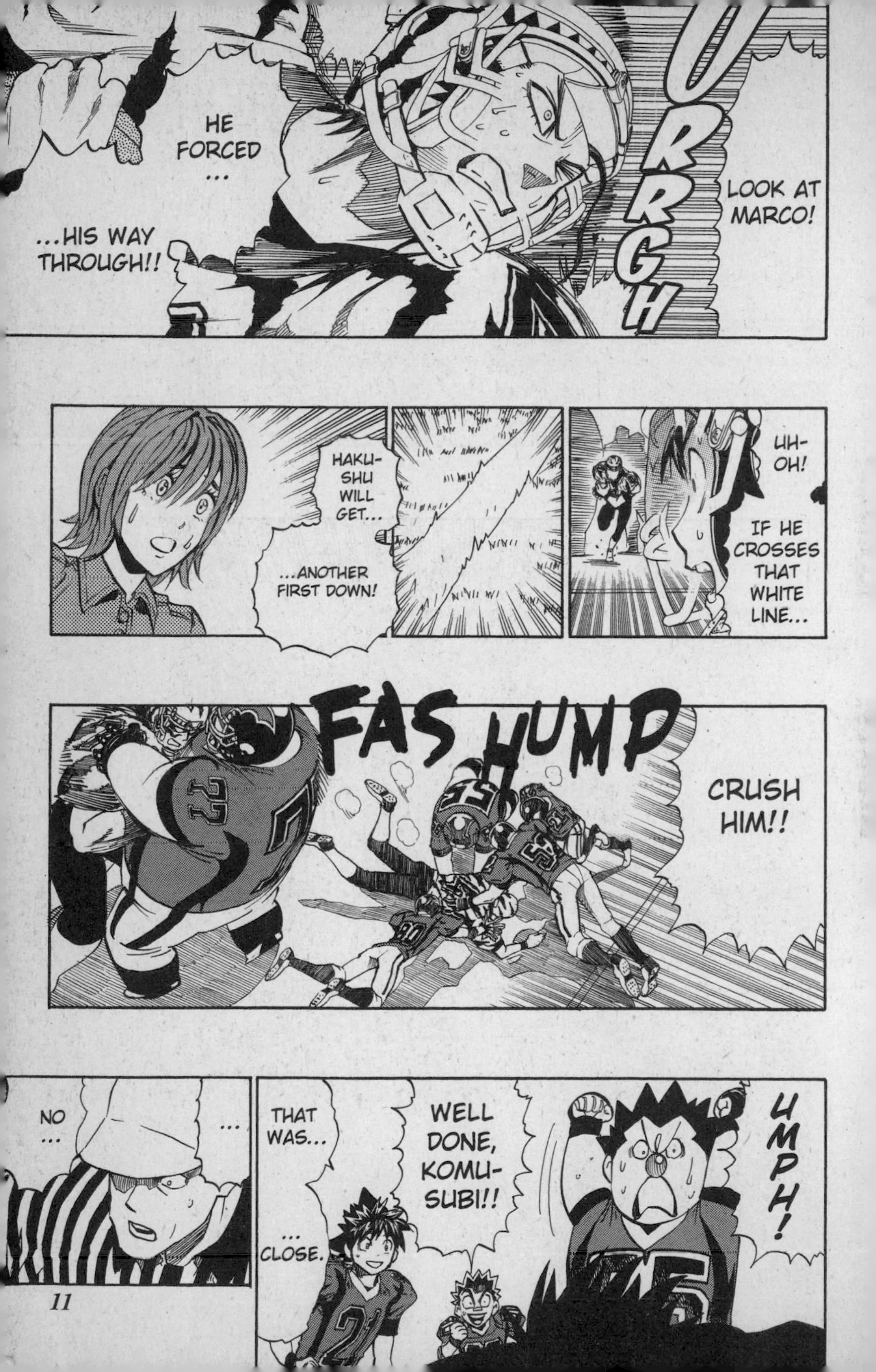
URRRGH
LOOK AT MARCO!
HE FORCED ...
...HIS WAY THROUGH!!
UH-OH!
IF HE CROSSES THAT WHITE LINE...
HAKU-SHU WILL GET...
...ANOTHER FIRST DOWN!
FASHUMP
CRUSH HIM!!
UMPH!
WELL DONE, KOMU-SUBI!!
THAT WAS...
...CLOSE.
NO ...
...

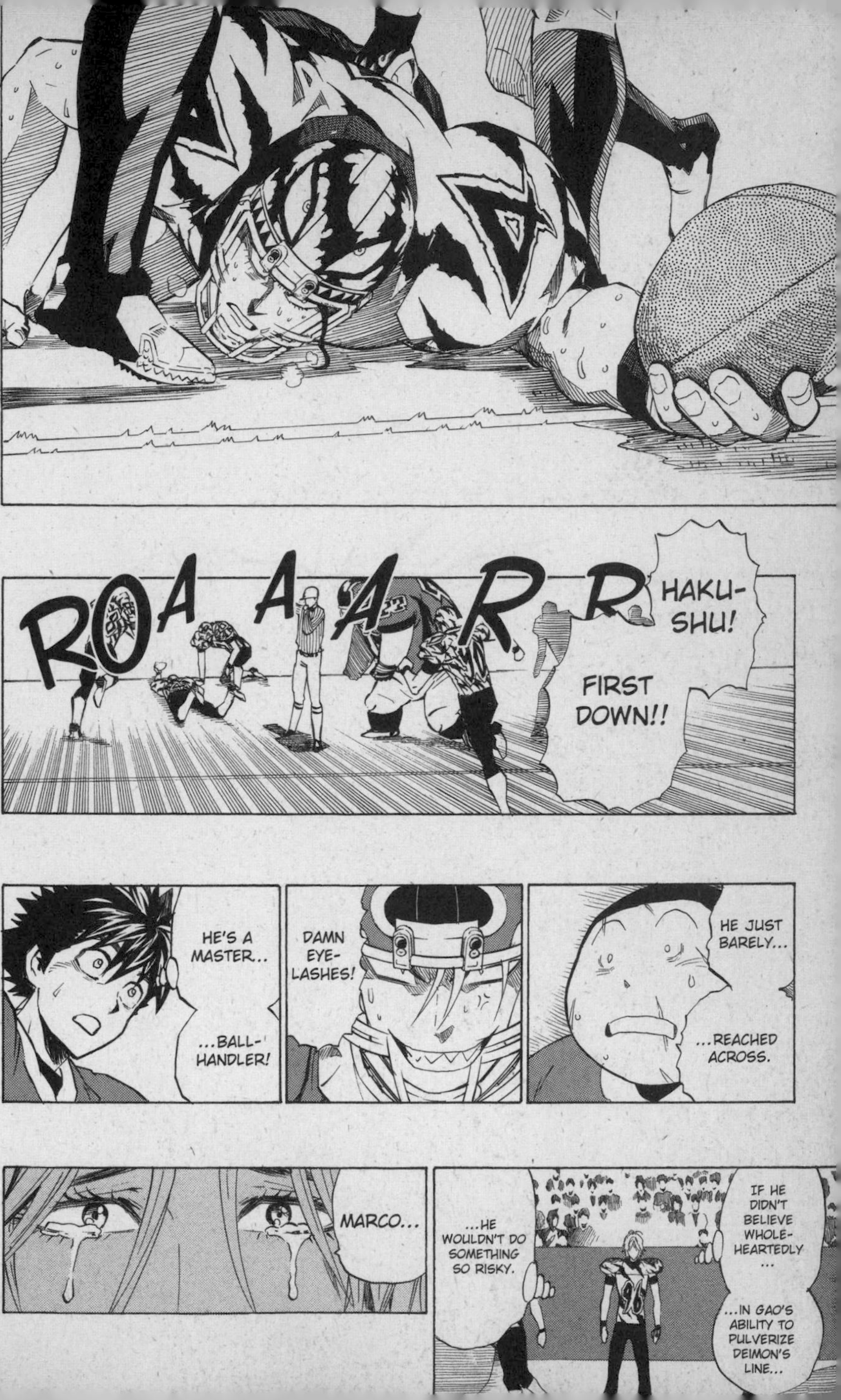
HAKU-SHU!
FIRST DOWN!!
ROAAARR
HE JUST BARELY...
...REACHED ACROSS.
DAMN EYE-LASHES!
HE'S A MASTER...
...BALL-HANDLER!
IF HE DIDN'T BELIEVE WHOLE-HEARTEDLY...
...IN GAO'S ABILITY TO PULVERIZE DEIMON'S LINE...
...HE WOULDN'T DO SOMETHING SO RISKY.
MARCO...

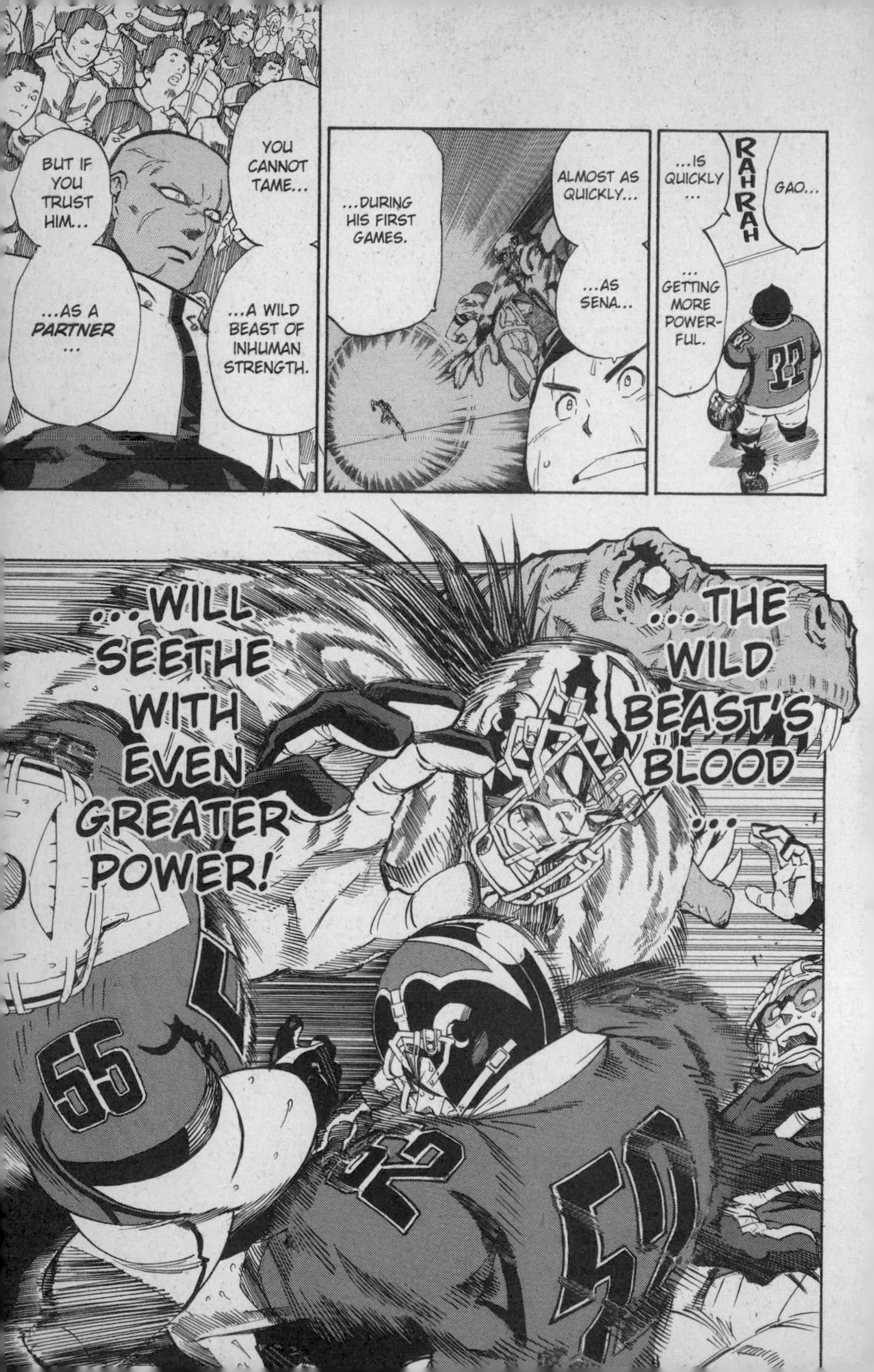
GAO...
RAHRAH
...IS QUICKLY...
...GETTING MORE POWER-FUL.
ALMOST AS QUICKLY...
...AS SENA...
...DURING HIS FIRST GAMES.
YOU CANNOT TAME...
...A WILD BEAST OF INHUMAN STRENGTH.
BUT IF YOU TRUST HIM...
...AS A *PARTNER*...
...THE WILD BEAST'S BLOOD...
...WILL SEETHE WITH EVEN GREATER POWER!

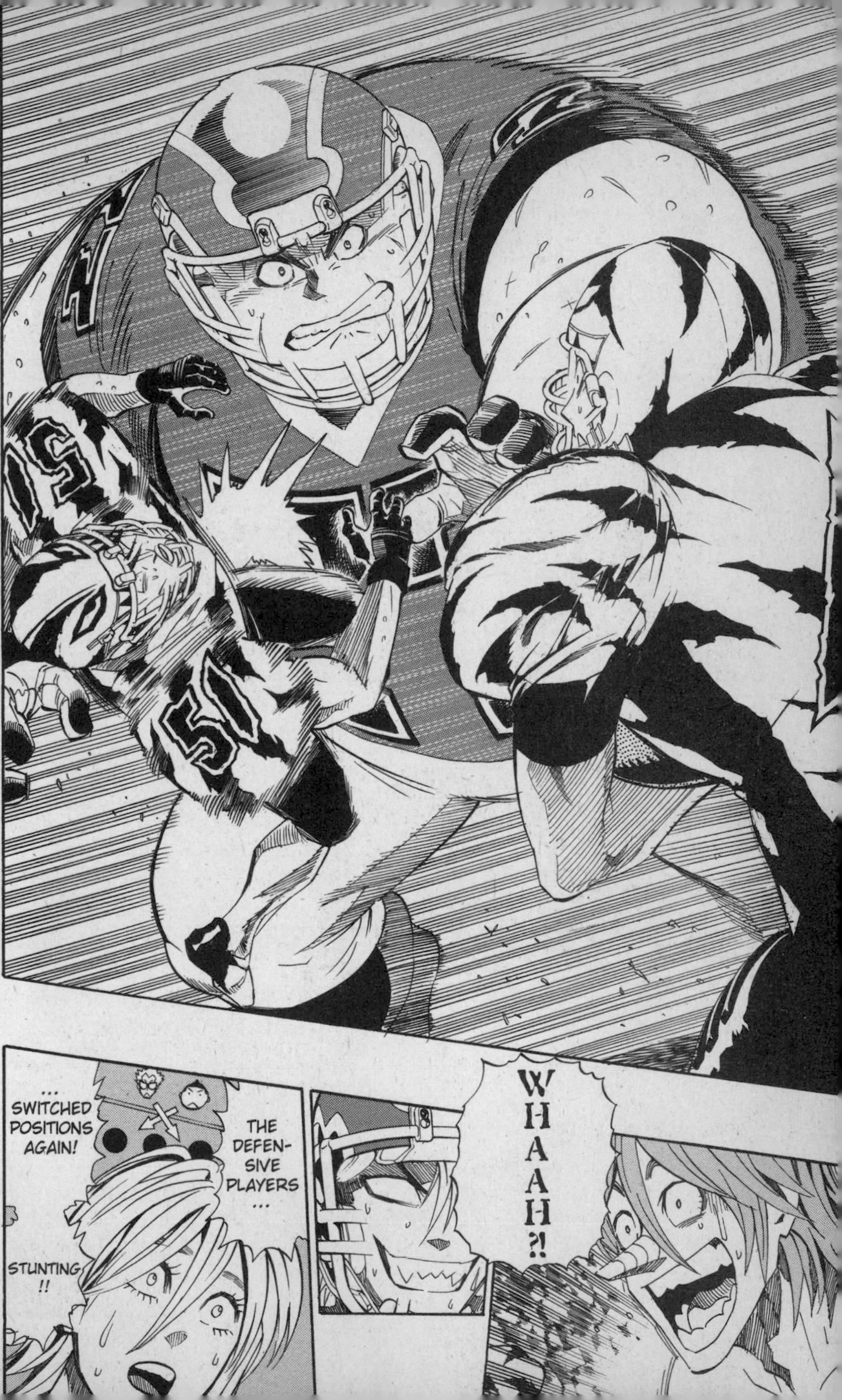
WHAAAH?!
THE DEFENSIVE PLAYERS...
...SWITCHED POSITIONS AGAIN!
STUNTING!!

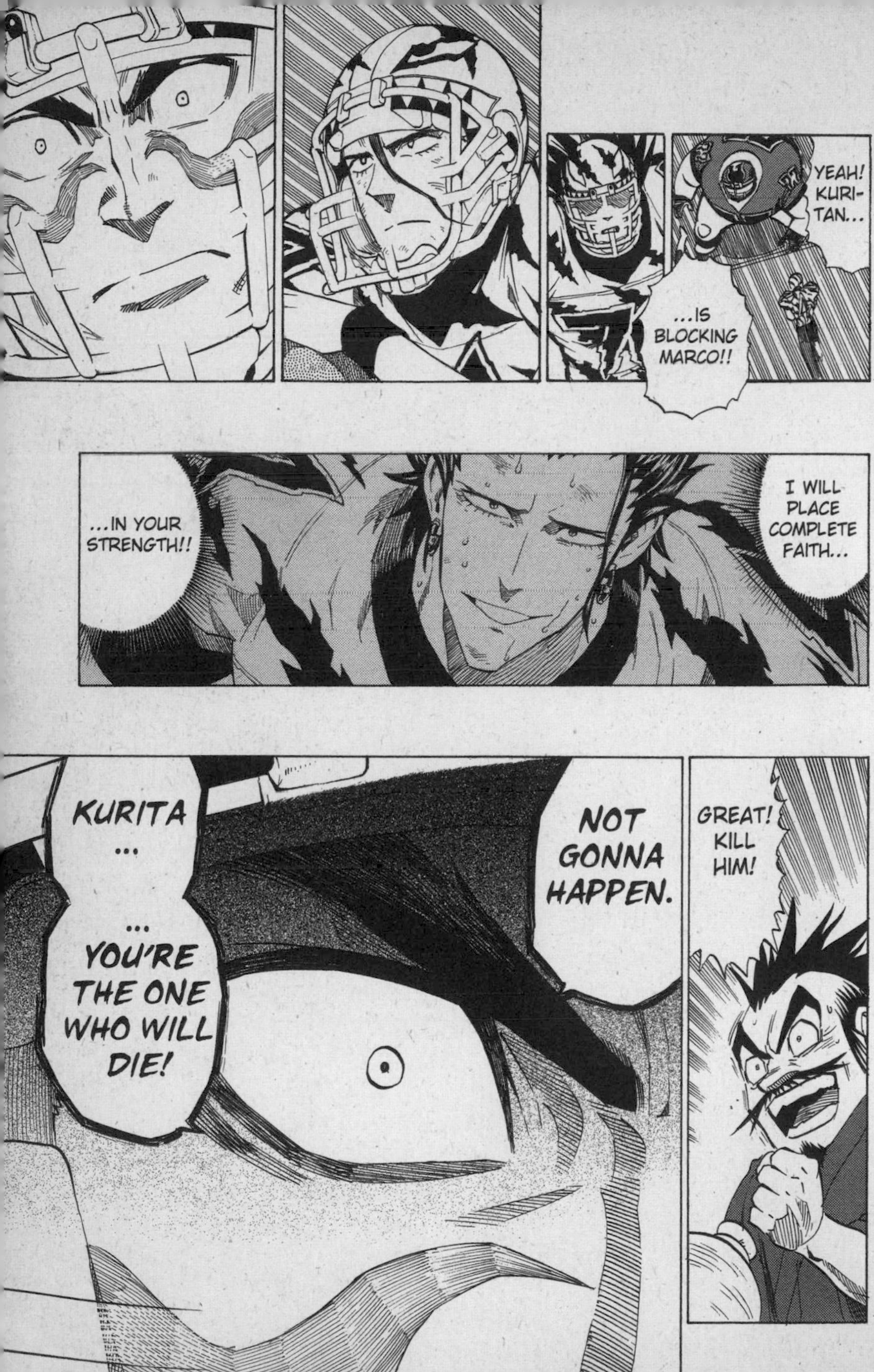
YEAH! KURI-TAN...
...IS BLOCKING MARCO!!
I WILL PLACE COMPLETE FAITH...
...IN YOUR STRENGTH!!
GREAT! KILL HIM!
NOT GONNA HAPPEN.
KURITA ...
... YOU'RE THE ONE WHO WILL DIE!

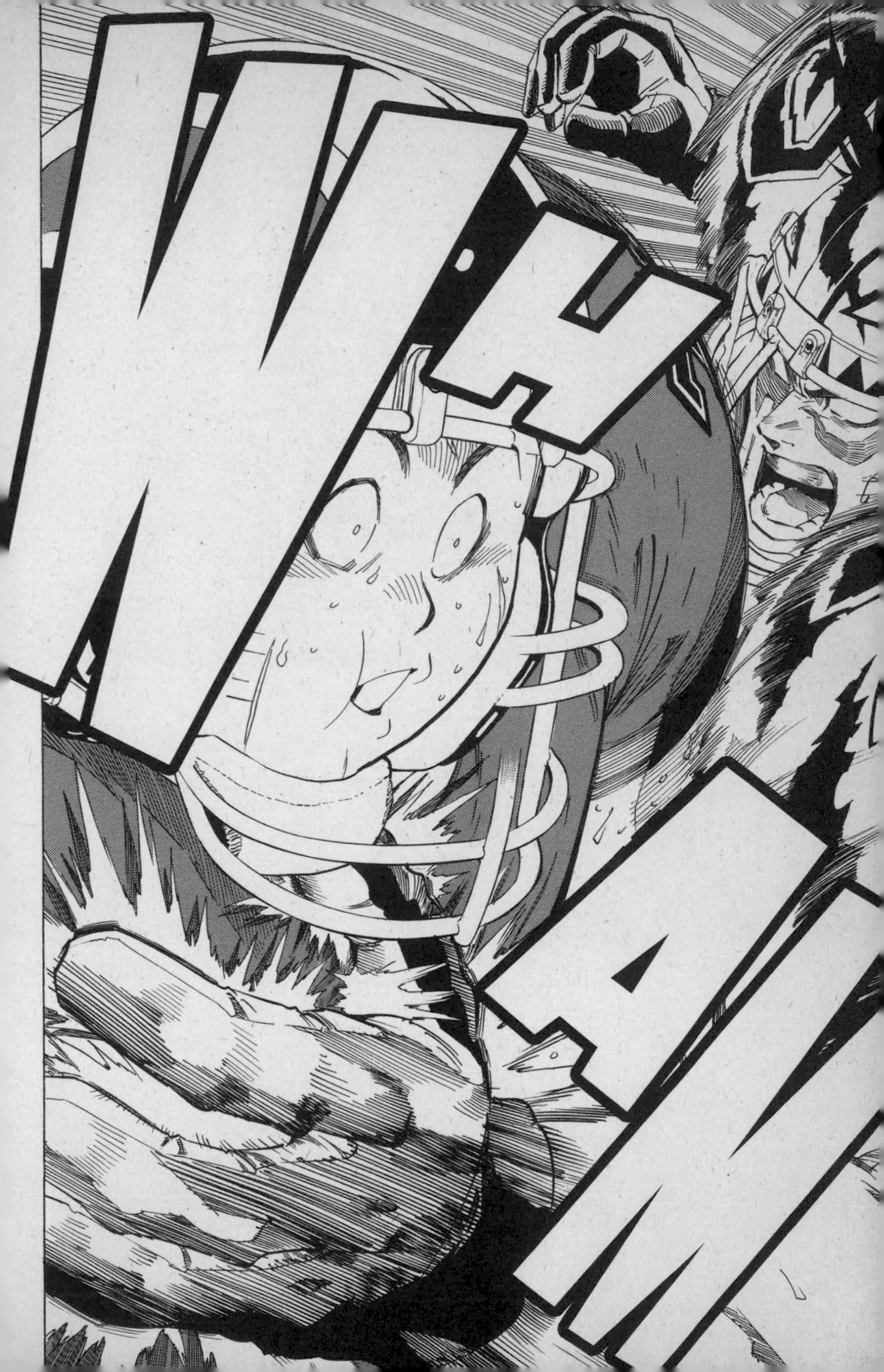
WHAM

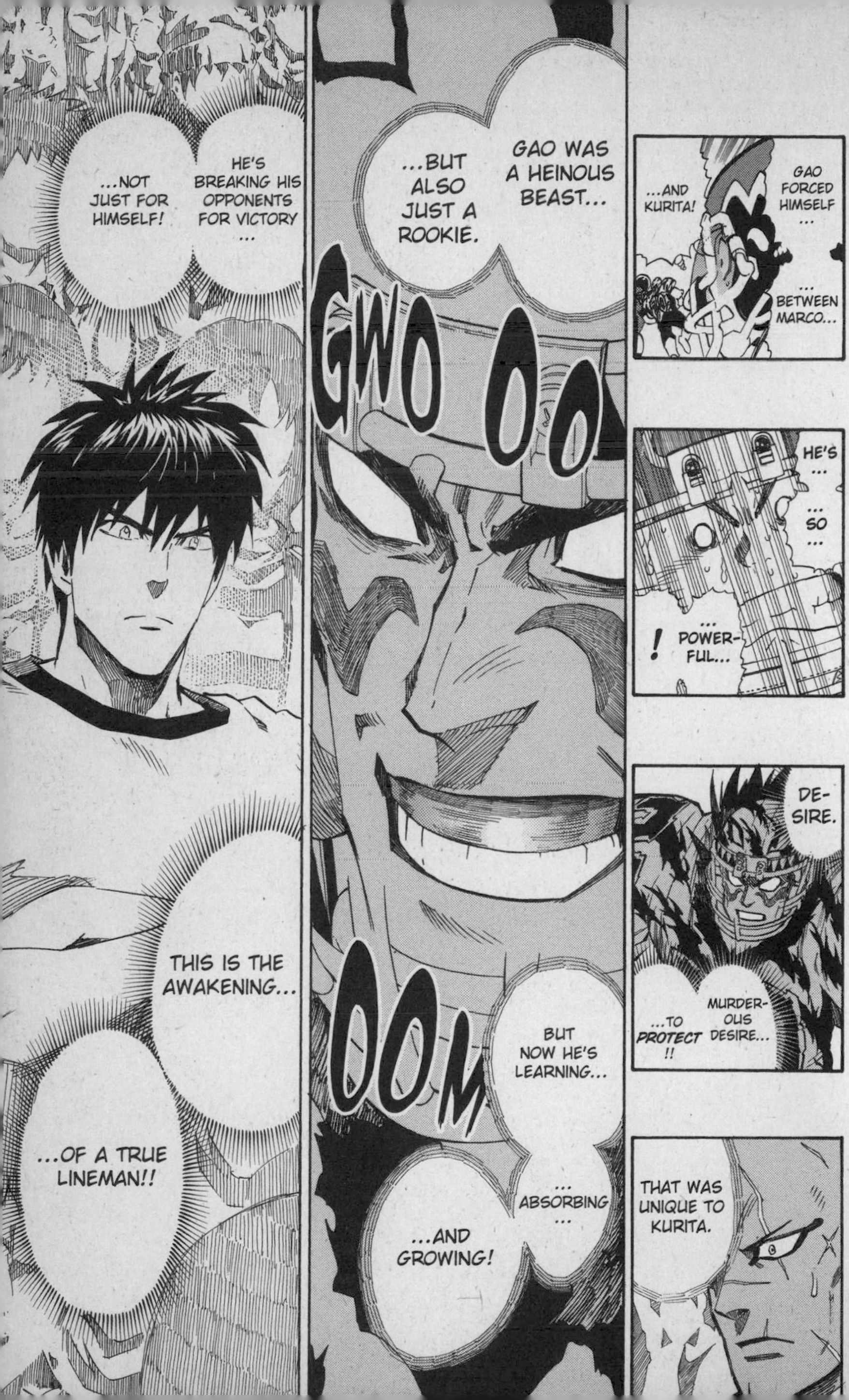
GAO FORCED HIMSELF ...
... BETWEEN MARCO...
...AND KURITA!
HE'S ...
... SO ...
... POWER-FUL...
!
DE-SIRE.
MURDER-OUS DESIRE...
...TO PROTECT !!
THAT WAS UNIQUE TO KURITA.
GAO WAS A HEINOUS BEAST...
...BUT ALSO JUST A ROOKIE.
GWOOOOOM
BUT NOW HE'S LEARNING...
... ABSORBING ...
...AND GROWING!
HE'S BREAKING HIS OPPONENTS FOR VICTORY ...
...NOT JUST FOR HIMSELF!
THIS IS THE AWAKENING...
...OF A TRUE LINEMAN!!

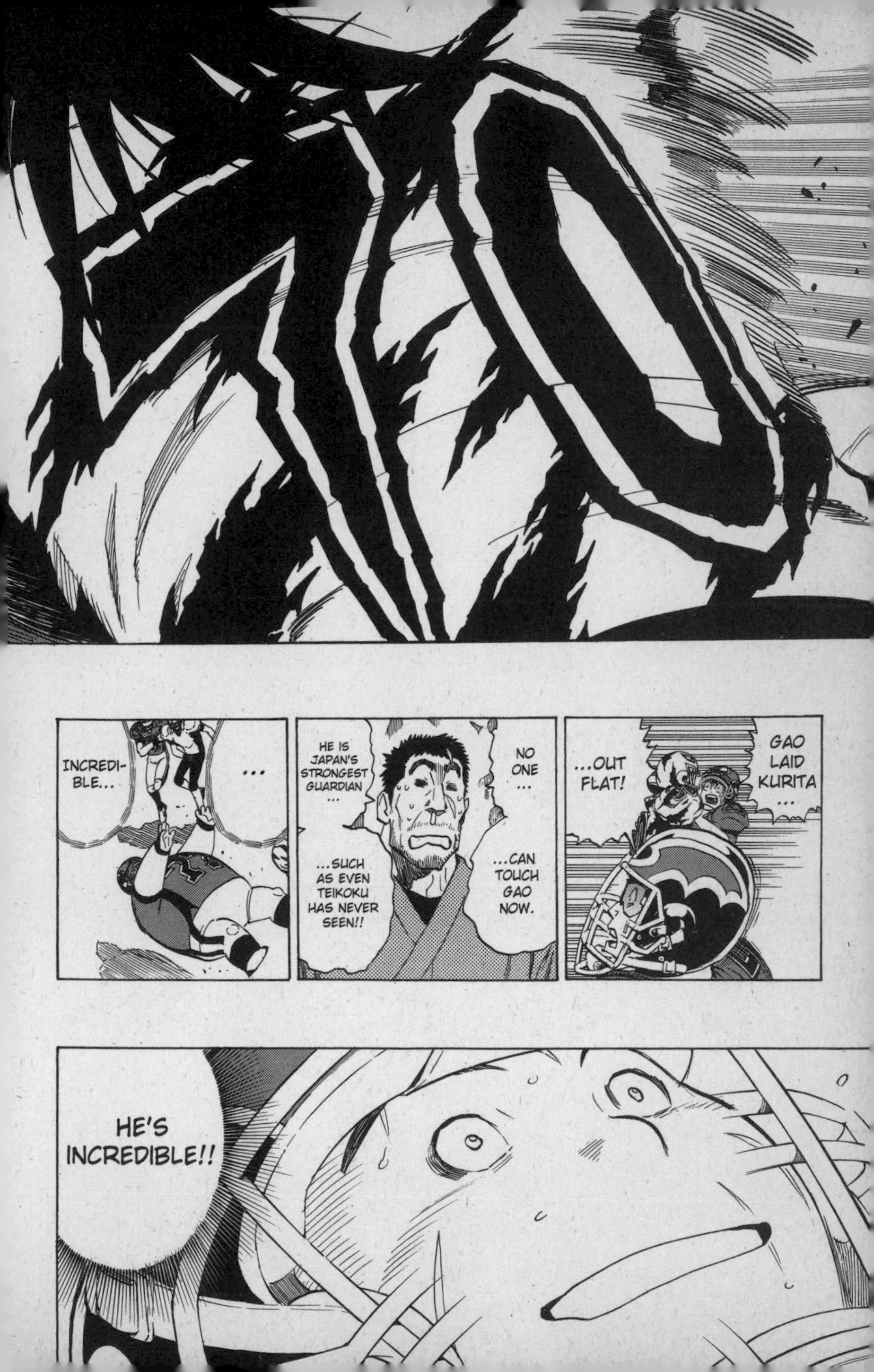
GAO LAID KURITA ...
...OUT FLAT!
NO ONE ...
...CAN TOUCH GAO NOW.
HE IS JAPAN'S STRONGEST GUARDIAN ...
...SUCH AS EVEN TEIKOKU HAS NEVER SEEN!!
...
INCREDI-BLE...
HE'S INCREDIBLE!!

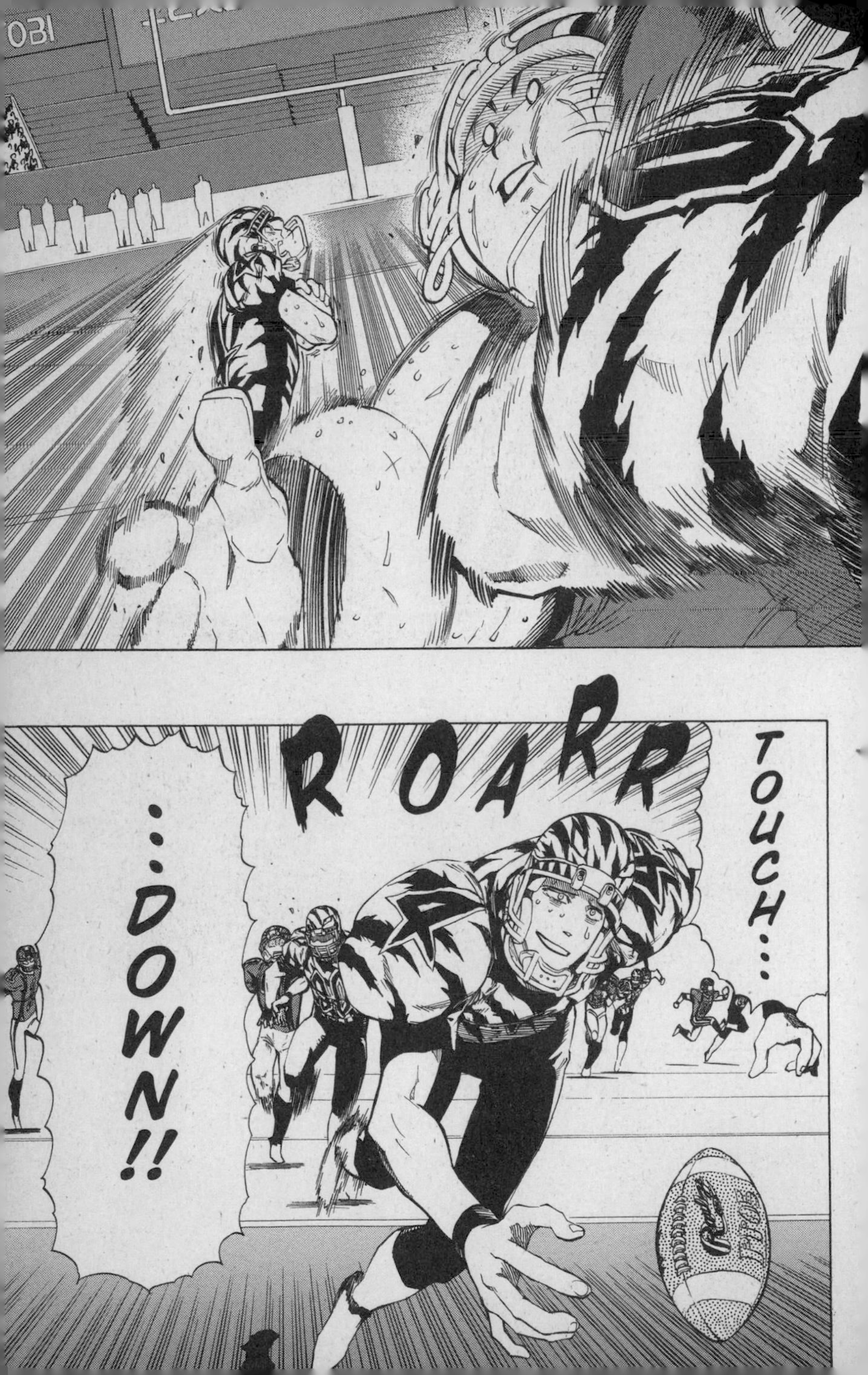
ROARR
TOUCH...
...DOWN!!

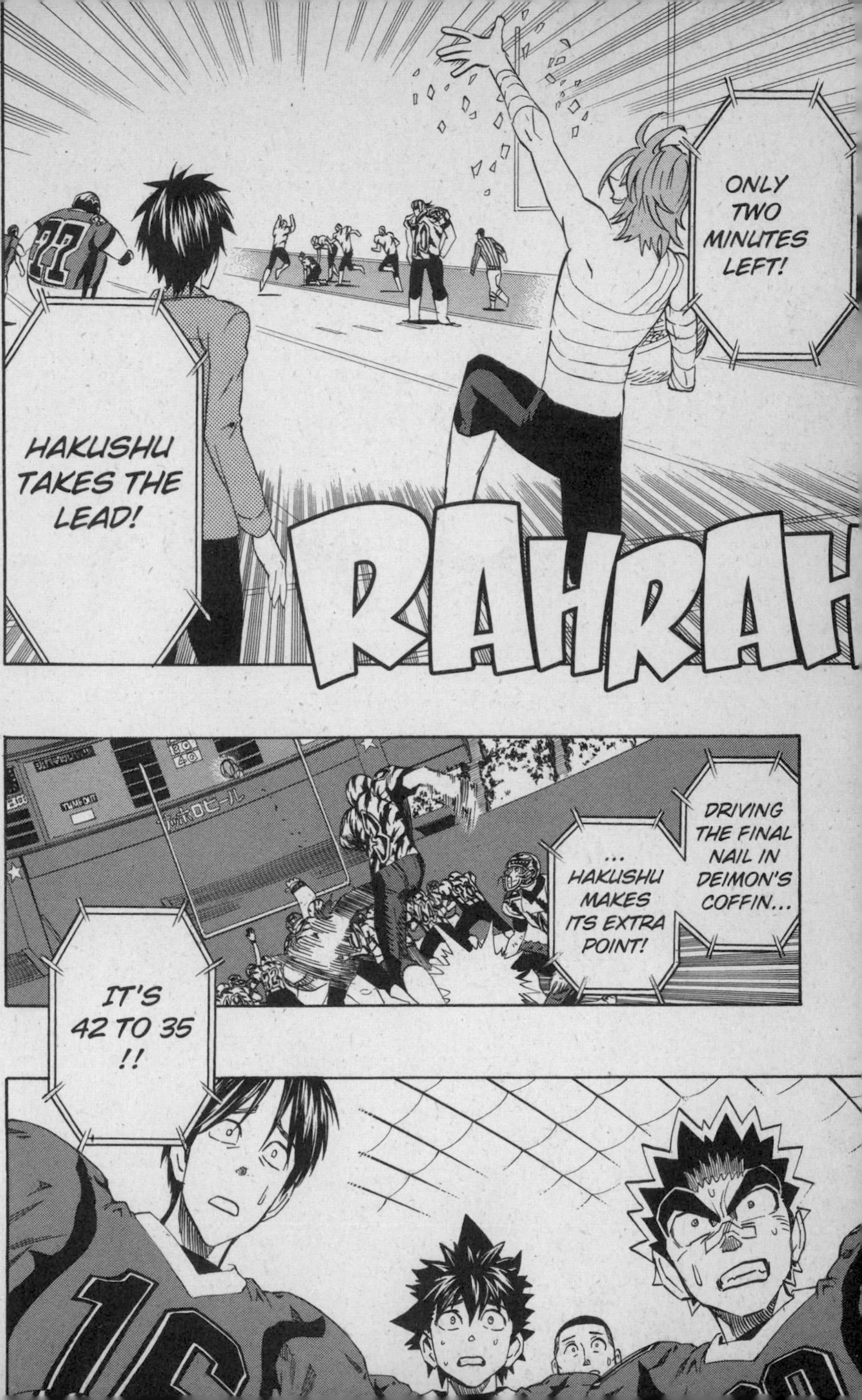
ONLY TWO MINUTES LEFT!
HAKUSHU TAKES THE LEAD!
RAHRAH
DRIVING THE FINAL NAIL IN DEIMON'S COFFIN...
... HAKUSHU MAKES ITS EXTRA POINT!
IT'S 42 TO 35 !!

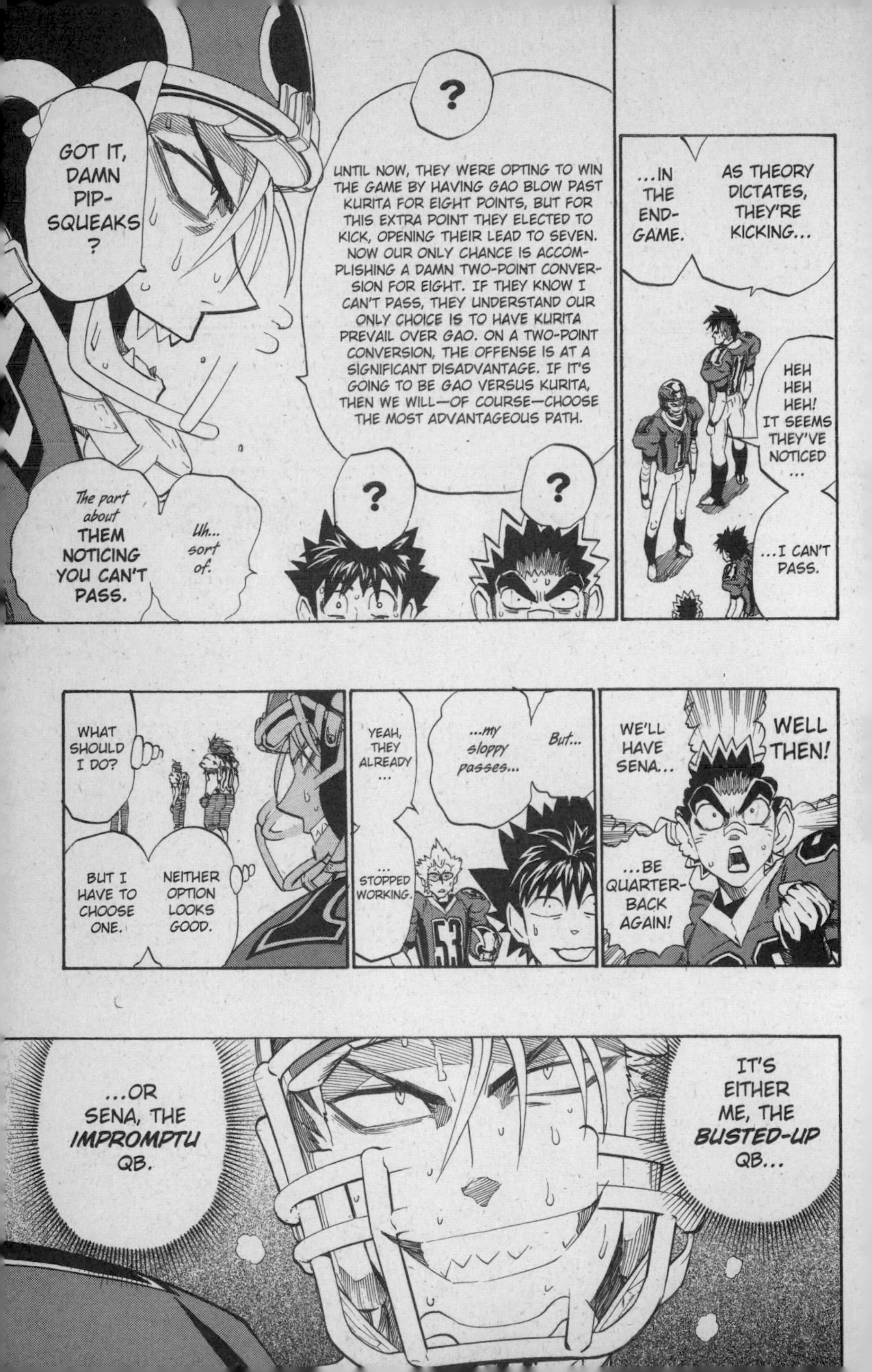
AS THEORY DICTATES, THEY'RE KICKING...
...IN THE END-GAME.
HEH HEH HEH! IT SEEMS THEY'VE NOTICED...
...I CAN'T PASS.
?
UNTIL NOW, THEY WERE OPTING TO WIN THE GAME BY HAVING GAO BLOW PAST KURITA FOR EIGHT POINTS, BUT FOR THIS EXTRA POINT THEY ELECTED TO KICK, OPENING THEIR LEAD TO SEVEN. NOW OUR ONLY CHANCE IS ACCOMPLISHING A DAMN TWO-POINT CONVERSION FOR EIGHT. IF THEY KNOW I CAN'T PASS, THEY UNDERSTAND OUR ONLY CHOICE IS TO HAVE KURITA PREVAIL OVER GAO. ON A TWO-POINT CONVERSION, THE OFFENSE IS AT A SIGNIFICANT DISADVANTAGE. IF IT'S GOING TO BE GAO VERSUS KURITA, THEN WE WILL—OF COURSE—CHOOSE THE MOST ADVANTAGEOUS PATH.
GOT IT, DAMN PIP-SQUEAKS?
?
?
Uh... sort of.
The part about THEM NOTICING YOU CAN'T PASS.
WELL THEN!
WE'LL HAVE SENA...
...BE QUARTER-BACK AGAIN!
But...
...my sloppy passes...
YEAH, THEY ALREADY...
...STOPPED WORKING.
WHAT SHOULD I DO?
NEITHER OPTION LOOKS GOOD.
BUT I HAVE TO CHOOSE ONE.
IT'S EITHER ME, THE BUSTED-UP QB...
...OR SENA, THE IMPROMPTU QB.

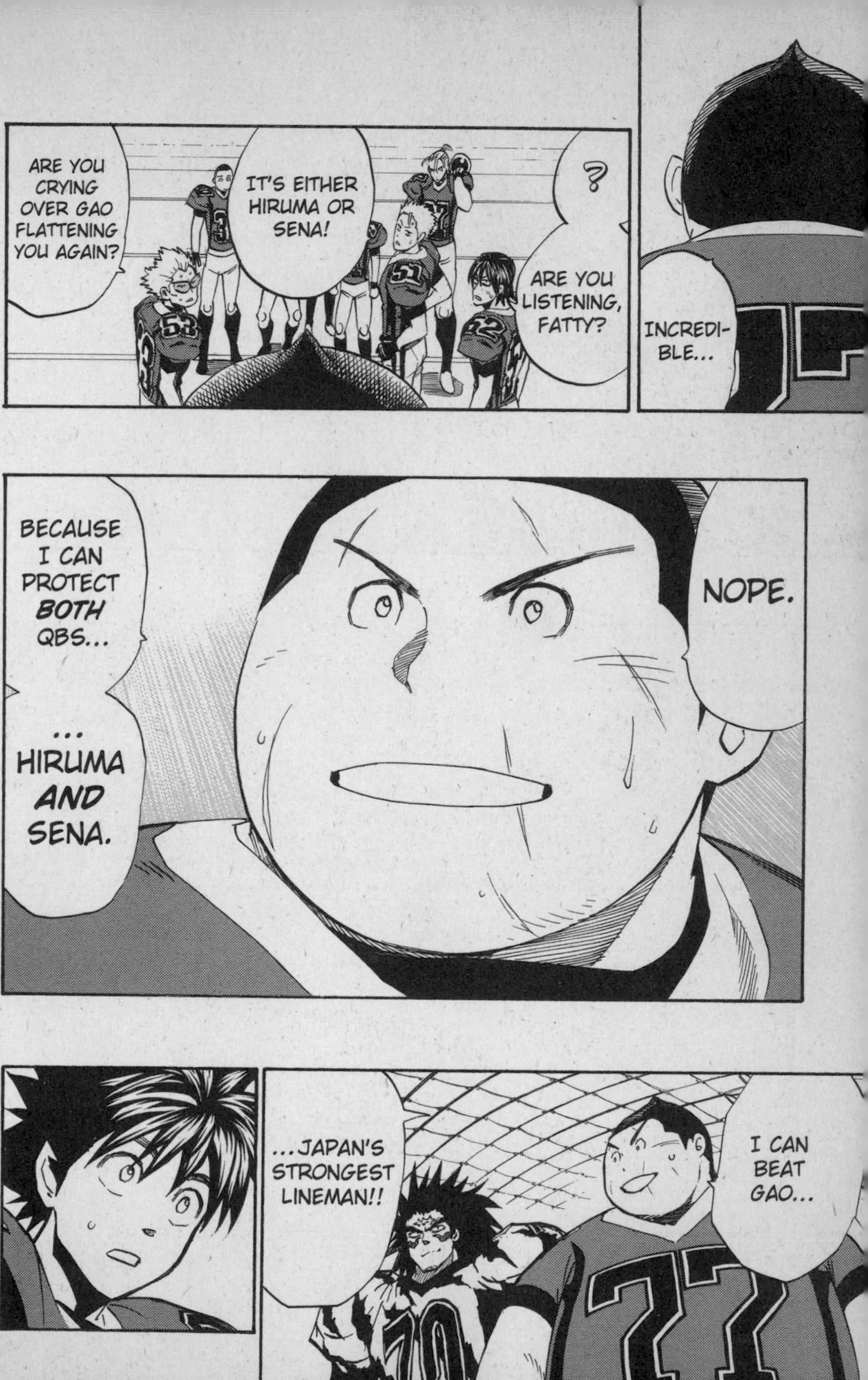
INCREDI-BLE...
?
ARE YOU LISTENING, FATTY?
IT'S EITHER HIRUMA OR SENA!
ARE YOU CRYING OVER GAO FLATTENING YOU AGAIN?
NOPE.
BECAUSE I CAN PROTECT *BOTH* QBS...
...HIRUMA *AND* SENA.
I CAN BEAT GAO...
...JAPAN'S STRONGEST LINEMAN!!

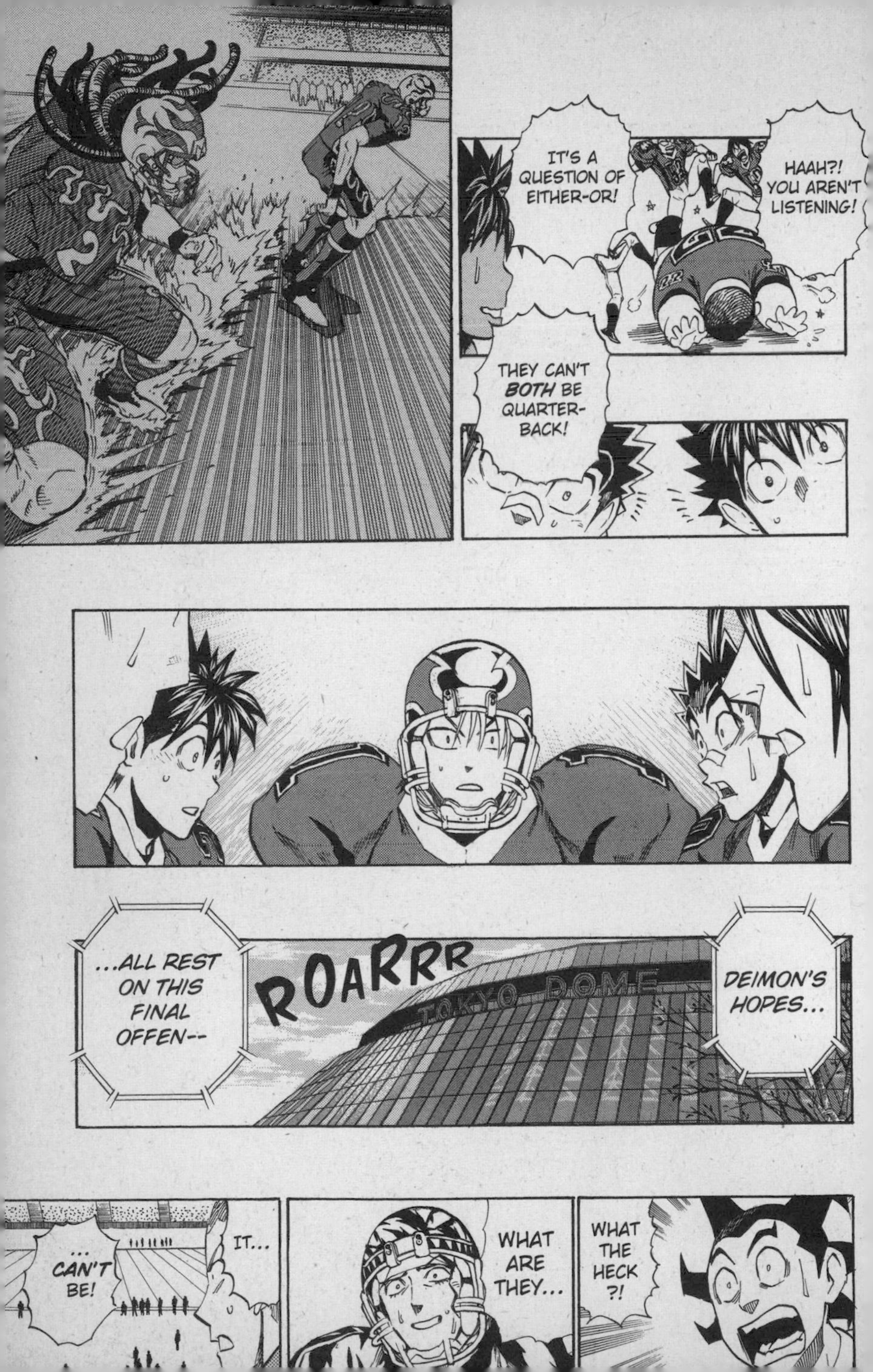
HAAH?! YOU AREN'T LISTENING!
IT'S A QUESTION OF EITHER-OR!
THEY CAN'T *BOTH* BE QUARTER-BACK!
DEIMON'S HOPES...
ROARRR
...ALL REST ON THIS FINAL OFFEN--
TOKYO DOME
WHAT THE HECK ?!
WHAT ARE THEY...
IT...
...CAN'T BE!

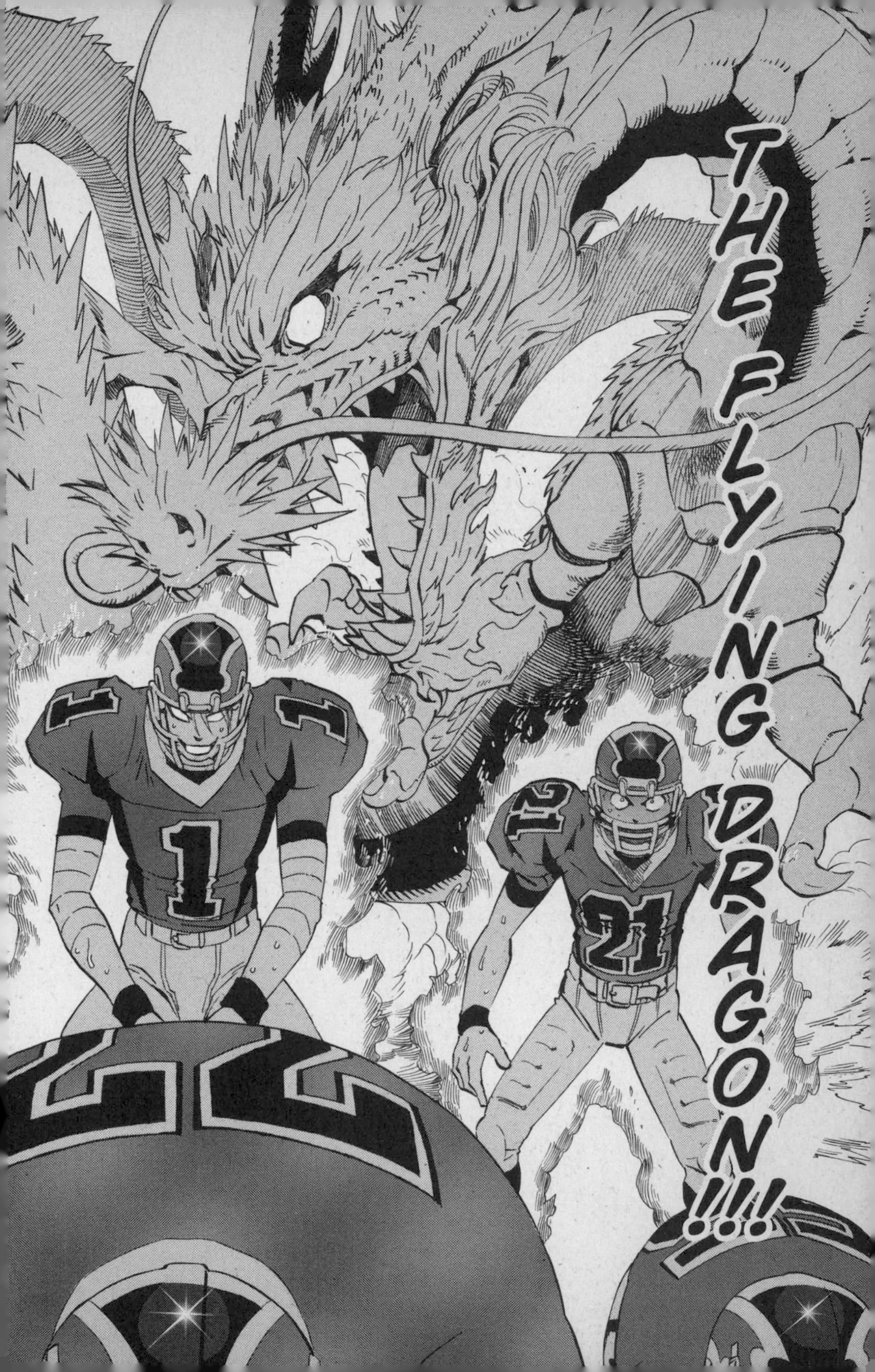
THE FLYING DRAGON!!!!

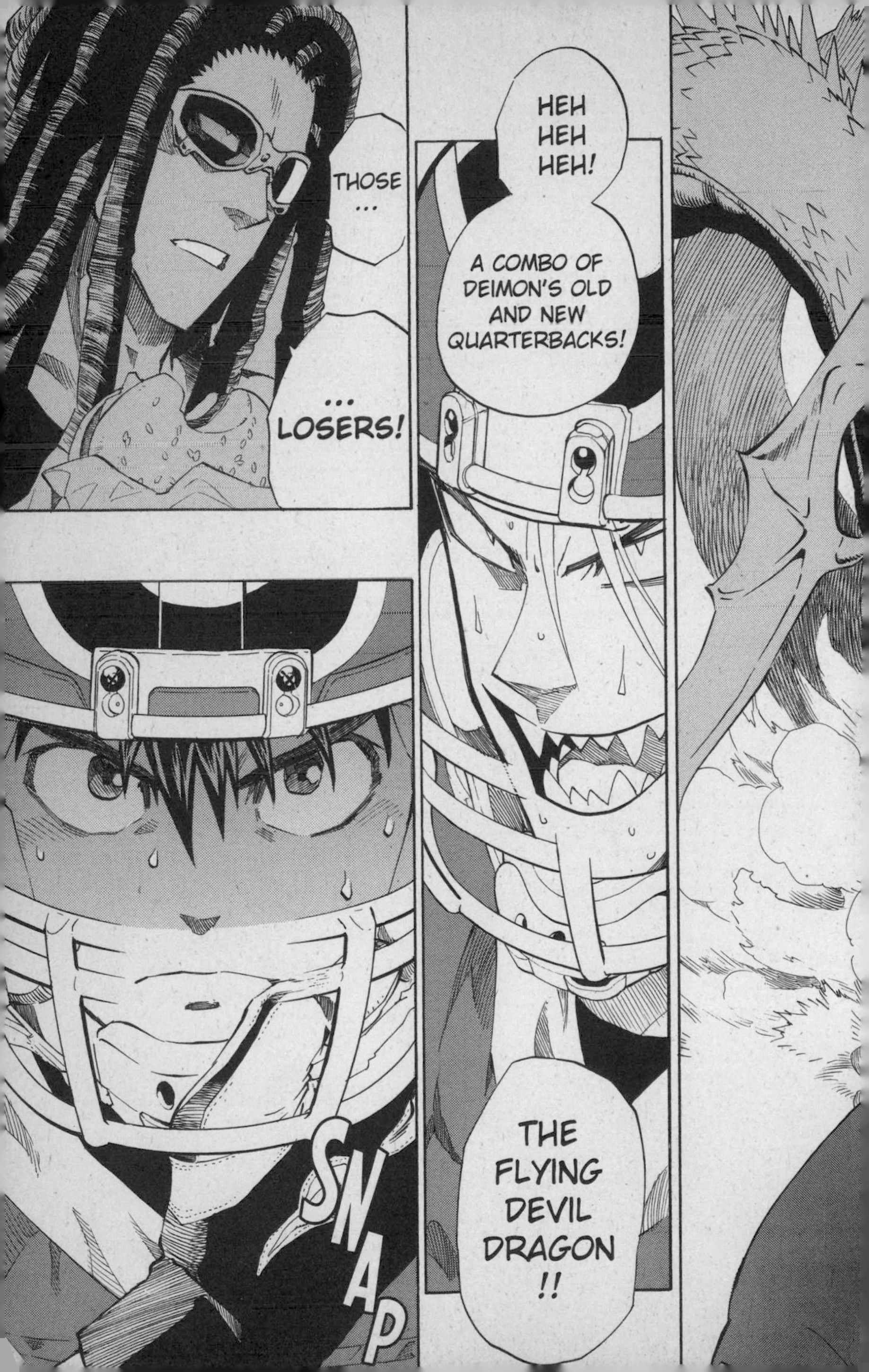
HEH HEH HEH!
A COMBO OF DEIMON'S OLD AND NEW QUARTERBACKS!
THE FLYING DEVIL DRAGON !!
THOSE ...
... LOSERS!
SNAP

Eyeshield 21 Survey Corner Devil Bat 021

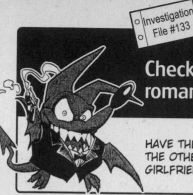

Investigation File #133

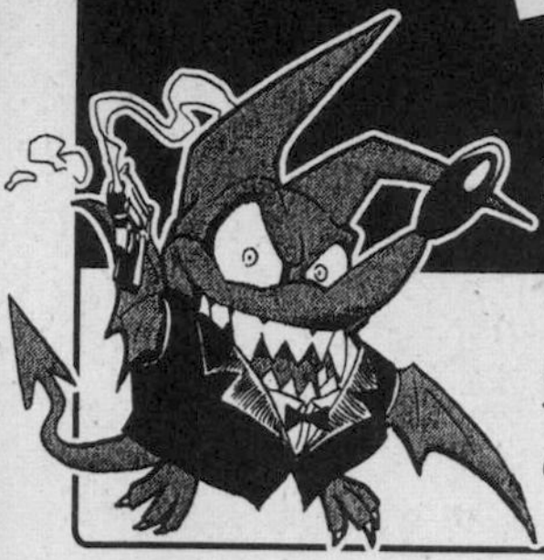

Check out the characters' romantic involvements!

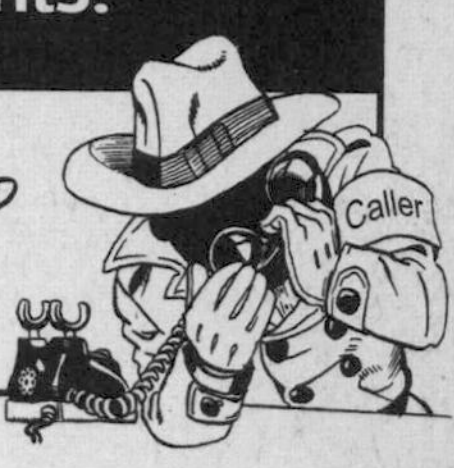
Caller

HAVE THE GUYS ON DEIMON AND THE OTHER TEAMS HAD GIRLFRIENDS?

Caller name: Nikumanjin in Saitama Prefecture

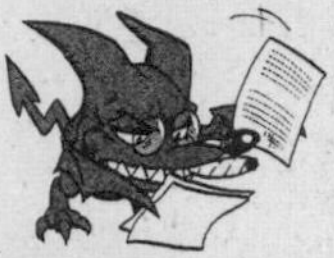

HERE'S THE SCOOP ON SOME OF THE GUYS.

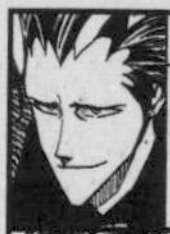	**Maruko** Hakushu manager Himuro used to be his girlfriend.	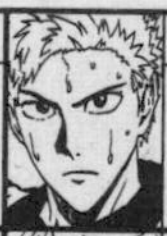	**Sakuraba** For a short time he had something like a girlfriend, but when he joined Jari Pro, they made him break it off.
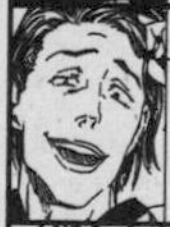	**Hatsujo** Currently has a girlfriend in his grade.	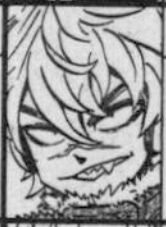	**Kamiya** Including his current girlfriend, he's had eight.
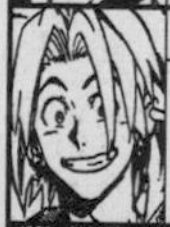	**Mizumachi** Went to an amusement park with a couple girls, but both times it didn't go any further.	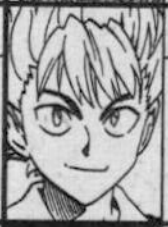	**Riku** A girl liked him in junior high, but it didn't go anywhere because he was too focused on football.
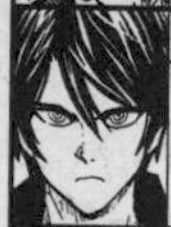	**Kakei** When he studied overseas, he dated a blonde with bad-girl tendencies, but it ended when he came back to Japan.	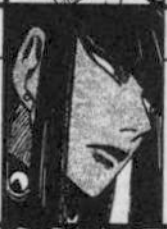	**Harao** Has three girls in his harem.
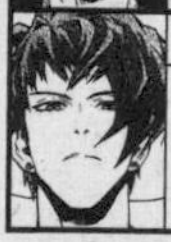	**Akaba** Dated a girl in his band but broke up with her because of a difference in harmonics.	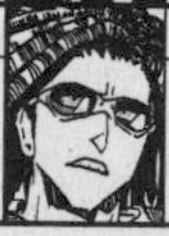	**Agon** He's always got lots of girls, but never officially dates any of them.

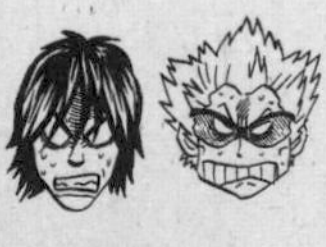

WHY ISN'T THERE ANYONE FROM DEIMON?! THE JERKS※!

※Guys who've got a real life.

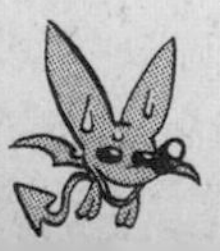

I TH-TH-TH-THINK THEY'RE A LITTLE JEALOUS!

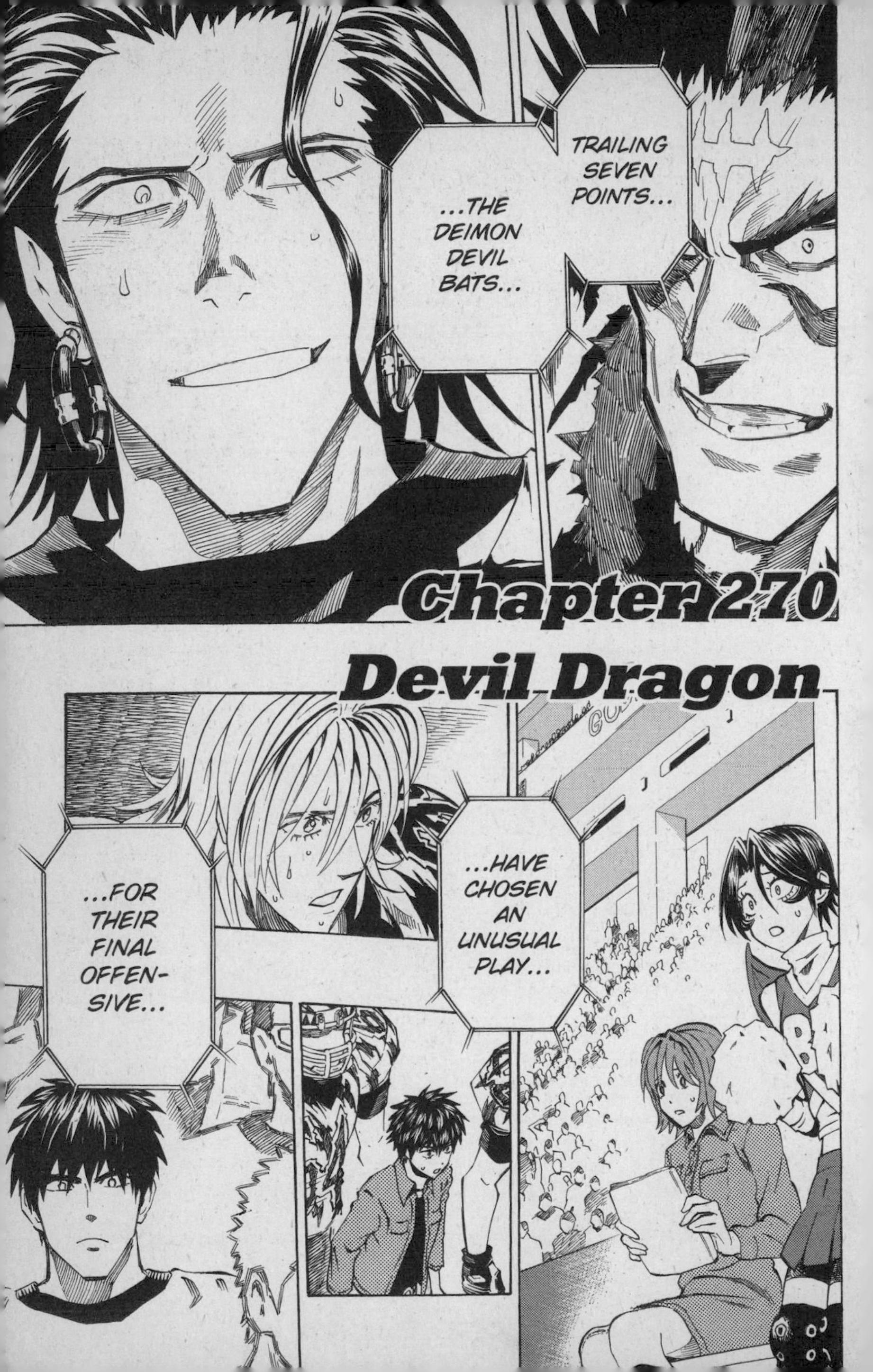
TRAILING SEVEN POINTS...
...THE DEIMON DEVIL BATS...
Chapter 270
Devil Dragon
...HAVE CHOSEN AN UNUSUAL PLAY...
...FOR THEIR FINAL OFFEN-SIVE...

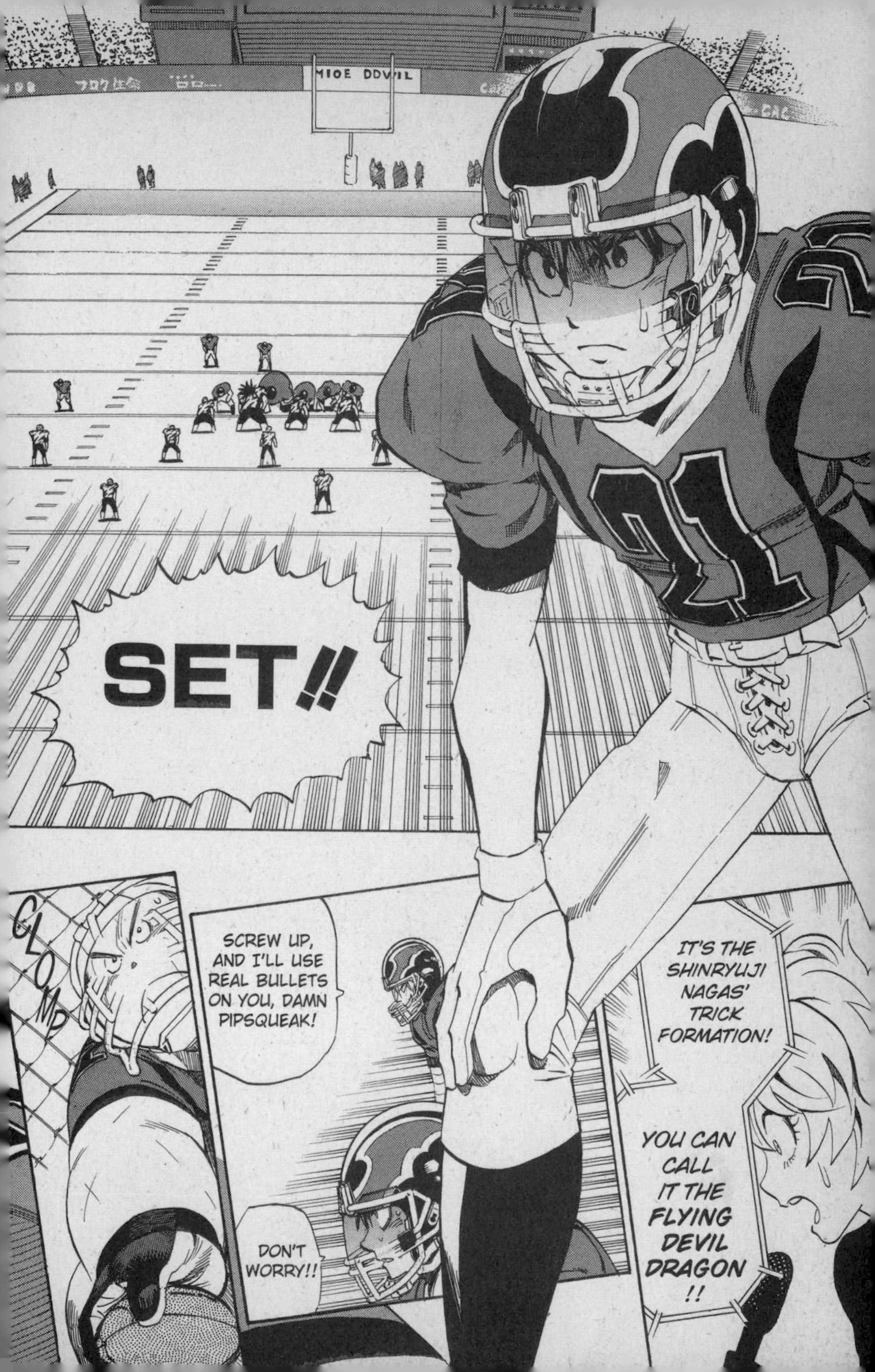
SET!!
IT'S THE SHINRYUJI NAGAS' TRICK FORMATION!
YOU CAN CALL IT THE FLYING DEVIL DRAGON!!
SCREW UP, AND I'LL USE REAL BULLETS ON YOU, DAMN PIPSQUEAK!
DON'T WORRY!!
CLOMP

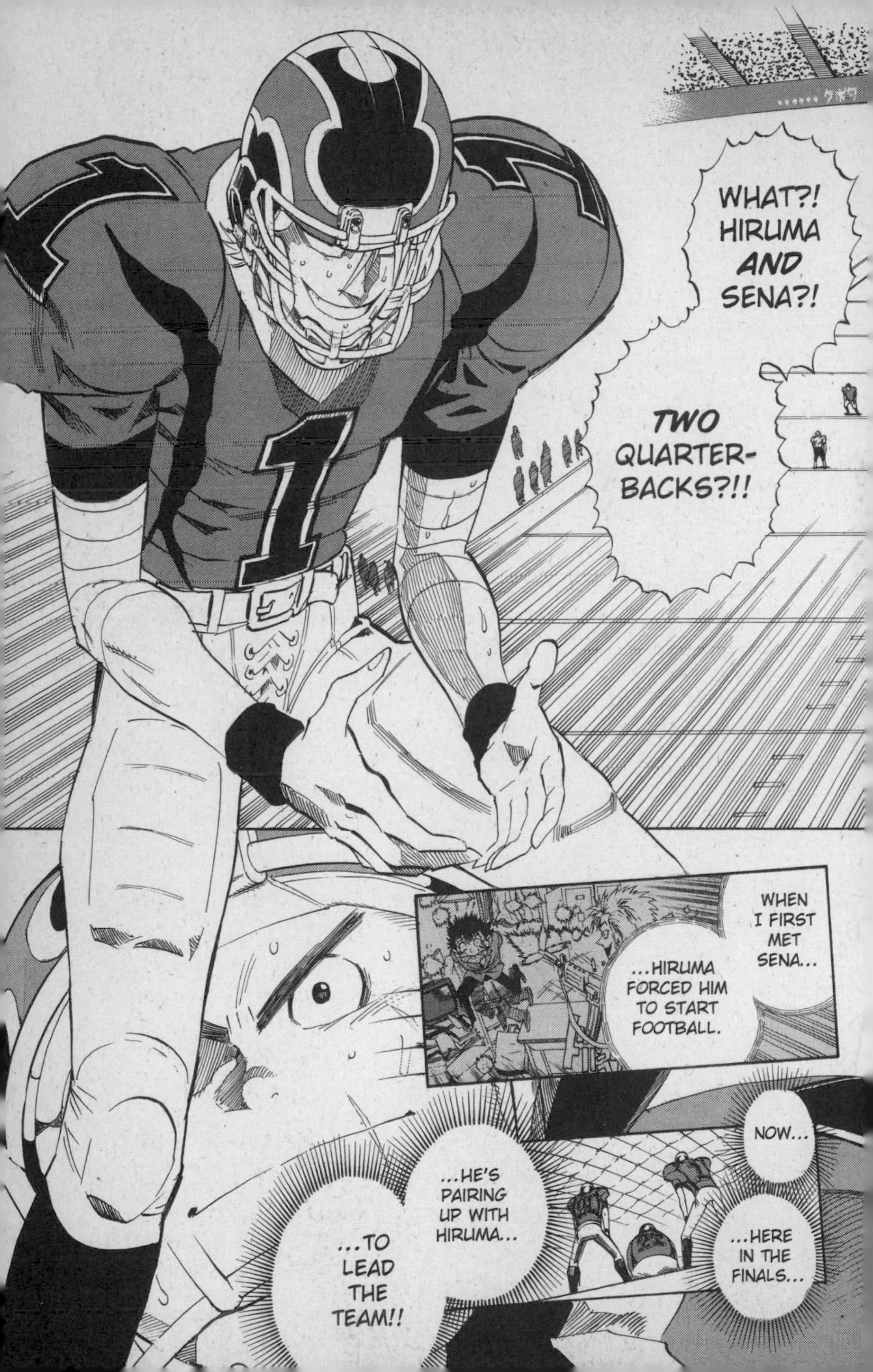
WHAT?! HIRUMA AND SENA?!
TWO QUARTER-BACKS?!!
WHEN I FIRST MET SENA...
...HIRUMA FORCED HIM TO START FOOTBALL.
NOW...
...HERE IN THE FINALS...
...HE'S PAIRING UP WITH HIRUMA...
...TO LEAD THE TEAM!!

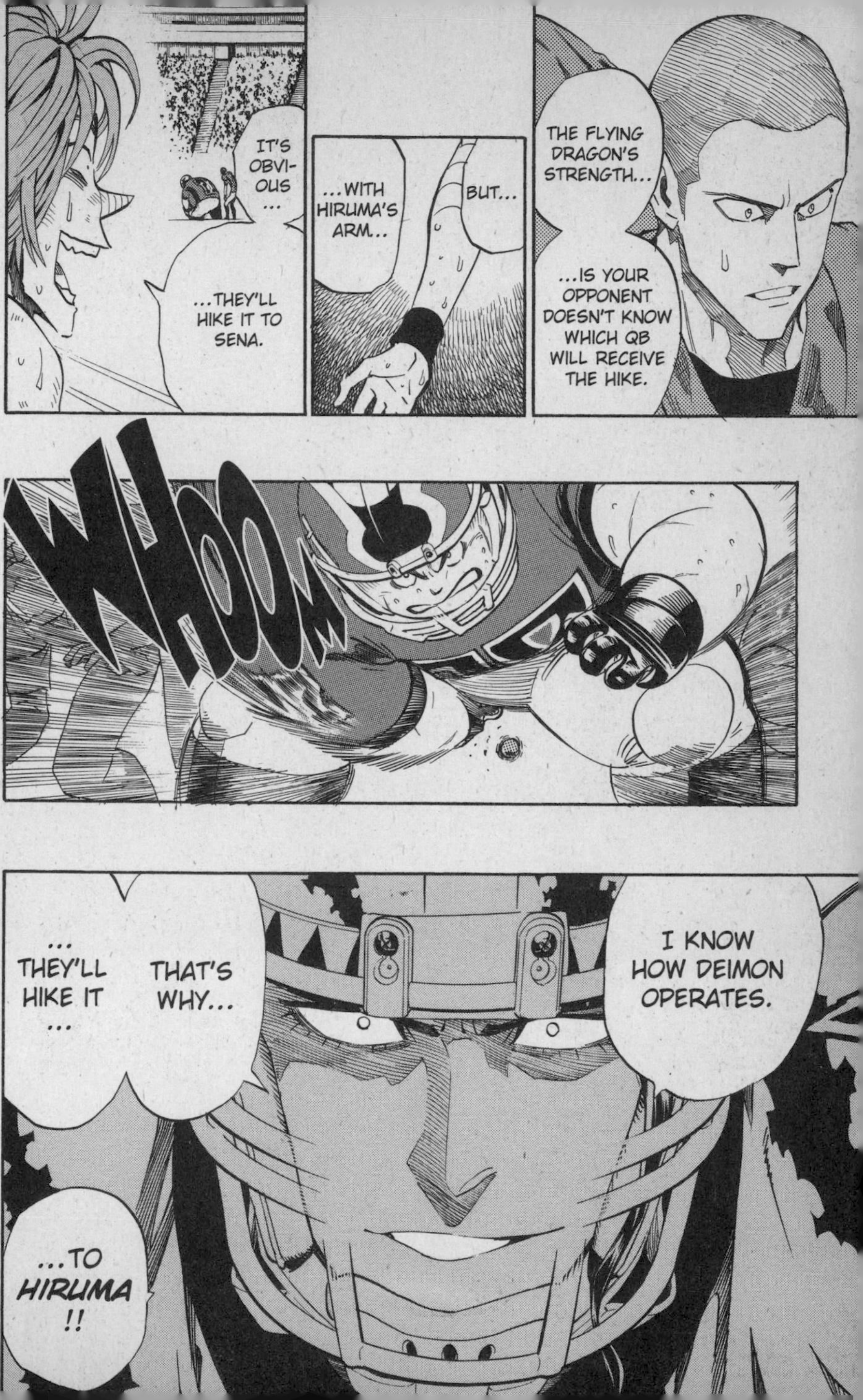
THE FLYING DRAGON'S STRENGTH...
...IS YOUR OPPONENT DOESN'T KNOW WHICH QB WILL RECEIVE THE HIKE.
BUT...
...WITH HIRUMA'S ARM...
IT'S OBVIOUS...
...THEY'LL HIKE IT TO SENA.
WHOOM
I KNOW HOW DEIMON OPERATES.
THAT'S WHY...
...THEY'LL HIKE IT...
...TO HIRUMA!!

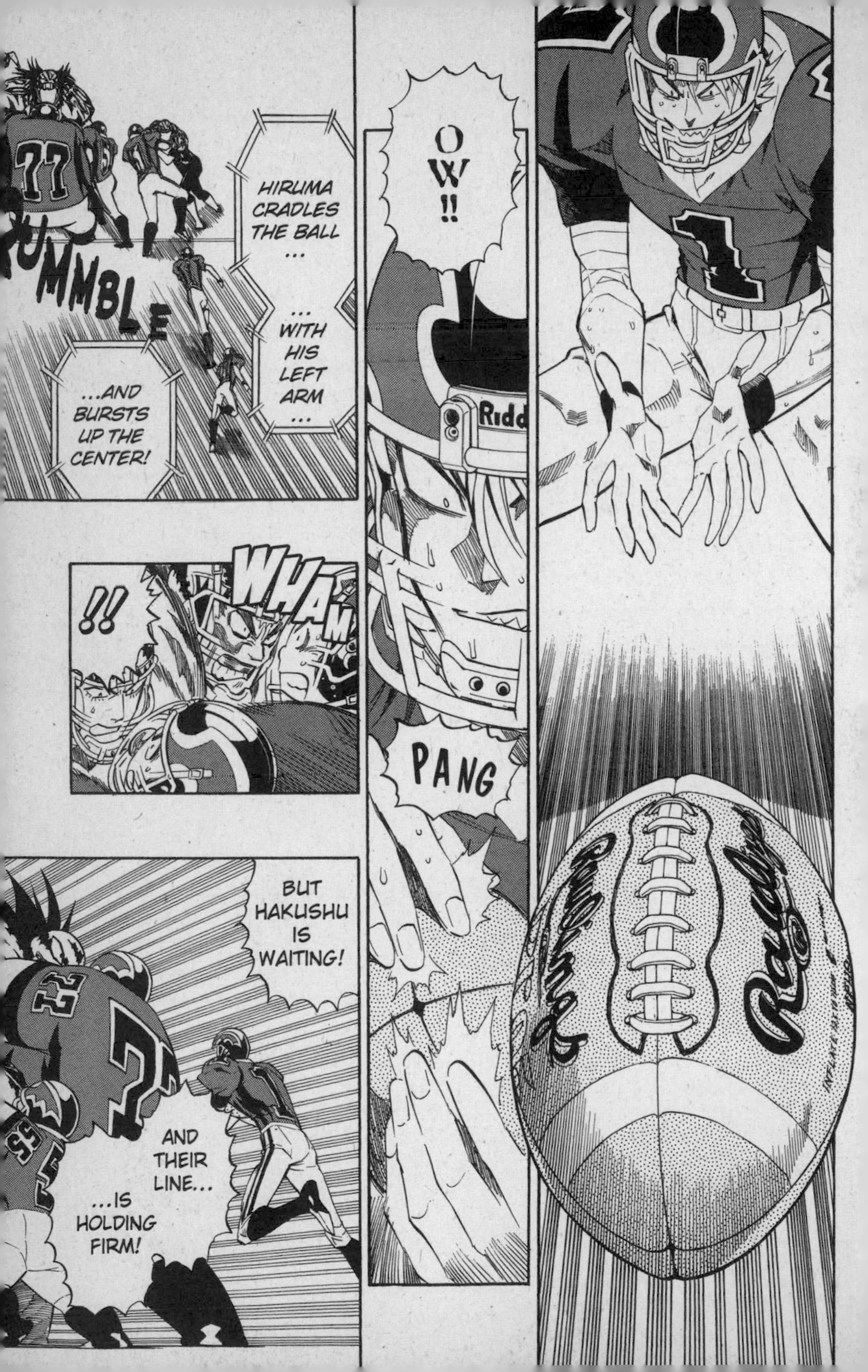
OW!!
PANG
RUMMBLE
HIRUMA CRADLES THE BALL...
...WITH HIS LEFT ARM...
...AND BURSTS UP THE CENTER!
WHAM
!!
BUT HAKUSHU IS WAITING!
AND THEIR LINE...
...IS HOLDING FIRM!

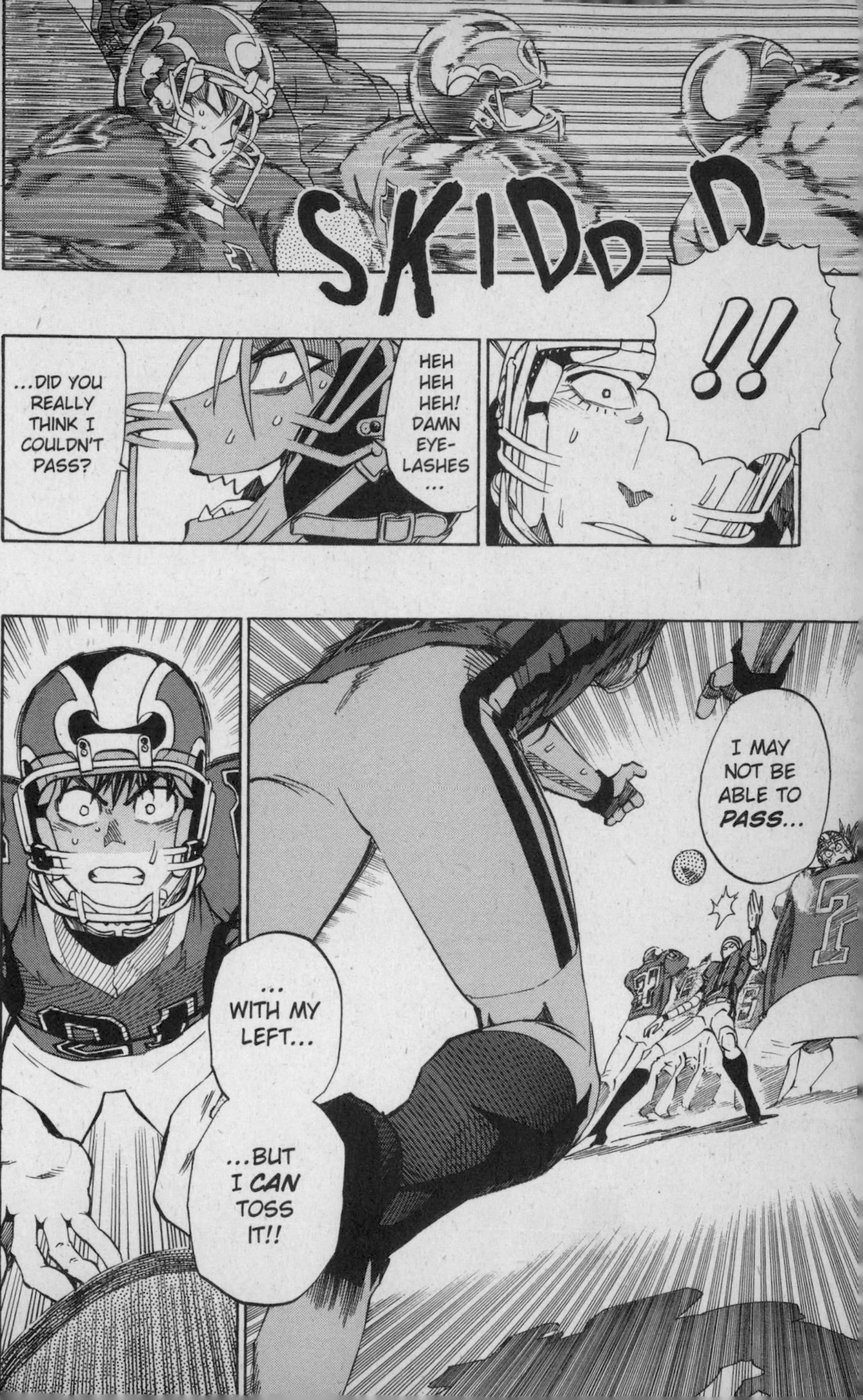
SKIDD D
!!
HEH HEH HEH! DAMN EYE-LASHES...
...DID YOU REALLY THINK I COULDN'T PASS?
I MAY NOT BE ABLE TO **PASS**...
...WITH MY LEFT...
...BUT I **CAN** TOSS IT!!

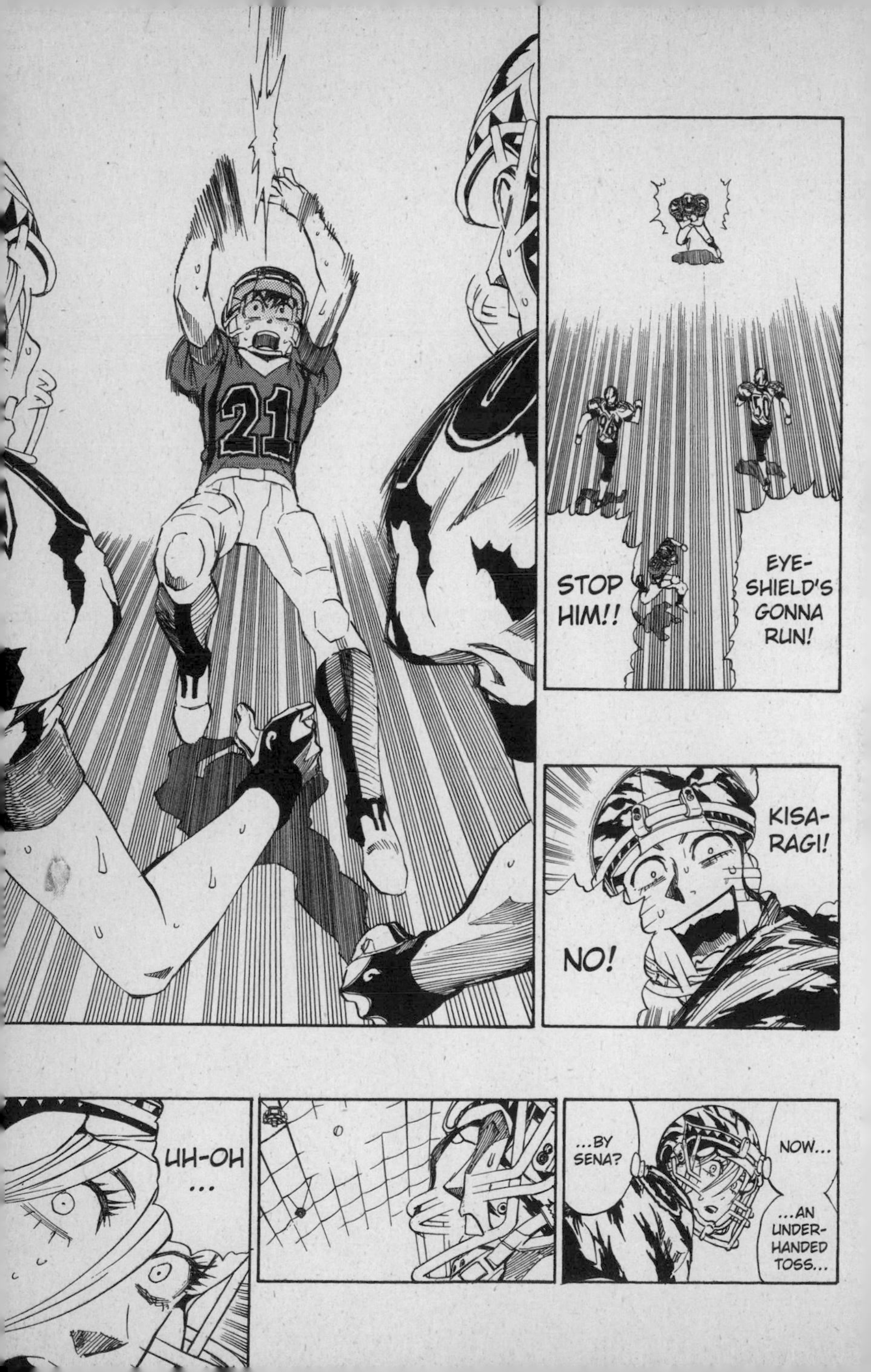
EYE-SHIELD'S GONNA RUN!
STOP HIM!!
KISA-RAGI!
NO!
NOW...
...AN UNDER-HANDED TOSS...
...BY SENA?
UH-OH ...

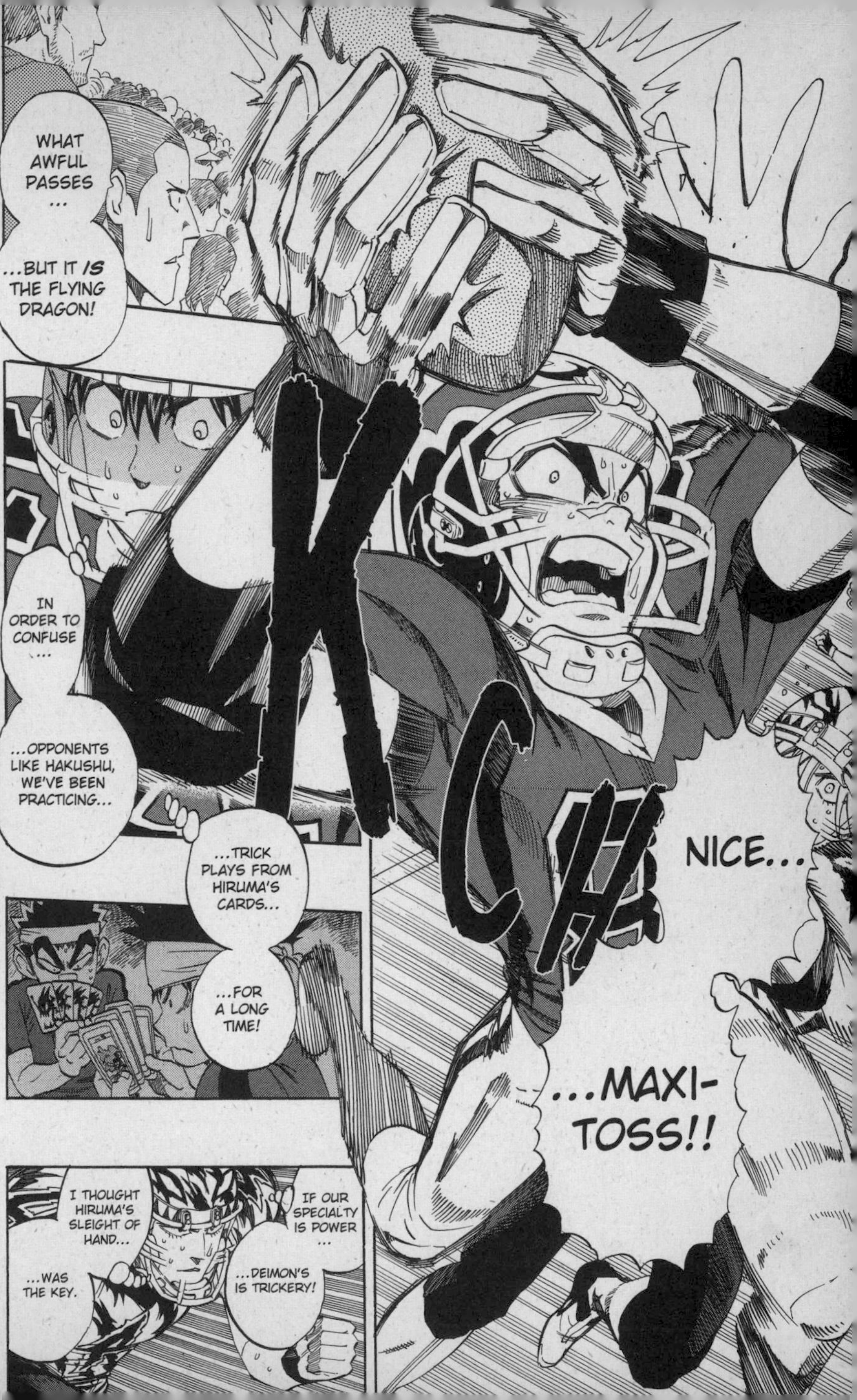
KCH
NICE...
...MAXI-TOSS!!
WHAT AWFUL PASSES...
...BUT IT *IS* THE FLYING DRAGON!
IN ORDER TO CONFUSE...
...OPPONENTS LIKE HAKUSHU, WE'VE BEEN PRACTICING...
...TRICK PLAYS FROM HIRUMA'S CARDS...
...FOR A LONG TIME!
IF OUR SPECIALTY IS POWER...
...DEIMON'S IS TRICKERY!
I THOUGHT HIRUMA'S SLEIGHT OF HAND...
...WAS THE KEY.

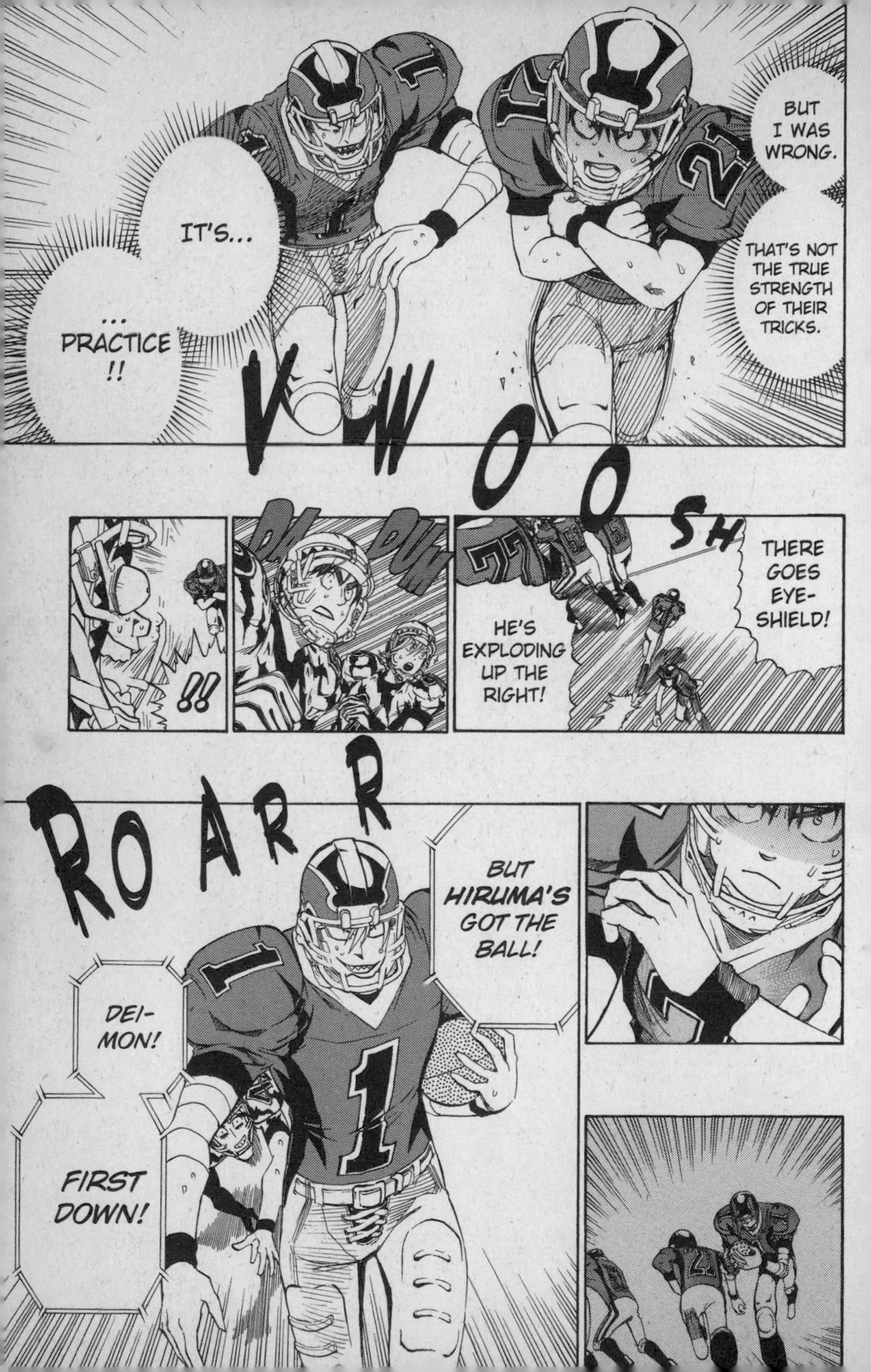
BUT I WAS WRONG.
THAT'S NOT THE TRUE STRENGTH OF THEIR TRICKS.
IT'S...
...PRACTICE !!
VWOOOSH
THERE GOES EYE-SHIELD!
HE'S EXPLODING UP THE RIGHT!
!!
ROARR
BUT HIRUMA'S GOT THE BALL!
DEI-MON!
FIRST DOWN!

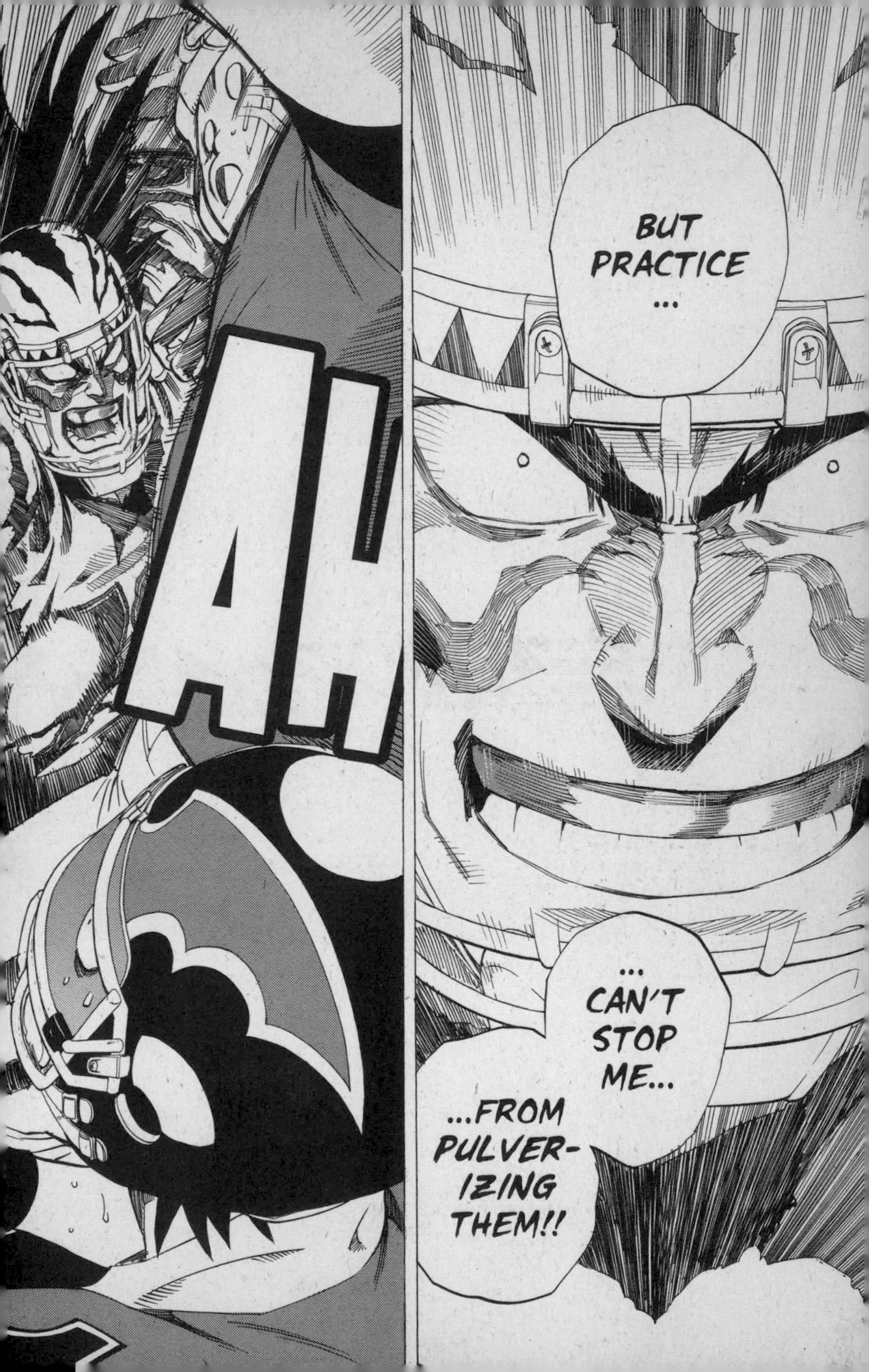
BUT PRACTICE ...
... CAN'T STOP ME...
...FROM PULVER-IZING THEM!!
AH

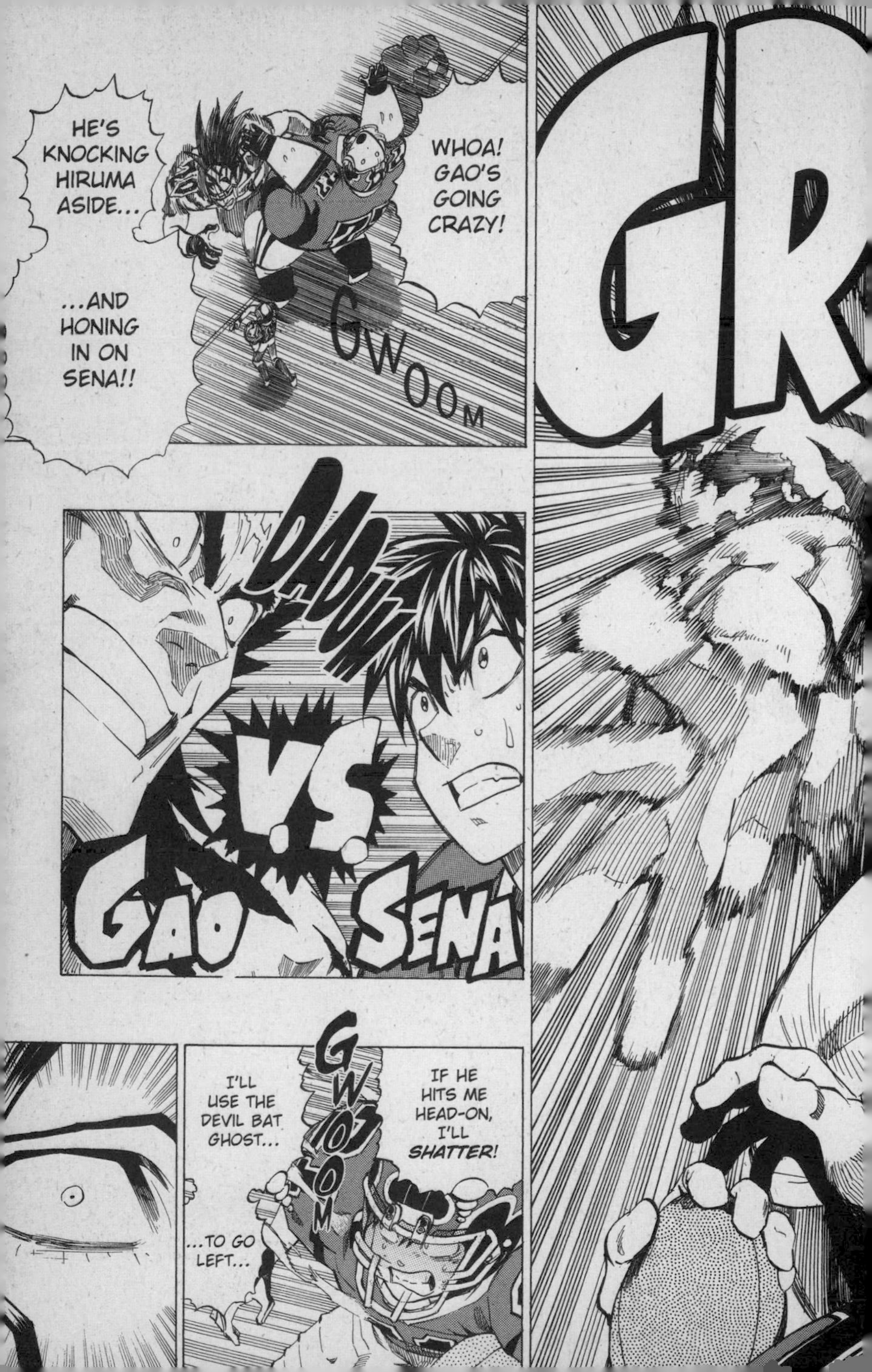
GR
WHOA! GAO'S GOING CRAZY!
HE'S KNOCKING HIRUMA ASIDE...
...AND HONING IN ON SENA!!
GWOOOM
DADUM
GAO VS SENA
IF HE HITS ME HEAD-ON, I'LL *SHATTER!*
GWOOOOM
I'LL USE THE DEVIL BAT GHOST...
...TO GO LEFT...

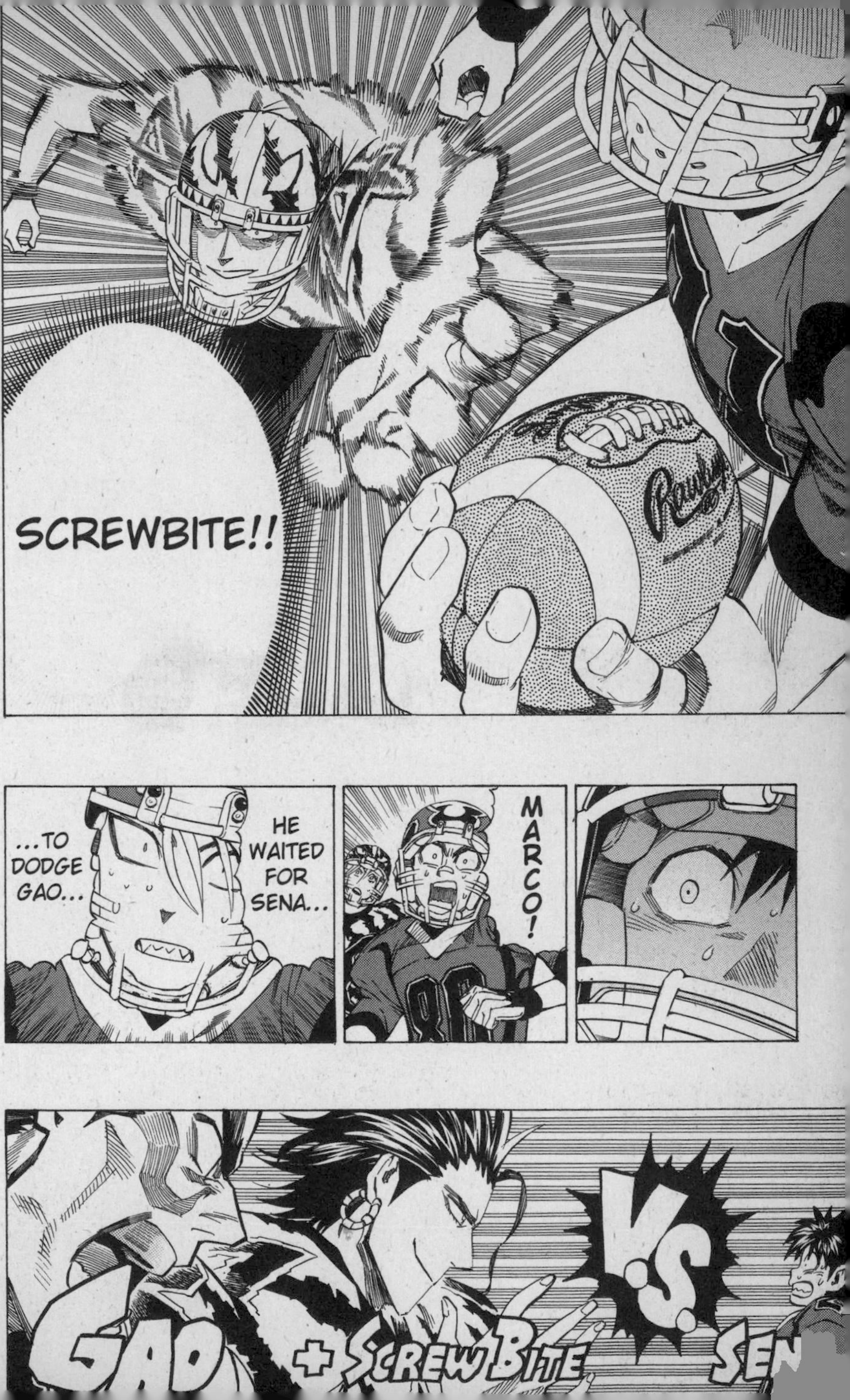
SCREWBITE!!
MARCO!
HE WAITED FOR SENA...
...TO DODGE GAO...
GAO + SCREW BITE V.S. SEN

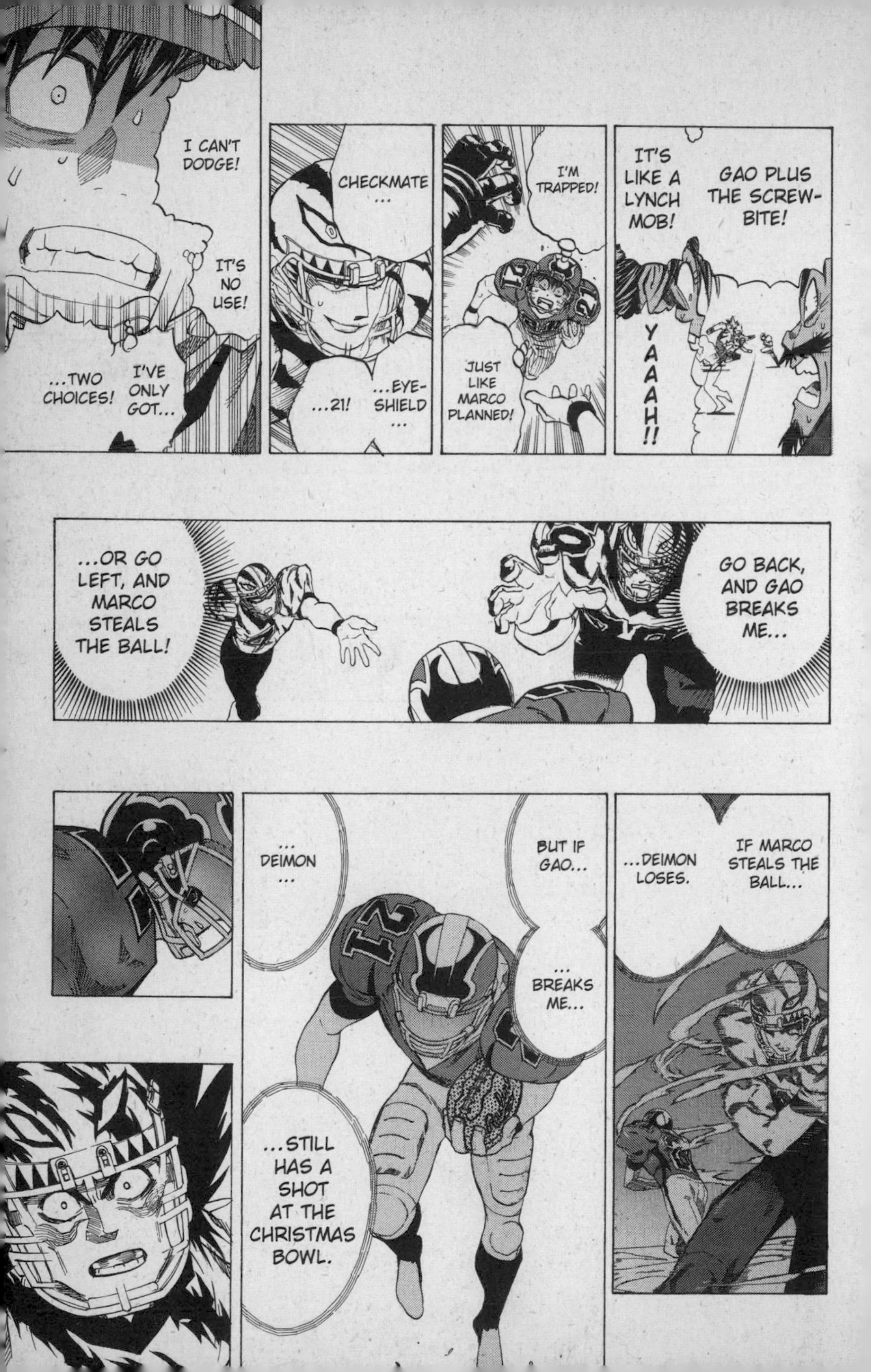
GAO PLUS THE SCREW-BITE!
IT'S LIKE A LYNCH MOB!
YAAAH!!
I'M TRAPPED!
JUST LIKE MARCO PLANNED!
CHECKMATE...
...EYE-SHIELD...
...21!
I CAN'T DODGE!
IT'S NO USE!
I'VE ONLY GOT...
...TWO CHOICES!
GO BACK, AND GAO BREAKS ME...
...OR GO LEFT, AND MARCO STEALS THE BALL!
IF MARCO STEALS THE BALL...
...DEIMON LOSES.
BUT IF GAO...
...BREAKS ME...
...DEIMON...
...STILL HAS A SHOT AT THE CHRISTMAS BOWL.

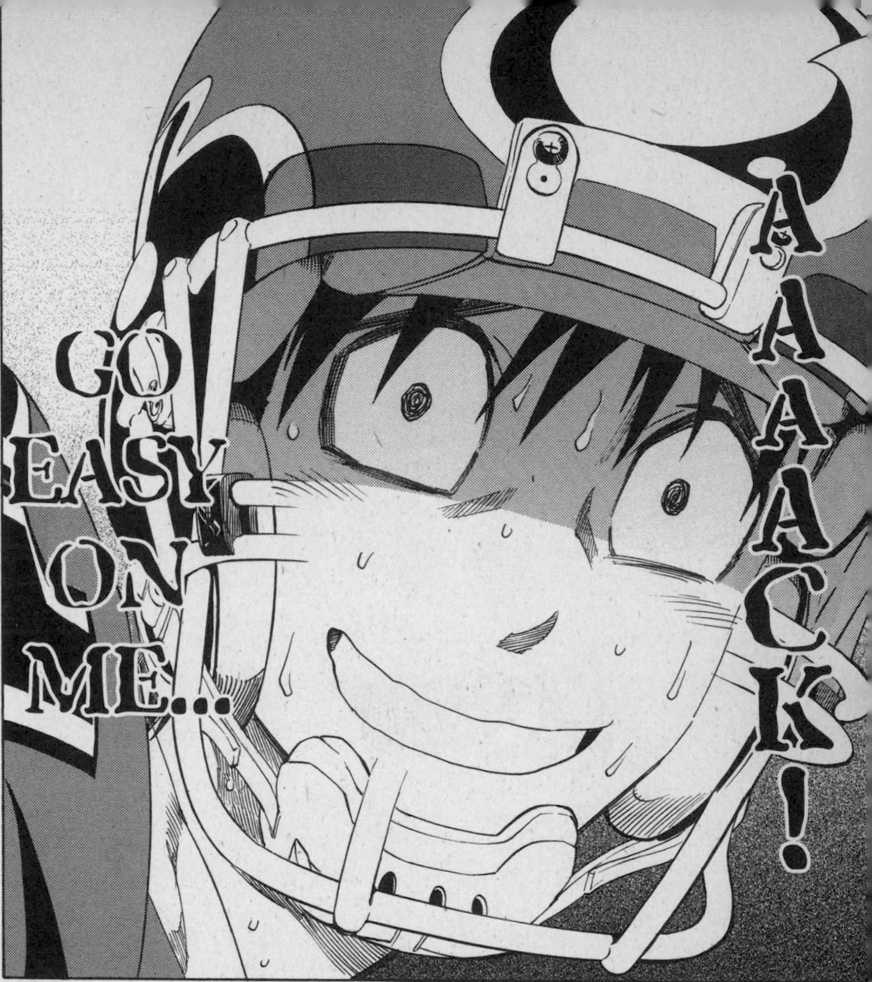
AAAACK!
GO EASY ON ME...
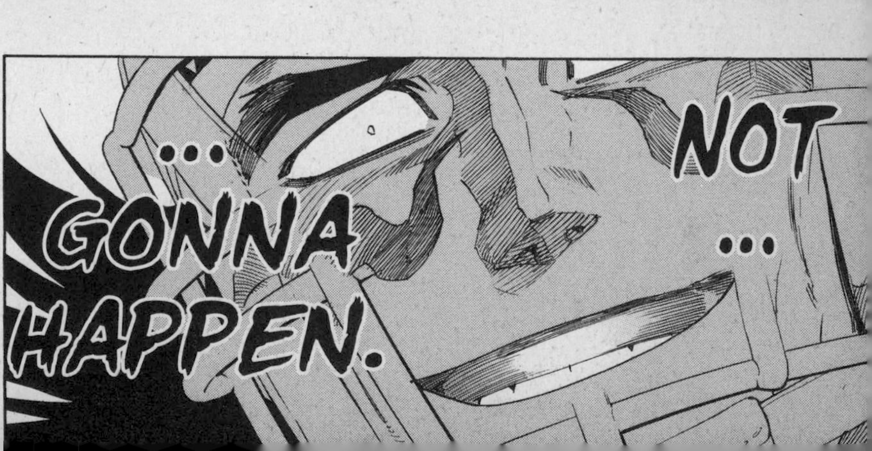
NOT ...
... GONNA HAPPEN.

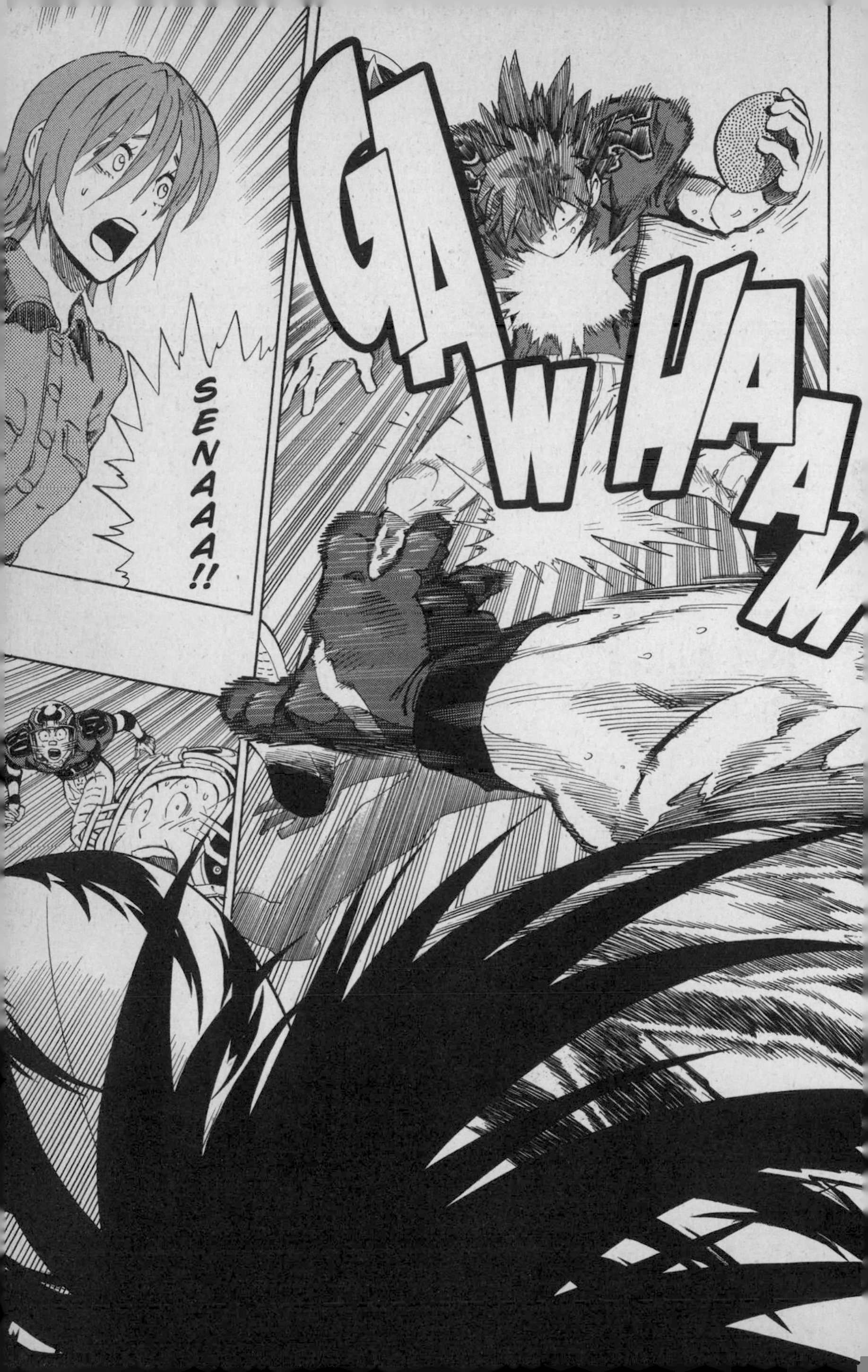
GAWHAAM
SENAAAA!!

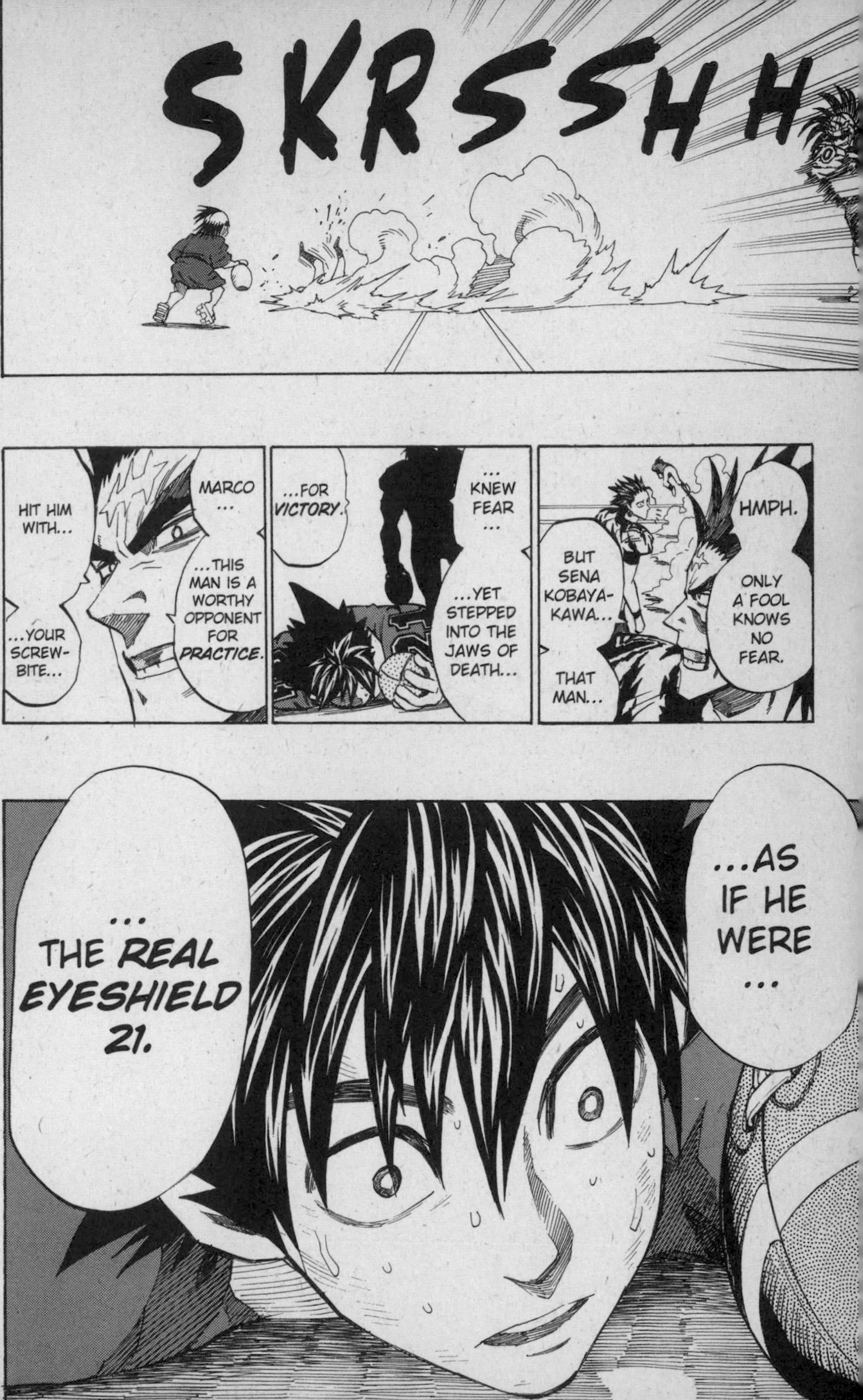
SKRSSHH
HMPH.
ONLY A FOOL KNOWS NO FEAR.
BUT SENA KOBAYAKAWA...
THAT MAN...
...KNEW FEAR...
...YET STEPPED INTO THE JAWS OF DEATH...
...FOR *VICTORY*.
MARCO...
...THIS MAN IS A WORTHY OPPONENT FOR *PRACTICE*.
HIT HIM WITH...
...YOUR SCREW-BITE...
...AS IF HE WERE...
...THE *REAL* EYESHIELD 21.

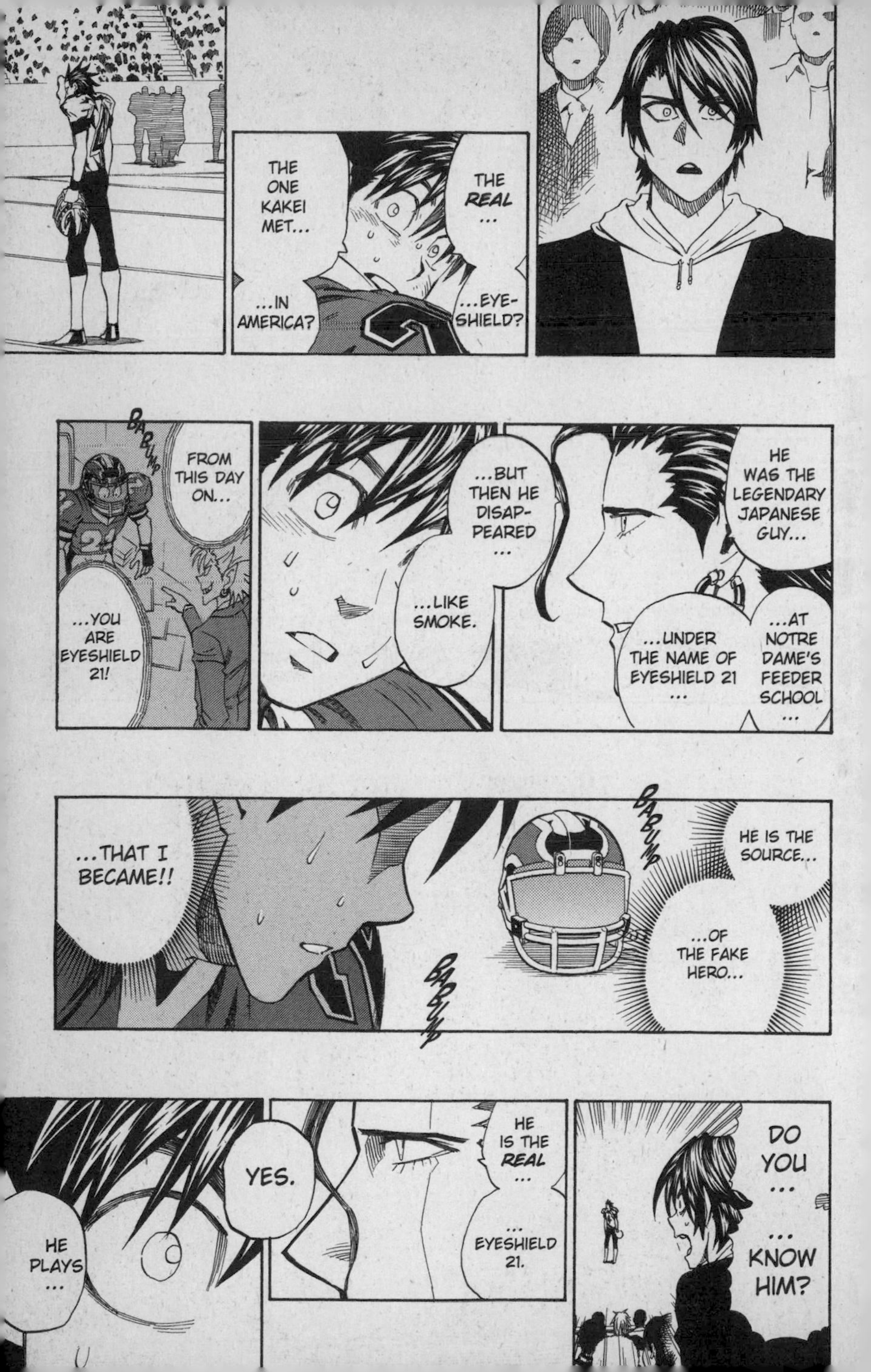
THE REAL ...
...EYE-SHIELD?
THE ONE KAKEI MET...
...IN AMERICA?
HE WAS THE LEGENDARY JAPANESE GUY...
...AT NOTRE DAME'S FEEDER SCHOOL ...
...UNDER THE NAME OF EYESHIELD 21 ...
...BUT THEN HE DISAP-PEARED ...
...LIKE SMOKE.
BABUMP
FROM THIS DAY ON...
...YOU ARE EYESHIELD 21!
BABUMP
HE IS THE SOURCE...
...OF THE FAKE HERO...
...THAT I BECAME!!
BABUMP
DO YOU ...
... KNOW HIM?
HE IS THE REAL ...
... EYESHIELD 21.
YES.
HE PLAYS ...

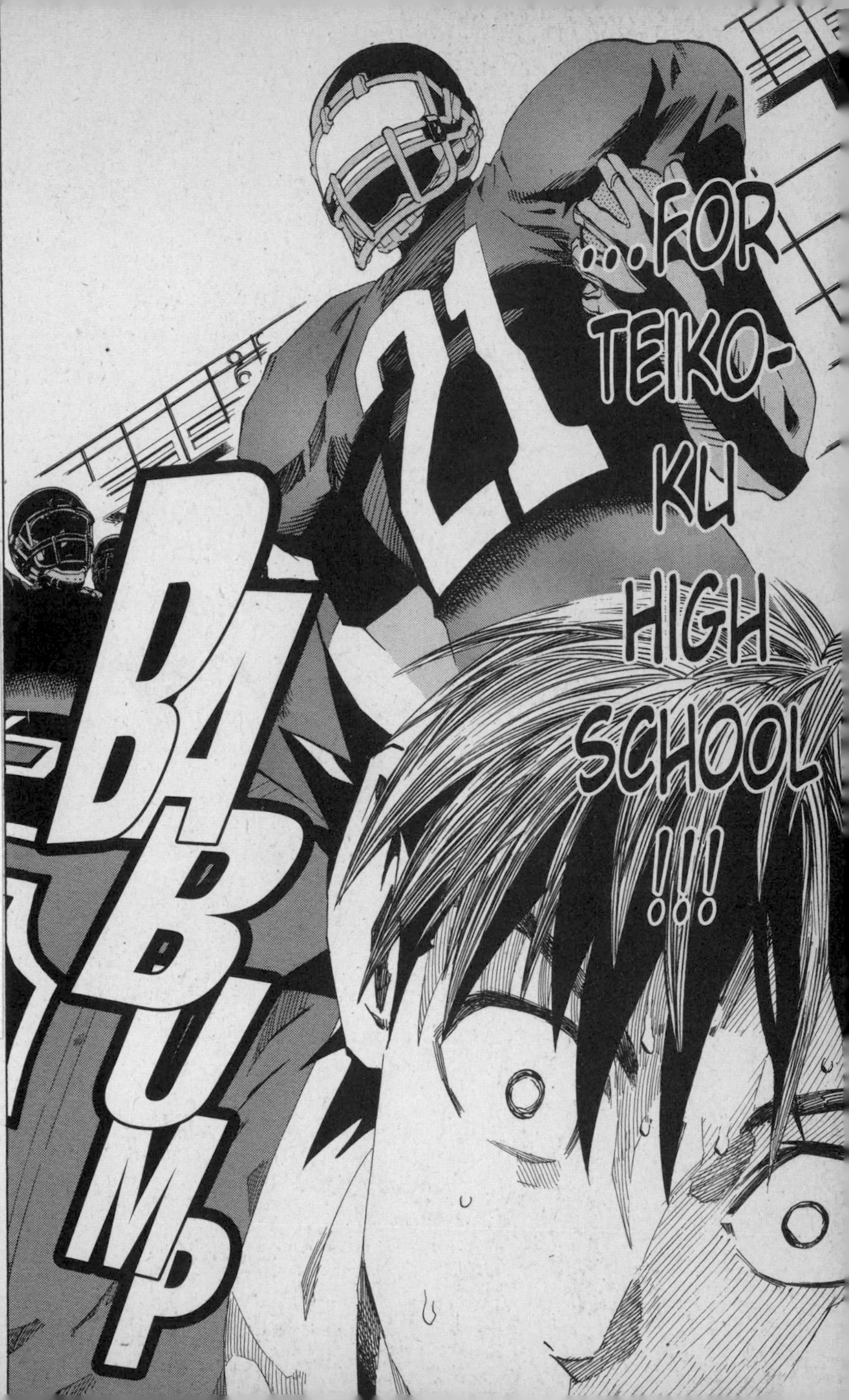
...FOR TEIKO-KU HIGH SCHOOL!!!
BA-BUMP

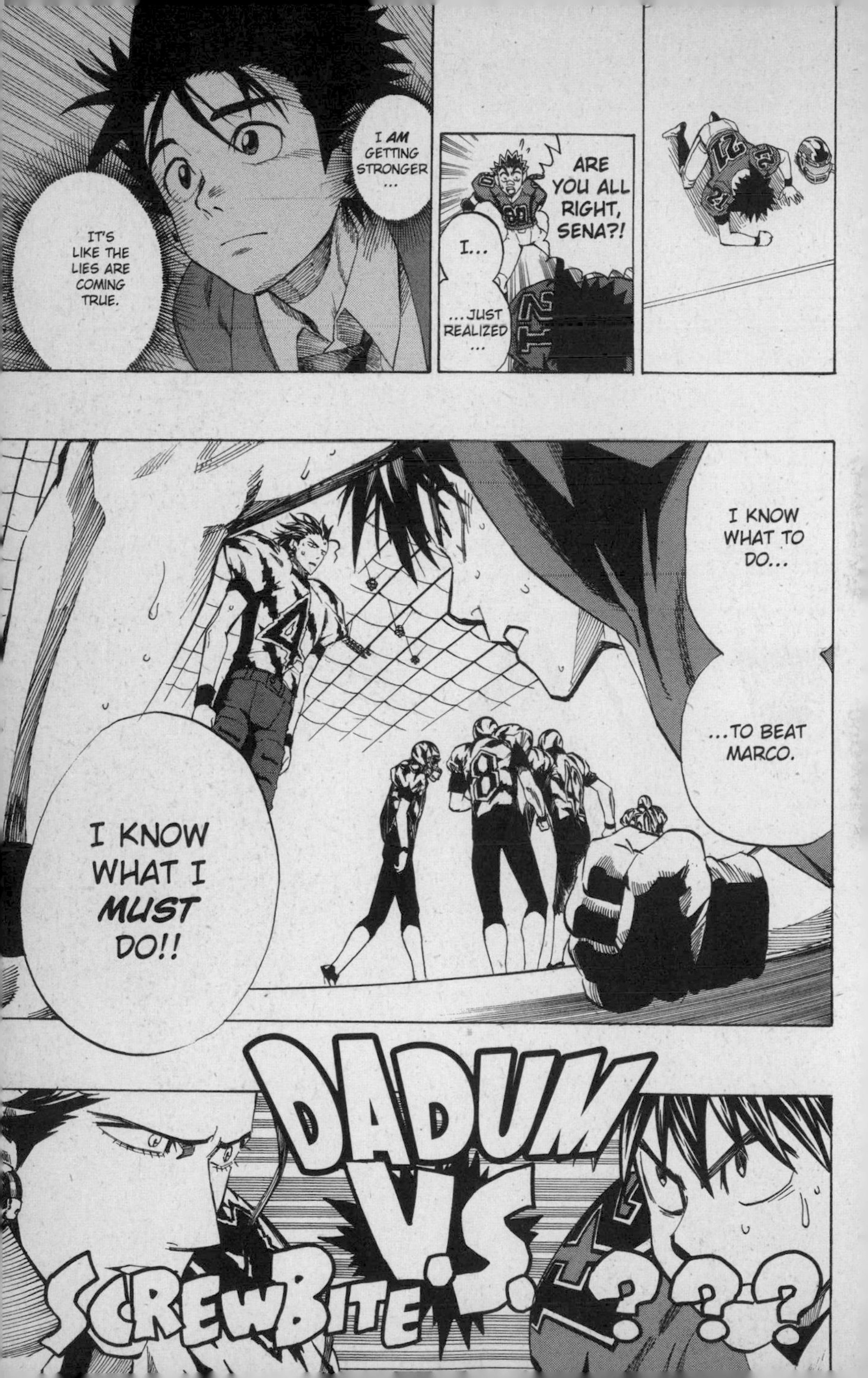
ARE YOU ALL RIGHT, SENA?!
I...
...JUST REALIZED...
I AM GETTING STRONGER...
IT'S LIKE THE LIES ARE COMING TRUE.
I KNOW WHAT TO DO...
...TO BEAT MARCO.
I KNOW WHAT I MUST DO!!
DADUM
SCREWBITE V.S. ???

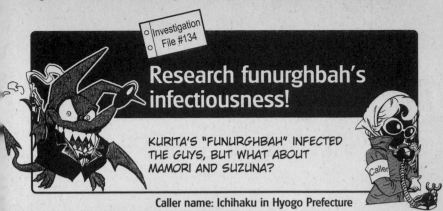

Investigation File #134

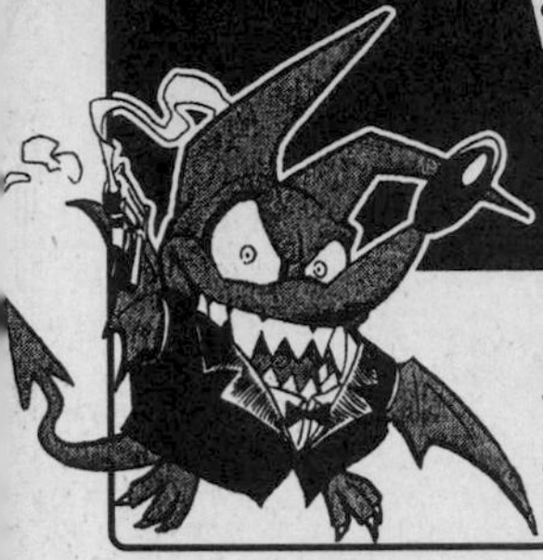

Research funurghbah's infectiousness!

KURITA'S "FUNURGHBAH" INFECTED THE GUYS, BUT WHAT ABOUT MAMORI AND SUZUNA?

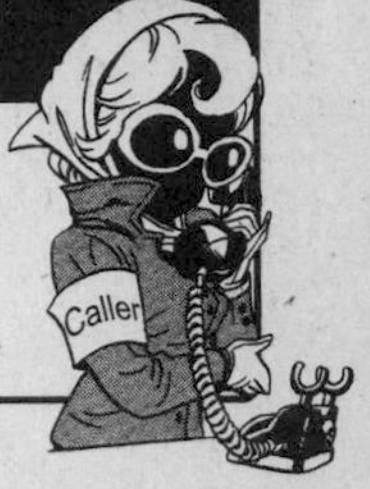
Caller

Caller name: Ichihaku in Hyogo Prefecture

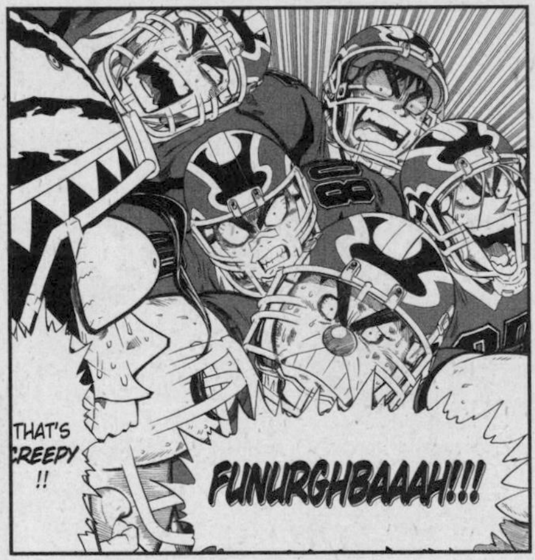
FUNURGHBAAAH!!!
THAT'S CREEPY !!

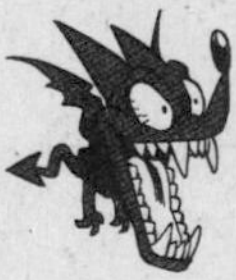

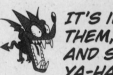

IT'S INFECTED THEM, HEART AND SOUL! YA-HA!!

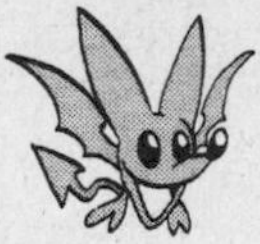

THEY DIDN'T WANT IT TO SHOW ON THEIR FACES, SO THEY PUT UP A FIGHT! IN THE END, THEIR FEMININE DEFENSES JUST BARELY SUPPRESSED IT!

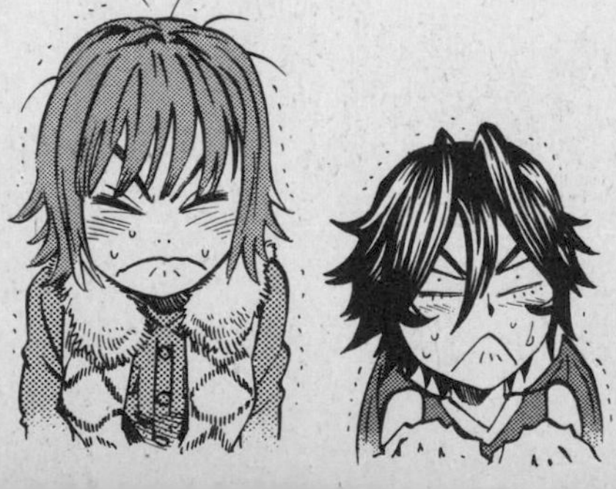

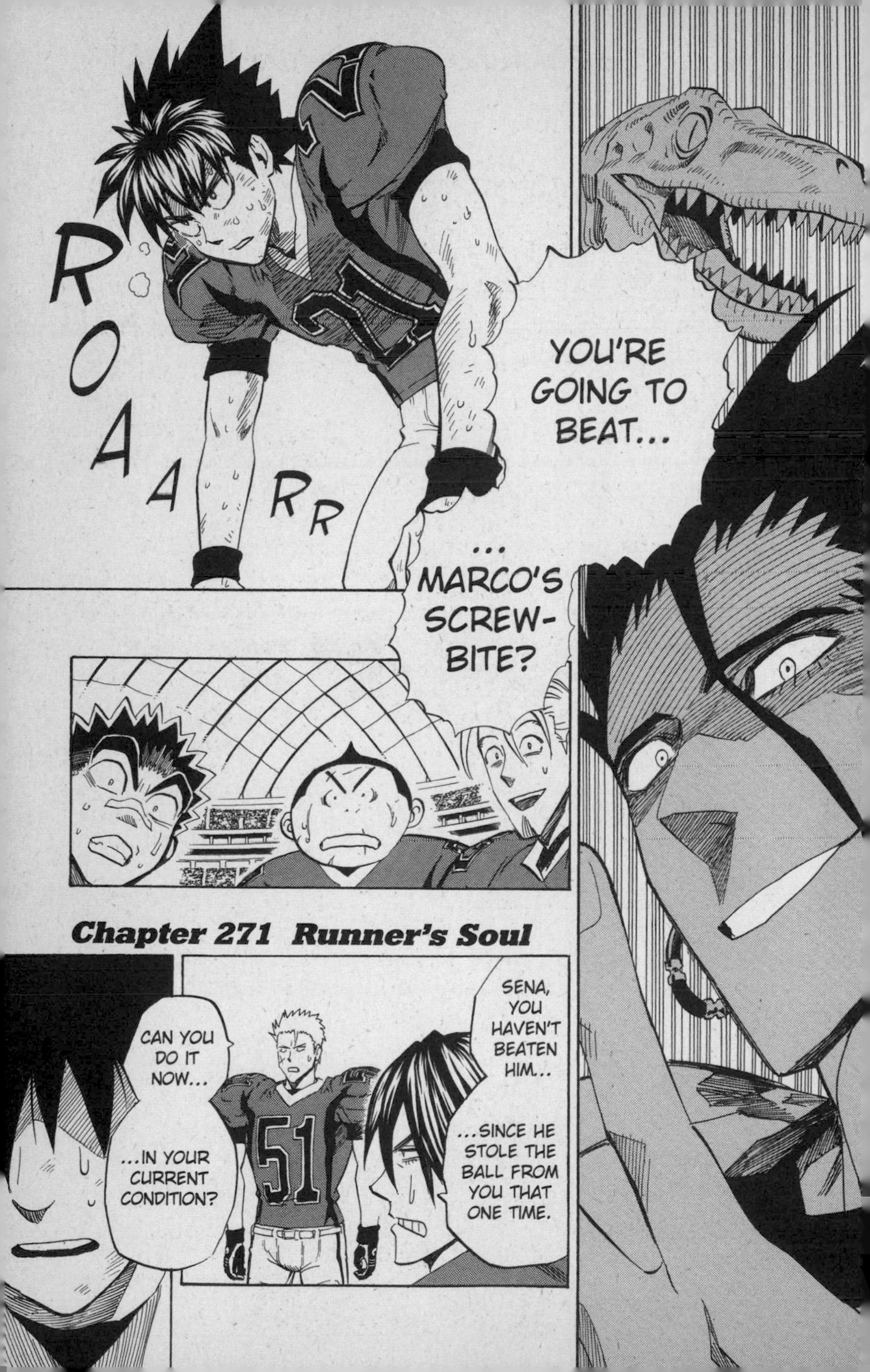
YOU'RE GOING TO BEAT...
...MARCO'S SCREW-BITE?
ROAAARR
Chapter 271 Runner's Soul
SENA, YOU HAVEN'T BEATEN HIM...
...SINCE HE STOLE THE BALL FROM YOU THAT ONE TIME.
CAN YOU DO IT NOW...
...IN YOUR CURRENT CONDITION?

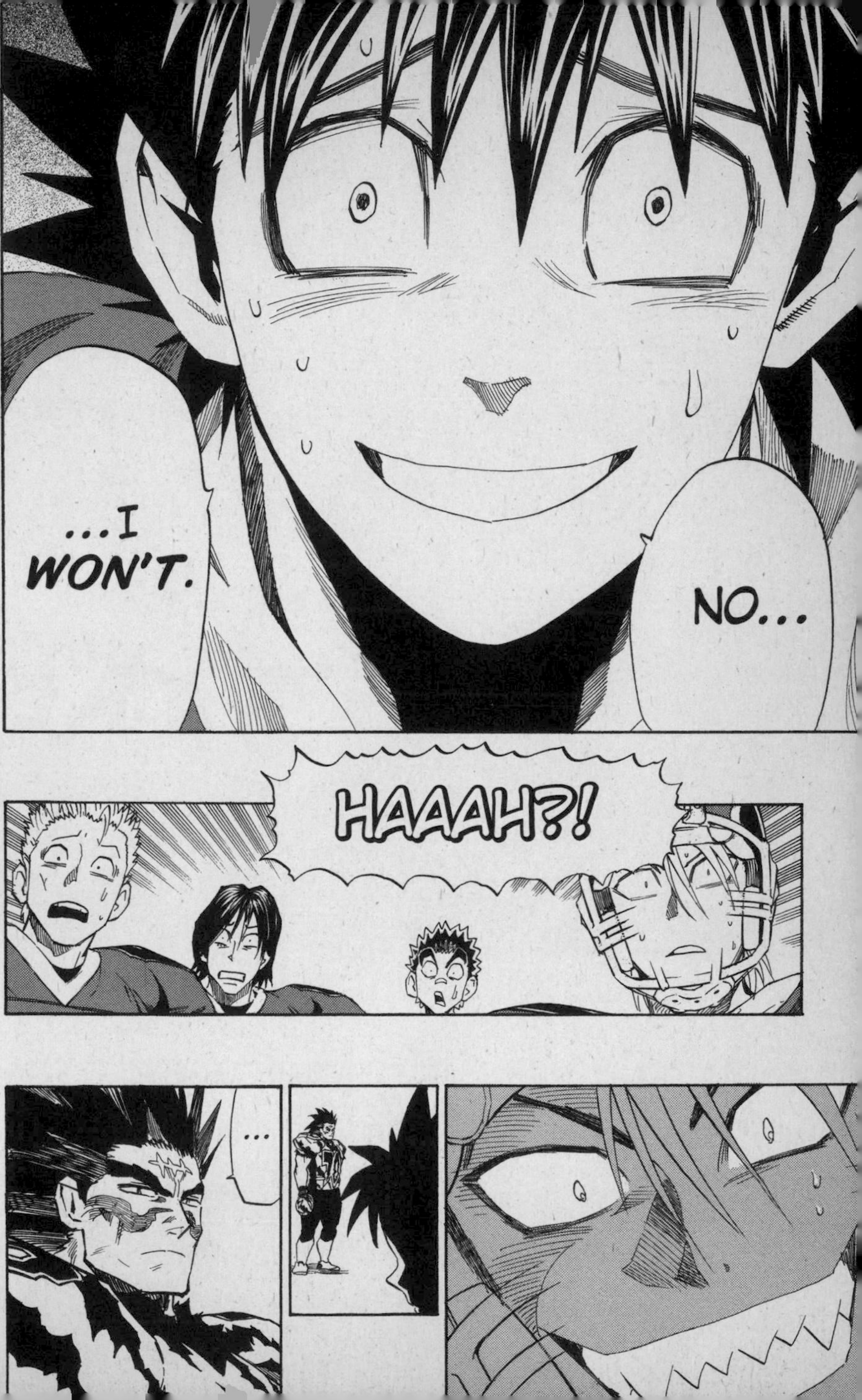
NO...
...I WON'T.
HAAAH?!
...

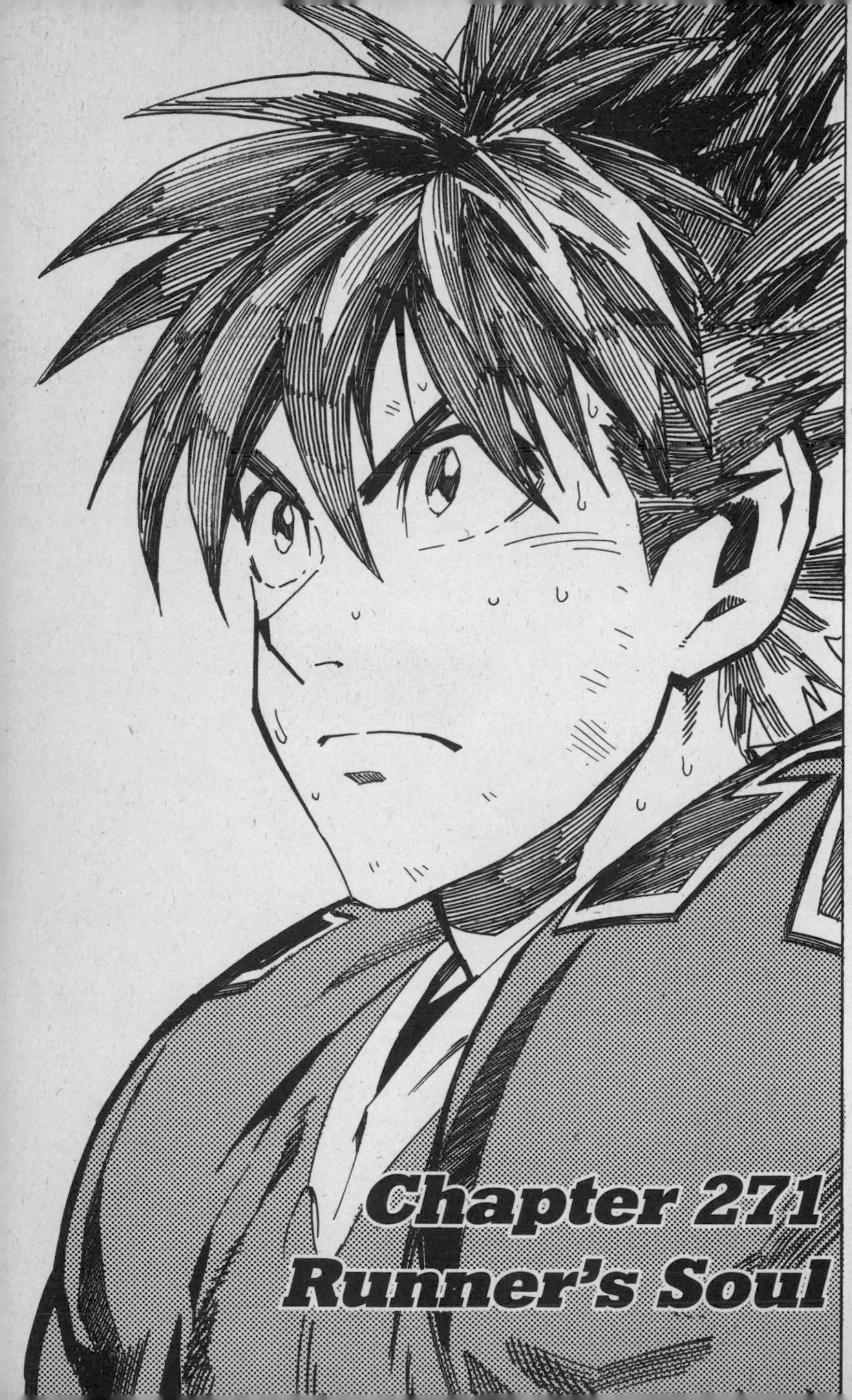
Chapter 271
Runner's Soul

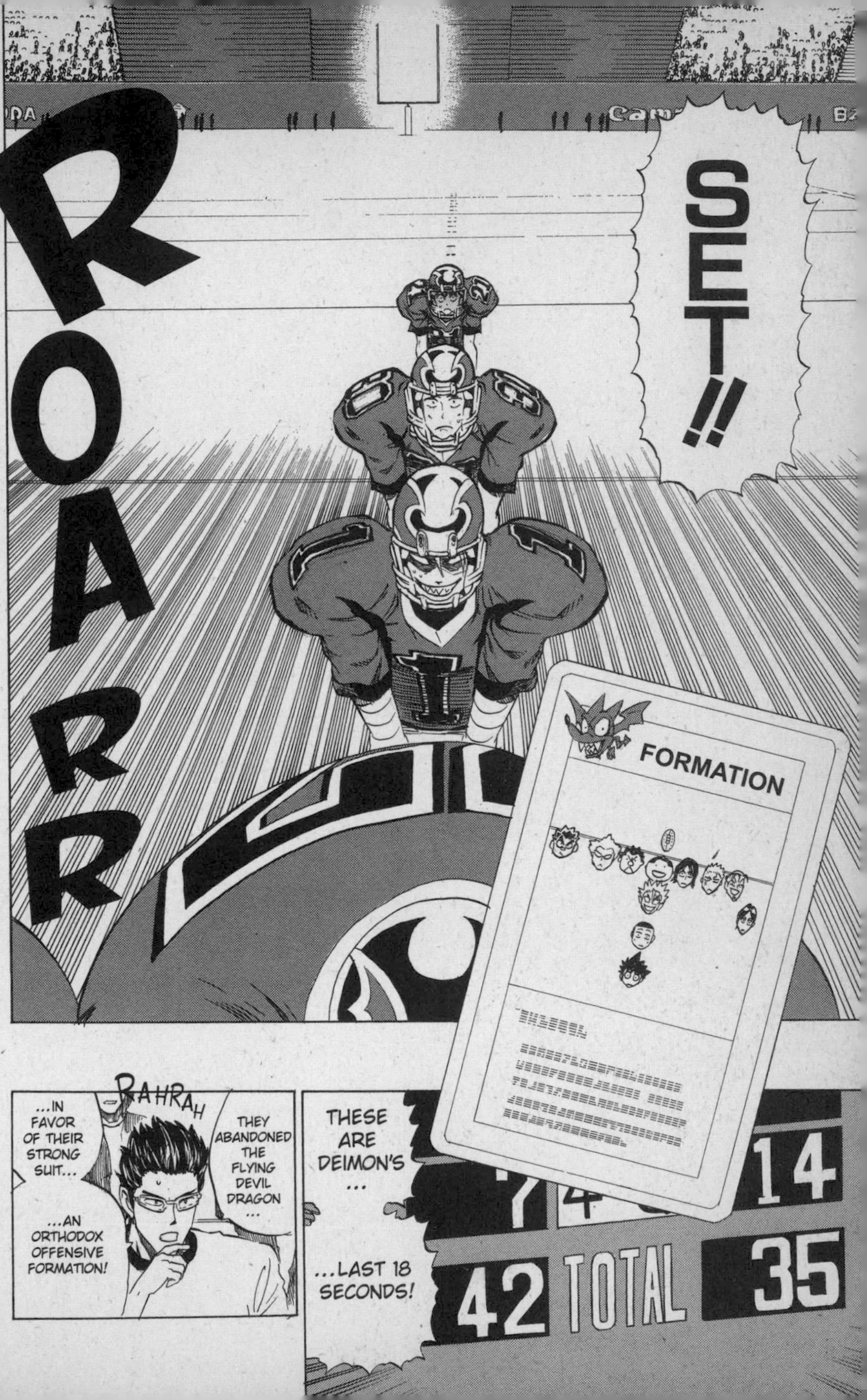
SET!!
ROARR
FORMATION
THESE ARE DEIMON'S ...
...LAST 18 SECONDS!
14
42
TOTAL
35
THEY ABANDONED THE FLYING DEVIL DRAGON ...
...IN FAVOR OF THEIR STRONG SUIT...
...AN ORTHODOX OFFENSIVE FORMATION!
RAHRAH

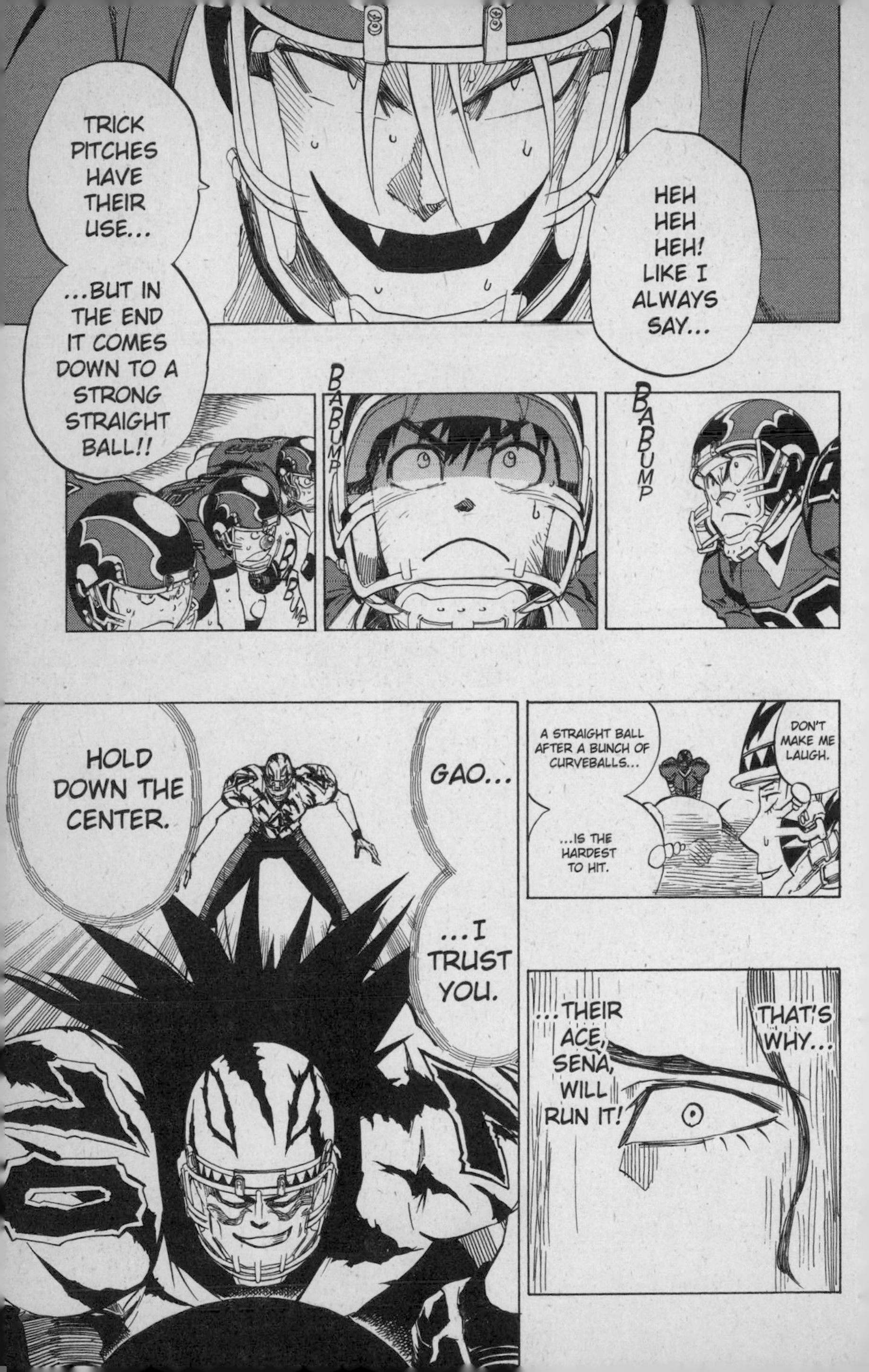
HEH HEH HEH! LIKE I ALWAYS SAY...
TRICK PITCHES HAVE THEIR USE...
...BUT IN THE END IT COMES DOWN TO A STRONG STRAIGHT BALL!!
BABUMP
BABUMP
BABUMP
DON'T MAKE ME LAUGH.
A STRAIGHT BALL AFTER A BUNCH OF CURVEBALLS...
...IS THE HARDEST TO HIT.
THAT'S WHY...
...THEIR ACE, SENA, WILL RUN IT!
GAO...
...I TRUST YOU.
HOLD DOWN THE CENTER.

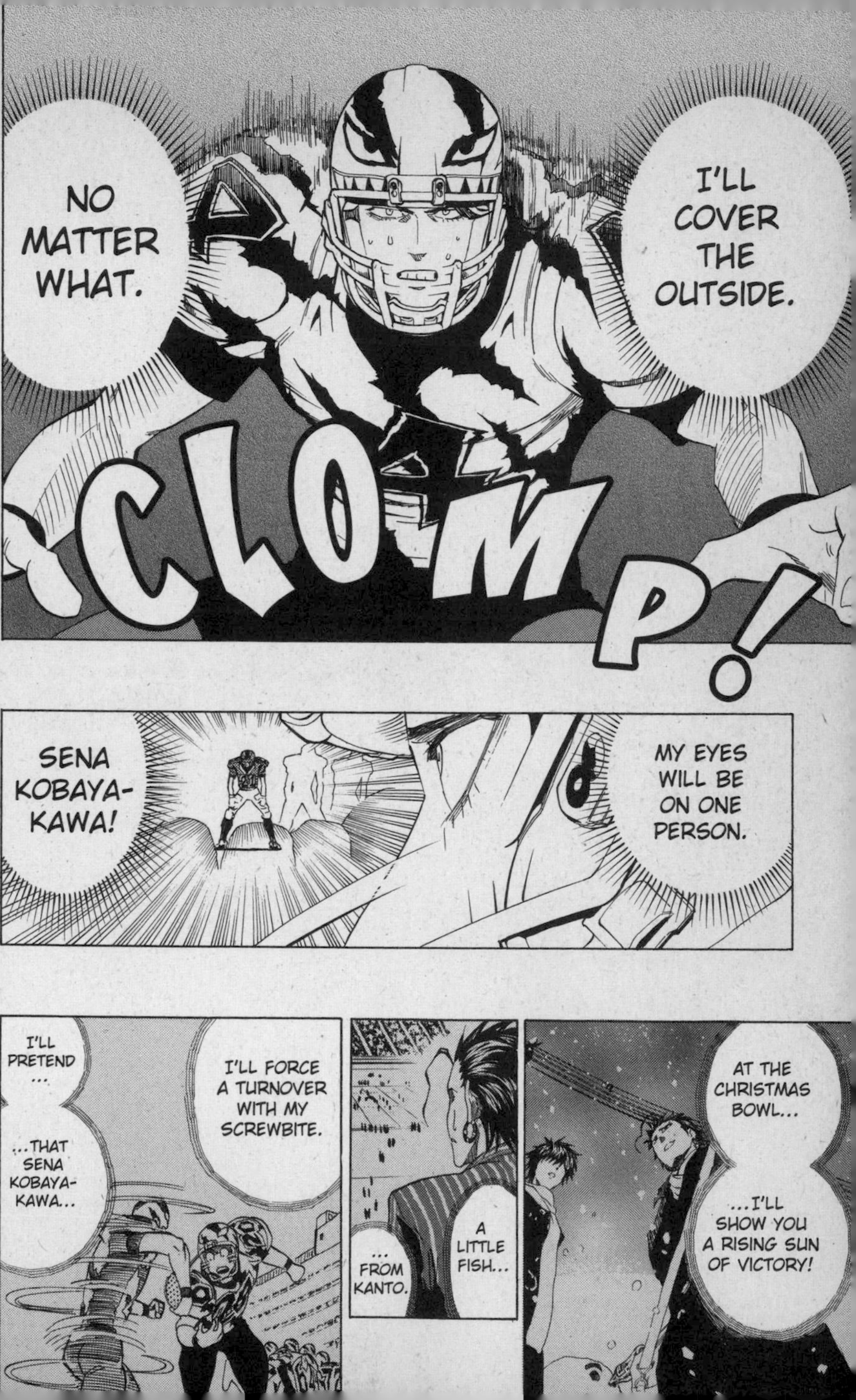
I'LL COVER THE OUTSIDE.
NO MATTER WHAT.
CLOMP!
MY EYES WILL BE ON ONE PERSON.
SENA KOBAYA-KAWA!
AT THE CHRISTMAS BOWL...
...I'LL SHOW YOU A RISING SUN OF VICTORY!
A LITTLE FISH...
...FROM KANTO.
I'LL FORCE A TURNOVER WITH MY SCREWBITE.
I'LL PRETEND...
...THAT SENA KOBAYA-KAWA...

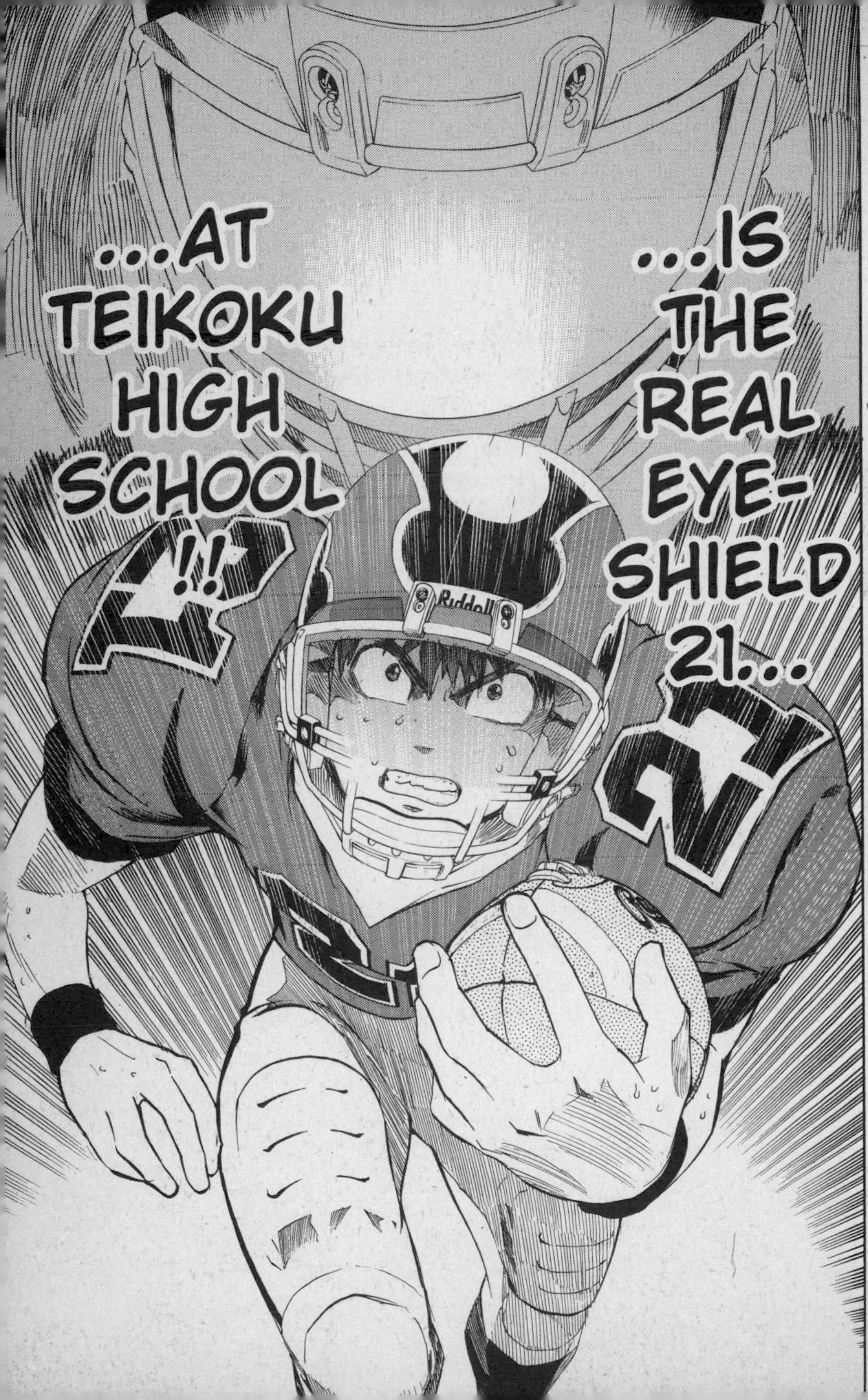
...IS THE REAL EYE-SHIELD 21...
...AT TEIKOKU HIGH SCHOOL!!

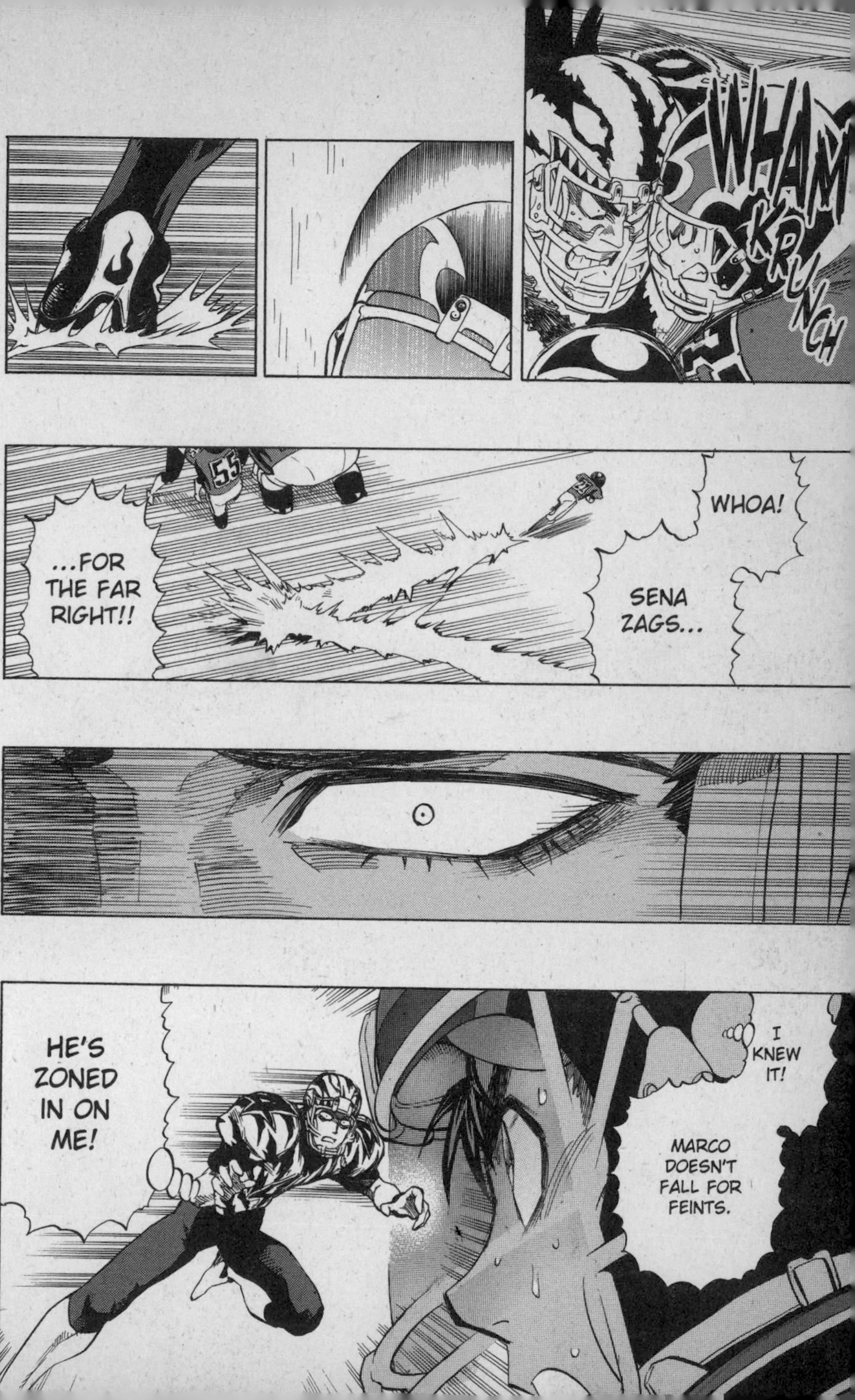
WHAM
KRUNCH
WHOA!
SENA ZAGS...
...FOR THE FAR RIGHT!!
I KNEW IT!
MARCO DOESN'T FALL FOR FEINTS.
HE'S ZONED IN ON ME!

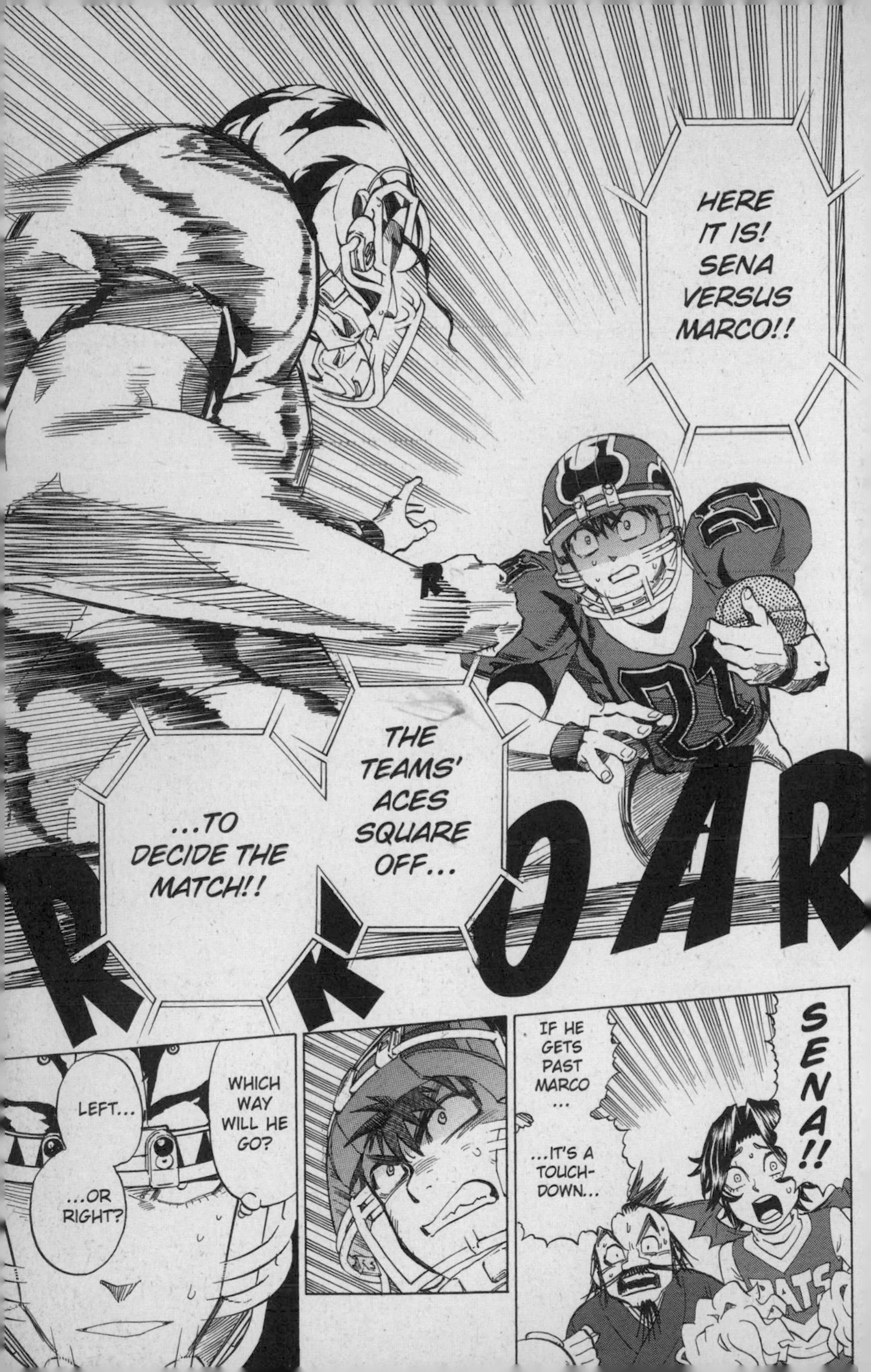
HERE IT IS! SENA VERSUS MARCO!!
THE TEAMS' ACES SQUARE OFF...
...TO DECIDE THE MATCH!!
RROAR
SENA!!
IF HE GETS PAST MARCO...
...IT'S A TOUCH-DOWN...
WHICH WAY WILL HE GO?
LEFT...
...OR RIGHT?

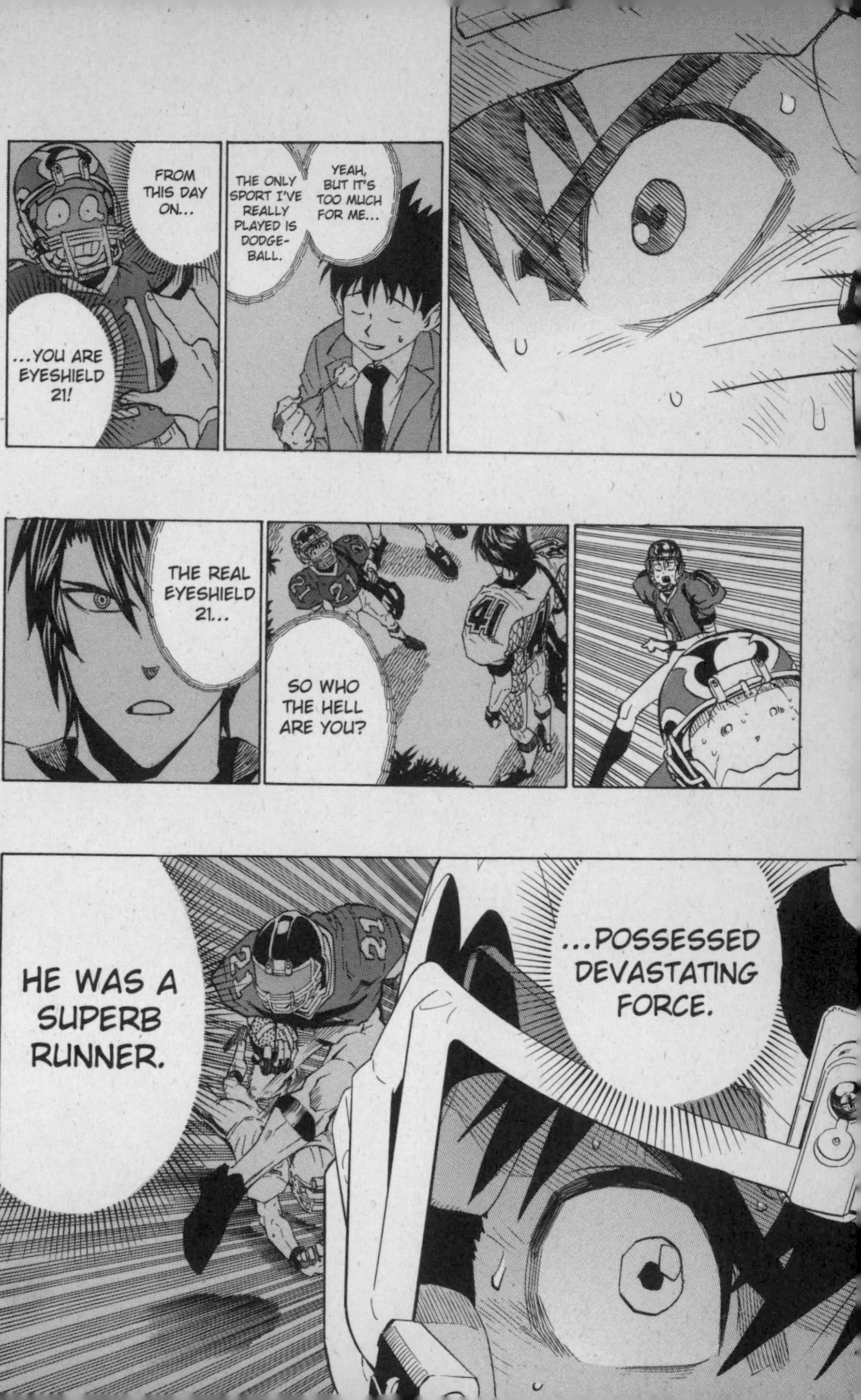
YEAH, BUT IT'S TOO MUCH FOR ME...
THE ONLY SPORT I'VE REALLY PLAYED IS DODGE-BALL.
FROM THIS DAY ON...
...YOU ARE EYESHIELD 21!
SO WHO THE HELL ARE YOU?
THE REAL EYESHIELD 21...
...POSSESSED DEVASTATING FORCE.
HE WAS A SUPERB RUNNER.

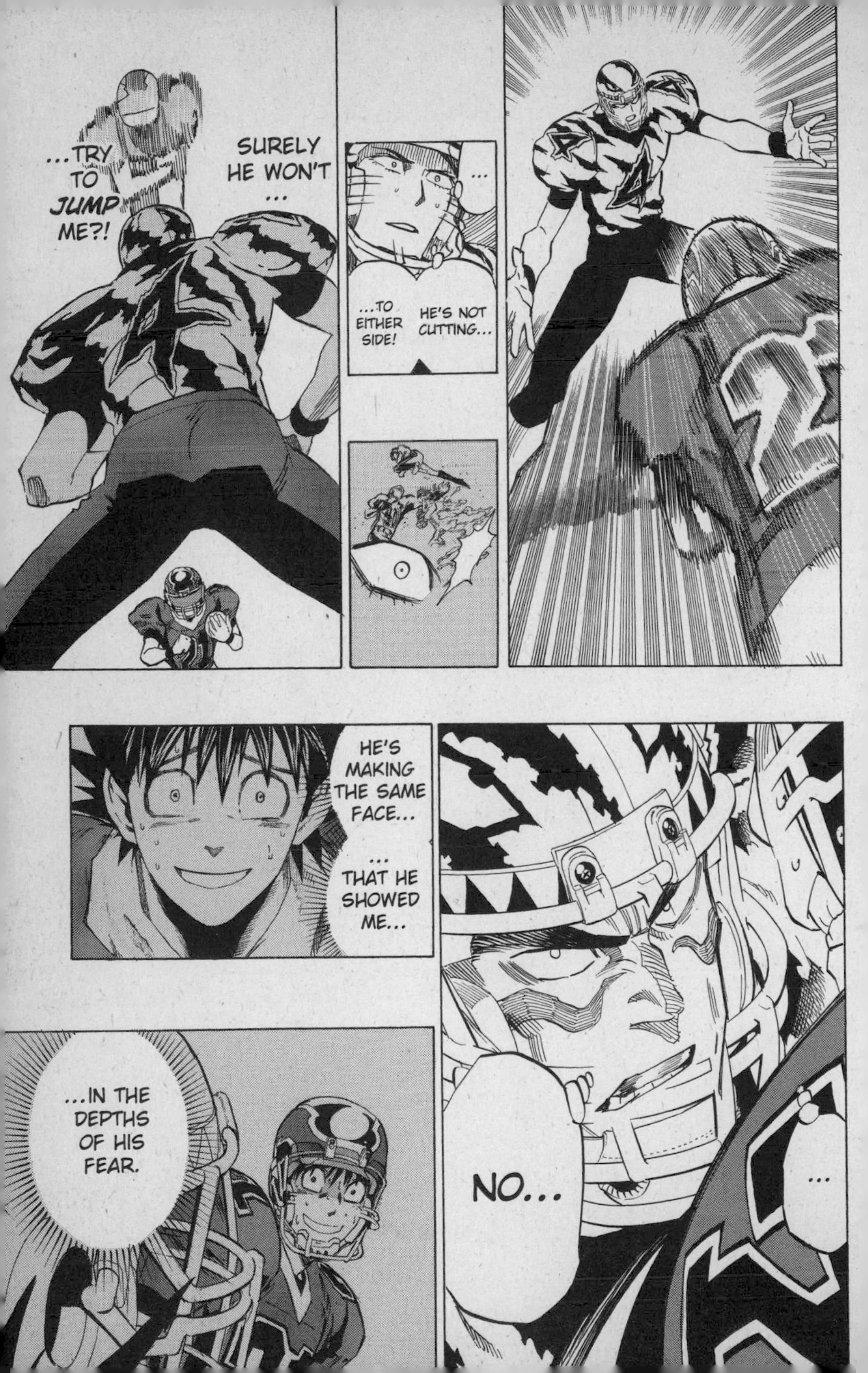
...
HE'S NOT CUTTING...
...TO EITHER SIDE!
SURELY HE WON'T ...
...TRY TO JUMP ME?!
...
NO...
HE'S MAKING THE SAME FACE...
... THAT HE SHOWED ME...
...IN THE DEPTHS OF HIS FEAR.

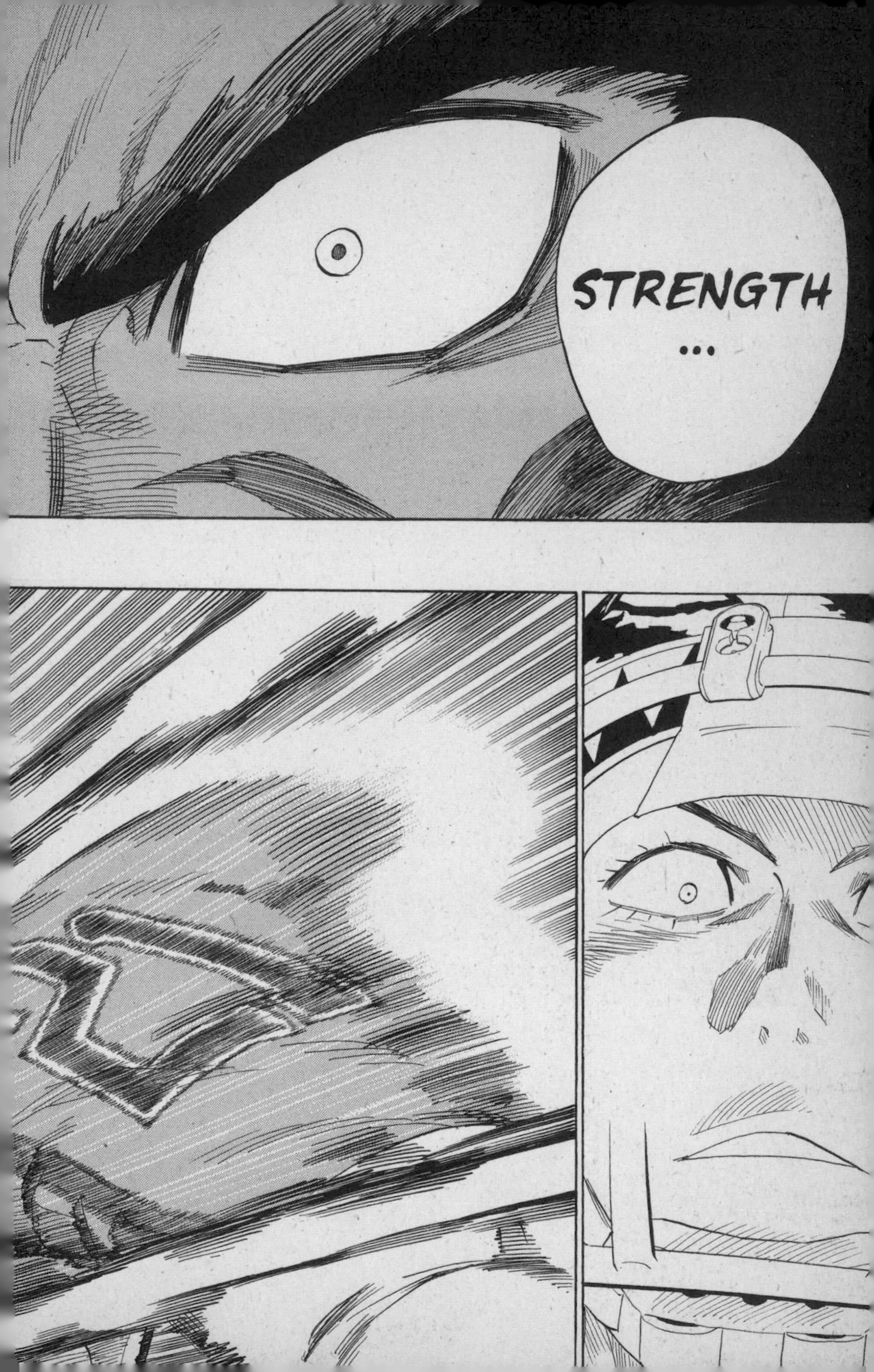
STRENGTH
...

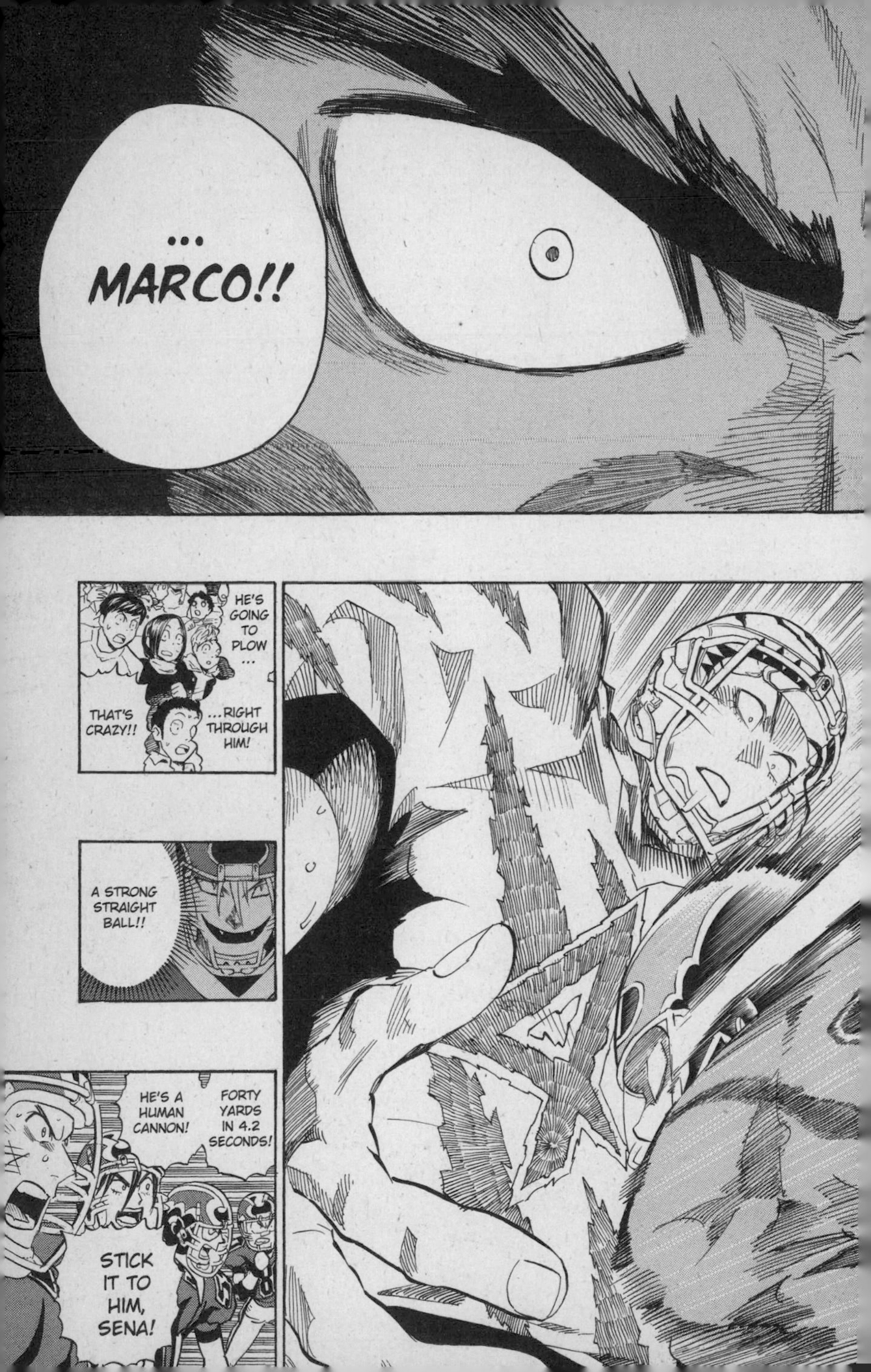
...
MARCO!!
HE'S GOING TO PLOW ...
...RIGHT THROUGH HIM!
THAT'S CRAZY!!
A STRONG STRAIGHT BALL!!
FORTY YARDS IN 4.2 SECONDS!
HE'S A HUMAN CANNON!
STICK IT TO HIM, SENA!

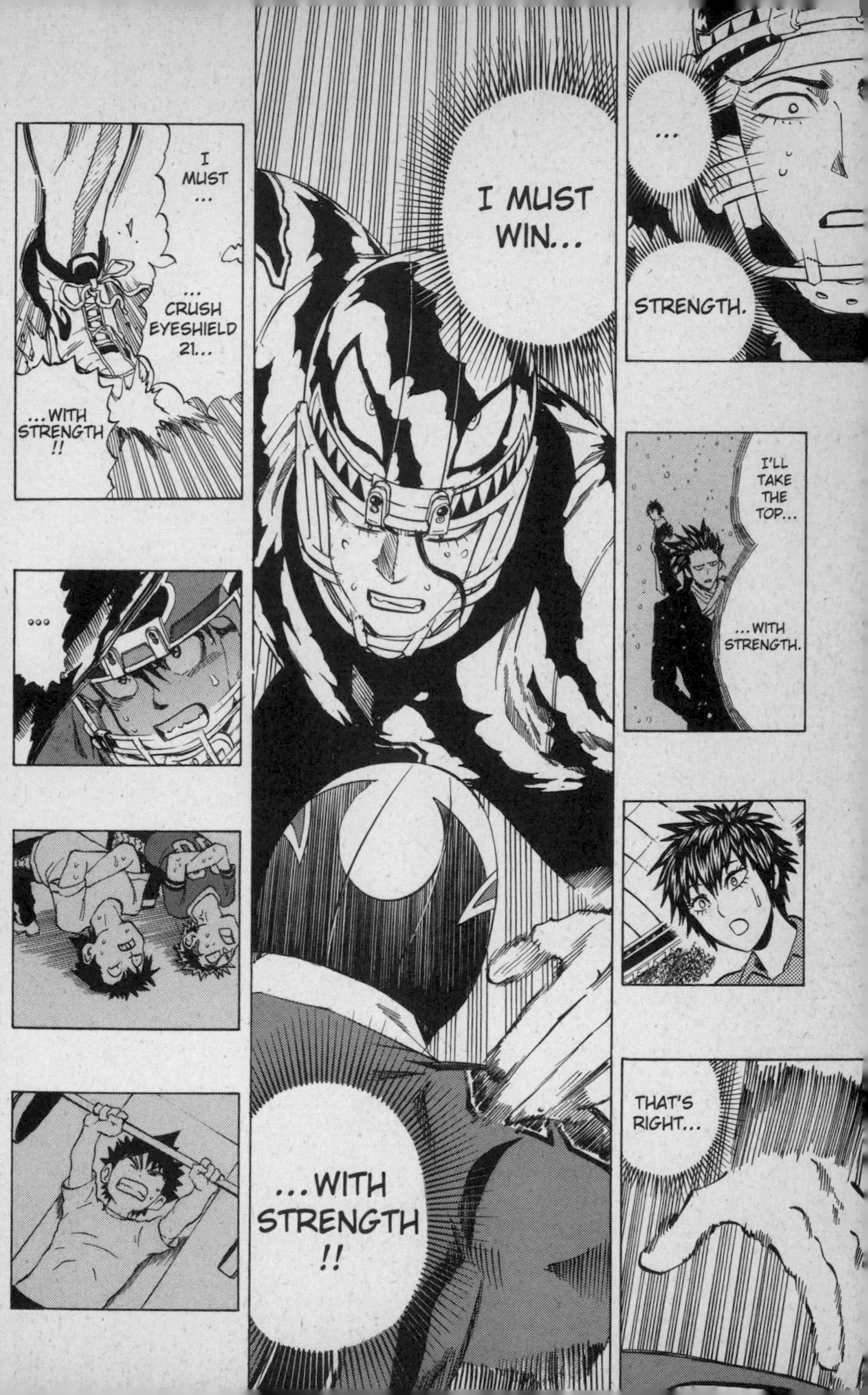
...
STRENGTH.
I'LL TAKE THE TOP...
...WITH STRENGTH.
THAT'S RIGHT...
I MUST WIN...
...WITH STRENGTH !!
I MUST ...
... CRUSH EYESHIELD 21...
...WITH STRENGTH !!
...

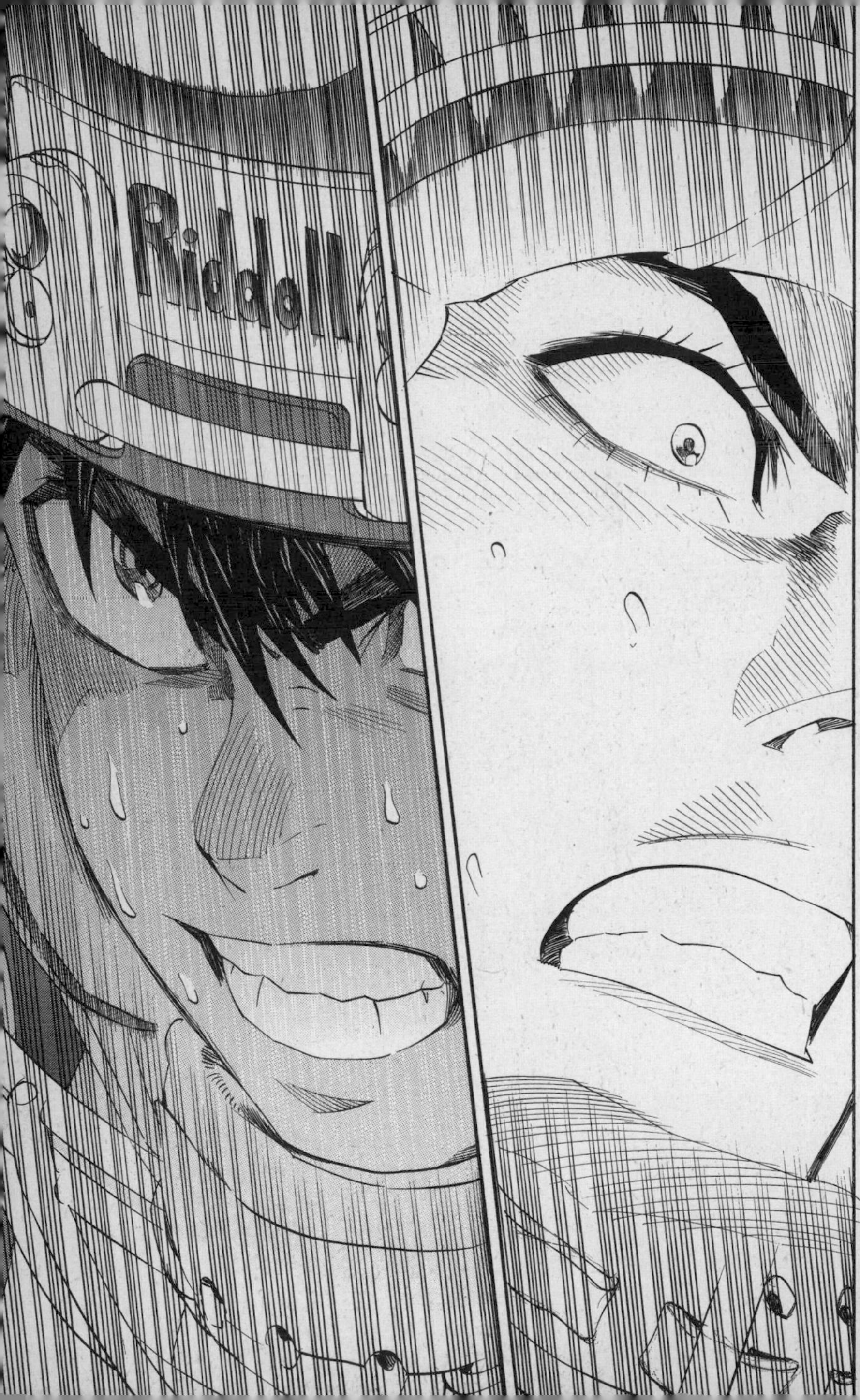
Riddell

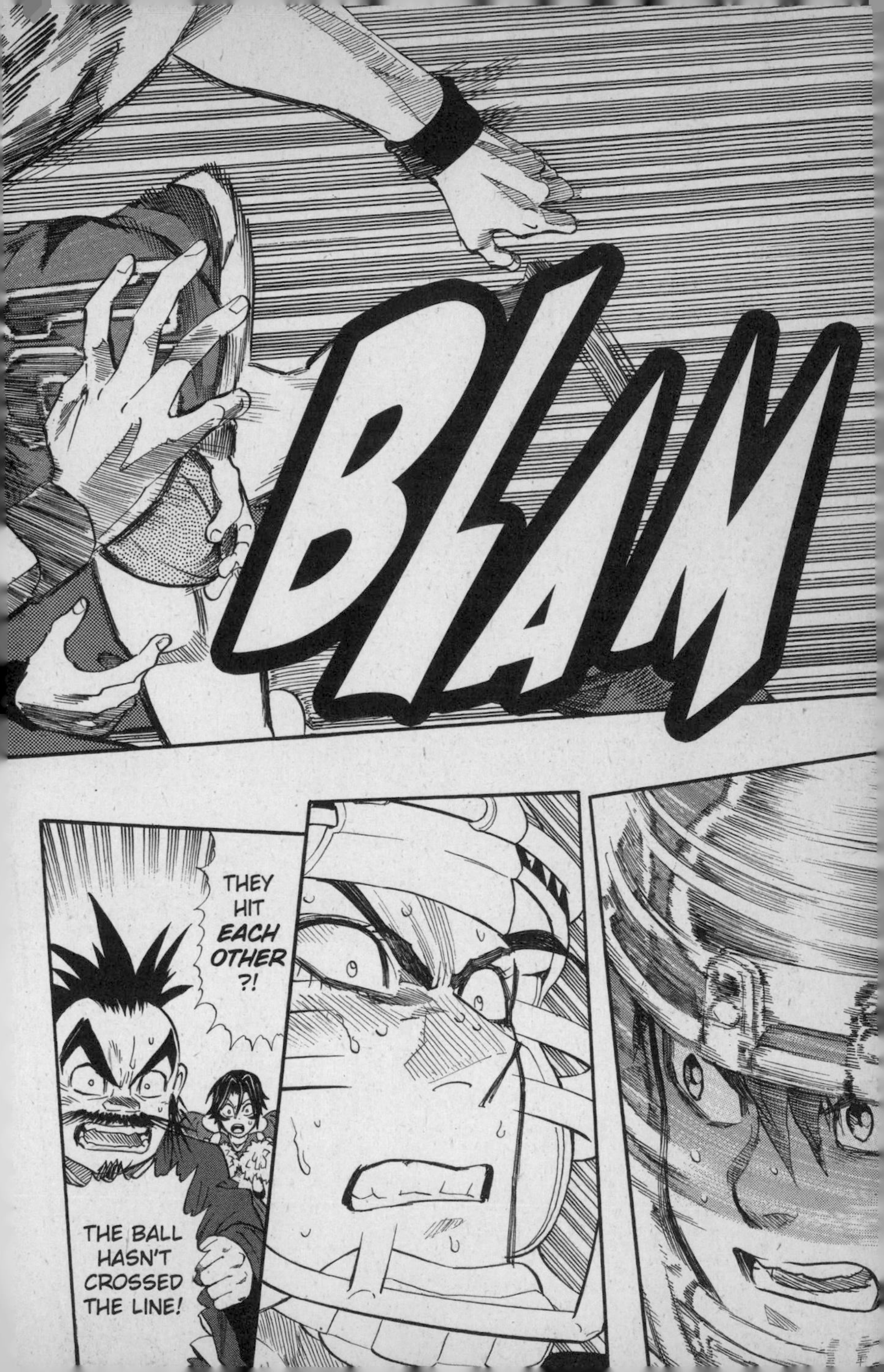
BLAM
THEY HIT EACH OTHER?!
THE BALL HASN'T CROSSED THE LINE!

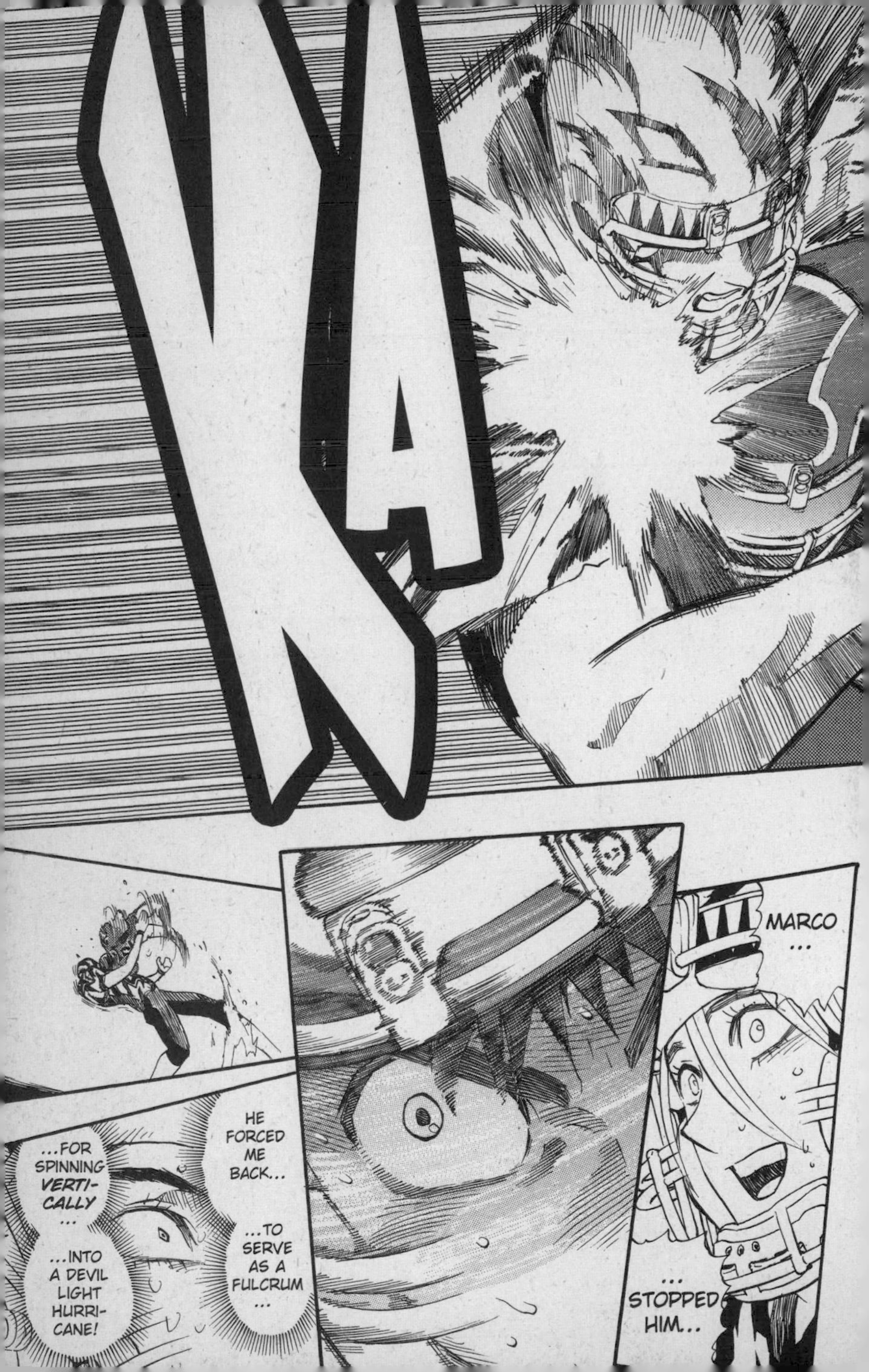
YA
MARCO ...
... STOPPED HIM...
HE FORCED ME BACK...
...TO SERVE AS A FULCRUM ...
...FOR SPINNING *VERTICALLY* ...
...INTO A DEVIL LIGHT HURRICANE!

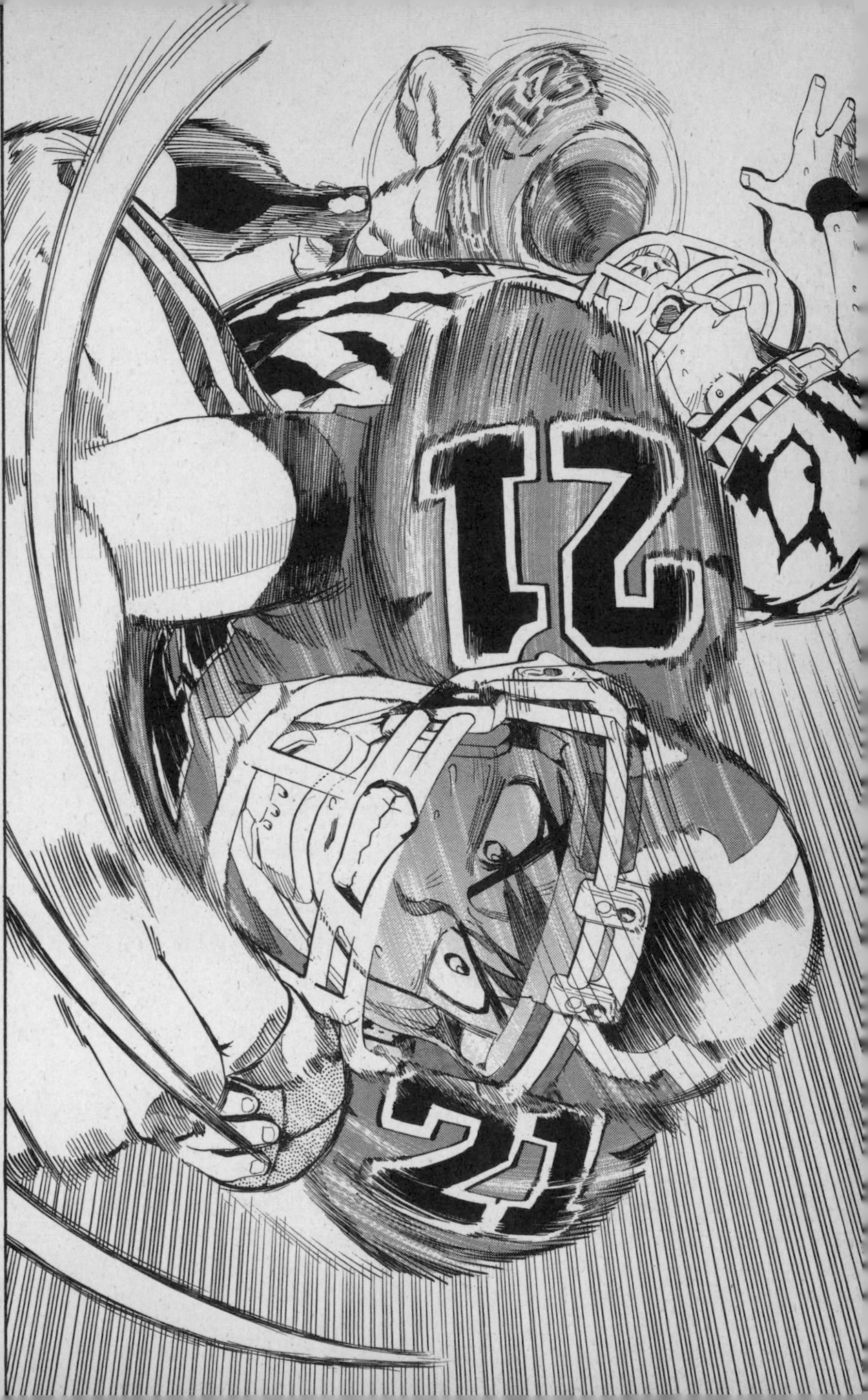

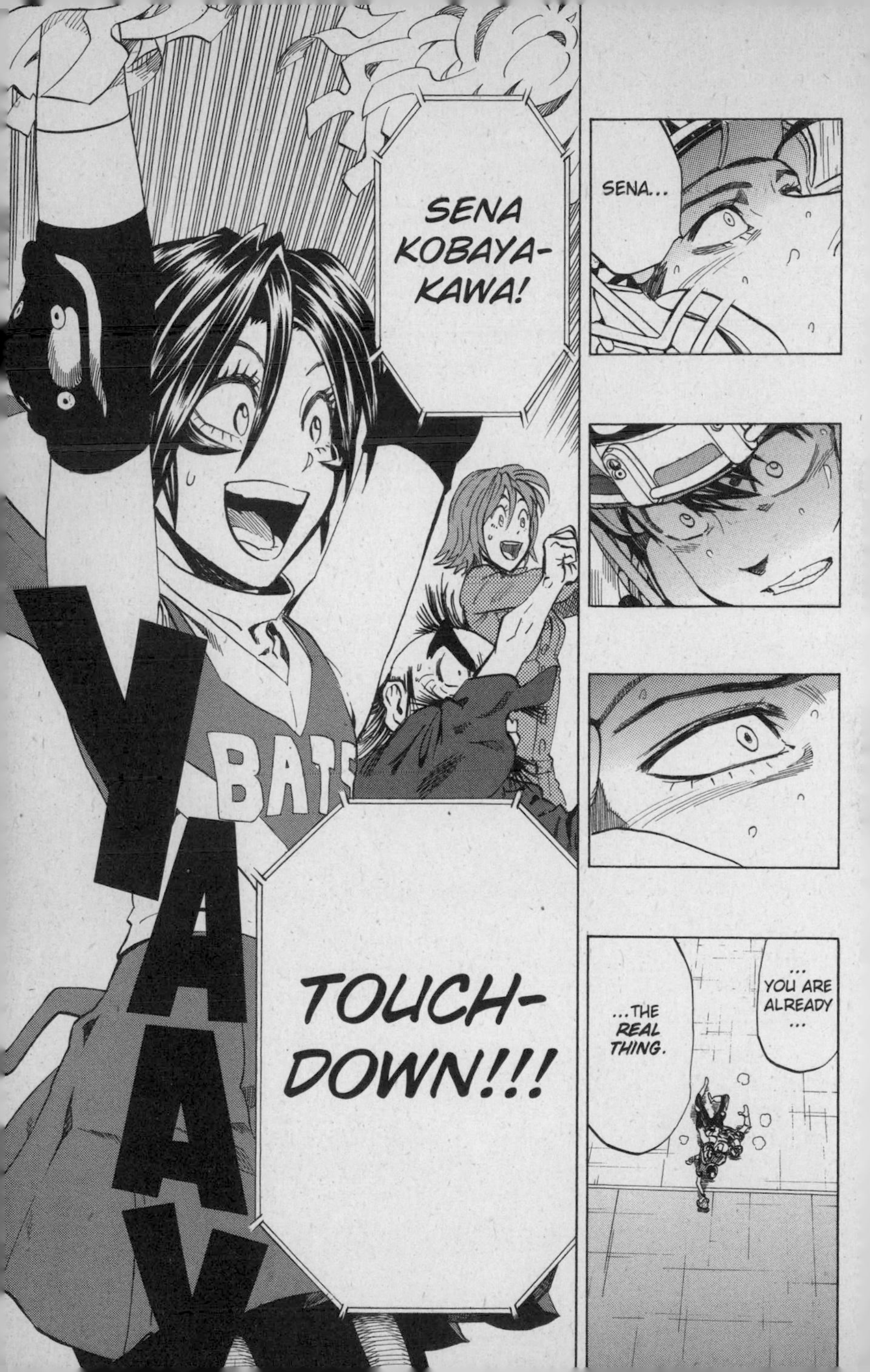
SENA...
... YOU ARE ALREADY ...
...THE REAL THING.
SENA KOBAYA-KAWA!
TOUCH-DOWN!!!
BATS
YAAAY

Investigation File #135

Reveal Cerberus's powers!!

IN CHAPTER 2 OF VOLUME 1, SENA WAS RUNNING AT A SPEED OF 40 YARDS IN 4.2 SECONDS, BUT CERBERUS CAUGHT HIM! JUST HOW FAST CAN THAT DOG RUN?!

Caller

Caller name: K.A. in Fukuoka Prefecture

The 40-yard Dash in Nature

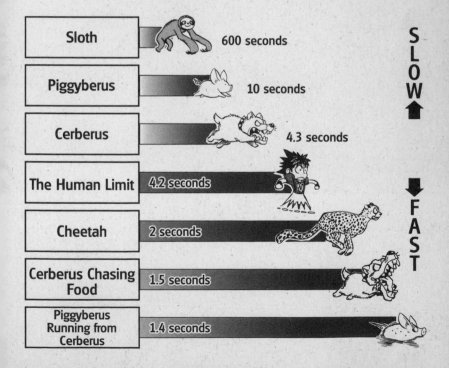

Sloth	600 seconds
Piggyberus	10 seconds
Cerberus	4.3 seconds
The Human Limit	4.2 seconds
Cheetah	2 seconds
Cerberus Chasing Food	1.5 seconds
Piggyberus Running from Cerberus	1.4 seconds

S L O W ↑

F A S T ↓

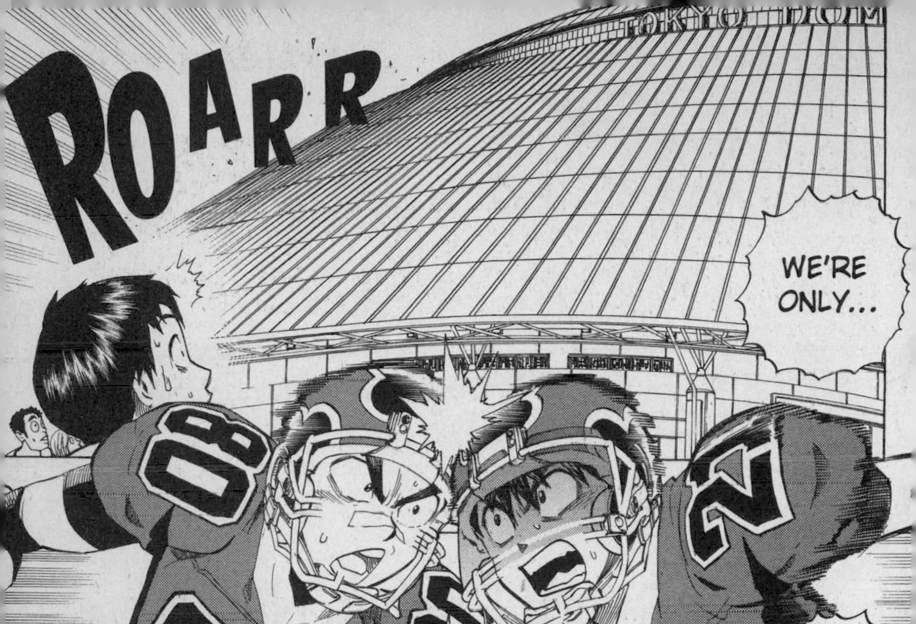
ROARR
WE'RE ONLY...
... ONE ...
TUNK
...POINT BEHIND !!!

Chapter 272 Win

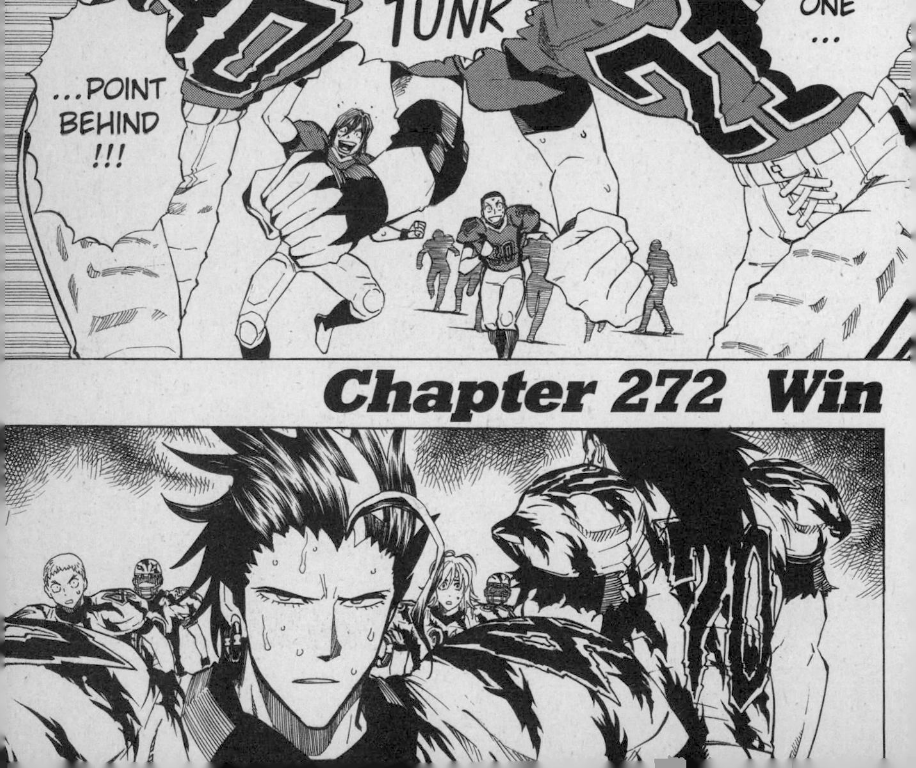

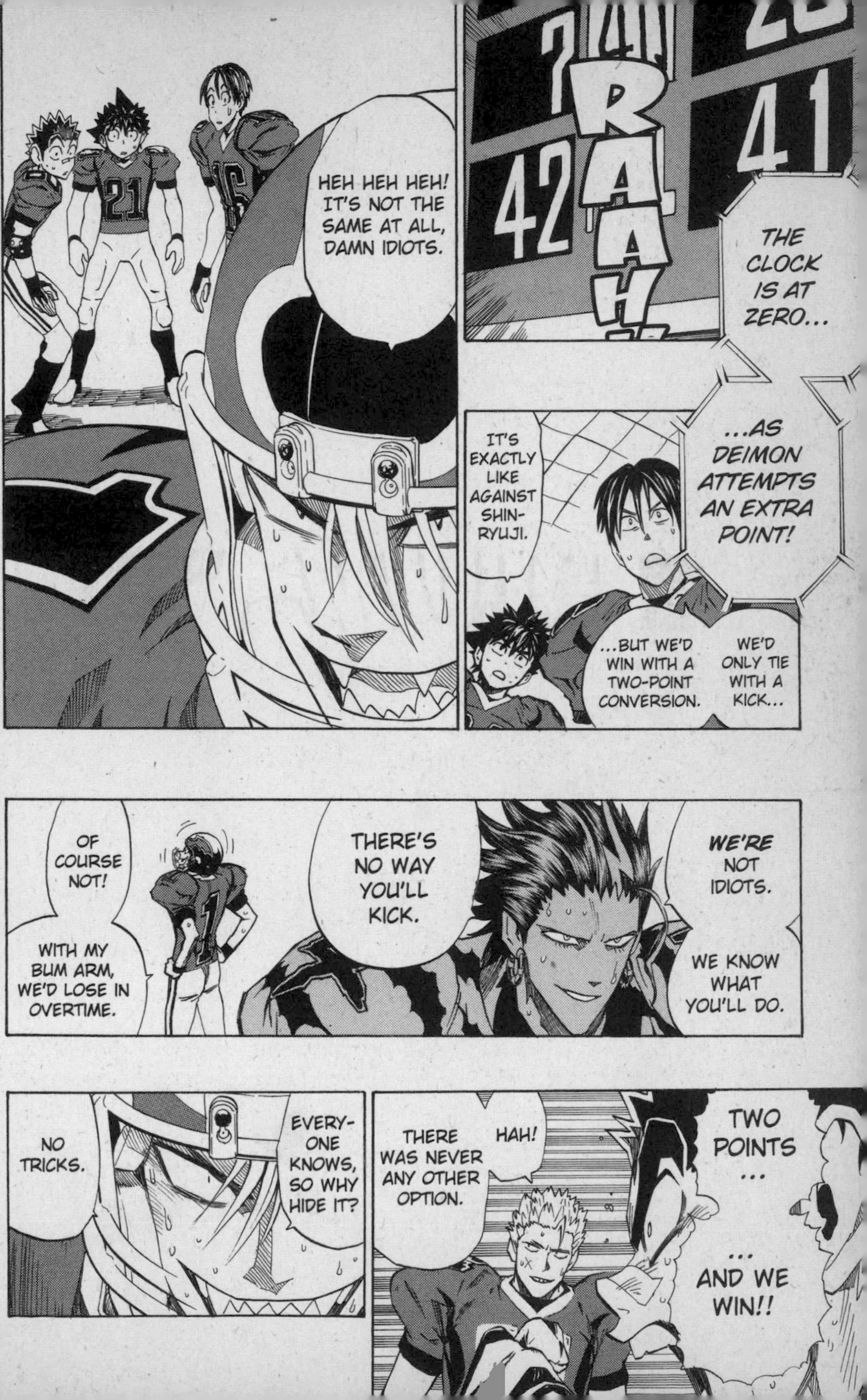
RAAH
THE CLOCK IS AT ZERO...
...AS DEIMON ATTEMPTS AN EXTRA POINT!
IT'S EXACTLY LIKE AGAINST SHIN-RYUJI.
WE'D ONLY TIE WITH A KICK...
...BUT WE'D WIN WITH A TWO-POINT CONVERSION.
HEH HEH HEH! IT'S NOT THE SAME AT ALL, DAMN IDIOTS.
WE'RE NOT IDIOTS.
WE KNOW WHAT YOU'LL DO.
THERE'S NO WAY YOU'LL KICK.
OF COURSE NOT!
WITH MY BUM ARM, WE'D LOSE IN OVERTIME.
TWO POINTS...
...AND WE WIN!!
HAH!
THERE WAS NEVER ANY OTHER OPTION.
EVERY-ONE KNOWS, SO WHY HIDE IT?
NO TRICKS.

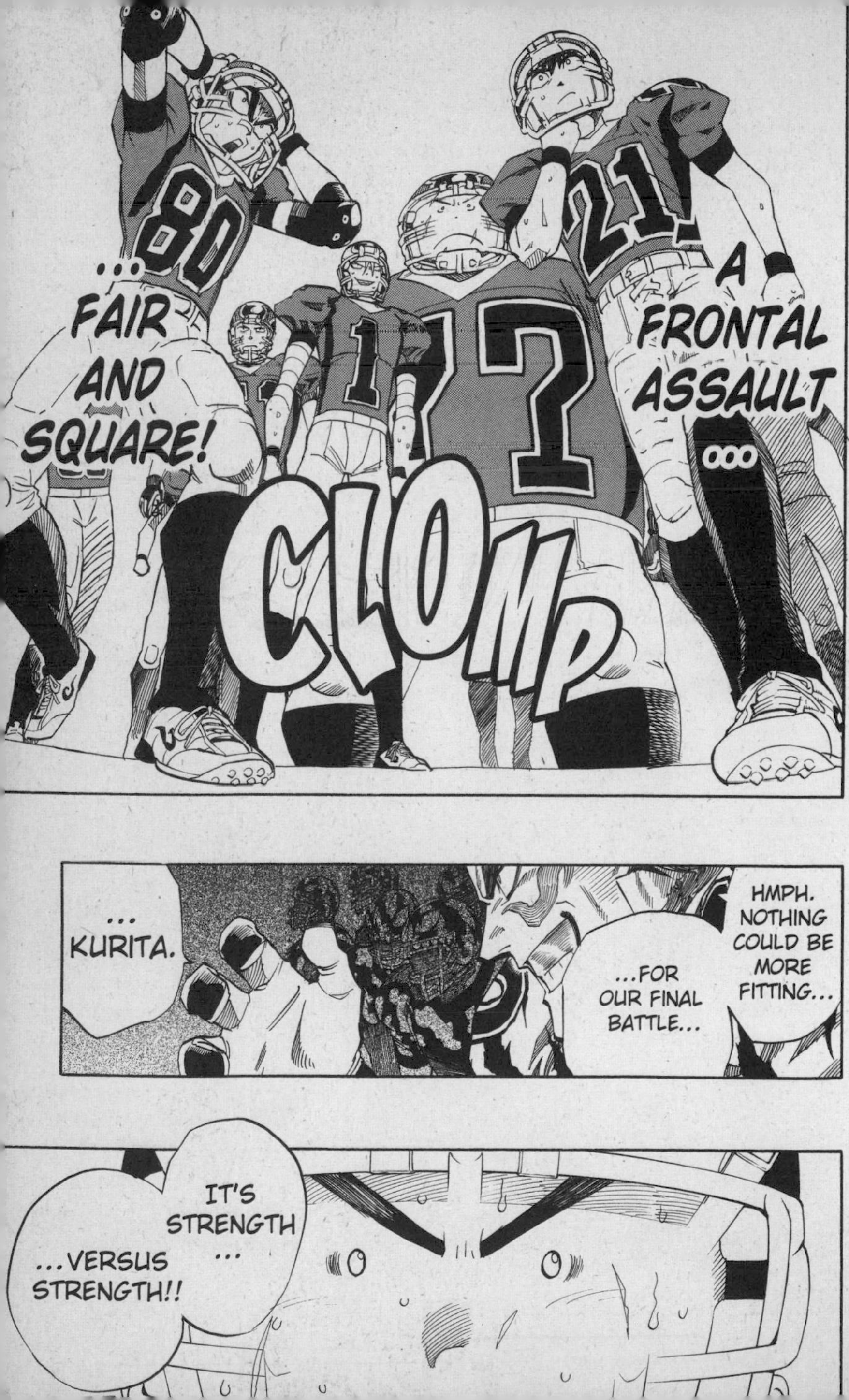
A FRONTAL ASSAULT...
...FAIR AND SQUARE!
CLOMP
HMPH. NOTHING COULD BE MORE FITTING...
...FOR OUR FINAL BATTLE...
...KURITA.
IT'S STRENGTH...
...VERSUS STRENGTH!!

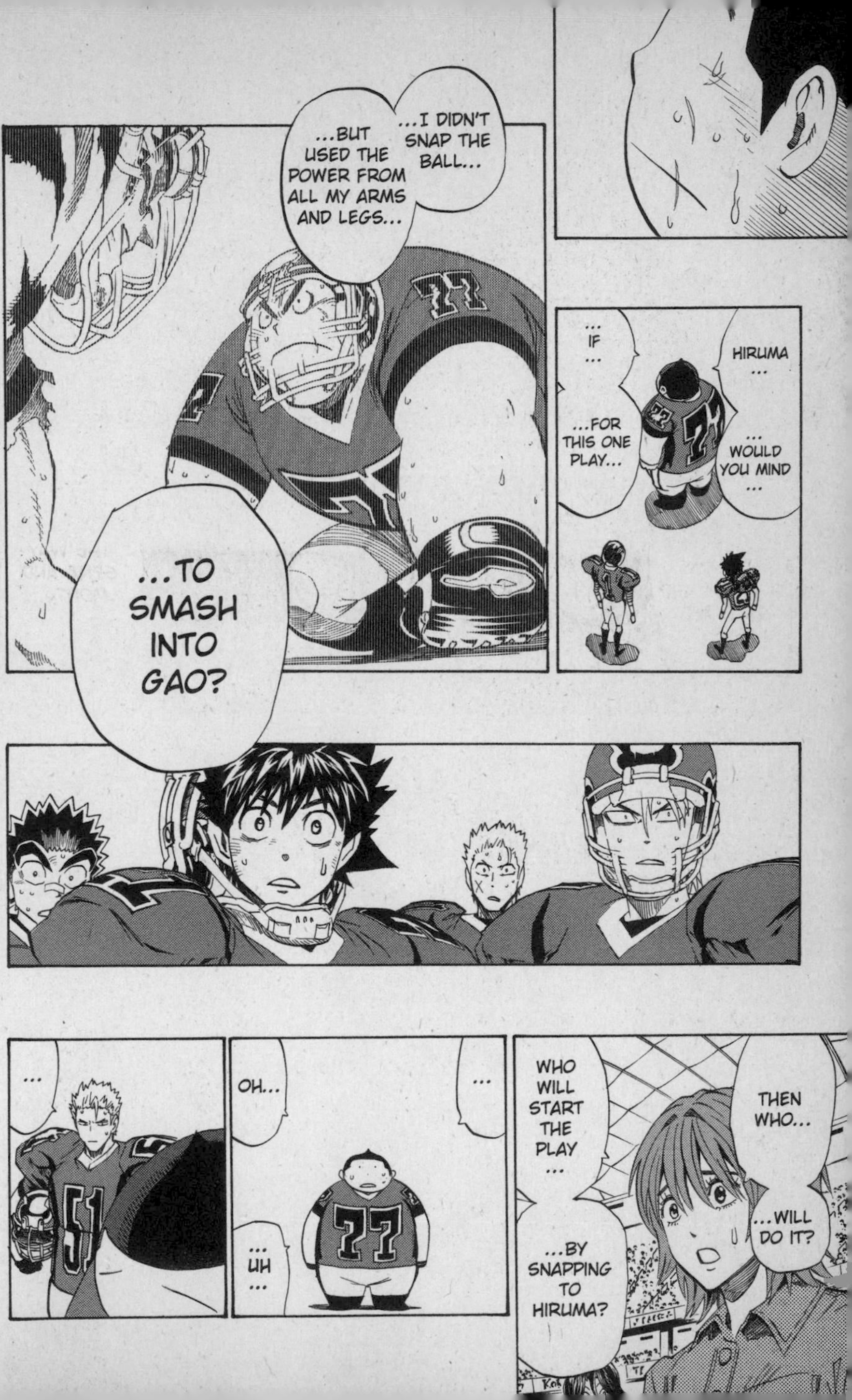
HIRUMA ...
... WOULD YOU MIND ...
... IF ...
...FOR THIS ONE PLAY...
...I DIDN'T SNAP THE BALL...
...BUT USED THE POWER FROM ALL MY ARMS AND LEGS...
...TO SMASH INTO GAO?
THEN WHO...
...WILL DO IT?
WHO WILL START THE PLAY ...
...BY SNAPPING TO HIRUMA?
...
OH...
... UH ...
...

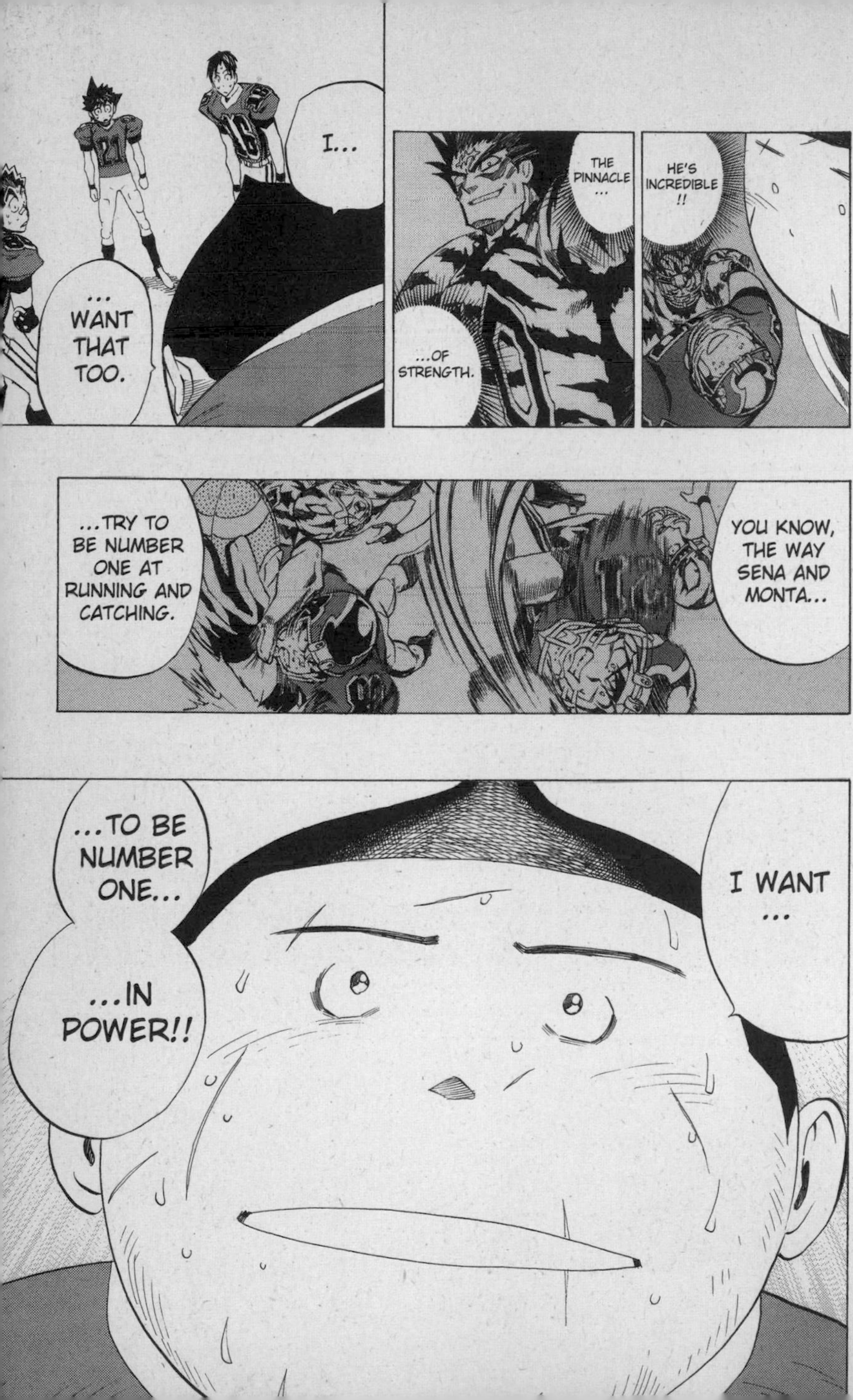
HE'S INCREDIBLE!!
THE PINNACLE...
...OF STRENGTH.
I...
...WANT THAT TOO.
YOU KNOW, THE WAY SENA AND MONTA...
...TRY TO BE NUMBER ONE AT RUNNING AND CATCHING.
I WANT...
...TO BE NUMBER ONE...
...IN POWER!!

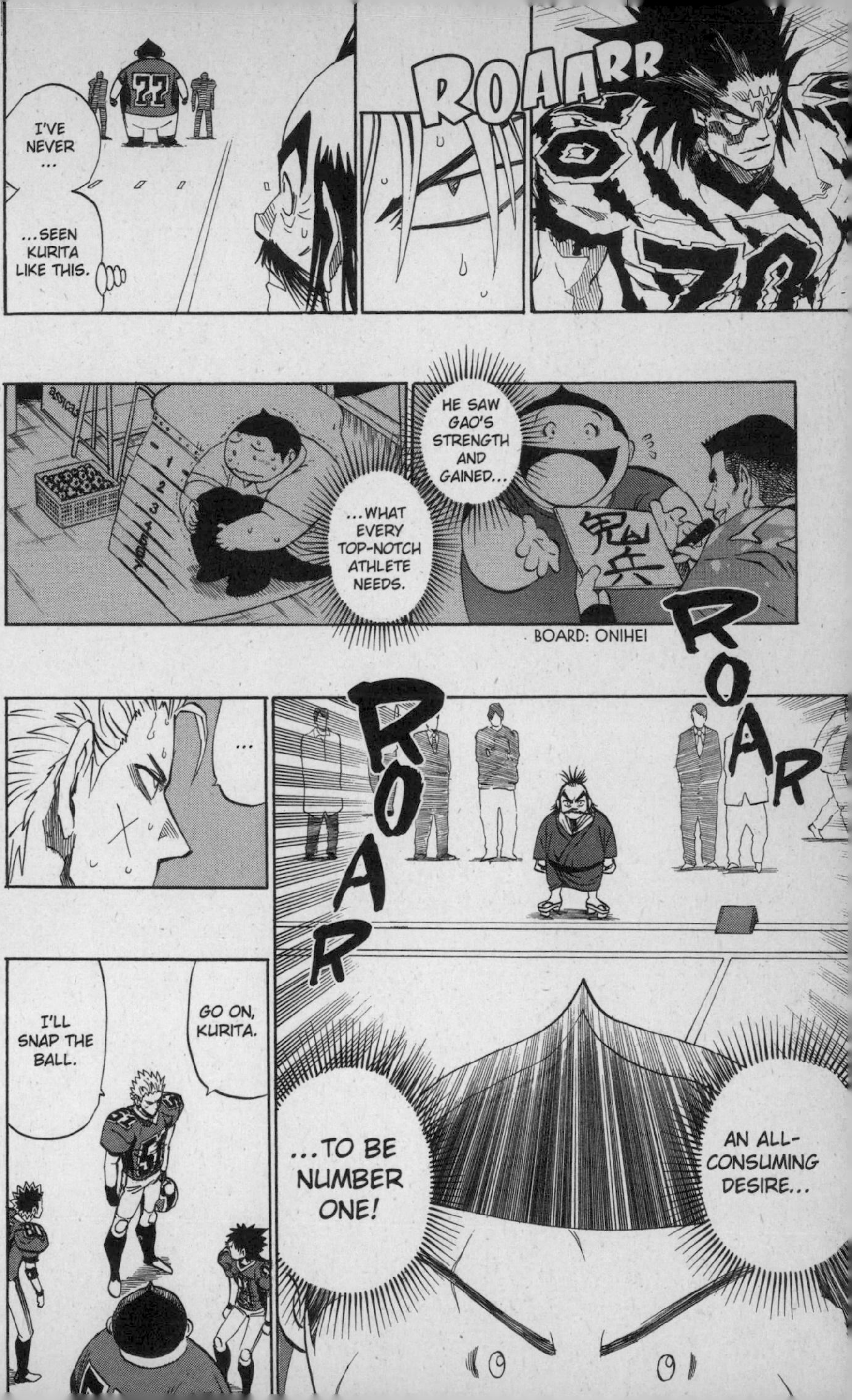
ROAAARR
I'VE NEVER ...
...SEEN KURITA LIKE THIS.
HE SAW GAO'S STRENGTH AND GAINED...
...WHAT EVERY TOP-NOTCH ATHLETE NEEDS.
BOARD: ONIHEI
ROAR
ROAR
...
AN ALL-CONSUMING DESIRE...
...TO BE NUMBER ONE!
GO ON, KURITA.
I'LL SNAP THE BALL.

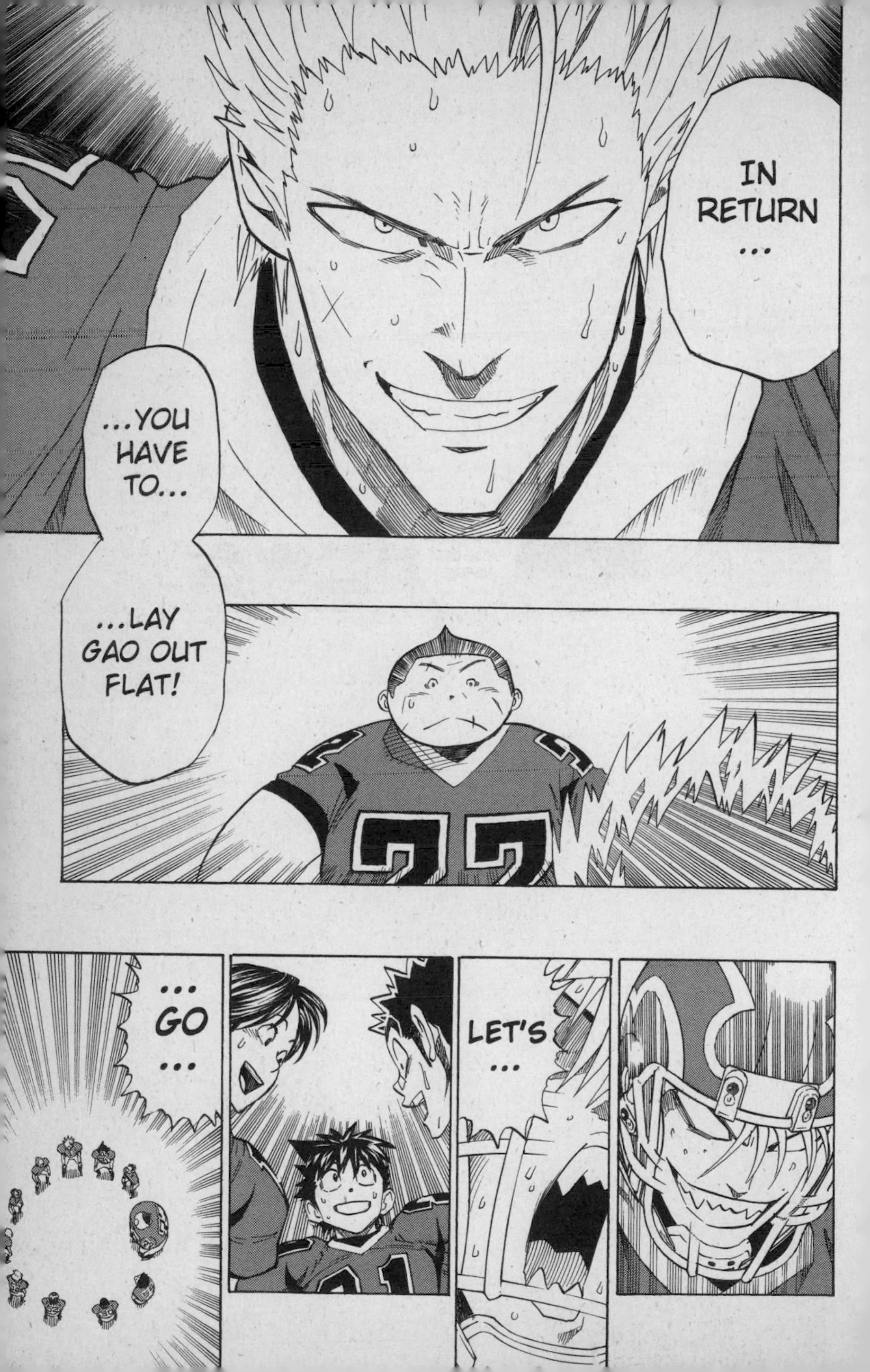
IN RETURN ...
...YOU HAVE TO...
...LAY GAO OUT FLAT!
LET'S ...
... GO ...

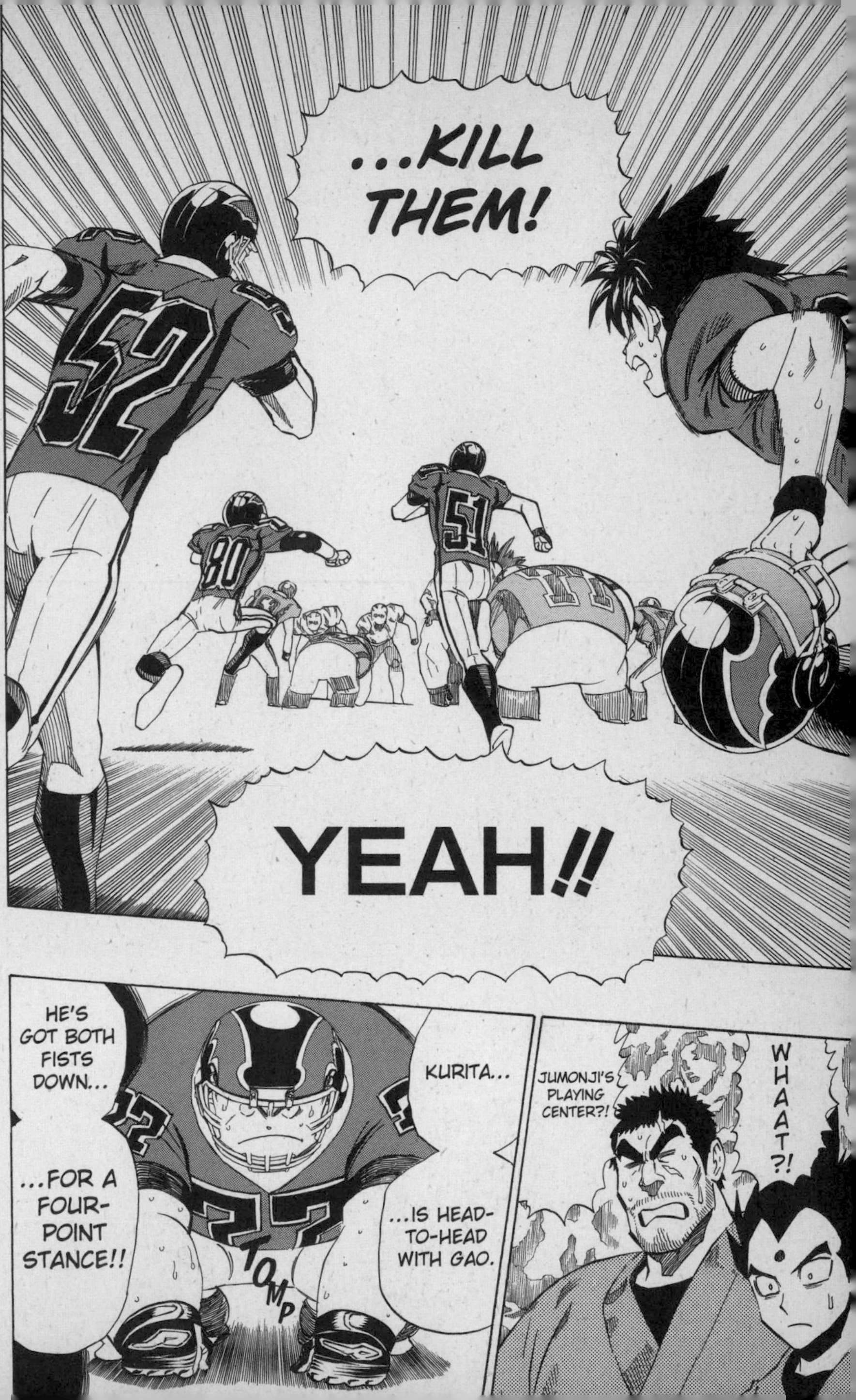
...KILL THEM!
YEAH!!
WHAAT?!
JUMONJI'S PLAYING CENTER?!
KURITA...
HE'S GOT BOTH FISTS DOWN...
...IS HEAD-TO-HEAD WITH GAO.
...FOR A FOUR-POINT STANCE!!
TOMP

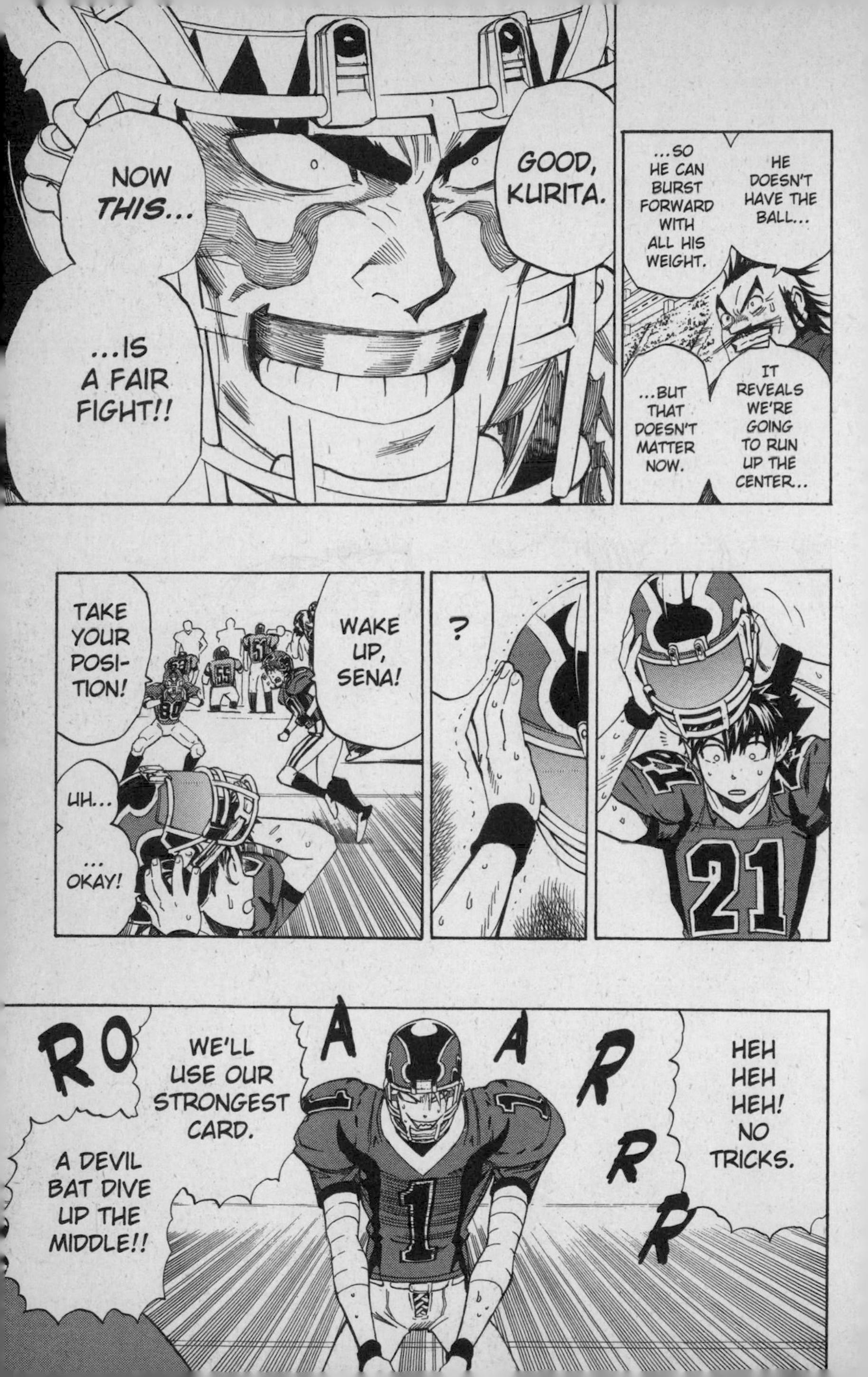
HE DOESN'T HAVE THE BALL...
...SO HE CAN BURST FORWARD WITH ALL HIS WEIGHT.
IT REVEALS WE'RE GOING TO RUN UP THE CENTER...
...BUT THAT DOESN'T MATTER NOW.
GOOD, KURITA.
NOW *THIS*...
...IS A FAIR FIGHT!!
?
WAKE UP, SENA!
TAKE YOUR POSITION!
UH...
...OKAY!
HEH HEH HEH! NO TRICKS.
ROAARRR
WE'LL USE OUR STRONGEST CARD.
A DEVIL BAT DIVE UP THE MIDDLE!!

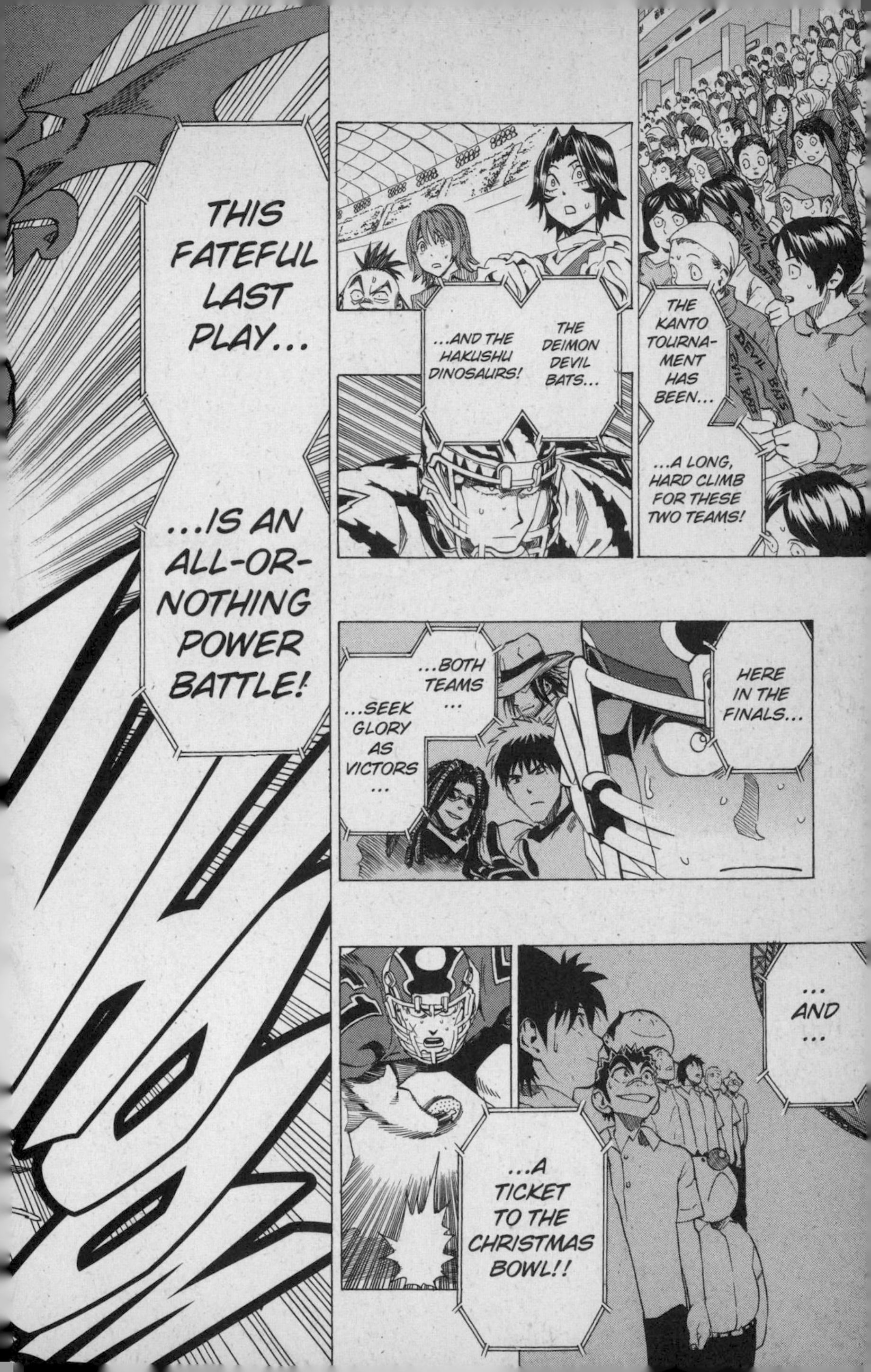

THE KANTO TOURNAMENT HAS BEEN...
...A LONG, HARD CLIMB FOR THESE TWO TEAMS!
THE DEIMON DEVIL BATS...
...AND THE HAKUSHU DINOSAURS!
HERE IN THE FINALS...
...BOTH TEAMS...
...SEEK GLORY AS VICTORS...
...AND...
...A TICKET TO THE CHRISTMAS BOWL!!
THIS FATEFUL LAST PLAY...
...IS AN ALL-OR-NOTHING POWER BATTLE!

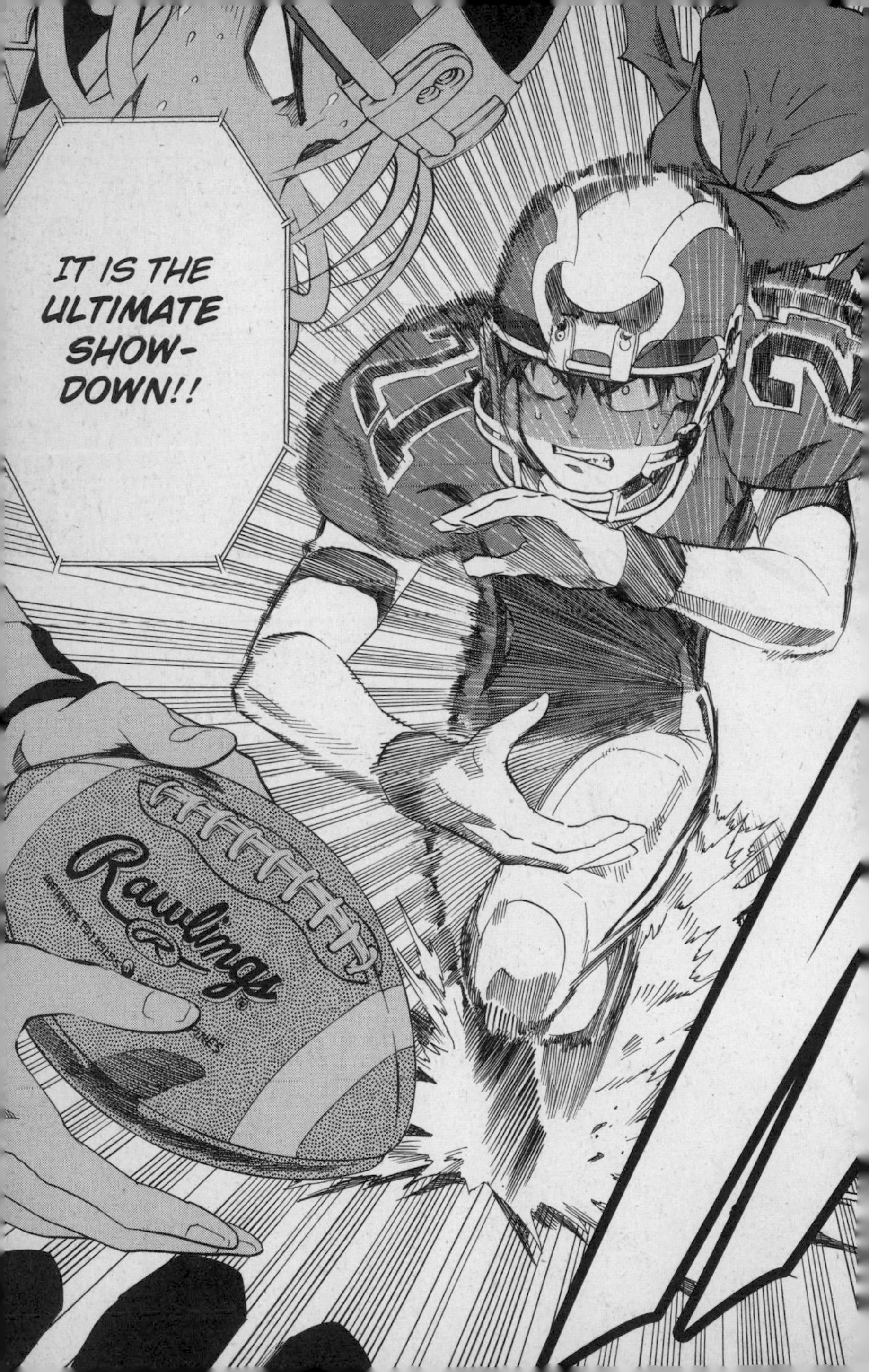
IT IS THE ULTIMATE SHOW-DOWN!!
Rawlings

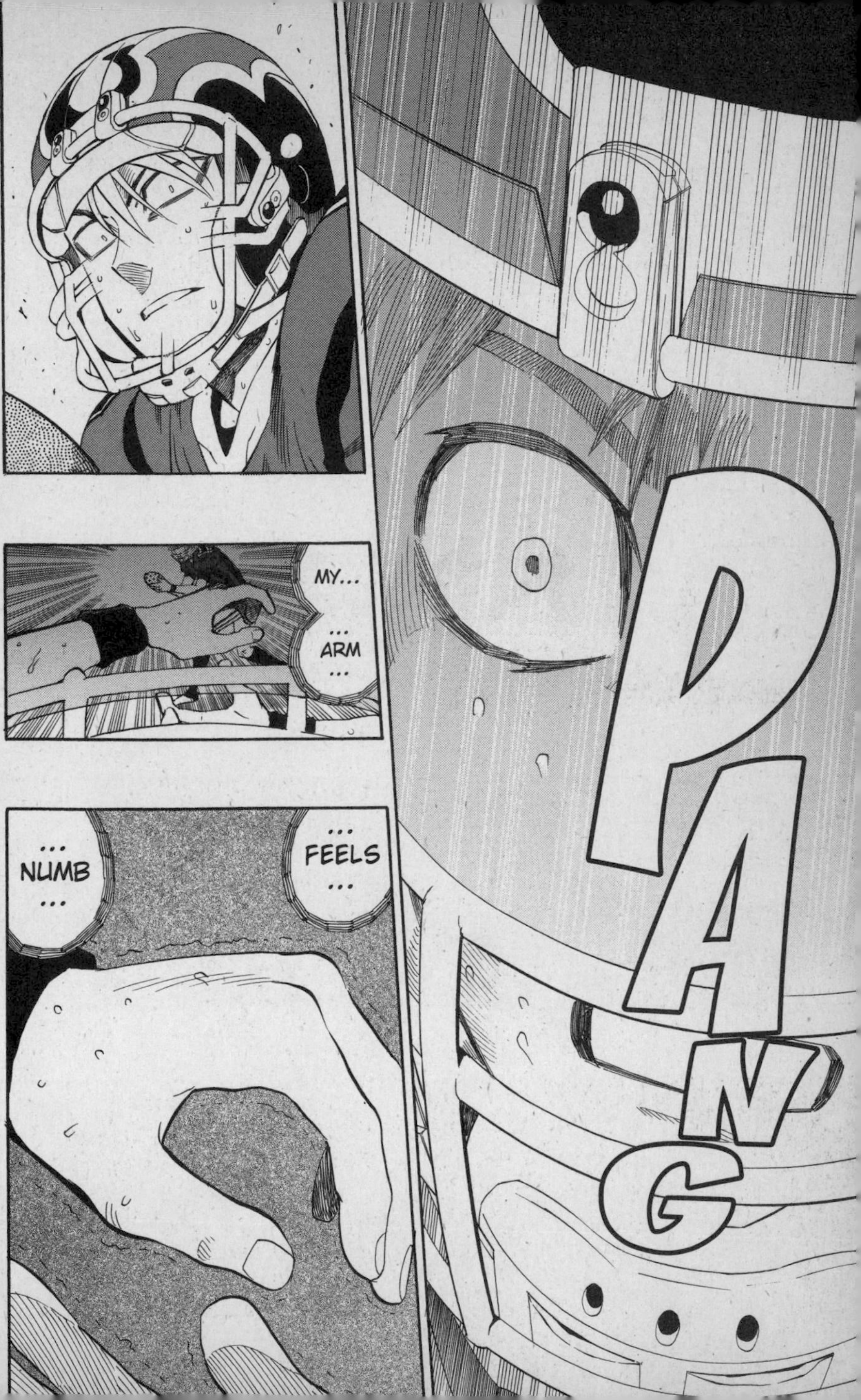
PANG
MY...
...ARM...
...FEELS...
...NUMB...

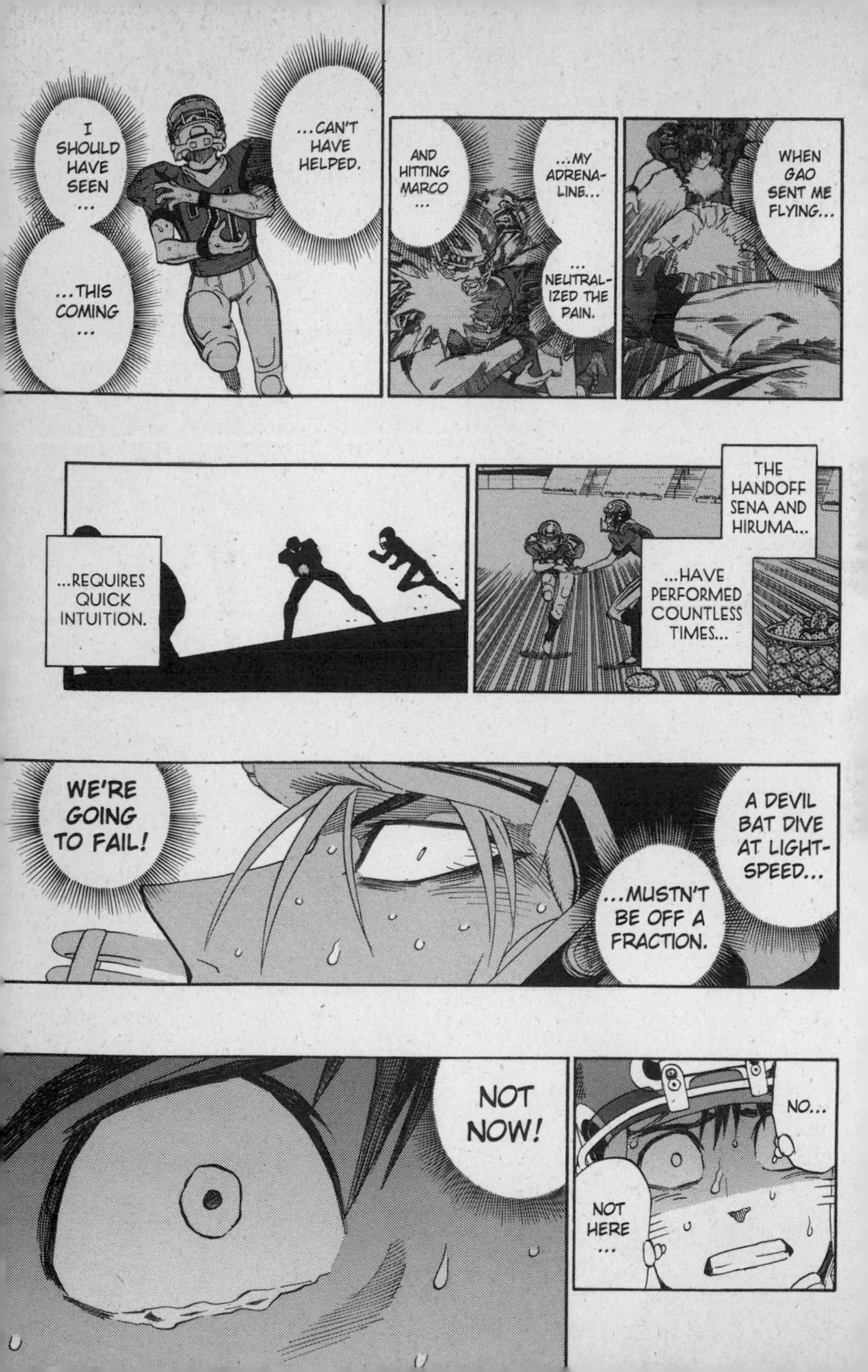
WHEN GAO SENT ME FLYING...
AND HITTING MARCO...
...MY ADRENALINE...
...NEUTRALIZED THE PAIN.
...CAN'T HAVE HELPED.
I SHOULD HAVE SEEN...
...THIS COMING...
THE HANDOFF SENA AND HIRUMA...
...HAVE PERFORMED COUNTLESS TIMES...
...REQUIRES QUICK INTUITION.
A DEVIL BAT DIVE AT LIGHT-SPEED...
...MUSTN'T BE OFF A FRACTION.
WE'RE GOING TO FAIL!
NO...
NOT HERE...
NOT NOW!

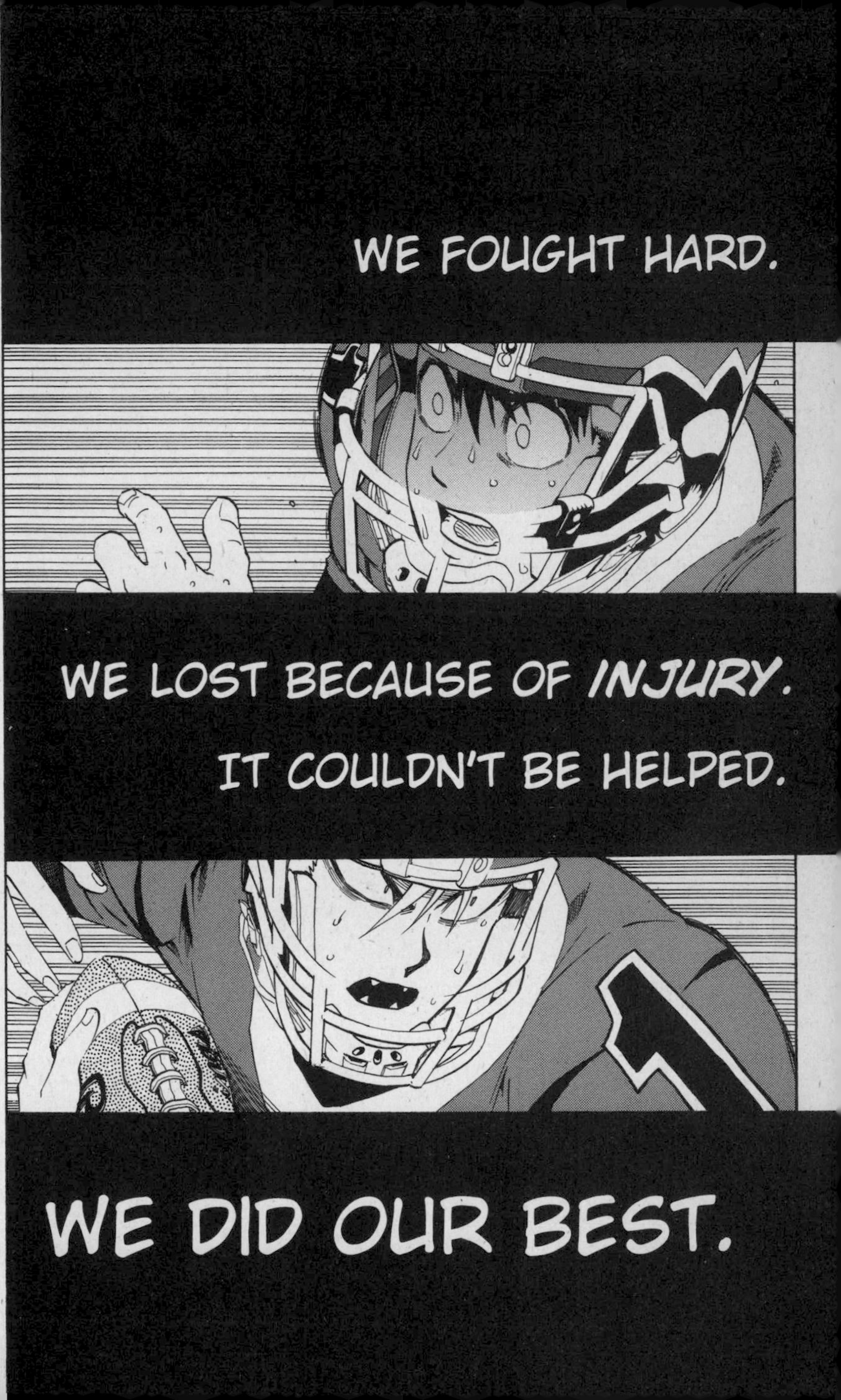
WE FOUGHT HARD.
WE LOST BECAUSE OF *INJURY*.
IT COULDN'T BE HELPED.
WE DID OUR BEST.

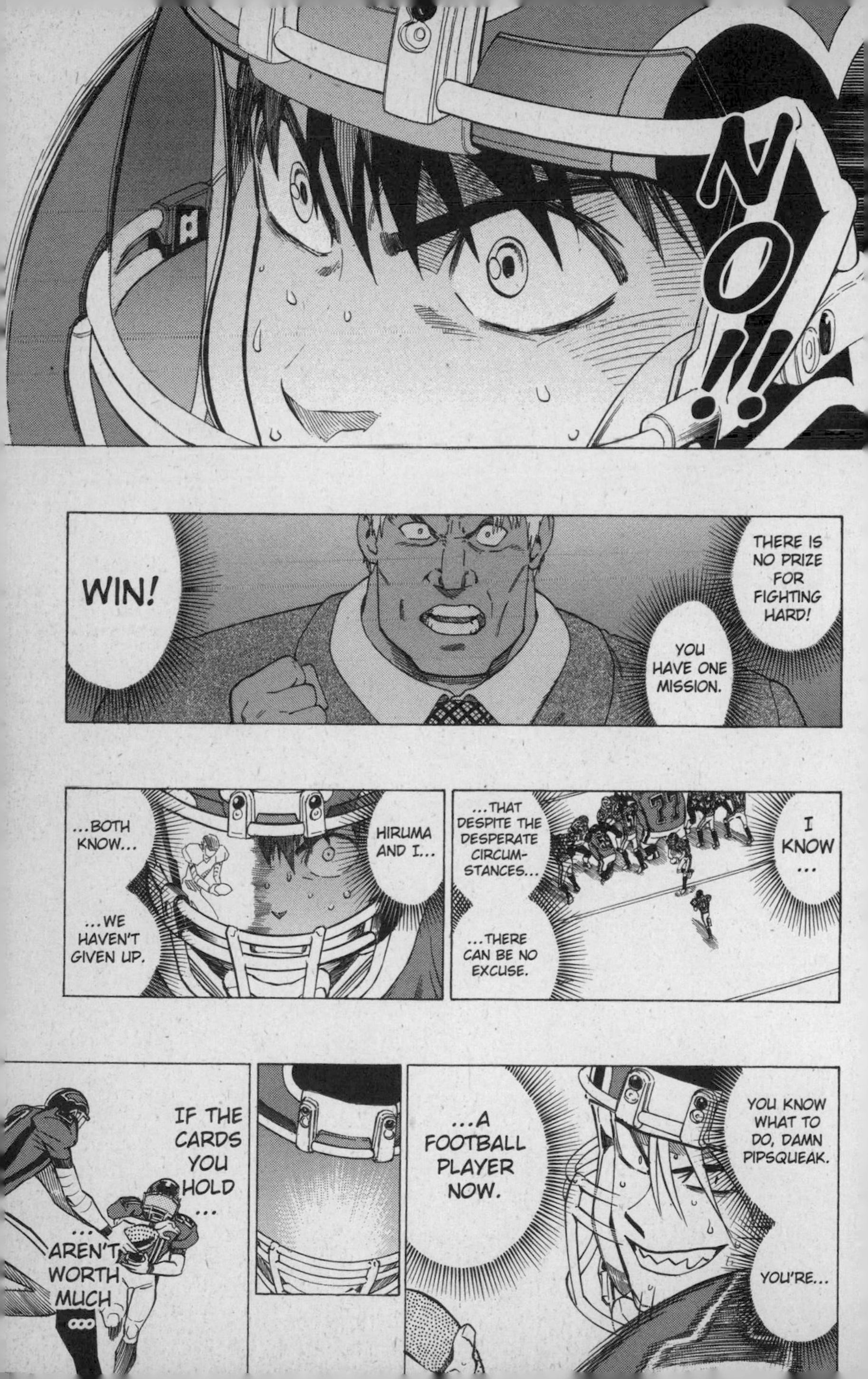
NO!!
THERE IS NO PRIZE FOR FIGHTING HARD!
YOU HAVE ONE MISSION.
WIN!
I KNOW...
...THAT DESPITE THE DESPERATE CIRCUM-STANCES...
...THERE CAN BE NO EXCUSE.
HIRUMA AND I...
...BOTH KNOW...
...WE HAVEN'T GIVEN UP.
YOU KNOW WHAT TO DO, DAMN PIPSQUEAK.
YOU'RE...
...A FOOTBALL PLAYER NOW.
IF THE CARDS YOU HOLD...
...AREN'T WORTH MUCH...

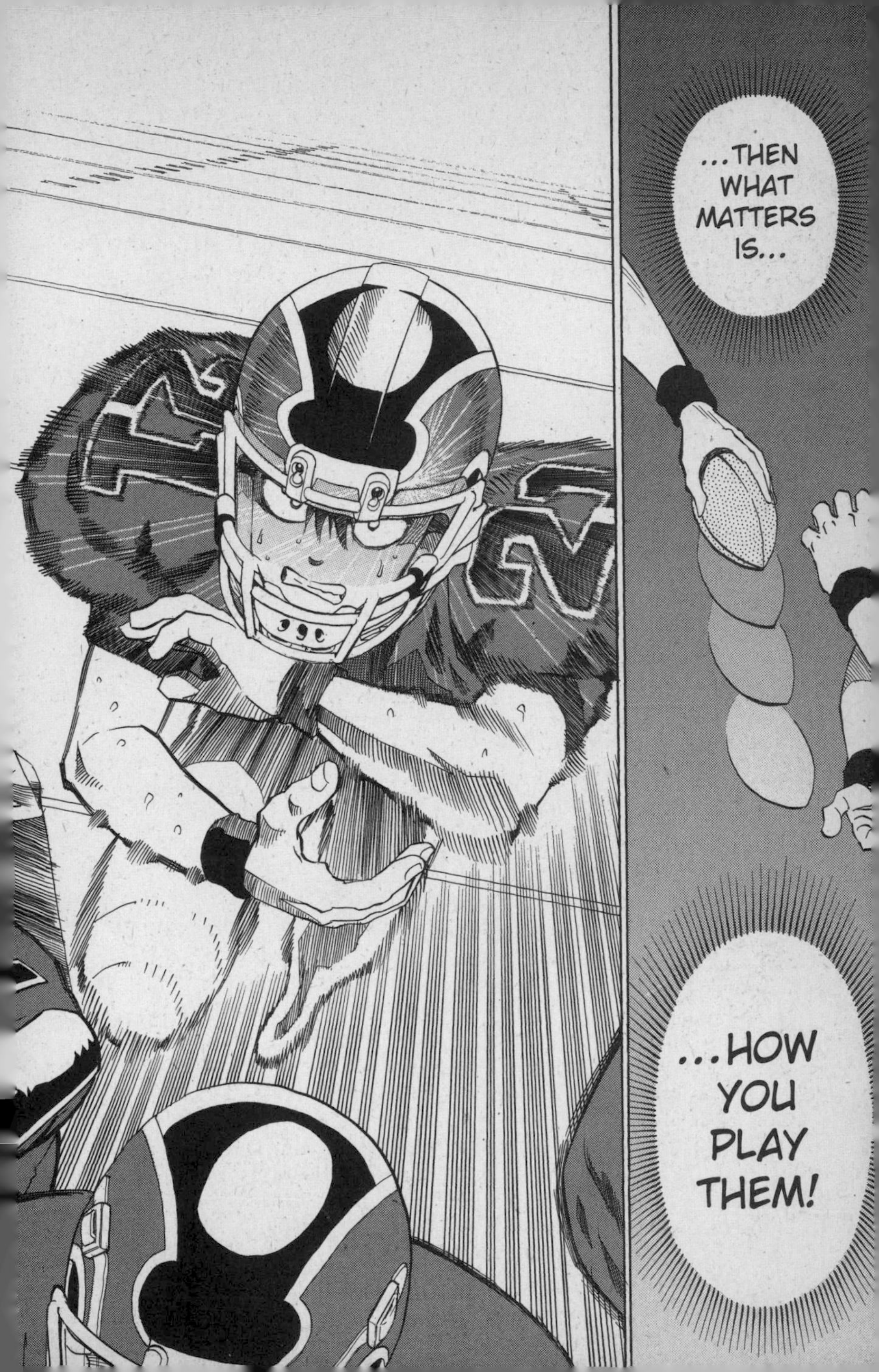
...THEN WHAT MATTERS IS...
...HOW YOU PLAY THEM!

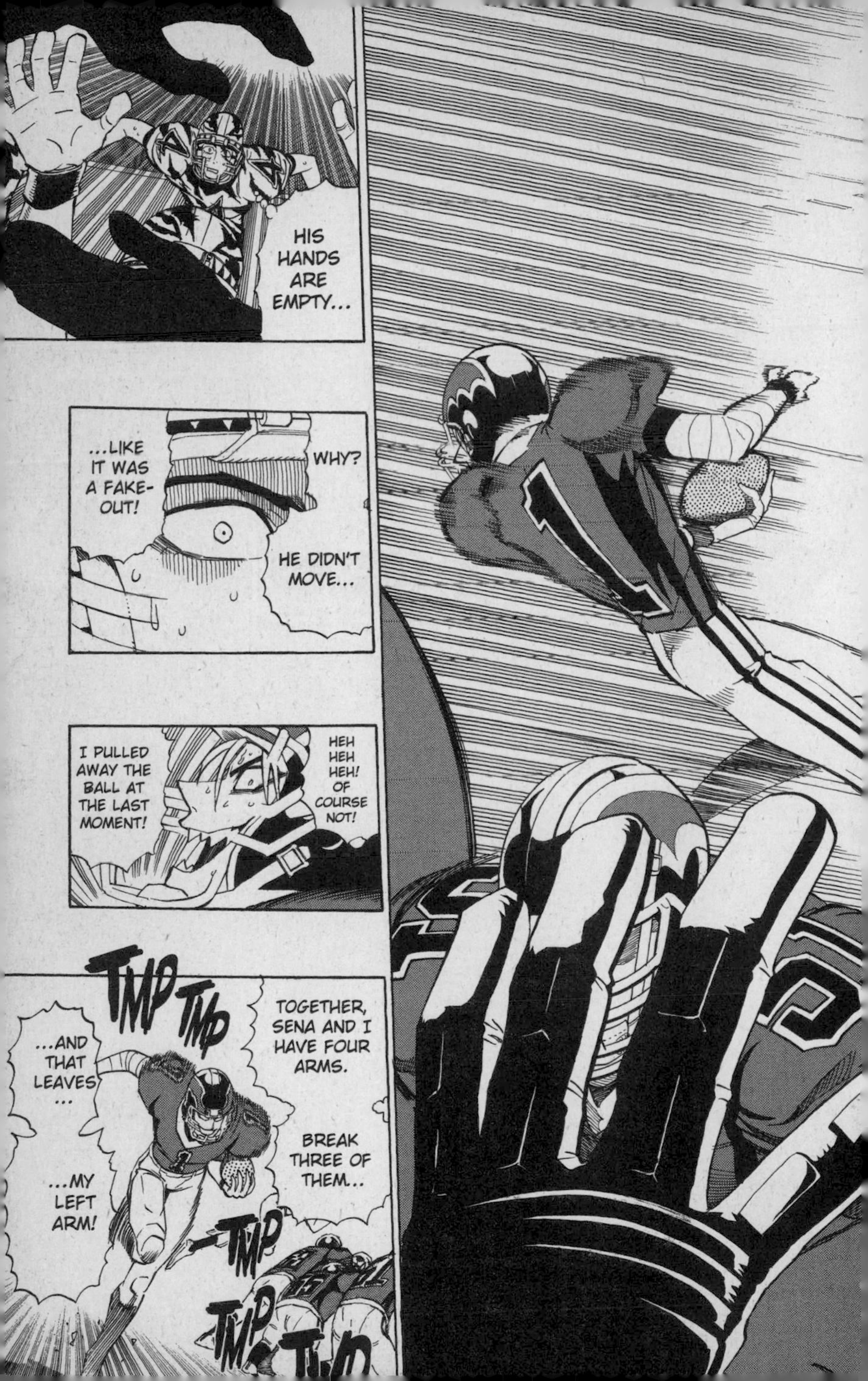
HIS HANDS ARE EMPTY...
WHY?
HE DIDN'T MOVE...
...LIKE IT WAS A FAKE-OUT!
HEH HEH HEH! OF COURSE NOT!
I PULLED AWAY THE BALL AT THE LAST MOMENT!
TMP TMP
TOGETHER, SENA AND I HAVE FOUR ARMS.
BREAK THREE OF THEM...
...AND THAT LEAVES...
...MY LEFT ARM!
TMP
TMP TMP

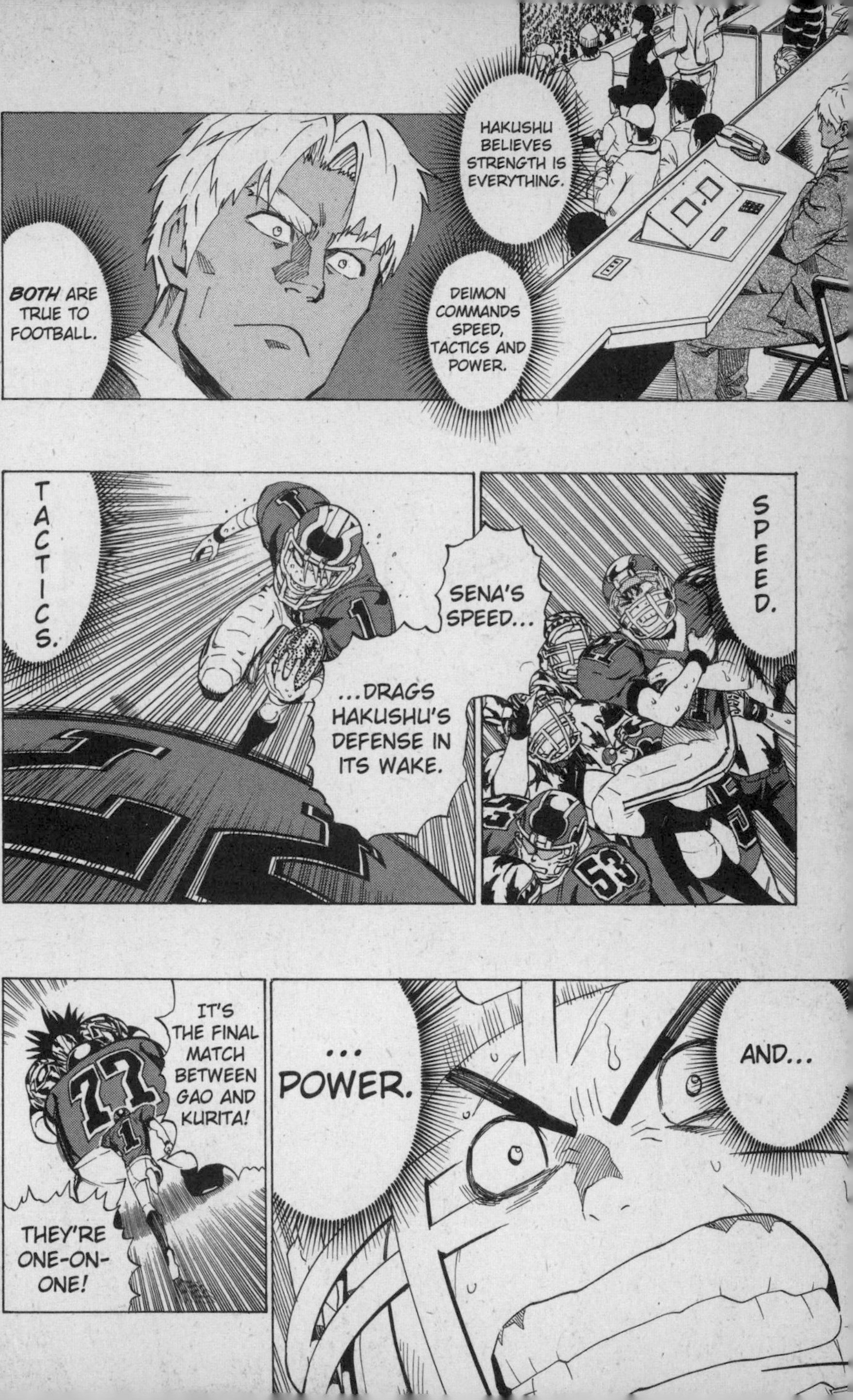
HAKUSHU BELIEVES STRENGTH IS EVERYTHING.
DEIMON COMMANDS SPEED, TACTICS AND POWER.
BOTH ARE TRUE TO FOOTBALL.
SPEED.
SENA'S SPEED...
...DRAGS HAKUSHU'S DEFENSE IN ITS WAKE.
TACTICS.
AND...
...POWER.
IT'S THE FINAL MATCH BETWEEN GAO AND KURITA!
THEY'RE ONE-ON-ONE!

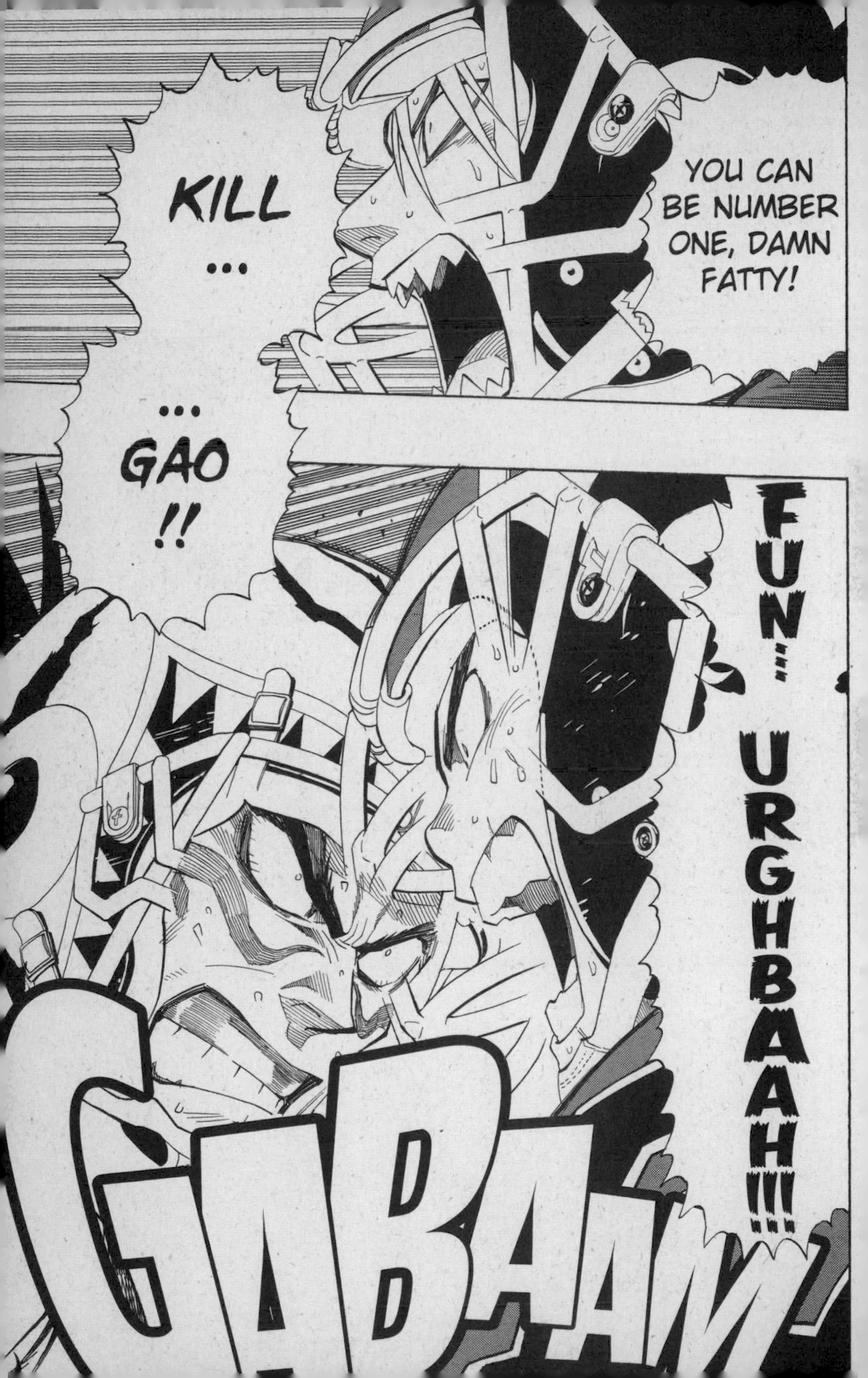
YOU CAN BE NUMBER ONE, DAMN FATTY!
KILL ... ... GAO!!
FUN!!
URGHBAAH!!!
GABAAM

Eyeshield 21 Survey Corner

Devil Bat 021

Investigation File #136

To commemorate volume 30, please do something for the extremely plain Ishimaru! He wears number 30!!

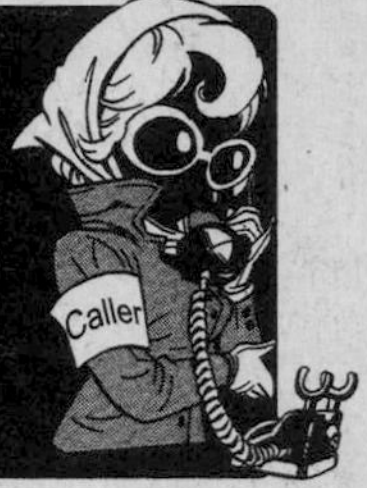
Caller

Caller name: A.K. in Fukuoka Prefecture

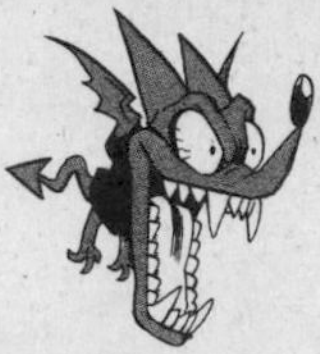

YOU'RE RIGHT. WE SHOULD MAKE HIM THE MAIN PROTAGONIST OF AN ENTIRE CHAPTER OR...

WELL, WOULD YOU LOOK AT THAT! IT'S ALREADY VOLUME 31!

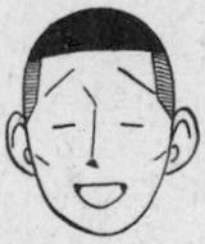

...

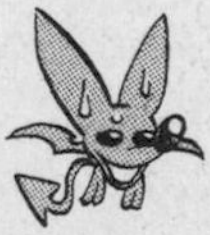

I'M CERTAIN HE DID THAT ON PURPOSE...

Send your queries for Devil Bat 021 here!!

Devil Bat 021
Shonen Jump Advanced/Eyeshield 21
c/o VIZ Media, LLC
P.O. Box 77010
San Francisco, CA 94107

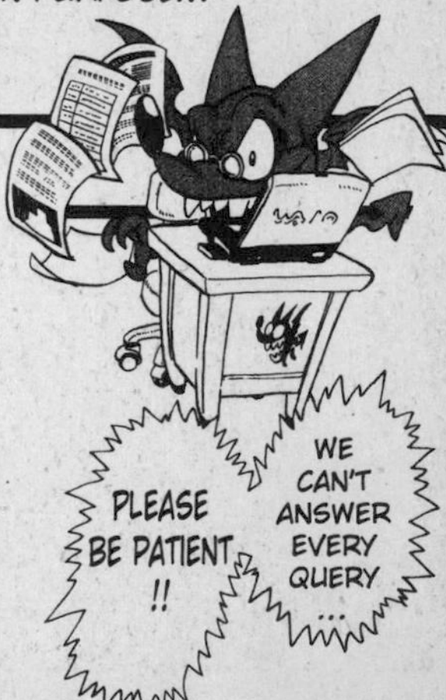
PLEASE BE PATIENT!!
WE CAN'T ANSWER EVERY QUERY...

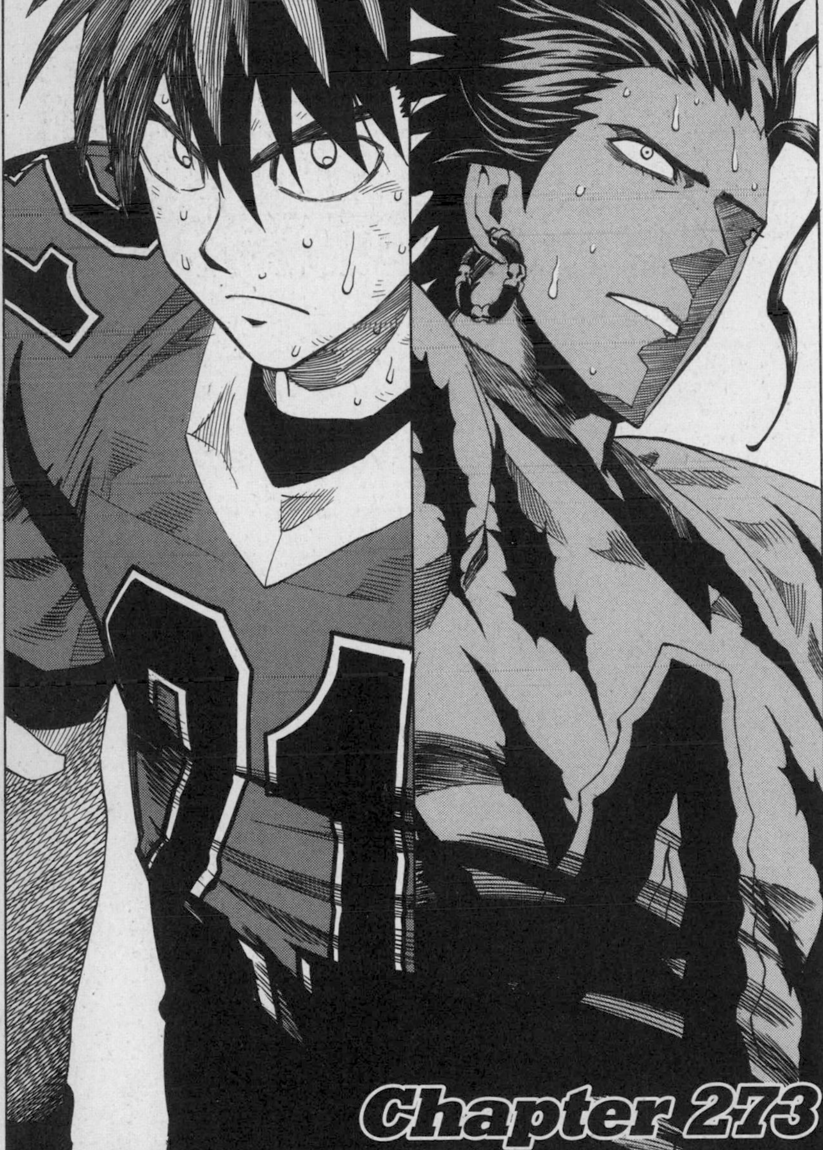
Chapter 273
And the Winner Is...

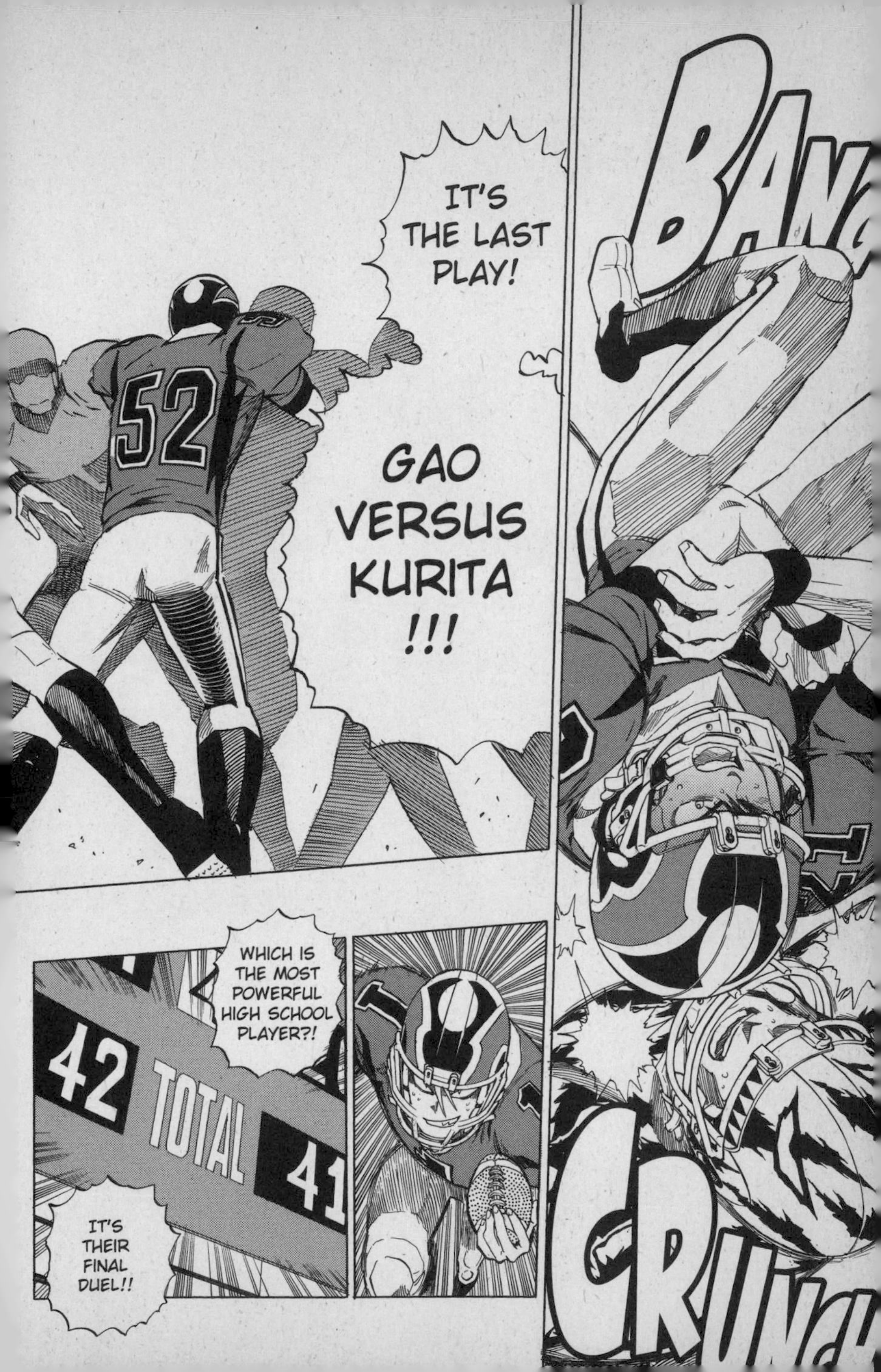
BAN
CRUNC
IT'S THE LAST PLAY!
52
GAO VERSUS KURITA!!!
WHICH IS THE MOST POWERFUL HIGH SCHOOL PLAYER?!
42 TOTAL 41
IT'S THEIR FINAL DUEL!!

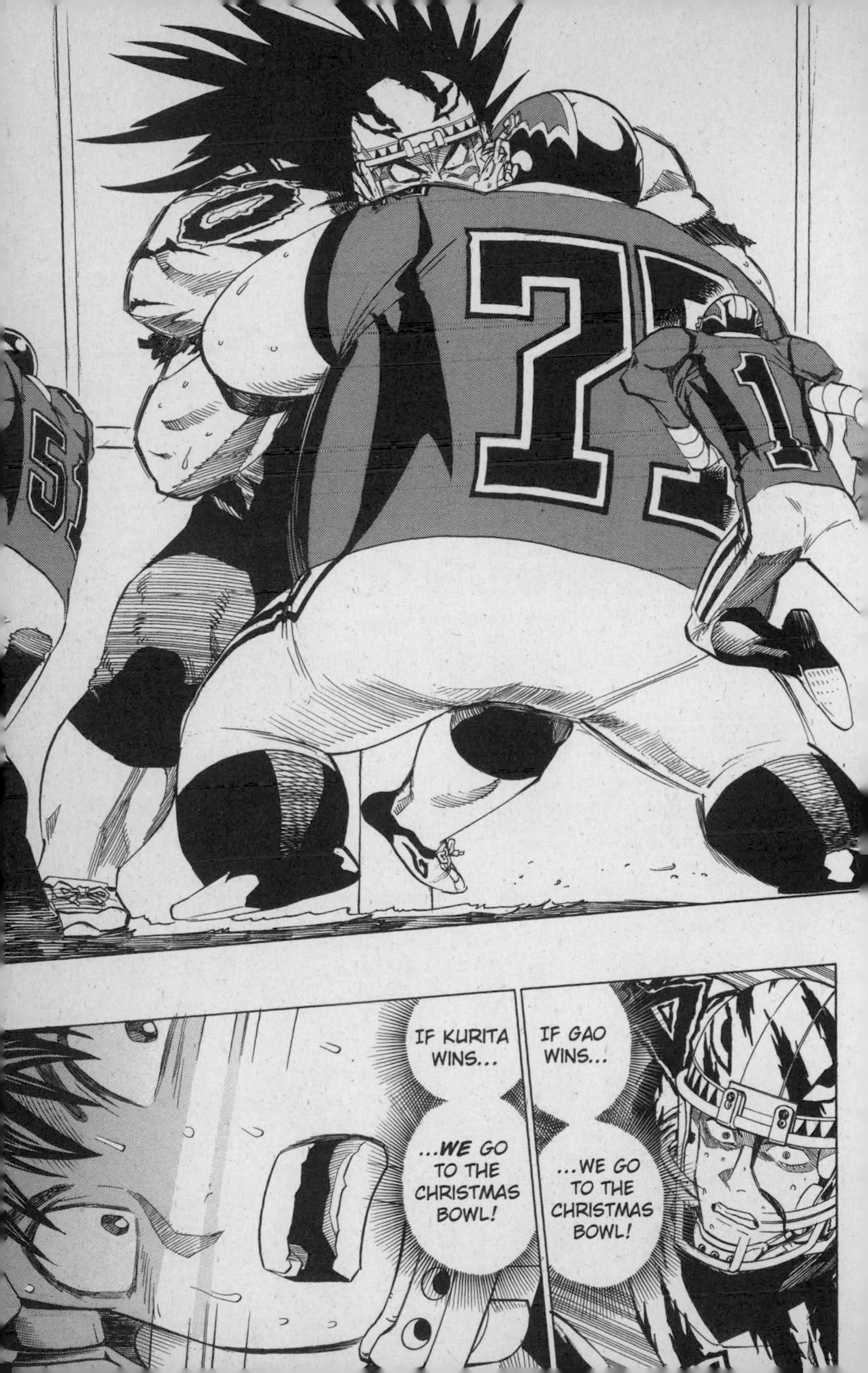
IF GAO WINS...
...WE GO TO THE CHRISTMAS BOWL!
IF KURITA WINS...
...WE GO TO THE CHRISTMAS BOWL!

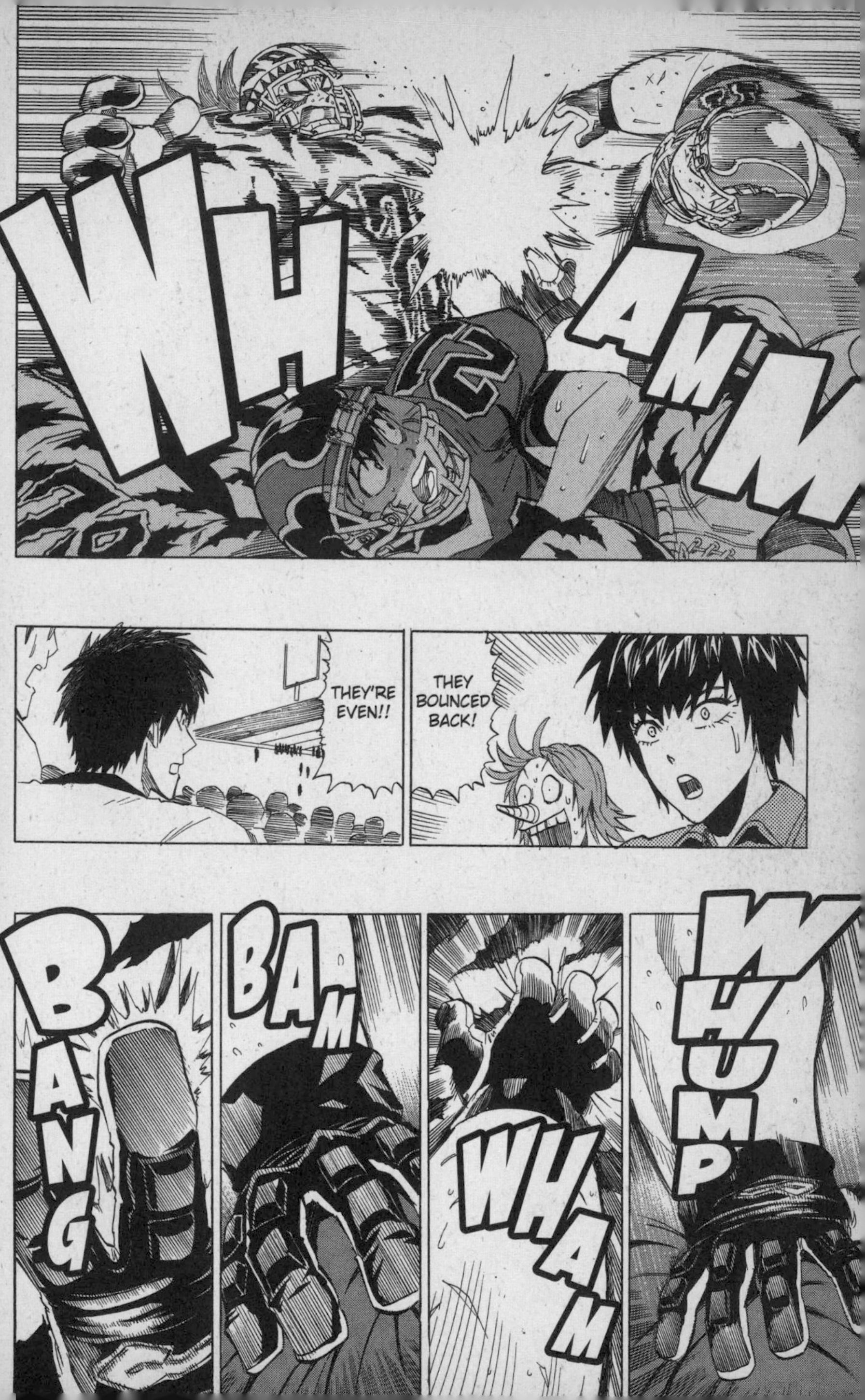
WHAMM
THEY BOUNCED BACK!
THEY'RE EVEN!!
WHUMP
WHAM
BAM
BANG

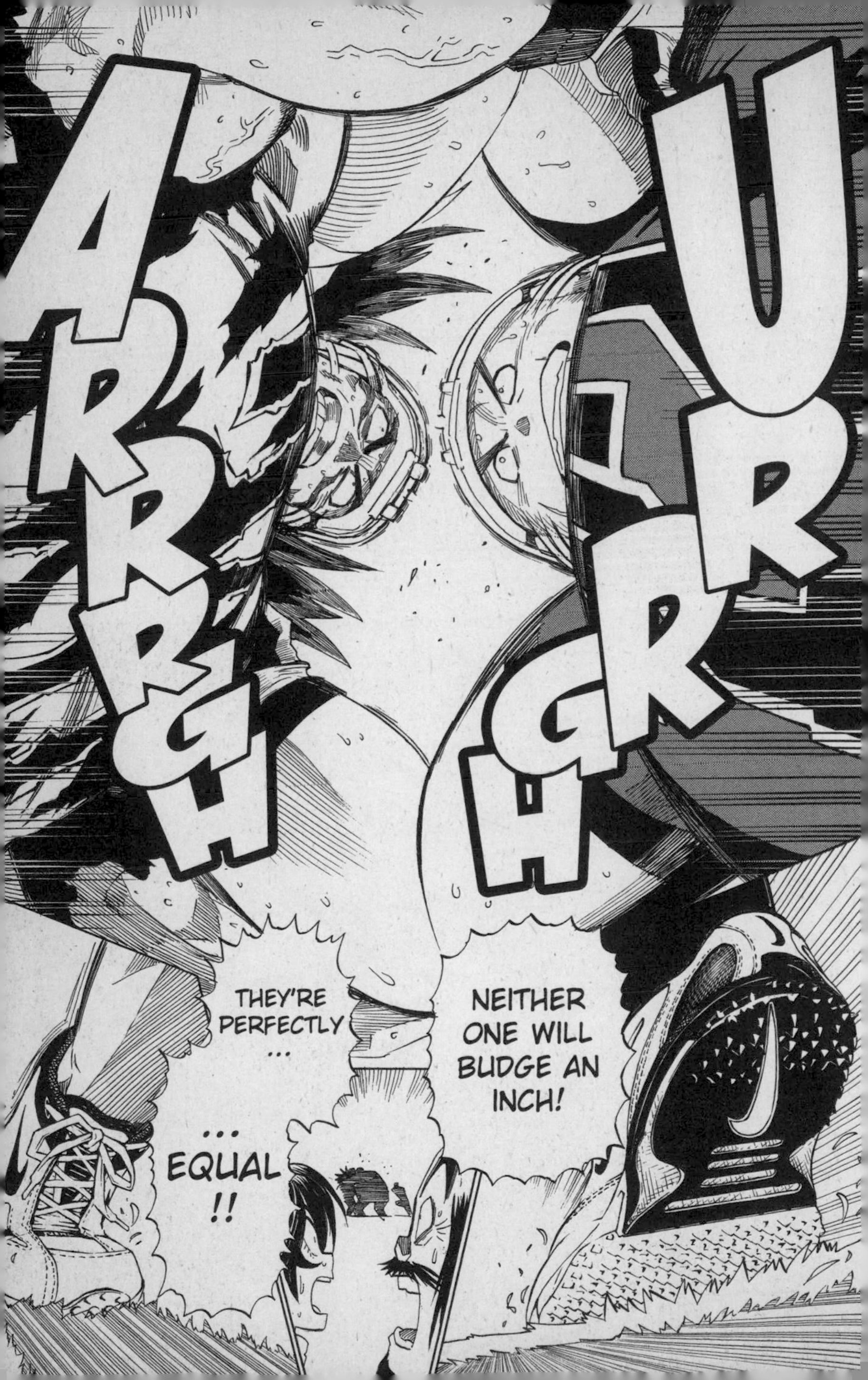
URRGH
ARRGH
NEITHER ONE WILL BUDGE AN INCH!
THEY'RE PERFECTLY ...
... EQUAL !!

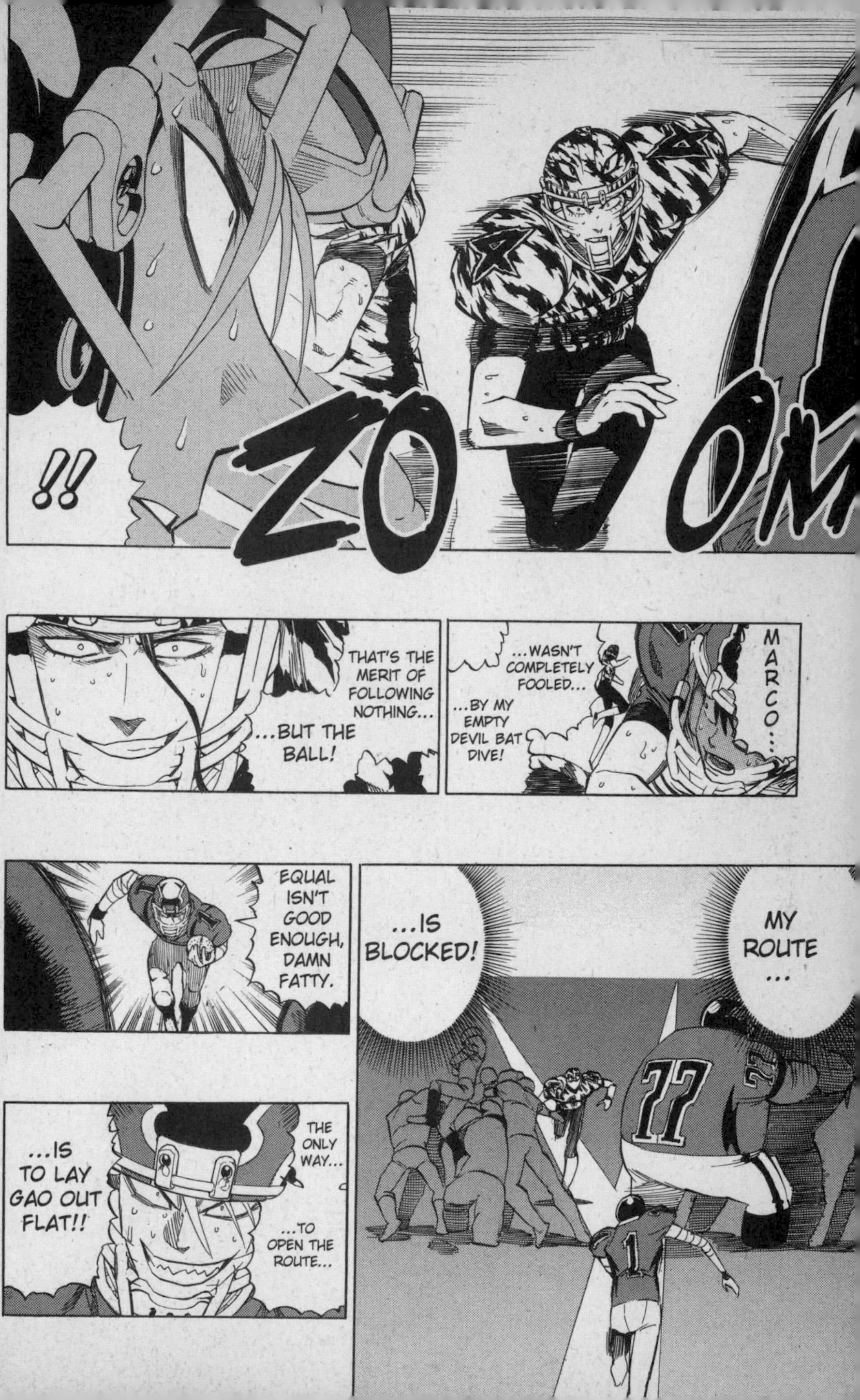
ZOOM
!!
MARCO...
...WASN'T COMPLETELY FOOLED...
...BY MY EMPTY DEVIL BAT DIVE!
THAT'S THE MERIT OF FOLLOWING NOTHING...
...BUT THE BALL!
MY ROUTE ...
...IS BLOCKED!
EQUAL ISN'T GOOD ENOUGH, DAMN FATTY.
THE ONLY WAY...
...TO OPEN THE ROUTE...
...IS TO LAY GAO OUT FLAT!!

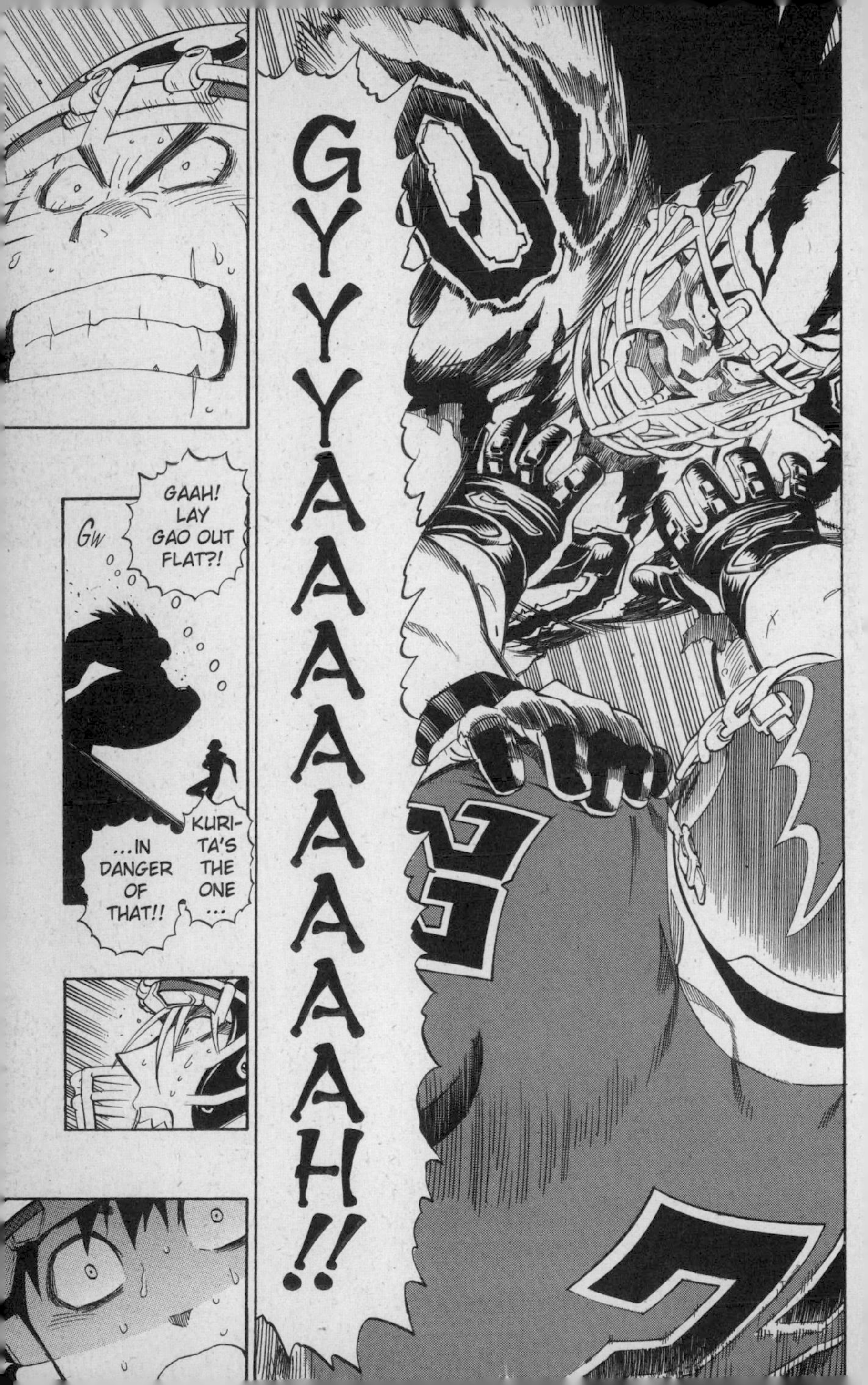
GYYAAAAAAAAH!!
GAAH! LAY GAO OUT FLAT?!
Gw
KURITA'S THE ONE...
...IN DANGER OF THAT!!

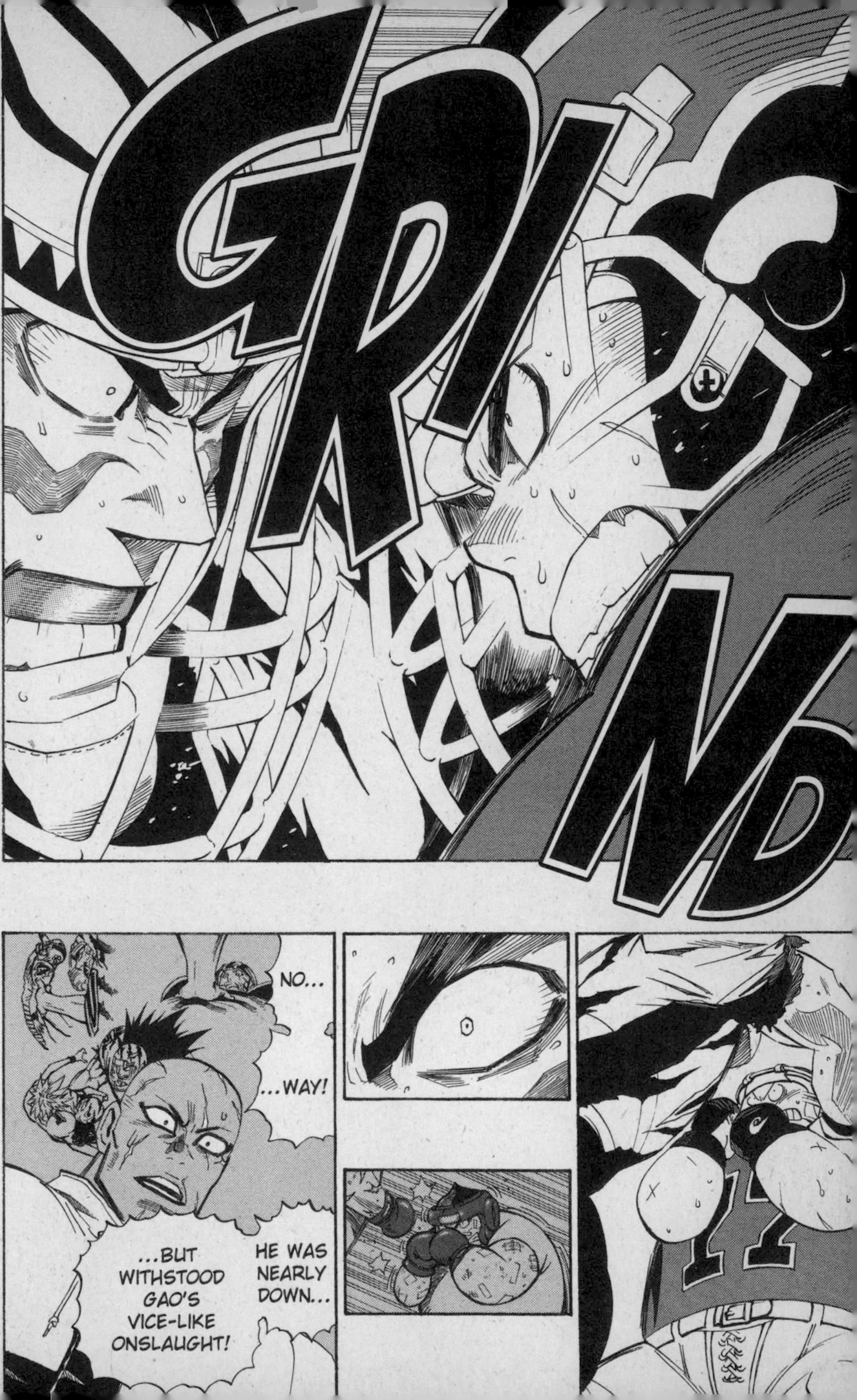
GRI
ND
NO...
...WAY!
HE WAS NEARLY DOWN...
...BUT WITHSTOOD GAO'S VICE-LIKE ONSLAUGHT!

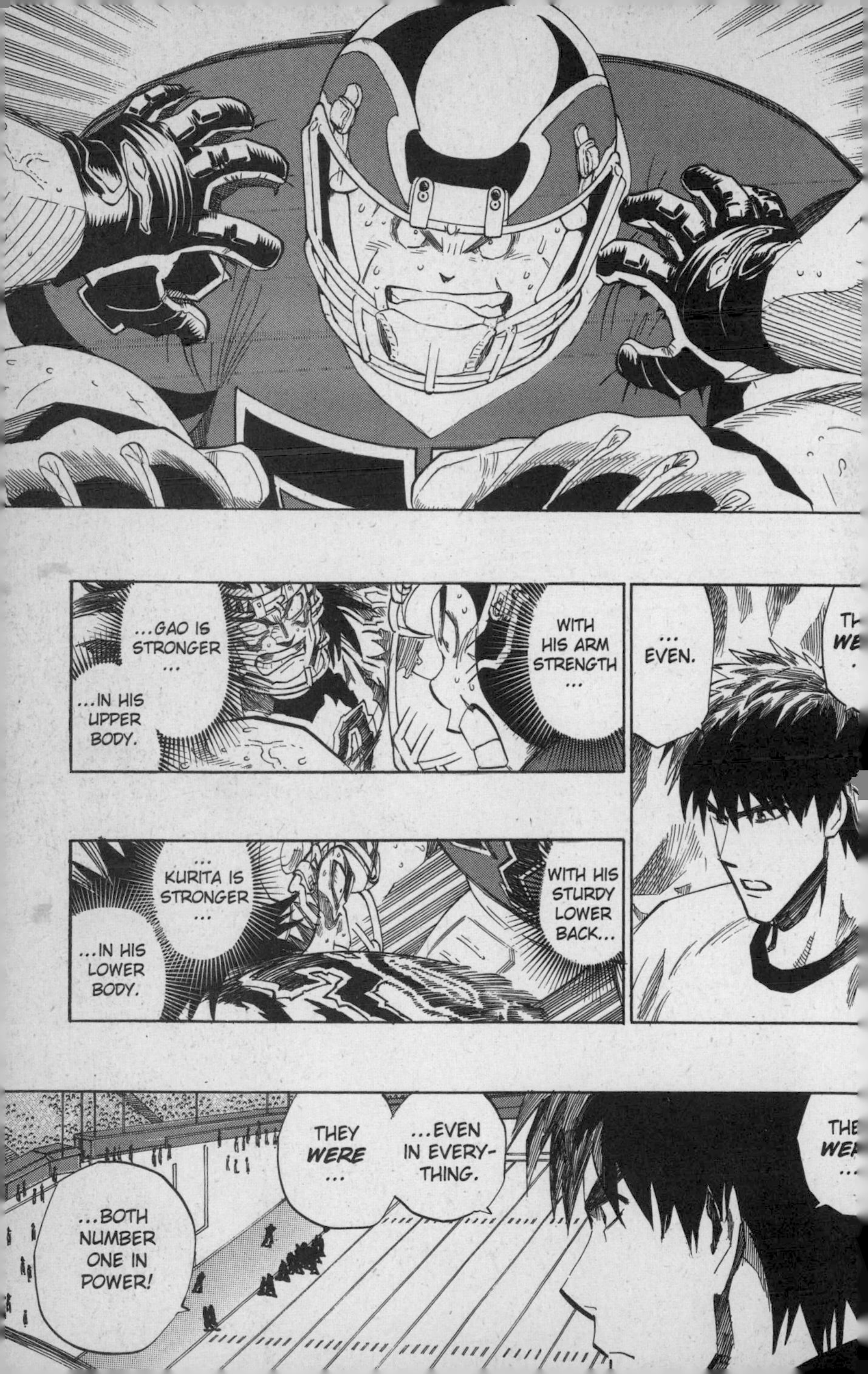

... EVEN.
WITH HIS ARM STRENGTH ...
...GAO IS STRONGER ...
...IN HIS UPPER BODY.
WITH HIS STURDY LOWER BACK...
... KURITA IS STRONGER ...
...IN HIS LOWER BODY.
...EVEN IN EVERY-THING.
THEY *WERE* ...
...BOTH NUMBER ONE IN POWER!

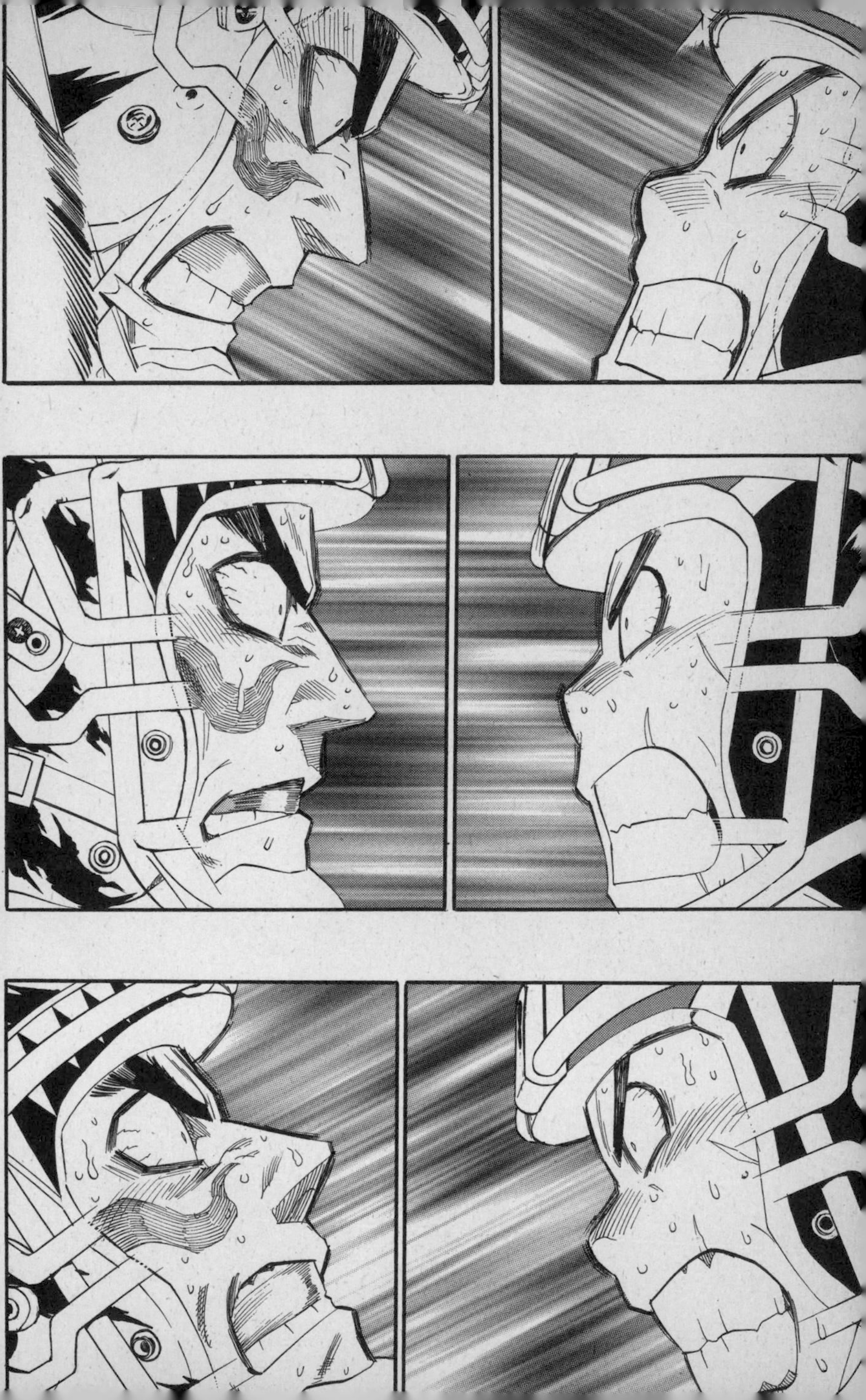

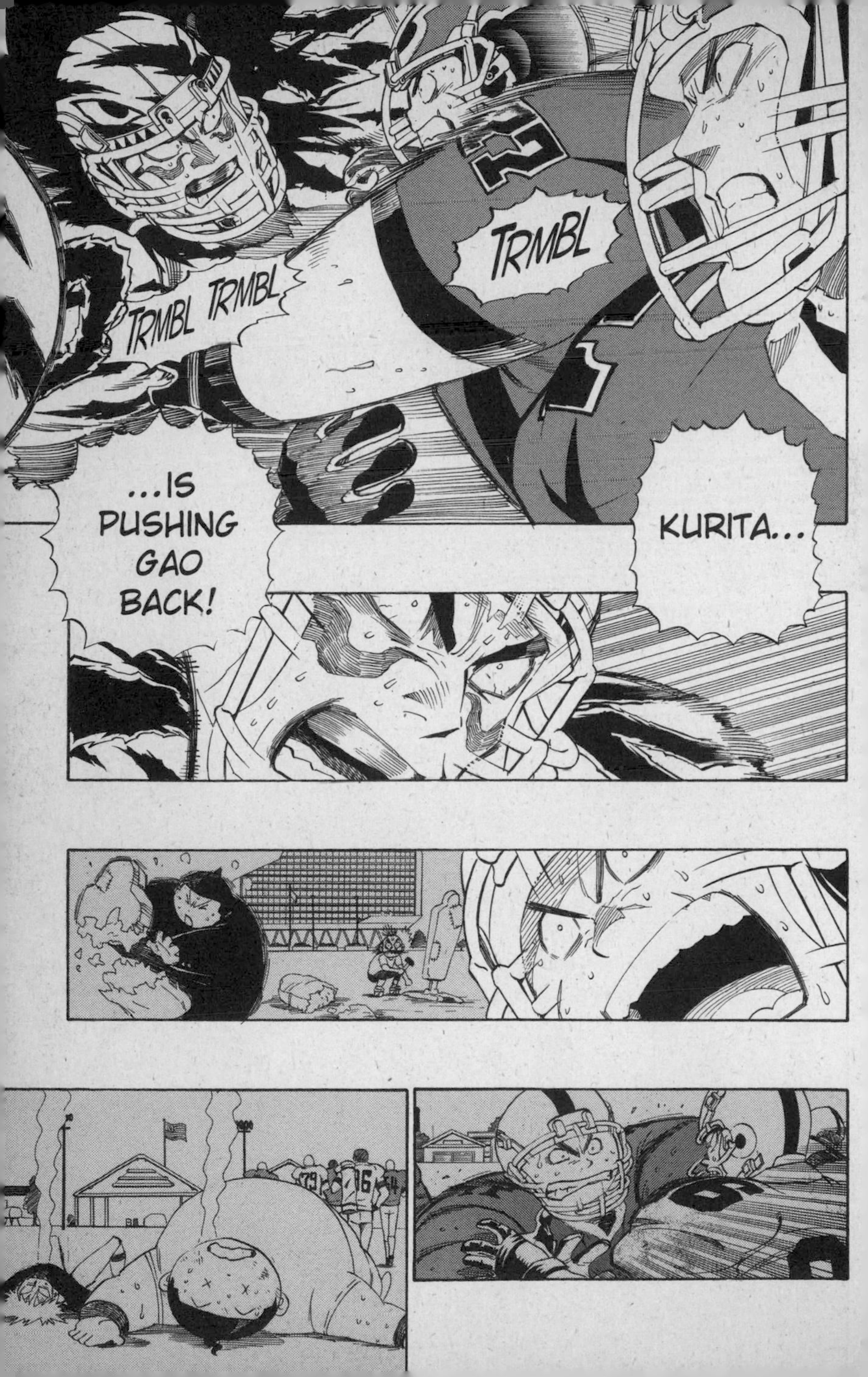
TRMBL
TRMBL TRMBL
KURITA...
...IS PUSHING GAO BACK!

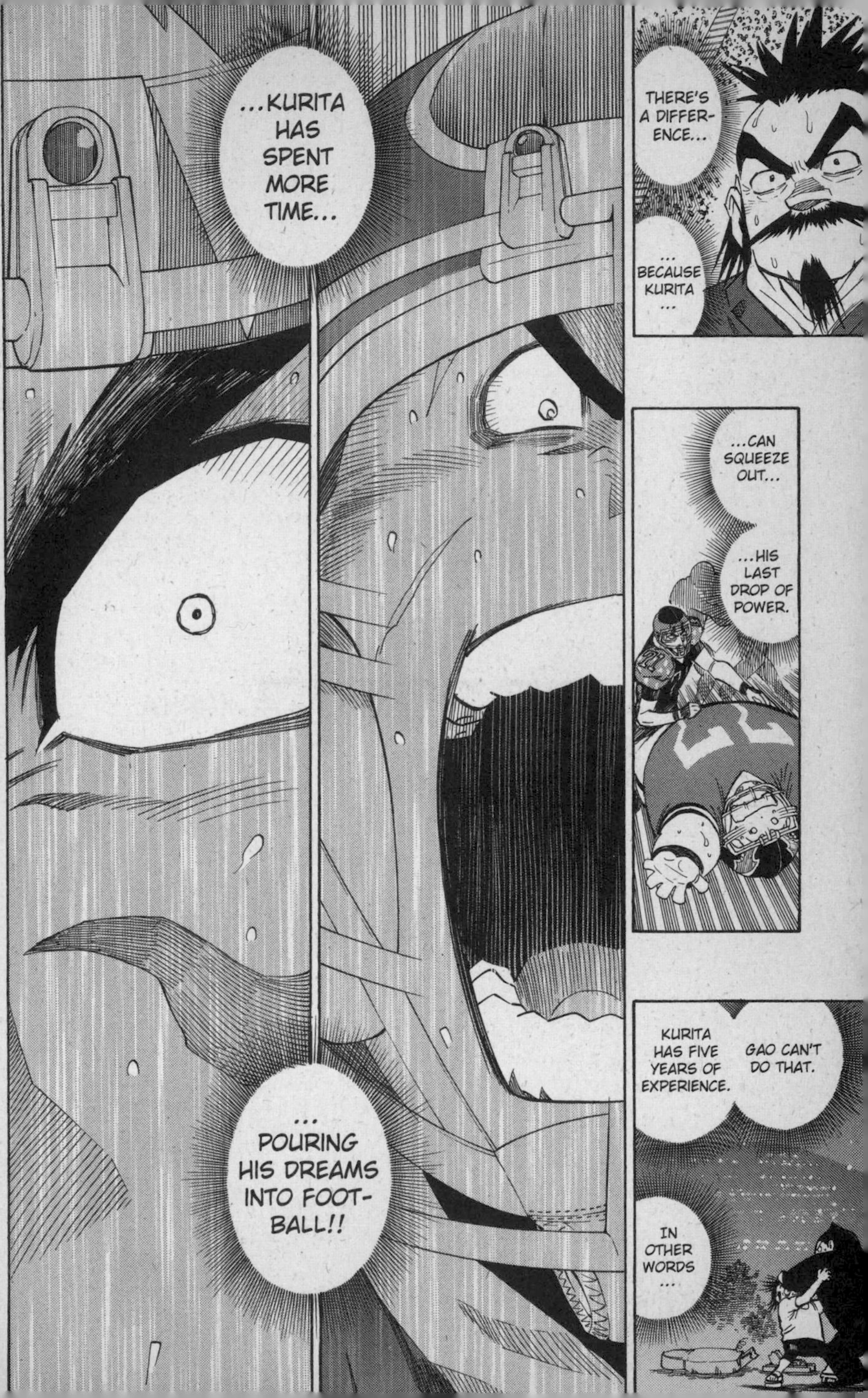
THERE'S A DIFFERENCE...
...BECAUSE KURITA...
...CAN SQUEEZE OUT...
...HIS LAST DROP OF POWER.
GAO CAN'T DO THAT.
KURITA HAS FIVE YEARS OF EXPERIENCE.
IN OTHER WORDS...
...KURITA HAS SPENT MORE TIME...
...POURING HIS DREAMS INTO FOOTBALL!!

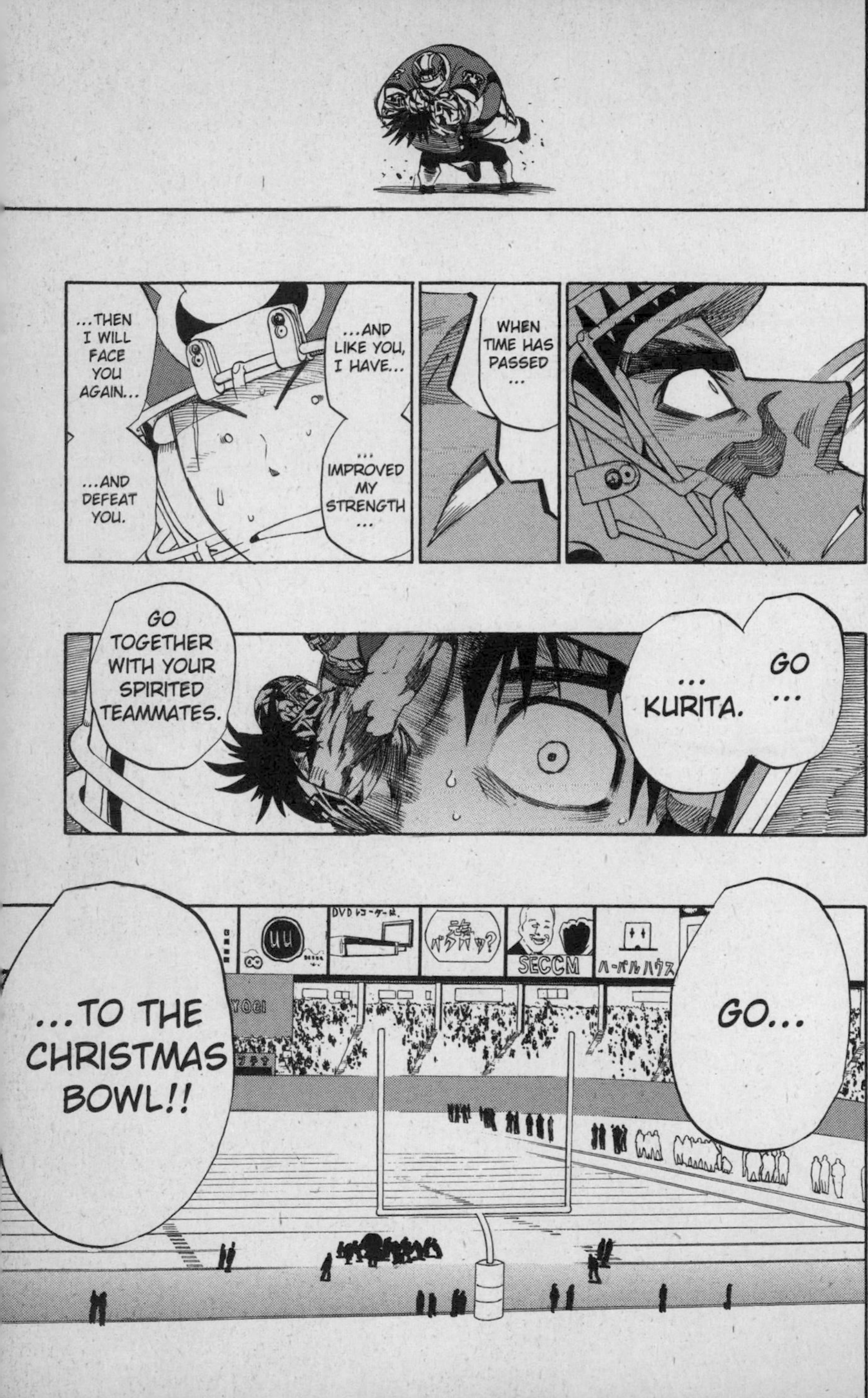
WHEN TIME HAS PASSED ...
...AND LIKE YOU, I HAVE...
... IMPROVED MY STRENGTH ...
...THEN I WILL FACE YOU AGAIN...
...AND DEFEAT YOU.
GO ... ... KURITA.
GO TOGETHER WITH YOUR SPIRITED TEAMMATES.
ハーバルハウス
SECCM
GO...
...TO THE CHRISTMAS BOWL!!

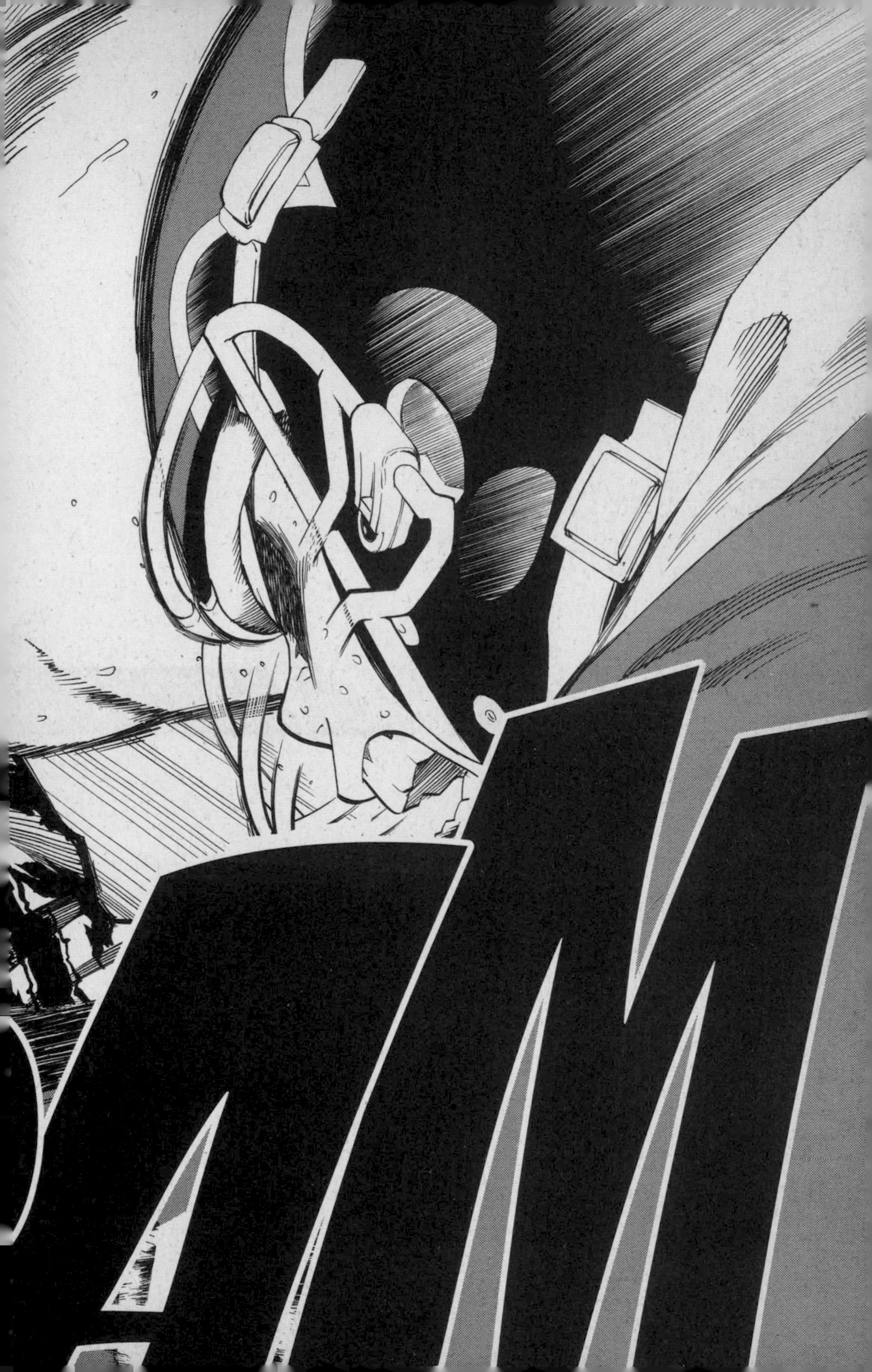
AM

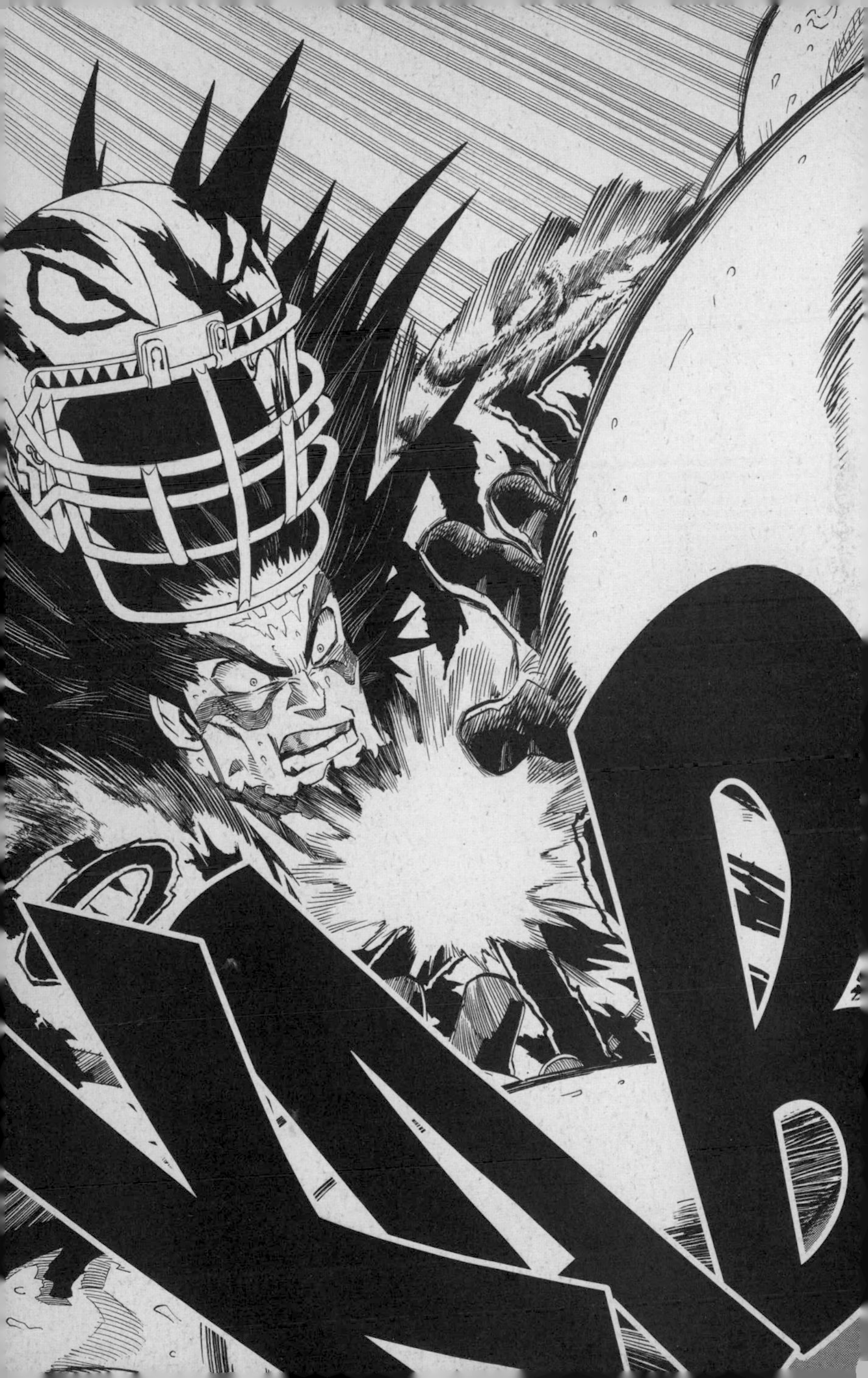

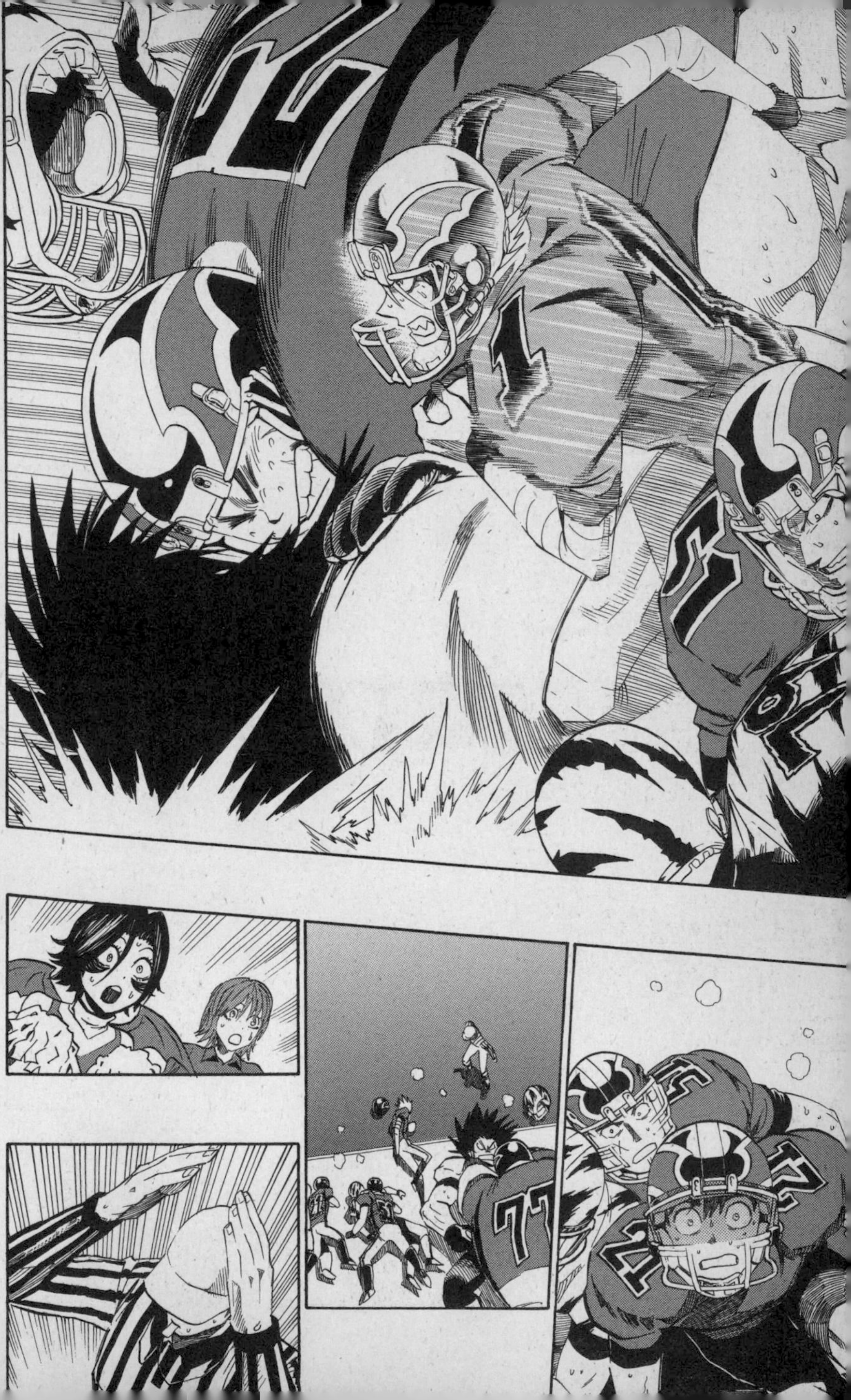

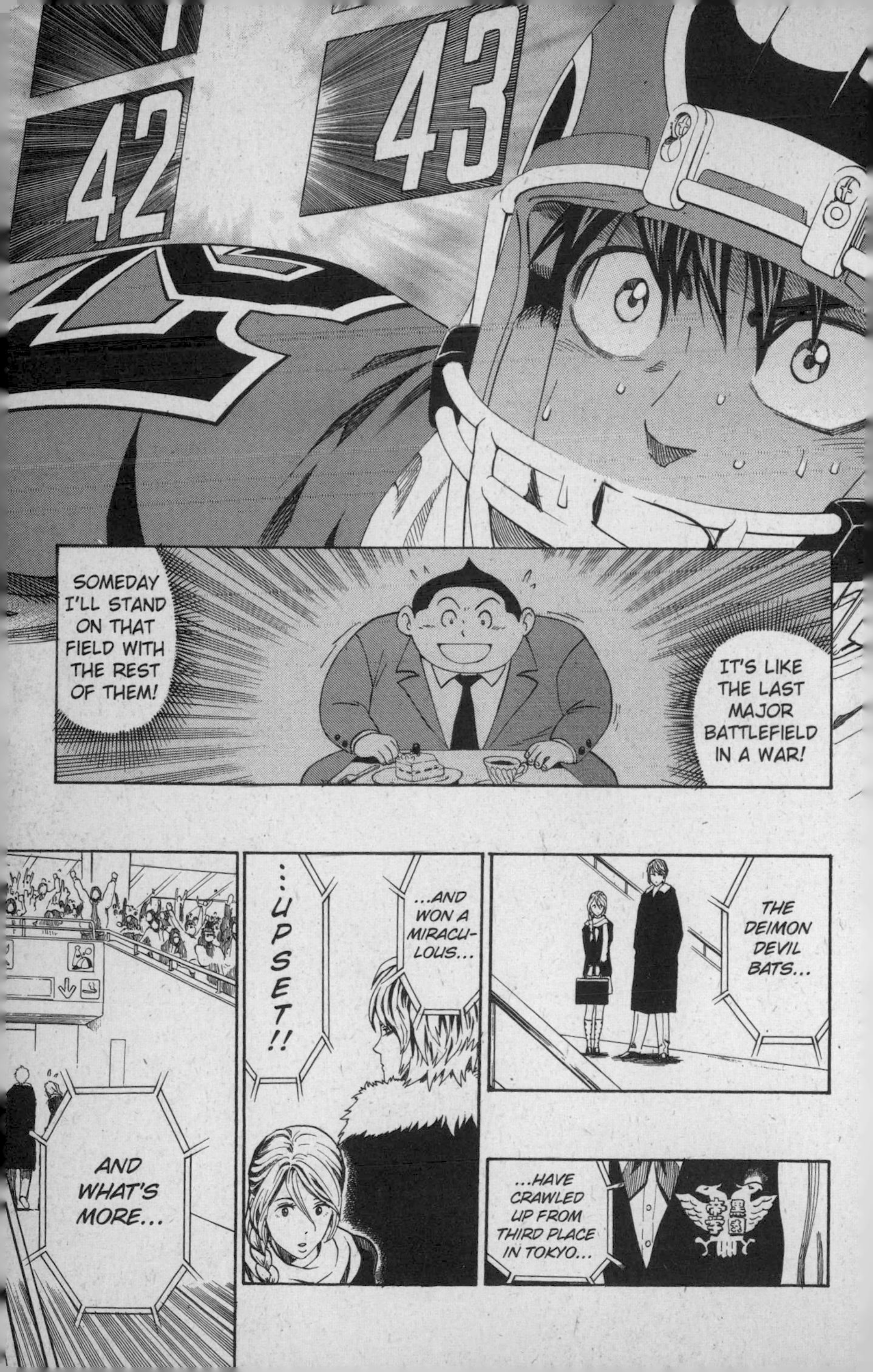
IT'S LIKE THE LAST MAJOR BATTLEFIELD IN A WAR!
SOMEDAY I'LL STAND ON THAT FIELD WITH THE REST OF THEM!
THE DEIMON DEVIL BATS...
...HAVE CRAWLED UP FROM THIRD PLACE IN TOKYO...
...AND WON A MIRACULOUS...
...UPSET!!
AND WHAT'S MORE...

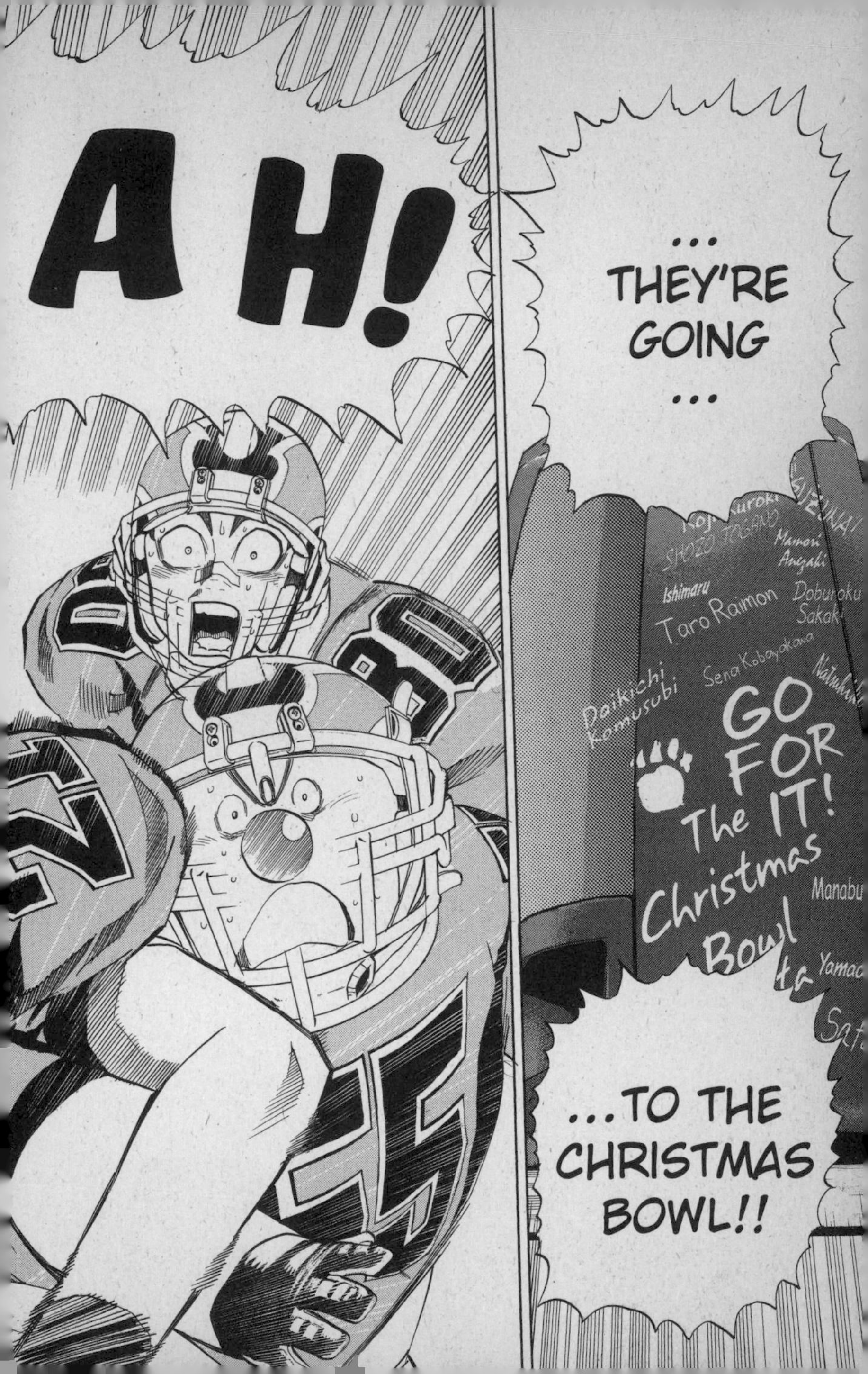
...THEY'RE GOING...
Koji Kuroki
SHOZO TOGANO
Mamori Anezaki
Ishimaru
Taro Raimon
Sena Kobayakawa
Daikichi Komusubi
GO FOR The Christmas Bowl
IT!
...TO THE CHRISTMAS BOWL!!
AH!

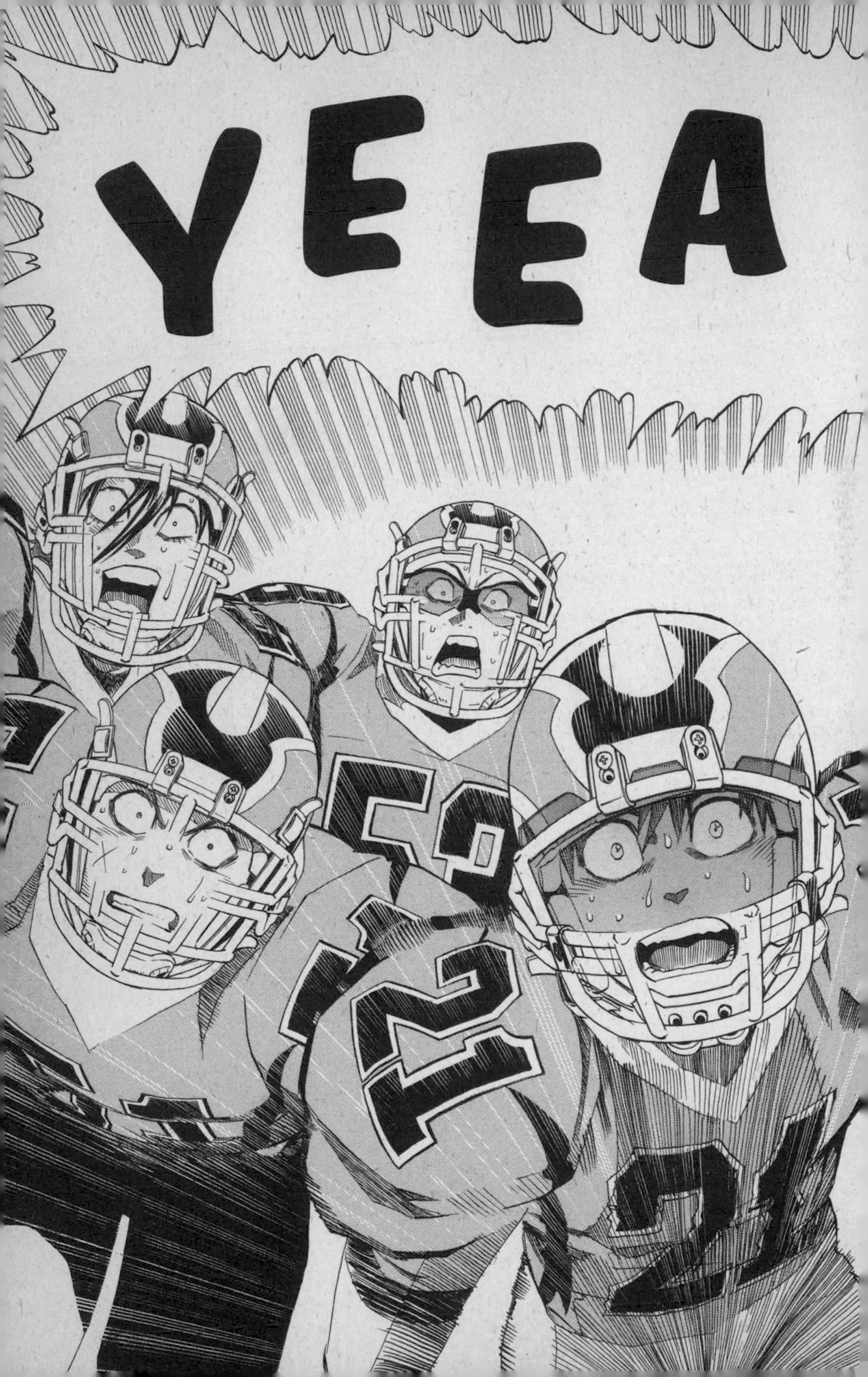
YEEA

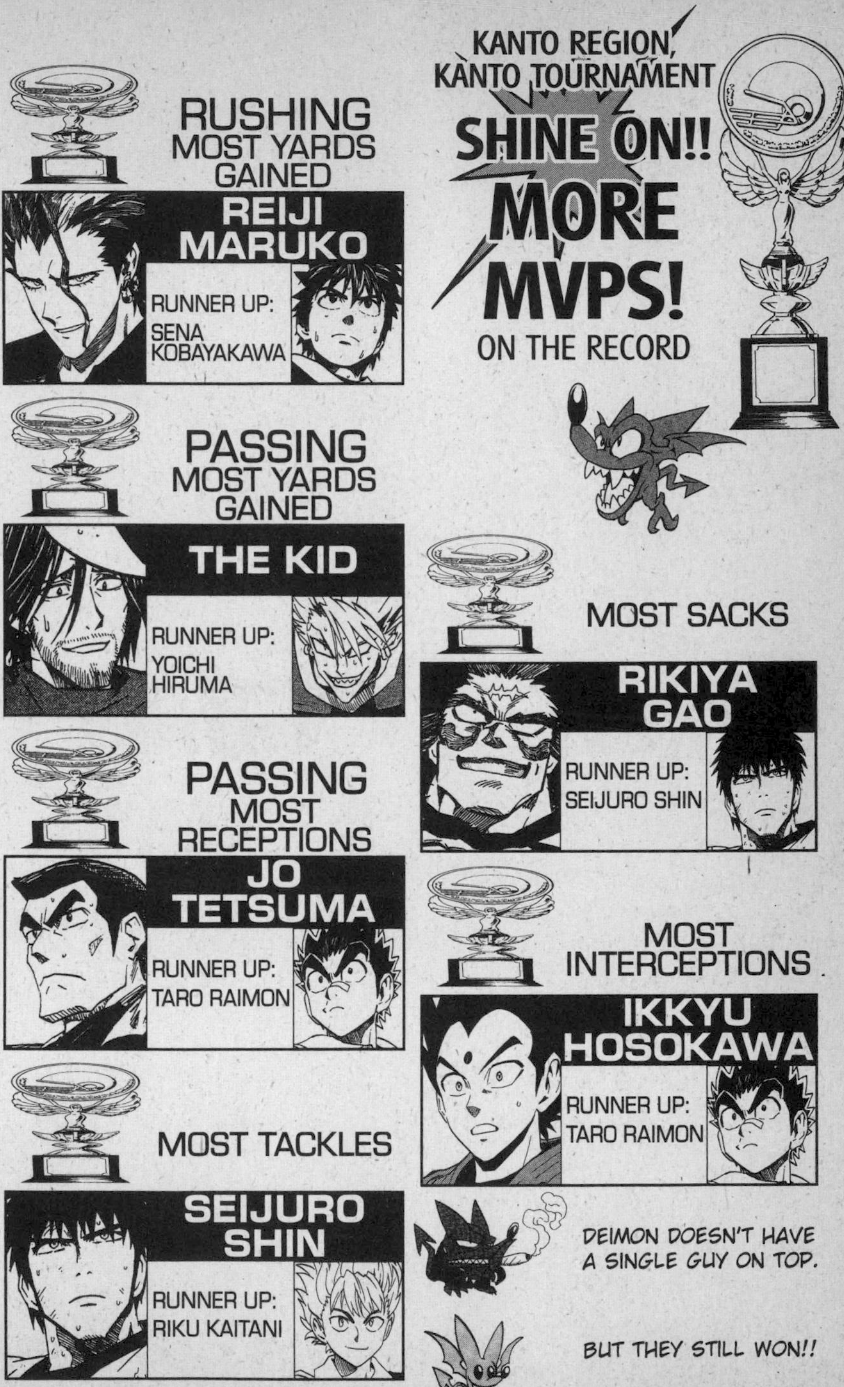
KANTO REGION, KANTO TOURNAMENT
SHINE ON!! MORE MVPS!
ON THE RECORD
MOST SACKS
RIKIYA GAO
RUNNER UP: SEIJURO SHIN
MOST INTERCEPTIONS
IKKYU HOSOKAWA
RUNNER UP: TARO RAIMON
DEIMON DOESN'T HAVE A SINGLE GUY ON TOP.
BUT THEY STILL WON!!
RUSHING MOST YARDS GAINED
REIJI MARUKO
RUNNER UP: SENA KOBAYAKAWA
PASSING MOST YARDS GAINED
THE KID
RUNNER UP: YOICHI HIRUMA
PASSING MOST RECEPTIONS
JO TETSUMA
RUNNER UP: TARO RAIMON
MOST TACKLES
SEIJURO SHIN
RUNNER UP: RIKU KAITANI

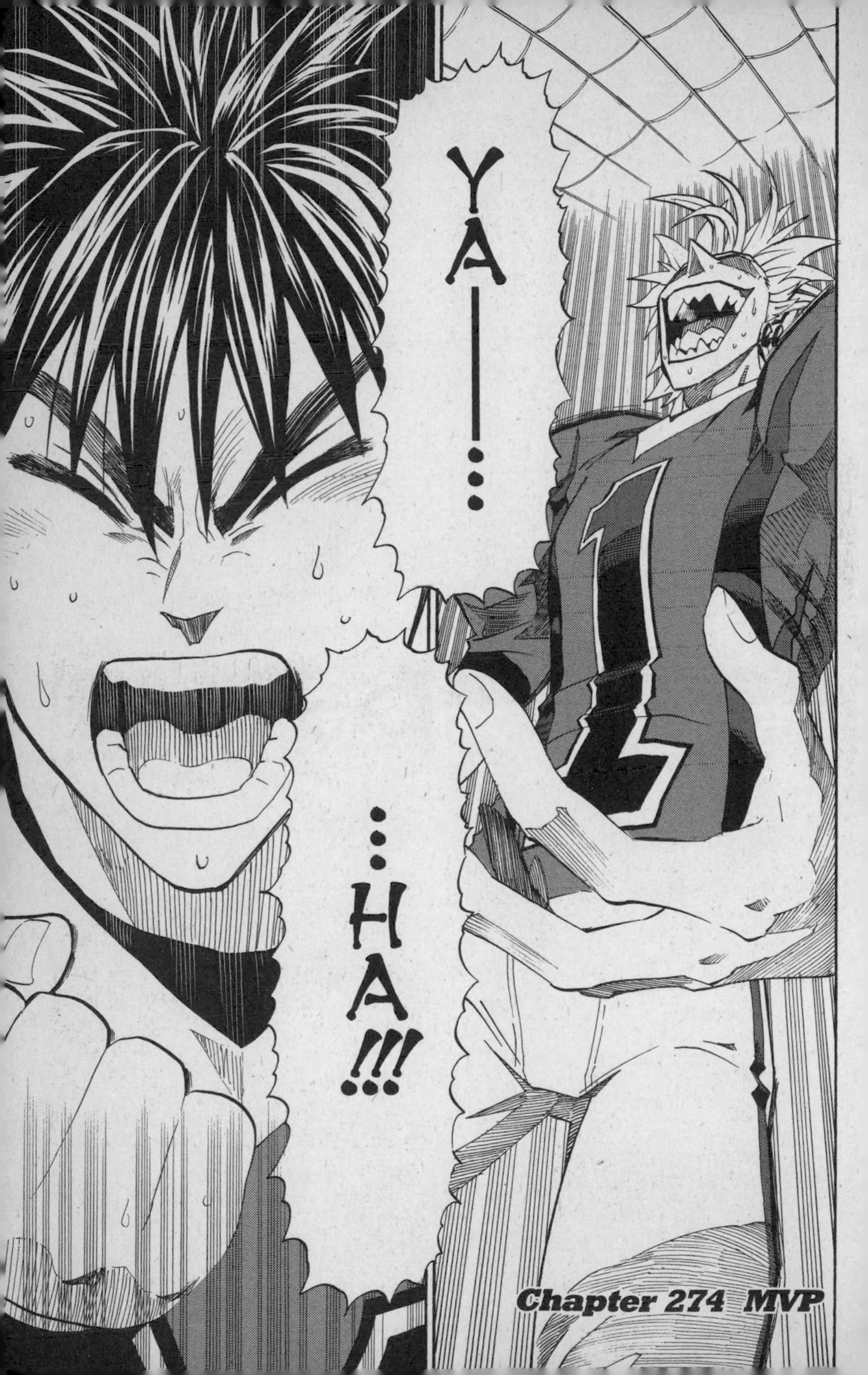
YA--...
...HA!!!
Chapter 274 MVP

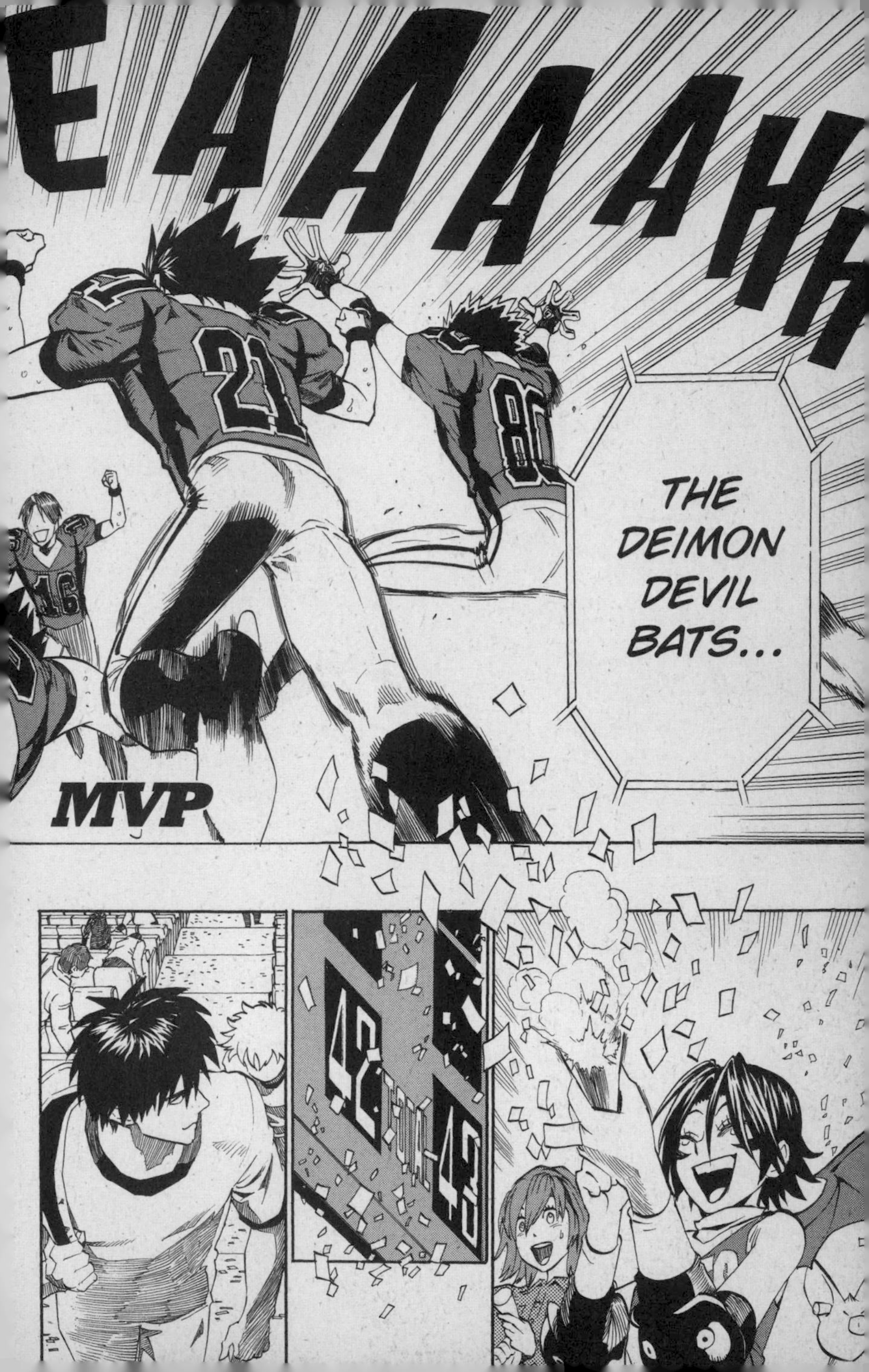
EAAAAAH
THE DEIMON DEVIL BATS...
MVP

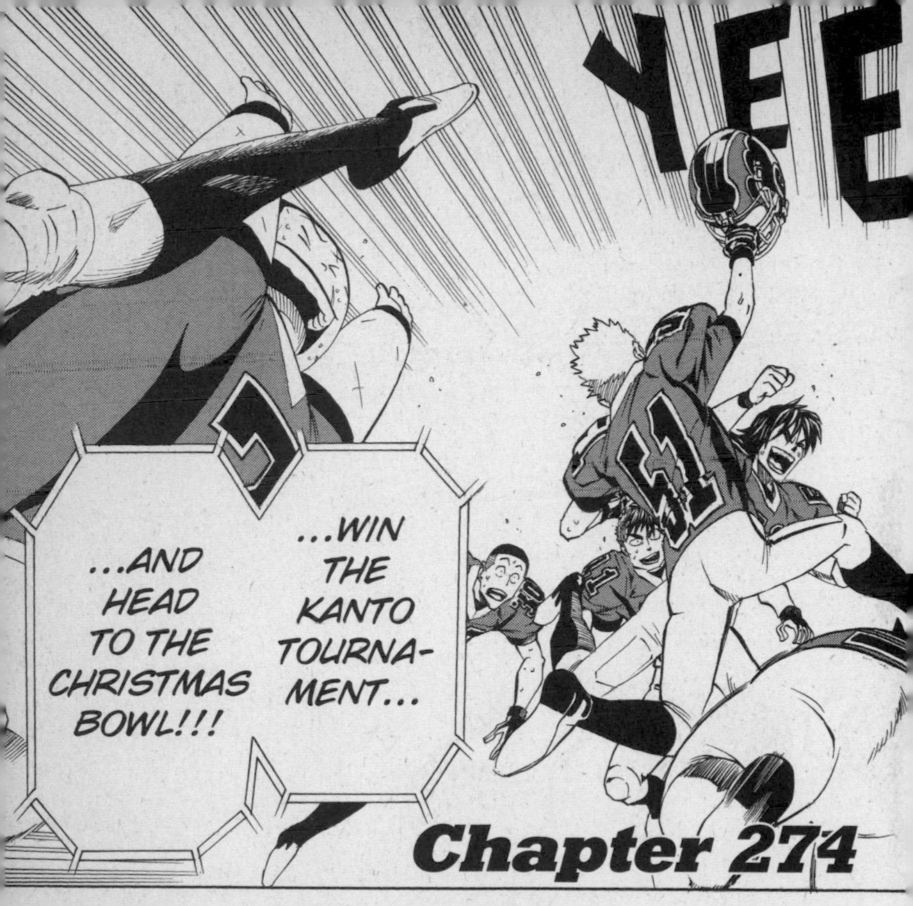
YEE
...WIN THE KANTO TOURNAMENT...
...AND HEAD TO THE CHRISTMAS BOWL!!!

Chapter 274

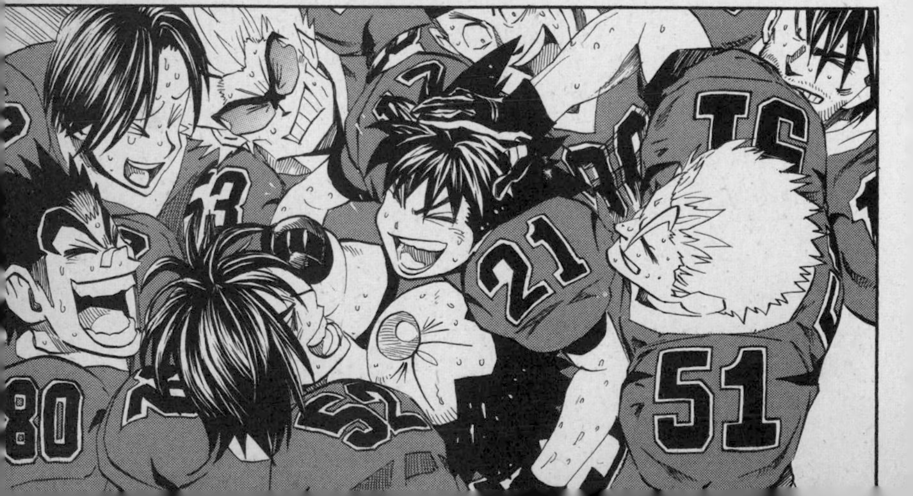

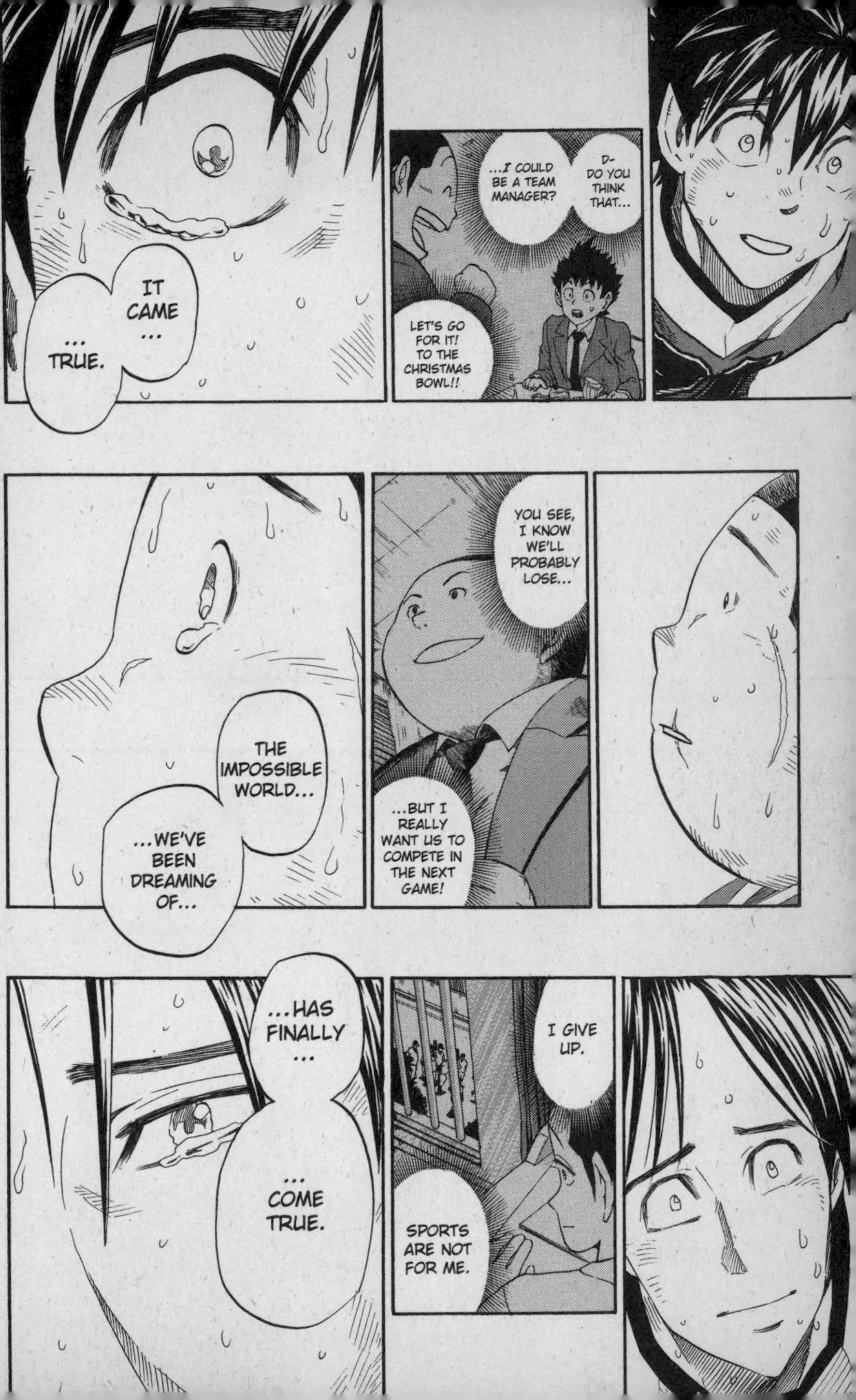
D- DO YOU THINK THAT...
...I COULD BE A TEAM MANAGER?
LET'S GO FOR IT! TO THE CHRISTMAS BOWL!!
IT CAME...
...TRUE.
YOU SEE, I KNOW WE'LL PROBABLY LOSE...
...BUT I REALLY WANT US TO COMPETE IN THE NEXT GAME!
THE IMPOSSIBLE WORLD...
...WE'VE BEEN DREAMING OF...
I GIVE UP.
SPORTS ARE NOT FOR ME.
...HAS FINALLY...
...COME TRUE.

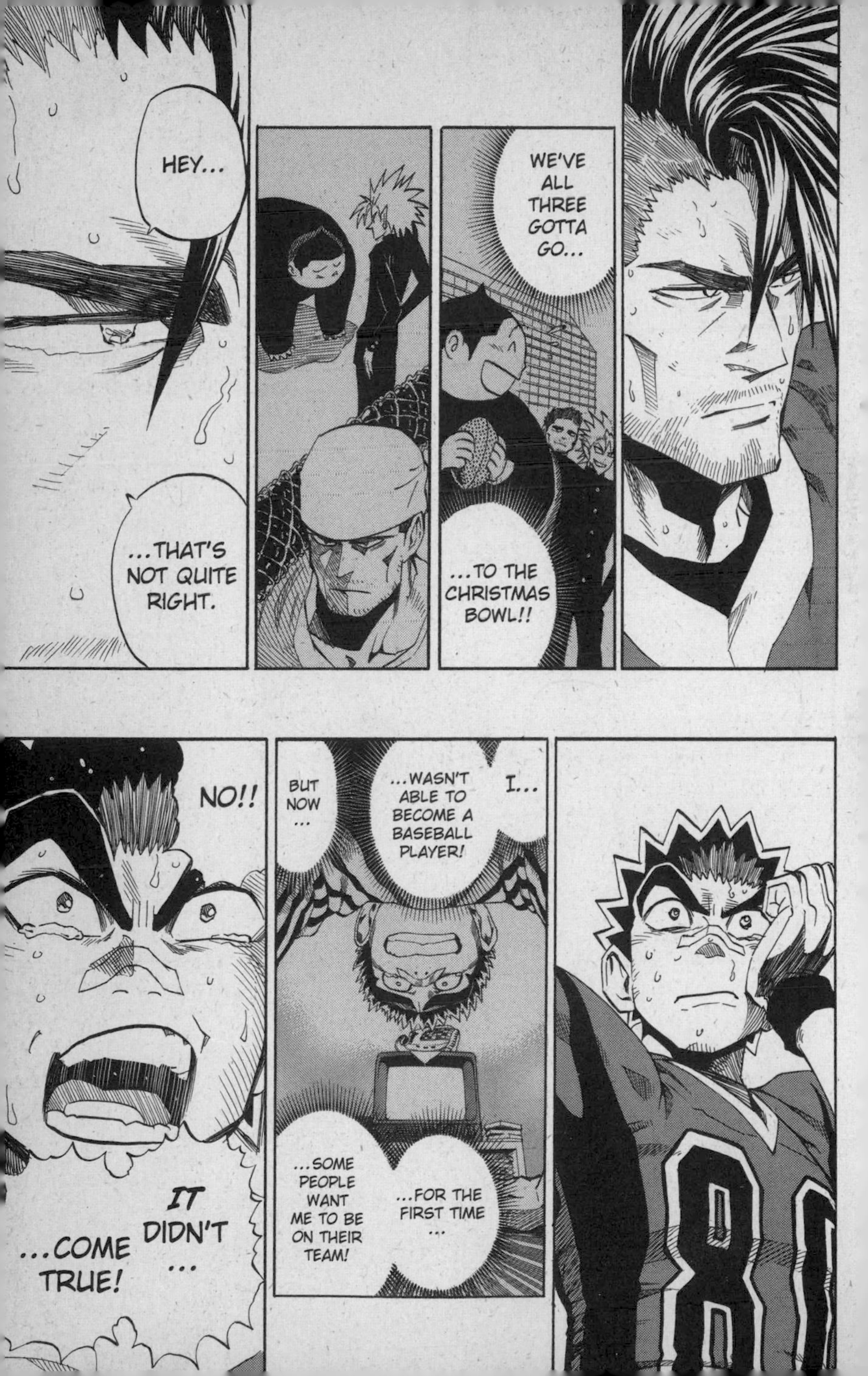
WE'VE ALL THREE GOTTA GO...
...TO THE CHRISTMAS BOWL!!
HEY...
...THAT'S NOT QUITE RIGHT.
I...
...WASN'T ABLE TO BECOME A BASEBALL PLAYER!
BUT NOW...
...FOR THE FIRST TIME...
...SOME PEOPLE WANT ME TO BE ON THEIR TEAM!
NO!!
IT DIDN'T...
...COME TRUE!

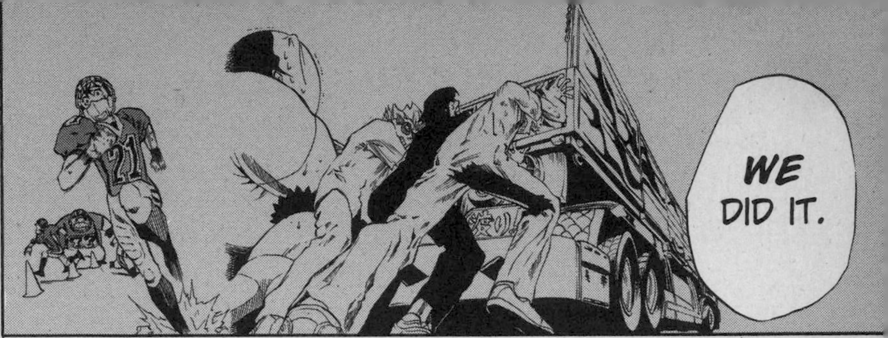
WE DID IT.

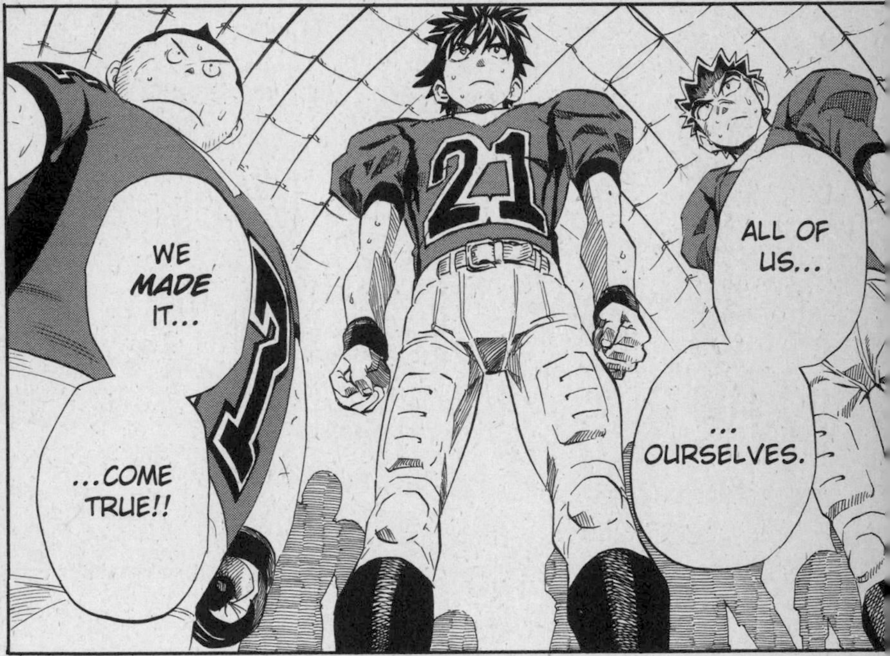
ALL OF US...
... OURSELVES.
WE MADE IT...
...COME TRUE!!

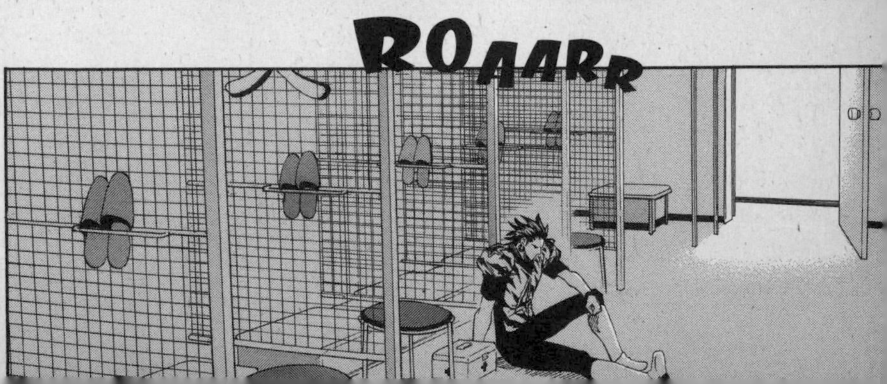
ROAARR

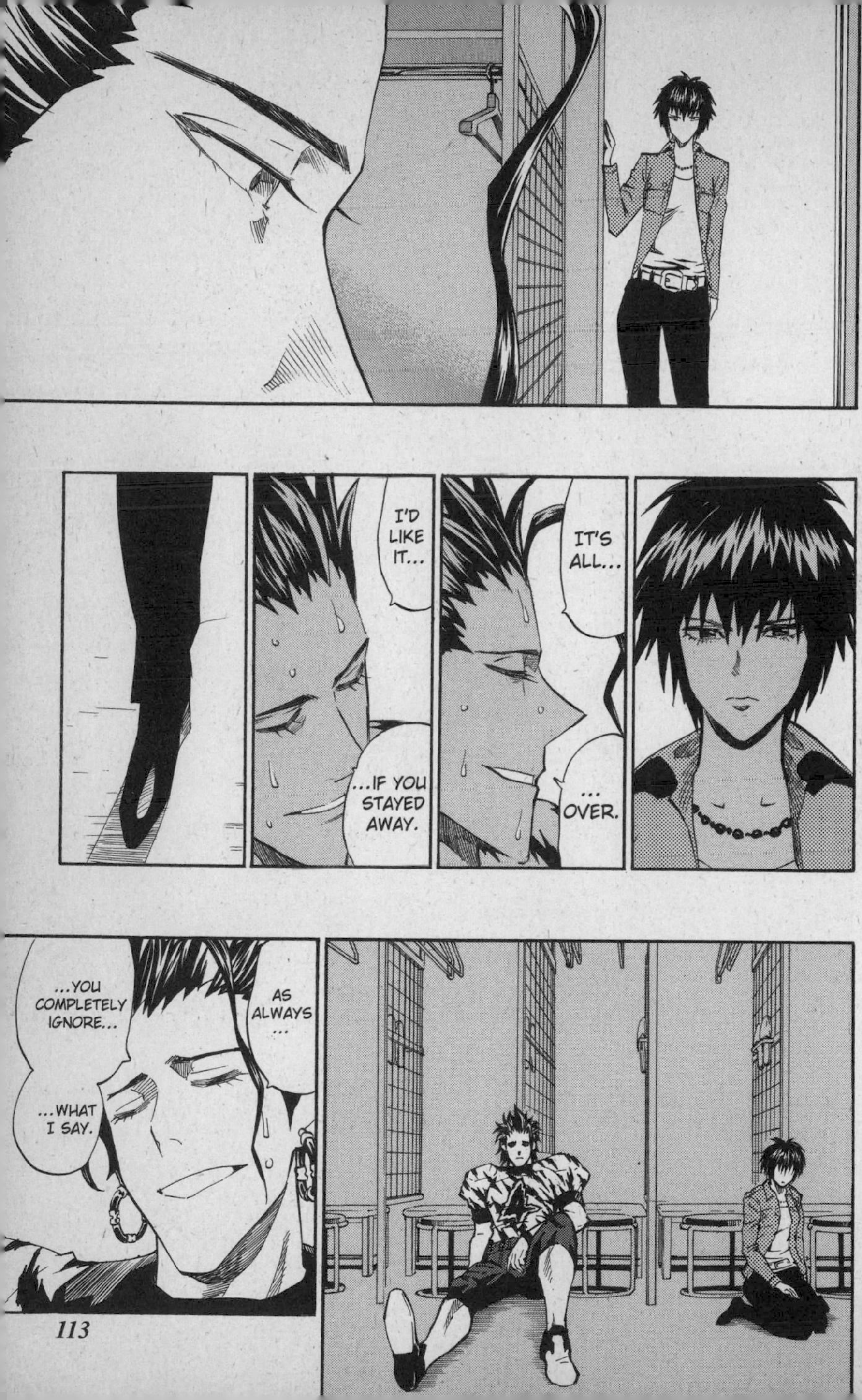
IT'S ALL...
...OVER.
I'D LIKE IT...
...IF YOU STAYED AWAY.
AS ALWAYS...
...YOU COMPLETELY IGNORE...
...WHAT I SAY.

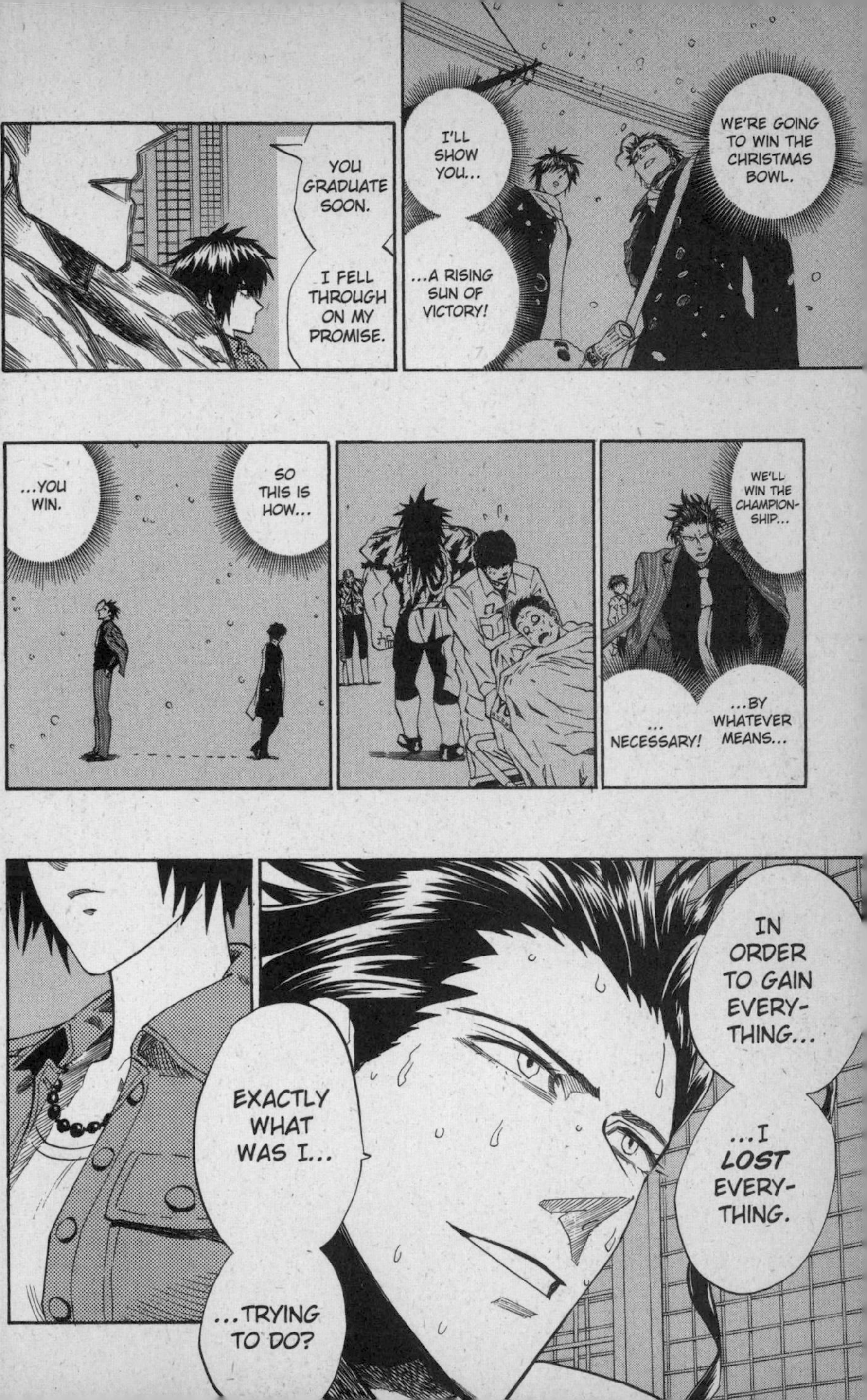
WE'RE GOING TO WIN THE CHRISTMAS BOWL.
I'LL SHOW YOU...
...A RISING SUN OF VICTORY!
YOU GRADUATE SOON.
I FELL THROUGH ON MY PROMISE.
WE'LL WIN THE CHAMPION-SHIP...
...BY WHATEVER MEANS...
...NECESSARY!
SO THIS IS HOW...
...YOU WIN.
IN ORDER TO GAIN EVERY-THING...
...I *LOST* EVERY-THING.
EXACTLY WHAT WAS I...
...TRYING TO DO?

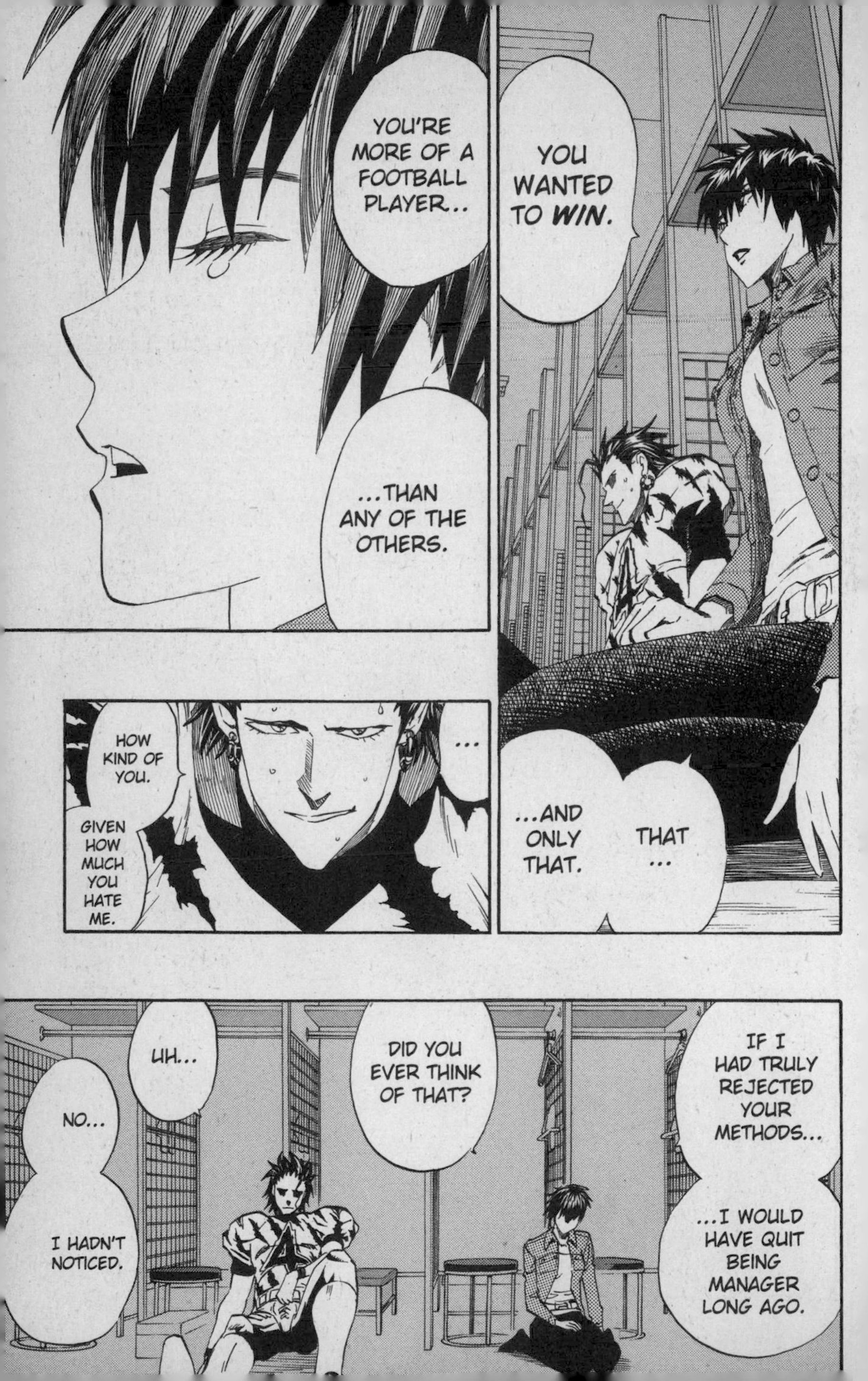
YOU WANTED TO WIN.
THAT...
...AND ONLY THAT.
YOU'RE MORE OF A FOOTBALL PLAYER...
...THAN ANY OF THE OTHERS.
...
HOW KIND OF YOU.
GIVEN HOW MUCH YOU HATE ME.
IF I HAD TRULY REJECTED YOUR METHODS...
...I WOULD HAVE QUIT BEING MANAGER LONG AGO.
DID YOU EVER THINK OF THAT?
UH...
NO...
I HADN'T NOTICED.

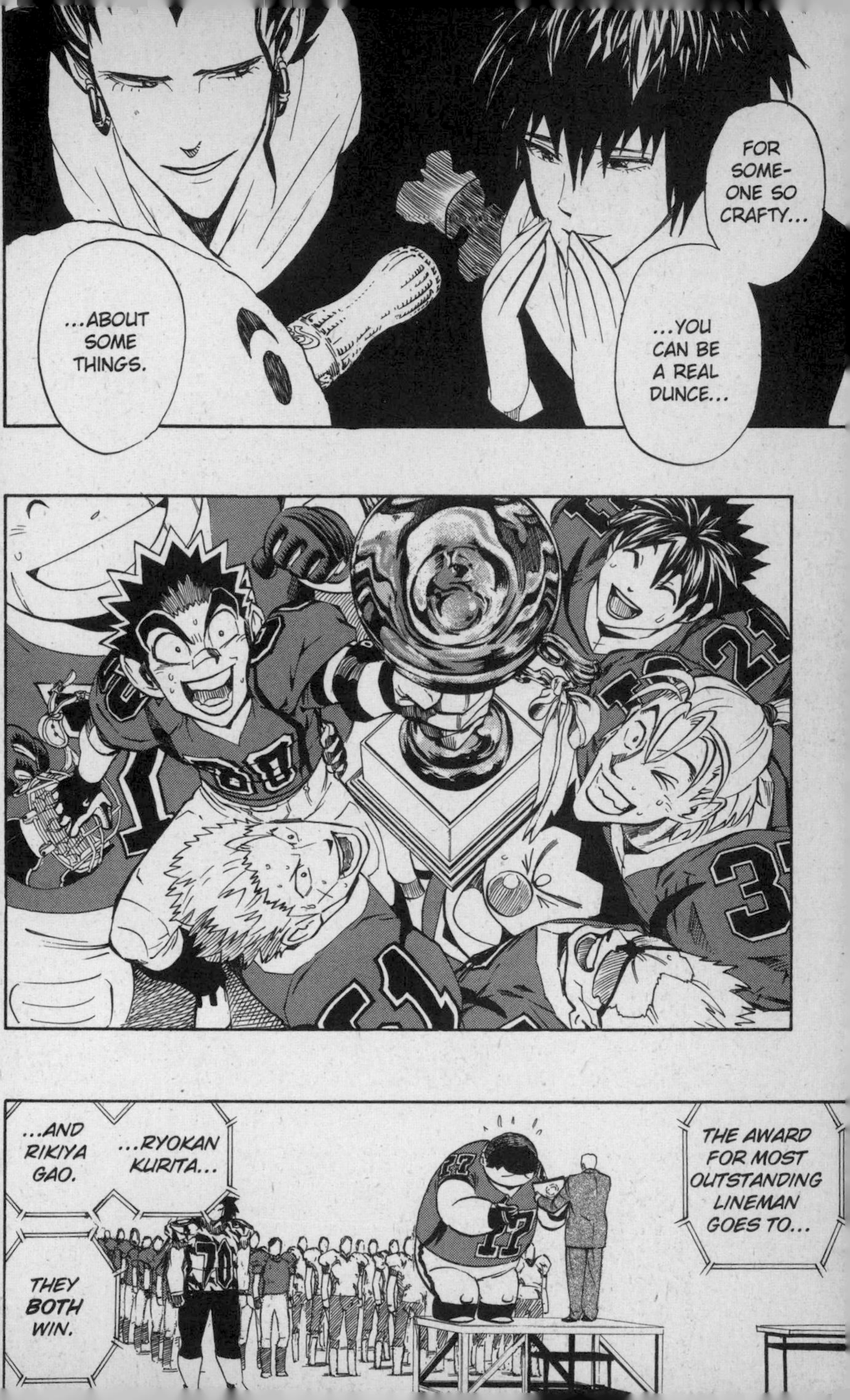
FOR SOMEONE SO CRAFTY...
...YOU CAN BE A REAL DUNCE...
...ABOUT SOME THINGS.
THE AWARD FOR MOST OUTSTANDING LINEMAN GOES TO...
...RYOKAN KURITA...
...AND RIKIYA GAO.
THEY BOTH WIN.

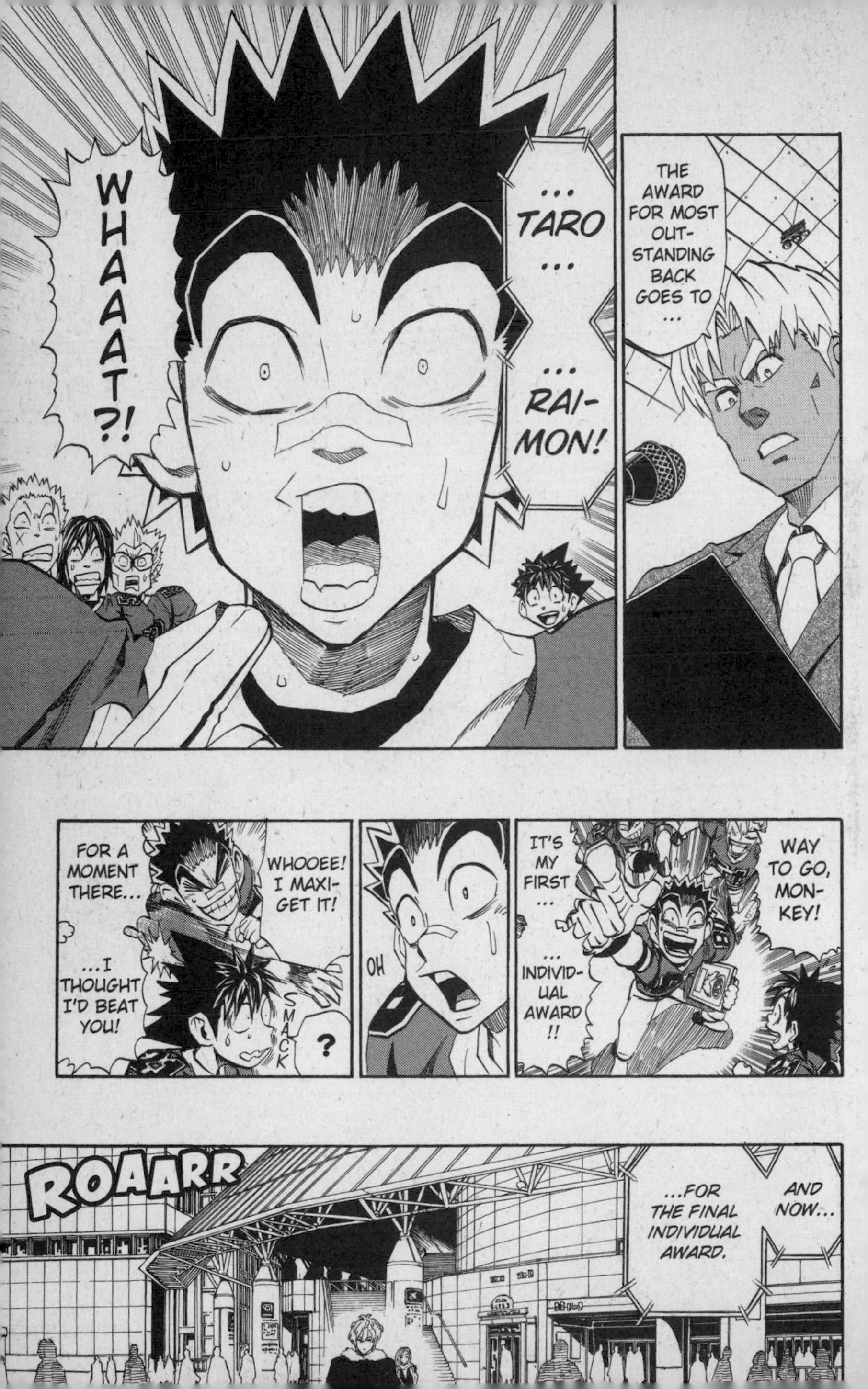
THE AWARD FOR MOST OUT-STANDING BACK GOES TO ...
... TARO ...
... RAI-MON!
WHAAAAT?!
WAY TO GO, MON-KEY!
IT'S MY FIRST ...
... INDIVID-UAL AWARD !!
OH
WHOOEE! I MAXI-GET IT!
SMACK
?
FOR A MOMENT THERE...
...I THOUGHT I'D BEAT YOU!
AND NOW...
...FOR THE FINAL INDIVIDUAL AWARD.
ROAARR

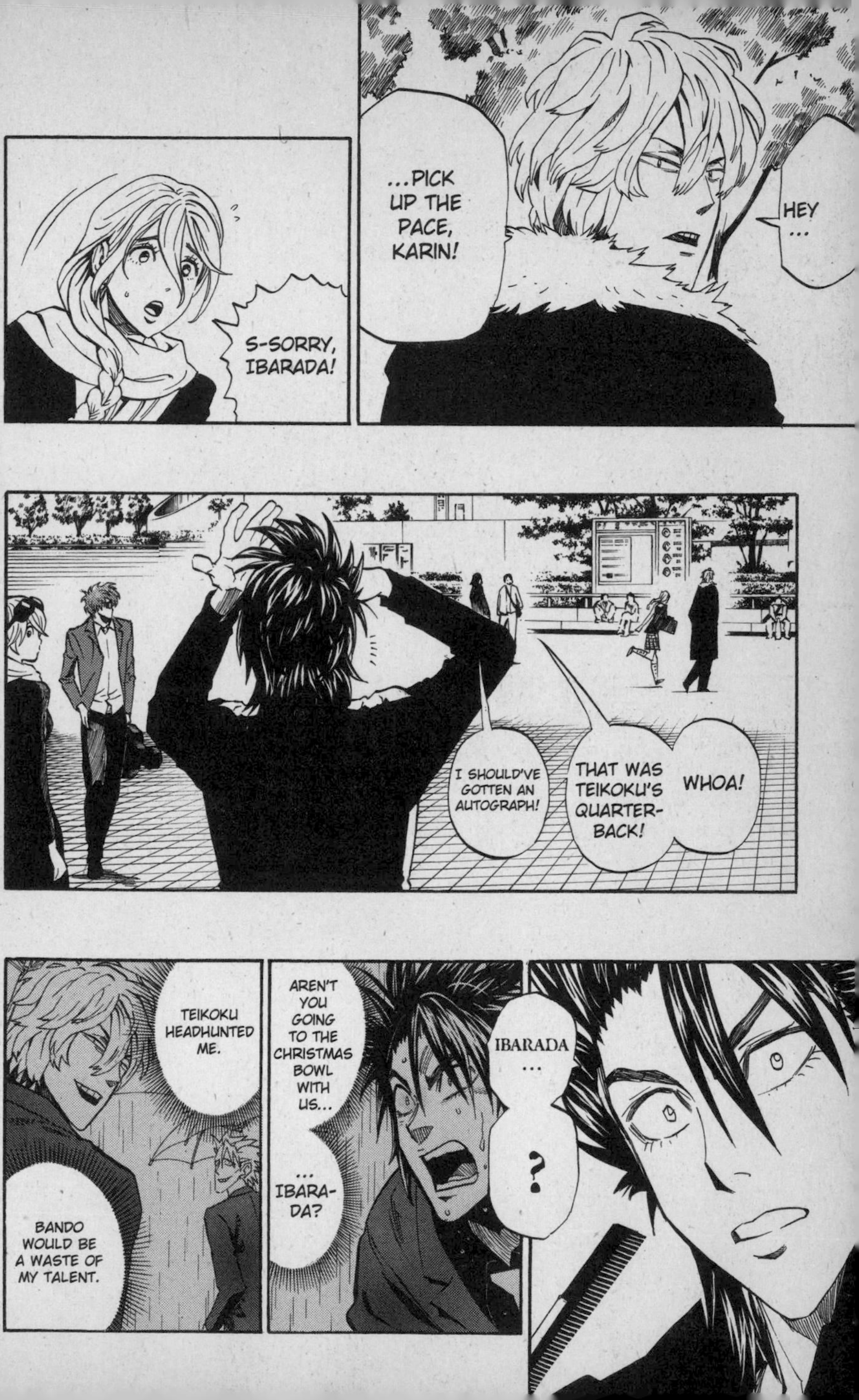
HEY ...
...PICK UP THE PACE, KARIN!
S-SORRY, IBARADA!
WHOA!
THAT WAS TEIKOKU'S QUARTER-BACK!
I SHOULD'VE GOTTEN AN AUTOGRAPH!
IBARADA ...
?
AREN'T YOU GOING TO THE CHRISTMAS BOWL WITH US...
... IBARA-DA?
TEIKOKU HEADHUNTED ME.
BANDO WOULD BE A WASTE OF MY TALENT.

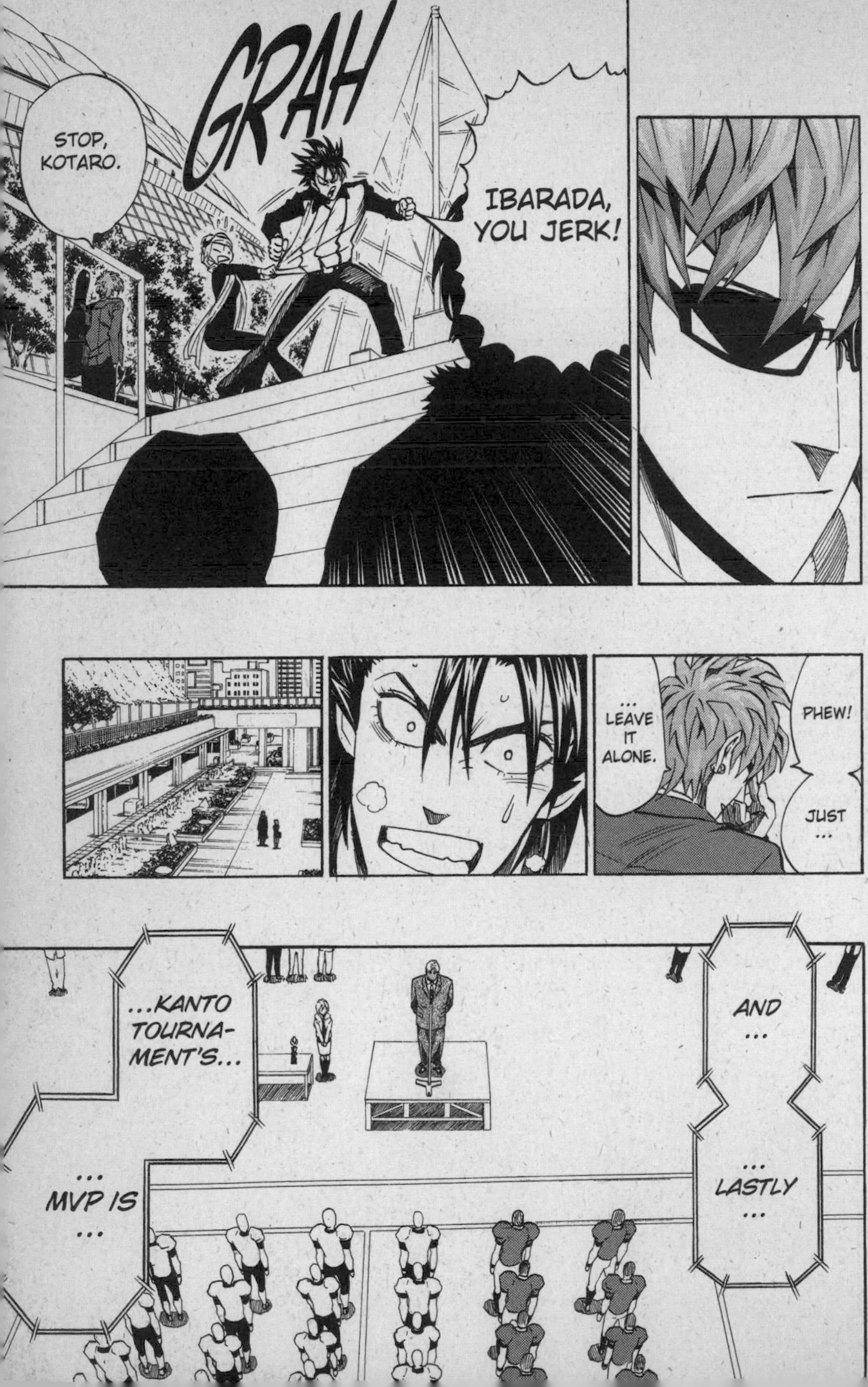
IBARADA, YOU JERK!
GRAH
STOP, KOTARO.
PHEW!
JUST ...
... LEAVE IT ALONE.
AND ...
... LASTLY ...
...KANTO TOURNAMENT'S...
... MVP IS ...

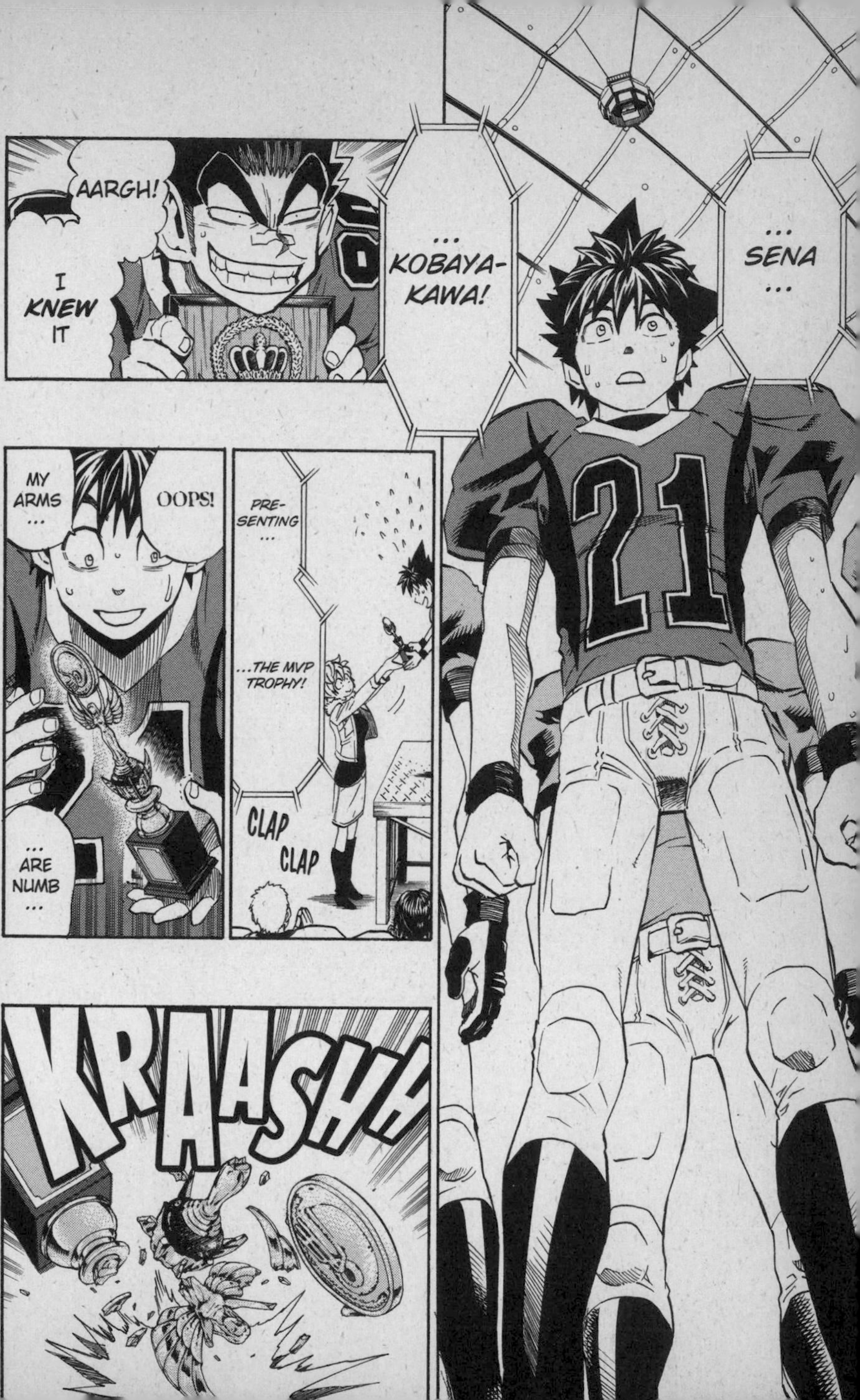

... SENA ...
... KOBAYA-KAWA!
AARGH!
I KNEW IT
PRE-SENTING ...
...THE MVP TROPHY!
CLAP CLAP
OOPS!
MY ARMS ...
... ARE NUMB ...
KRAASH

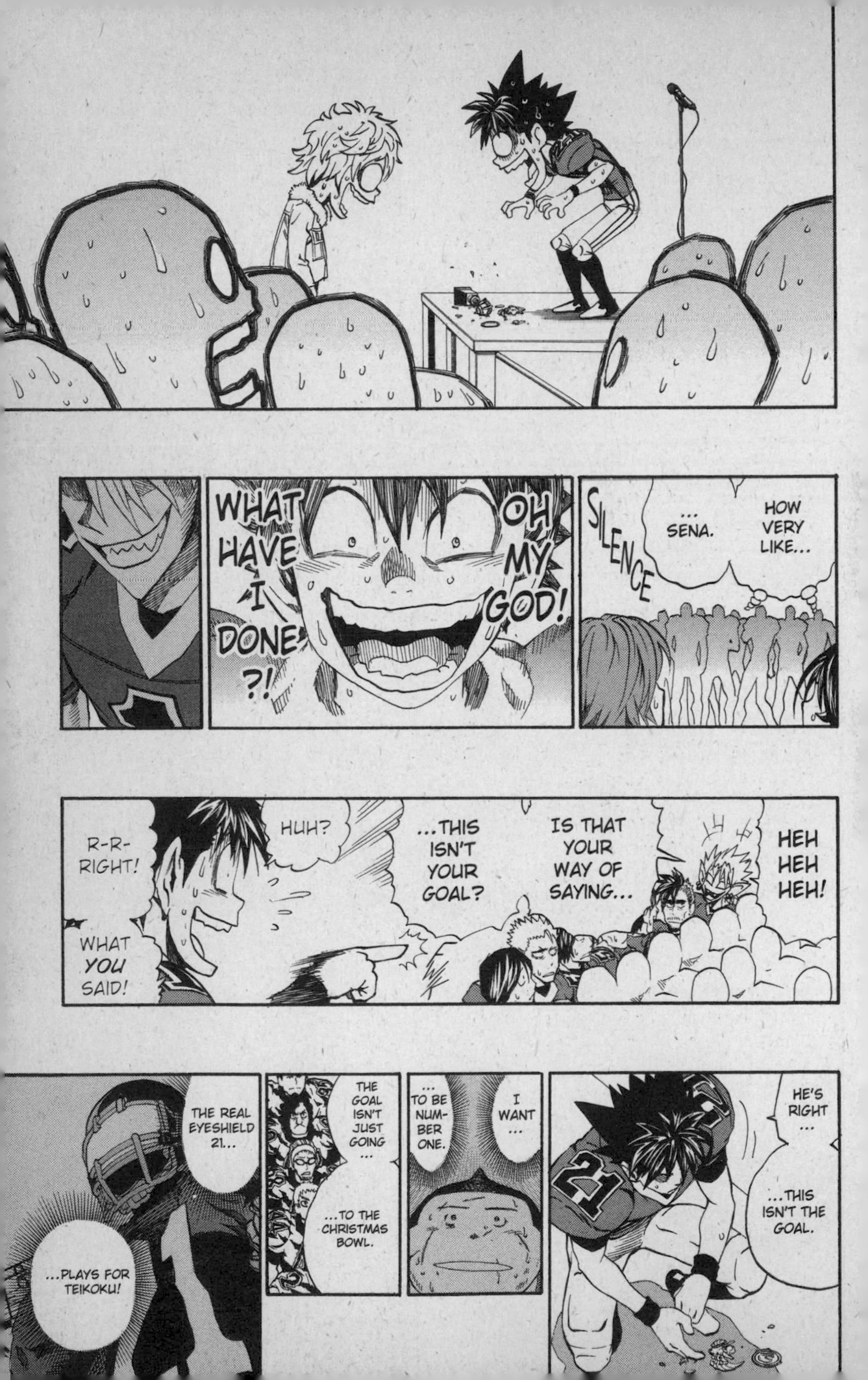
HOW VERY LIKE...
... SENA.
SILENCE
OH MY GOD!
WHAT HAVE I DONE?!
HEH HEH HEH!
IS THAT YOUR WAY OF SAYING...
...THIS ISN'T YOUR GOAL?
HUH?
R-R-RIGHT!
WHAT YOU SAID!
HE'S RIGHT...
...THIS ISN'T THE GOAL.
I WANT...
...TO BE NUM-BER ONE.
THE GOAL ISN'T JUST GOING...
...TO THE CHRISTMAS BOWL.
THE REAL EYESHIELD 21...
...PLAYS FOR TEIKOKU!

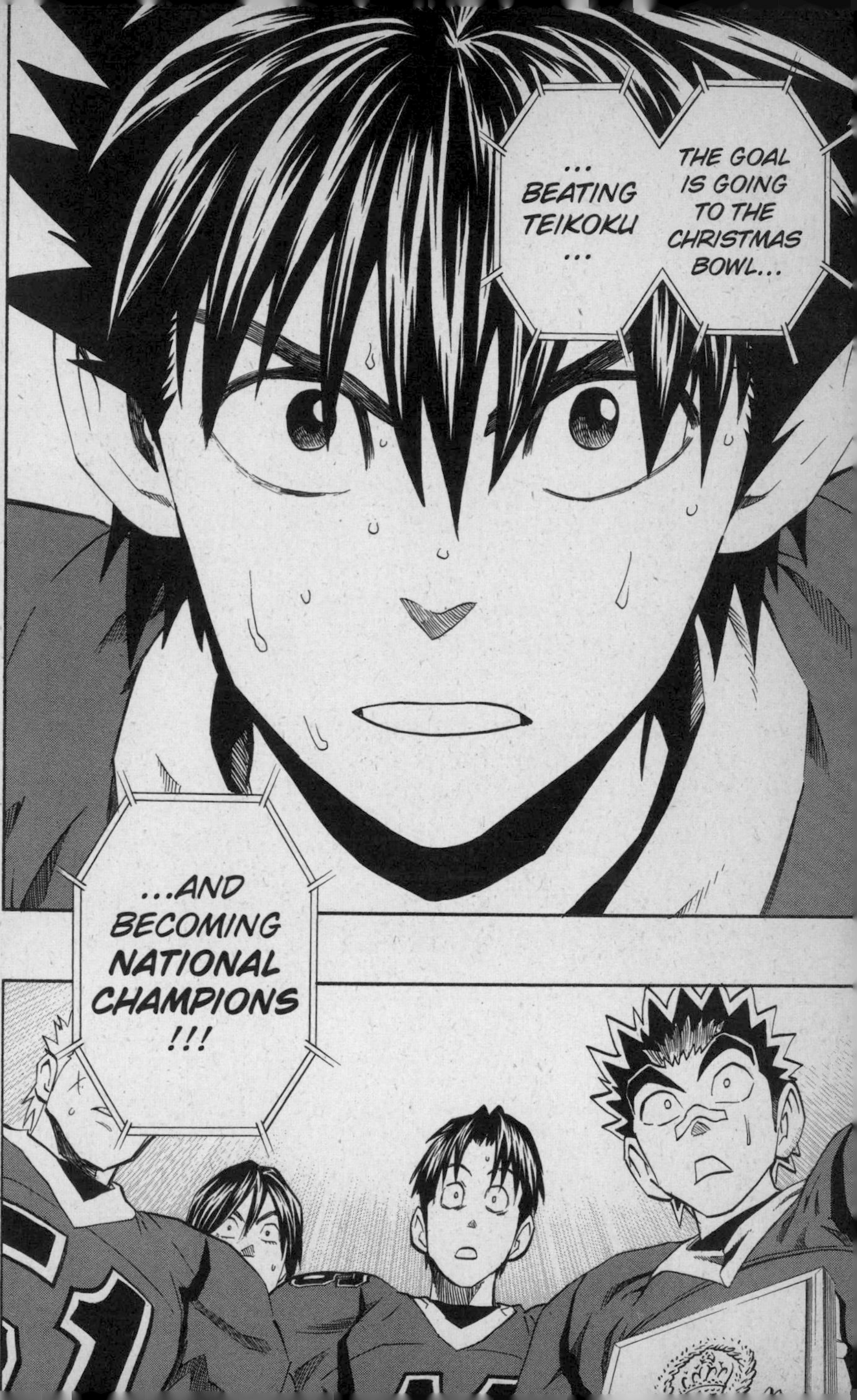
THE GOAL IS GOING TO THE CHRISTMAS BOWL...
...BEATING TEIKOKU...
...AND BECOMING NATIONAL CHAMPIONS!!!

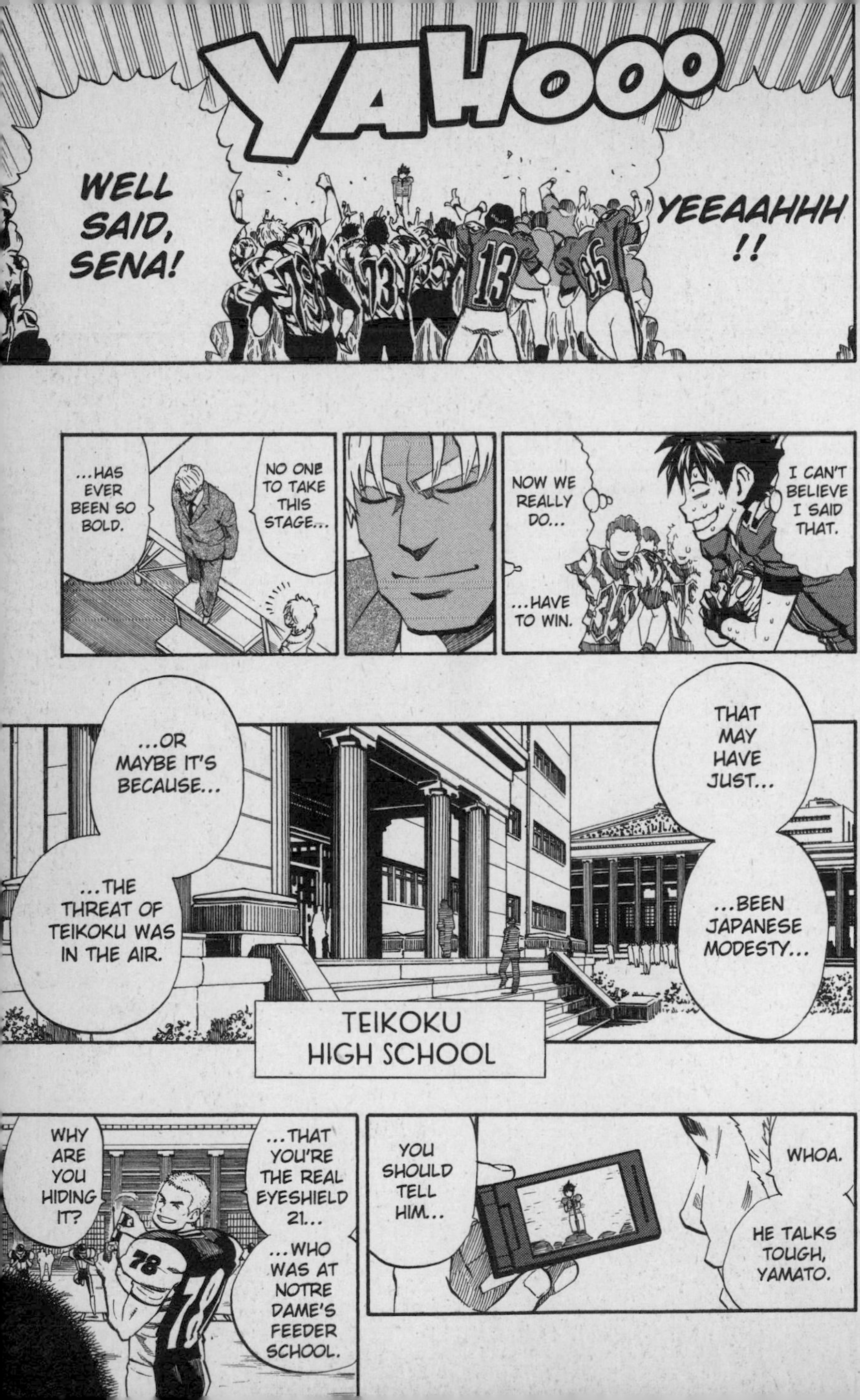
YAHOOO
YEEAAHHH!!
WELL SAID, SENA!
I CAN'T BELIEVE I SAID THAT.
NOW WE REALLY DO...
...HAVE TO WIN.
NO ONE TO TAKE THIS STAGE...
...HAS EVER BEEN SO BOLD.
THAT MAY HAVE JUST...
...BEEN JAPANESE MODESTY...
...OR MAYBE IT'S BECAUSE...
...THE THREAT OF TEIKOKU WAS IN THE AIR.
TEIKOKU HIGH SCHOOL
WHOA.
HE TALKS TOUGH, YAMATO.
YOU SHOULD TELL HIM...
...THAT YOU'RE THE REAL EYESHIELD 21...
...WHO WAS AT NOTRE DAME'S FEEDER SCHOOL.
WHY ARE YOU HIDING IT?
78

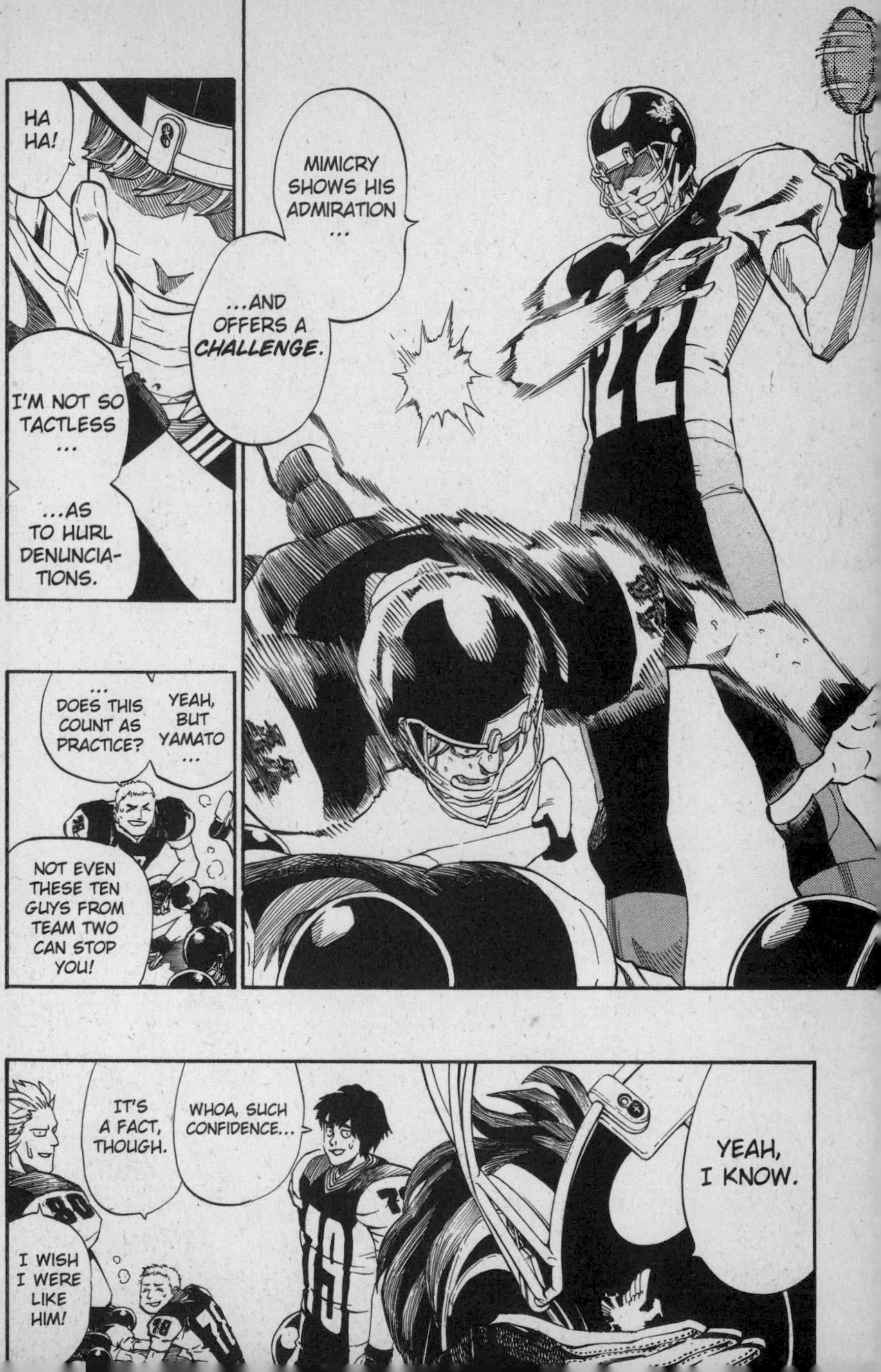
MIMICRY SHOWS HIS ADMIRATION ...
...AND OFFERS A CHALLENGE.
HA HA!
I'M NOT SO TACTLESS ...
...AS TO HURL DENUNCIATIONS.
... DOES THIS COUNT AS PRACTICE?
YEAH, BUT YAMATO ...
NOT EVEN THESE TEN GUYS FROM TEAM TWO CAN STOP YOU!
YEAH, I KNOW.
WHOA, SUCH CONFIDENCE...
IT'S A FACT, THOUGH.
I WISH I WERE LIKE HIM!

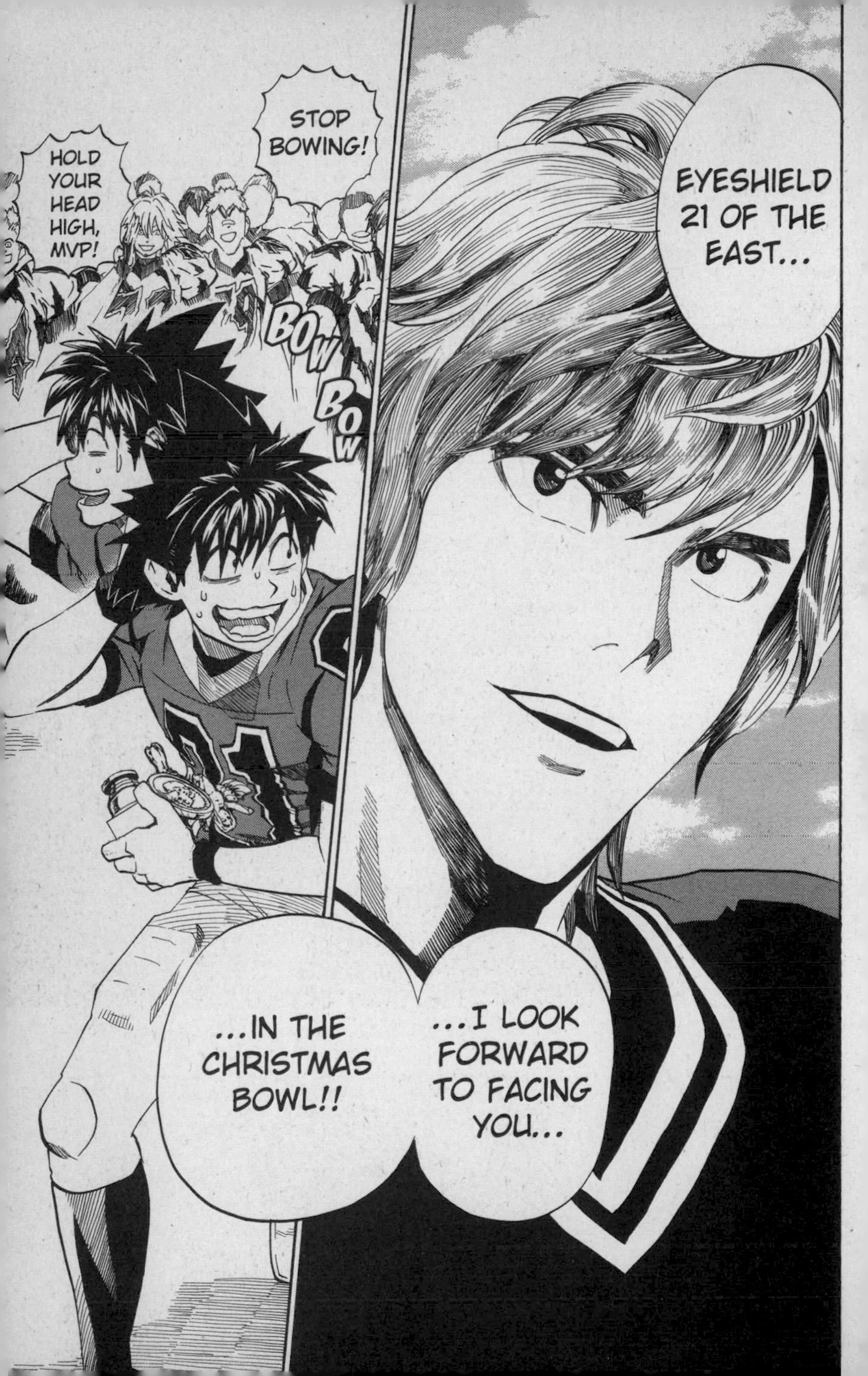
EYESHIELD 21 OF THE EAST...
...I LOOK FORWARD TO FACING YOU...
...IN THE CHRISTMAS BOWL!!
STOP BOWING!
HOLD YOUR HEAD HIGH, MVP!
BOW
BOW

KANTO REGION, KANTO TOURNAMENT

SHINE ON!! MORE MVPS!

BACKGROUND DATA

MOST HOURS TRAINED

RYOKAN KURITA

RUNNER UP: SEIJURO SHIN

TRICKED THE MOST TIMES

MAKOTO OTAWARA

RUNNER UP: HANATAKA TENGU

LEAST HOURS TRAINED

AGON KONGO

RUNNER UP: TAIGA KAMIYA

MOST PROTEIN CONSUMED

GANJO IWASHIGE

RUNNER UP: ATSUSHI MUNAKATA

MOST DATA ANALYZED

HAYATO AKABA

RUNNER UP: YOICHI HIRUMA

MOST BAD PREDICTIONS

ONIHEI YAMAMOTO

RUNNER UP: SEIBU'S COACH

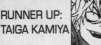

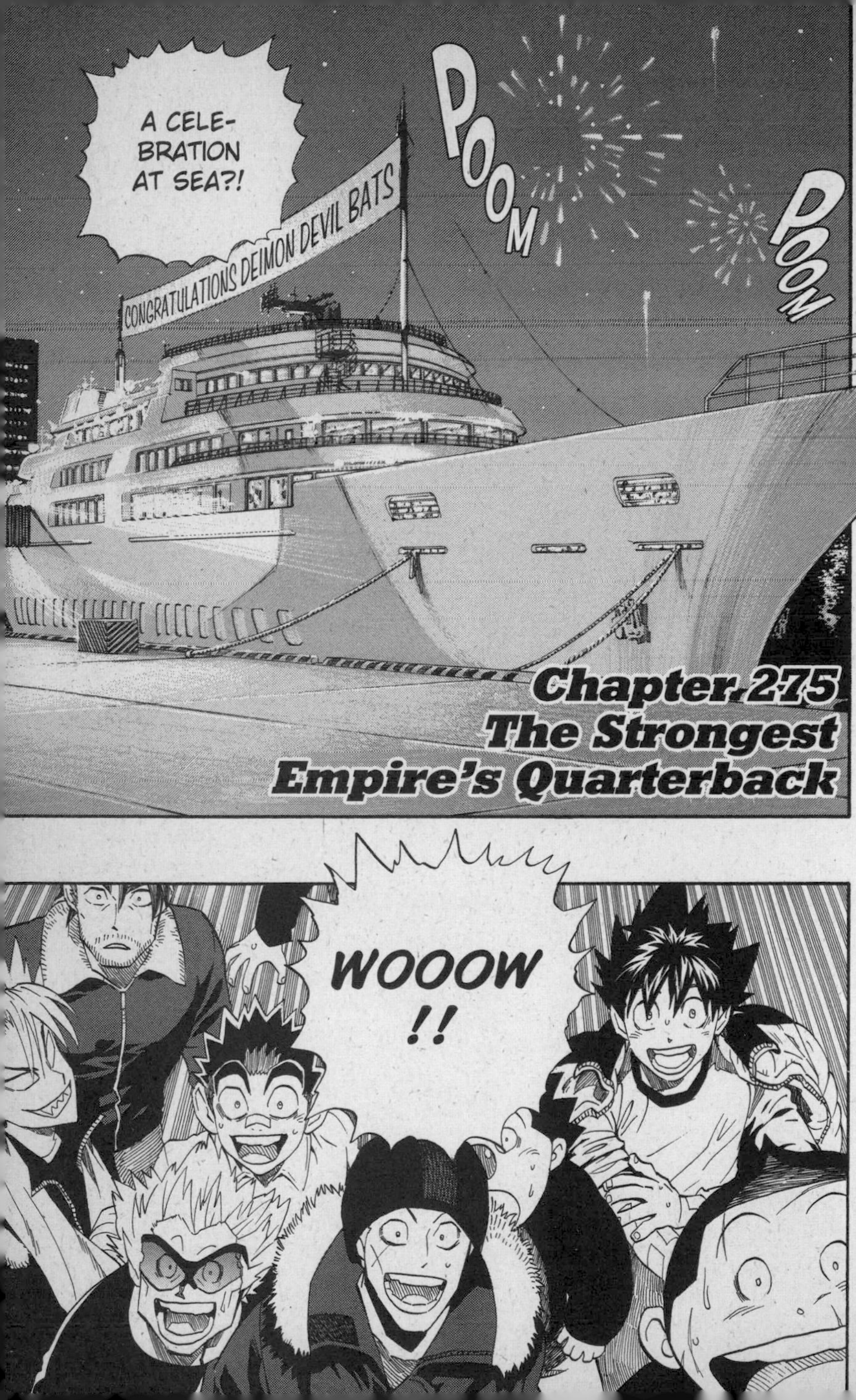
POOM
POOM
A CELE-BRATION AT SEA?!
CONGRATULATIONS DEIMON DEVIL BATS
Chapter 275
The Strongest Empire's Quarterback
WOOOW !!

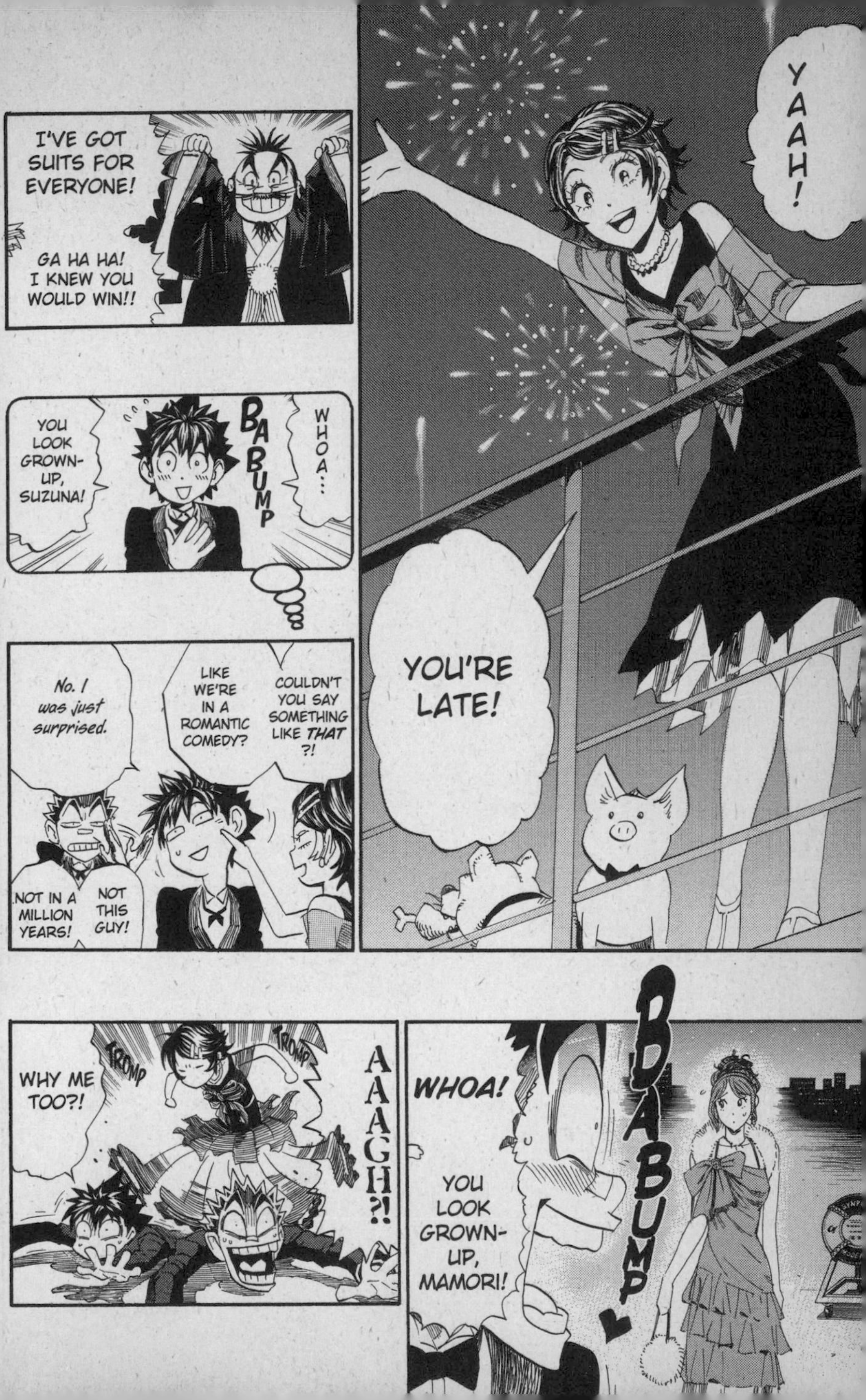
YAAH!
YOU'RE LATE!
I'VE GOT SUITS FOR EVERYONE!
GA HA HA! I KNEW YOU WOULD WIN!!
WHOA...
BABUMP
YOU LOOK GROWN-UP, SUZUNA!
COULDN'T YOU SAY SOMETHING LIKE *THAT*?!
LIKE WE'RE IN A ROMANTIC COMEDY?
No. I was just surprised.
NOT THIS GUY!
NOT IN A MILLION YEARS!
BABUMP
WHOA!
YOU LOOK GROWN-UP, MAMORI!
AAAGH?!
TROMP
TROMP
WHY ME TOO?!

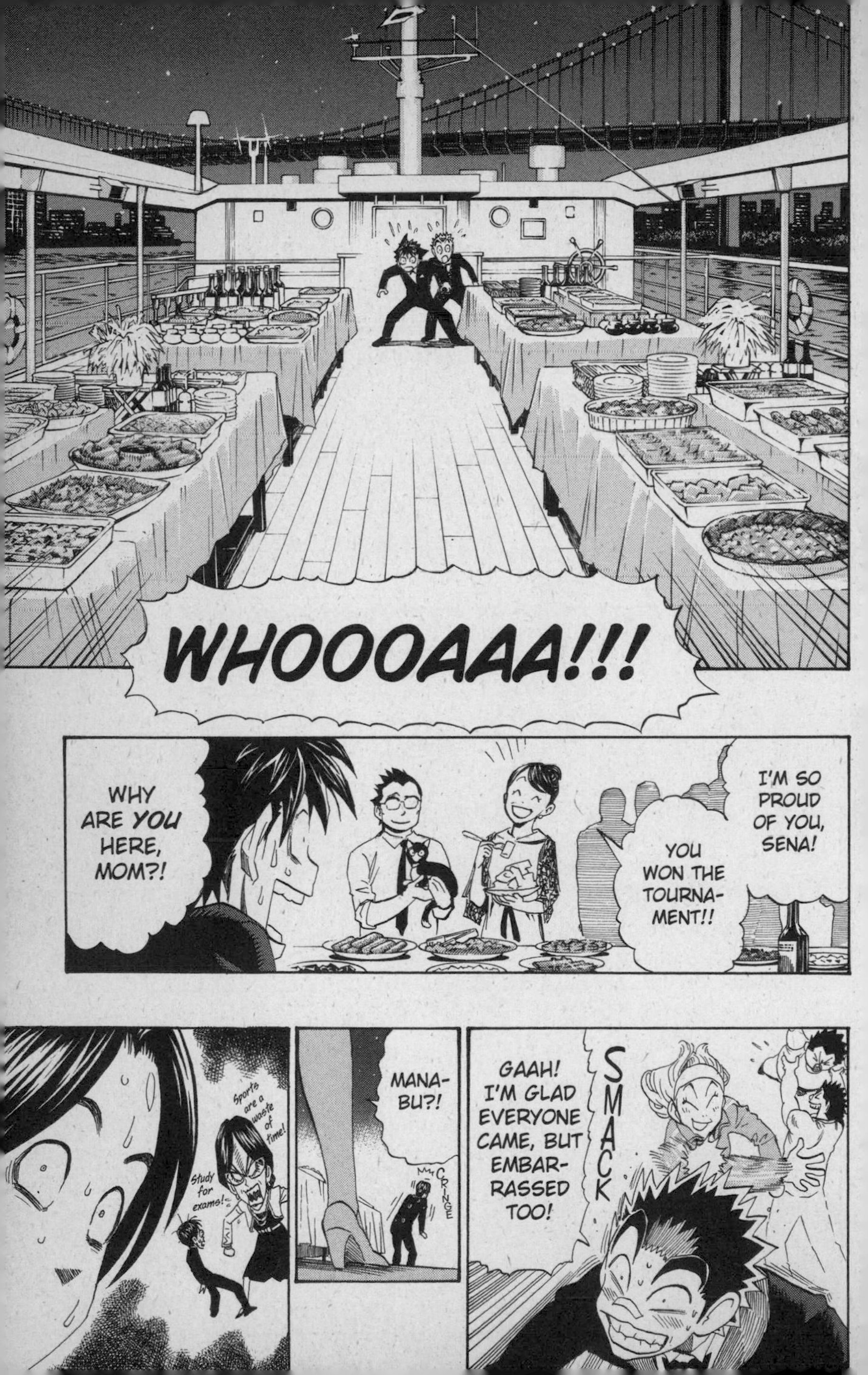
WHOOOAAA!!!
I'M SO PROUD OF YOU, SENA!
YOU WON THE TOURNAMENT!!
WHY ARE YOU HERE, MOM?!
SMACK
GAAH! I'M GLAD EVERYONE CAME, BUT EMBARRASSED TOO!
MANABU?!
CRINGE
Sports are a waste of time!
Study for exams!

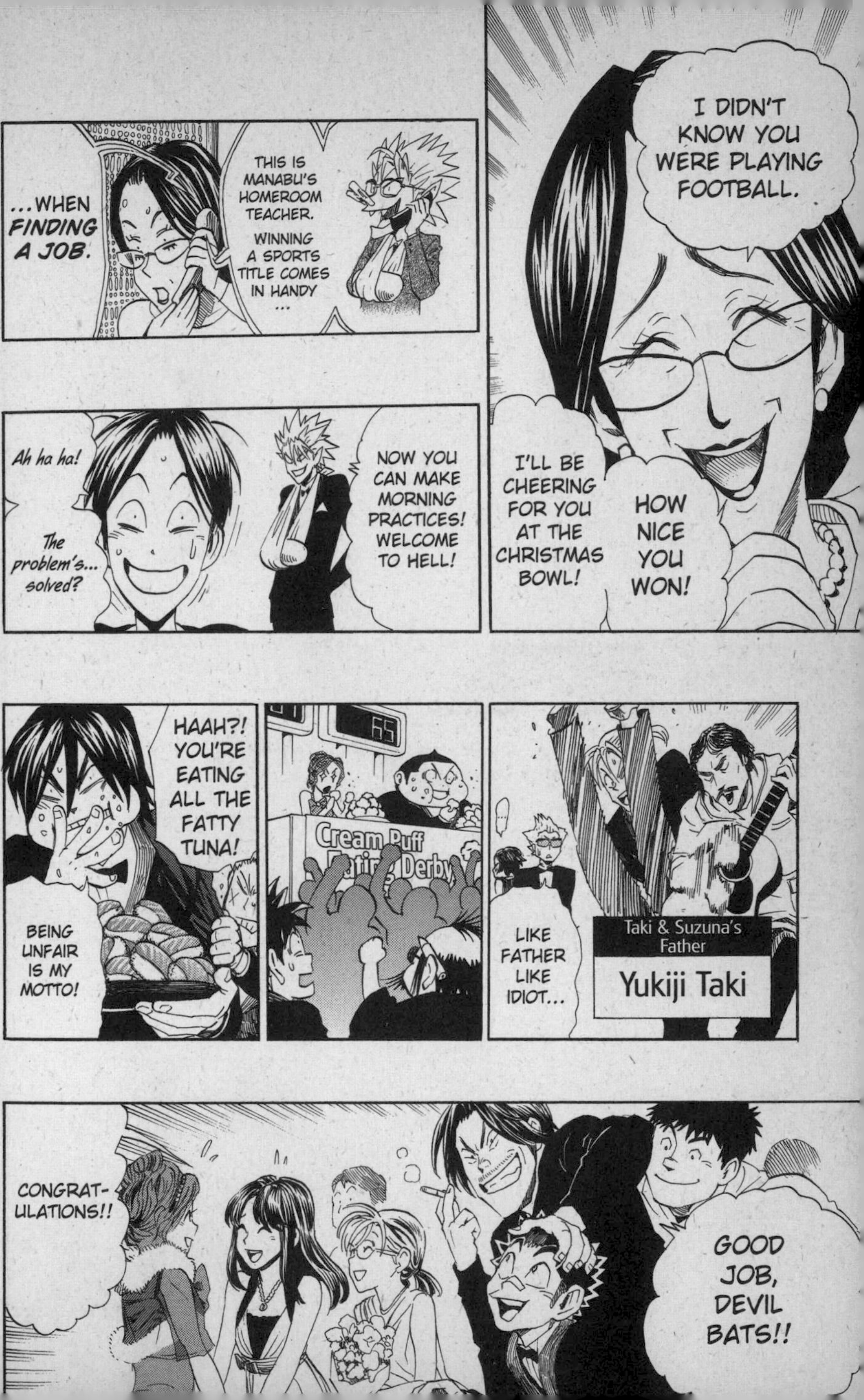
I DIDN'T KNOW YOU WERE PLAYING FOOTBALL.
HOW NICE YOU WON!
I'LL BE CHEERING FOR YOU AT THE CHRISTMAS BOWL!
THIS IS MANABU'S HOMEROOM TEACHER.
WINNING A SPORTS TITLE COMES IN HANDY ...
...WHEN *FINDING A JOB*.
NOW YOU CAN MAKE MORNING PRACTICES! WELCOME TO HELL!
Ah ha ha!
The problem's... solved?
Taki & Suzuna's Father
Yukiji Taki
LIKE FATHER LIKE IDIOT...
65
Cream Puff Eating Derby
HAAH?! YOU'RE EATING ALL THE FATTY TUNA!
BEING UNFAIR IS MY MOTTO!
GOOD JOB, DEVIL BATS!!
CONGRAT-ULATIONS!!

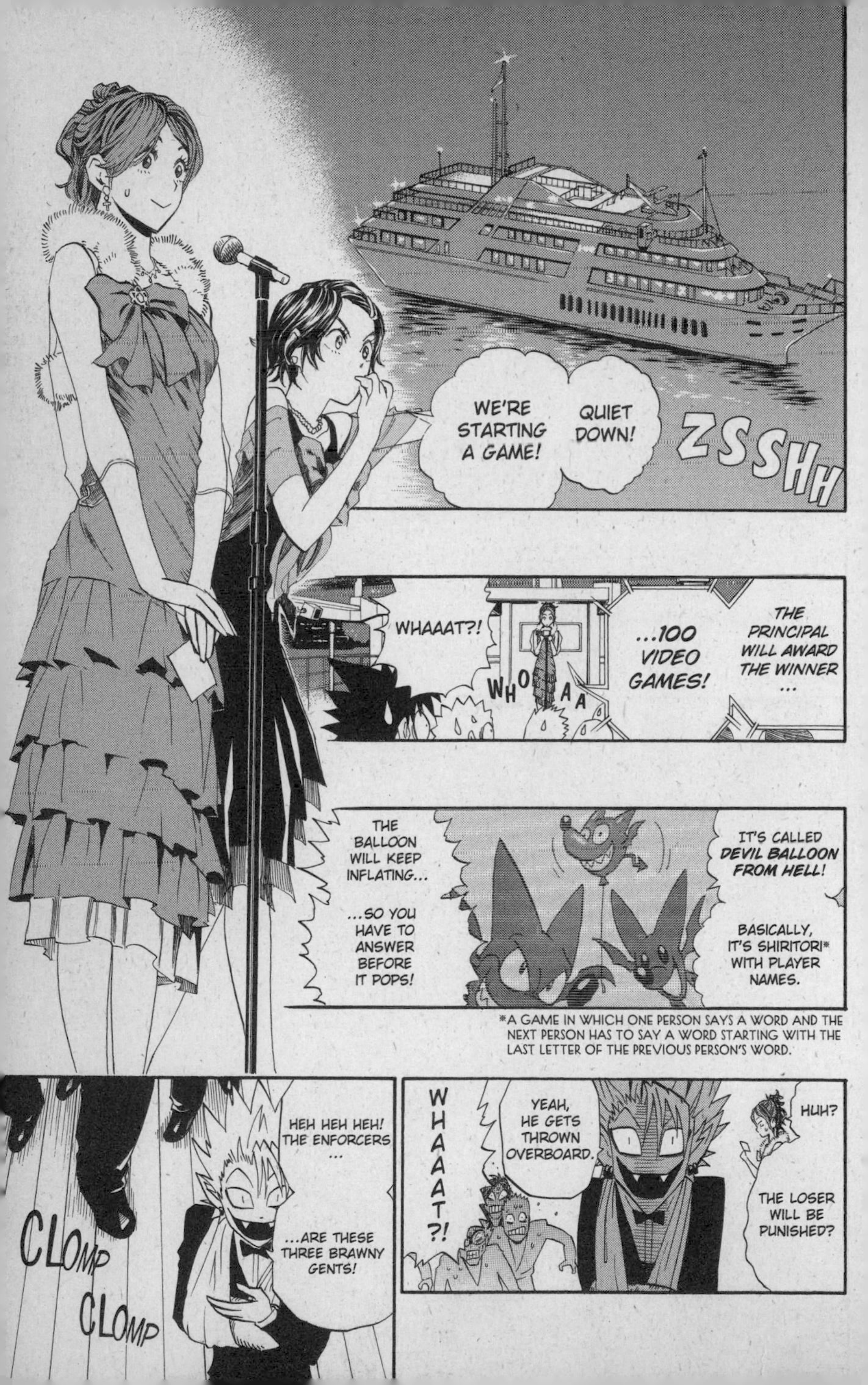
QUIET DOWN!
WE'RE STARTING A GAME!
ZSSHH
THE PRINCIPAL WILL AWARD THE WINNER ...
...100 VIDEO GAMES!
WHAAAT?!
WHOAAA
IT'S CALLED *DEVIL BALLOON FROM HELL!*
BASICALLY, IT'S SHIRITORI* WITH PLAYER NAMES.
THE BALLOON WILL KEEP INFLATING...
...SO YOU HAVE TO ANSWER BEFORE IT POPS!
HUH?
THE LOSER WILL BE PUNISHED?
YEAH, HE GETS THROWN OVERBOARD.
WHAAAAT?!
HEH HEH HEH! THE ENFORCERS ...
...ARE THESE THREE BRAWNY GENTS!
CLOMP
CLOMP

*A GAME IN WHICH ONE PERSON SAYS A WORD AND THE NEXT PERSON HAS TO SAY A WORD STARTING WITH THE LAST LETTER OF THE PREVIOUS PERSON'S WORD.

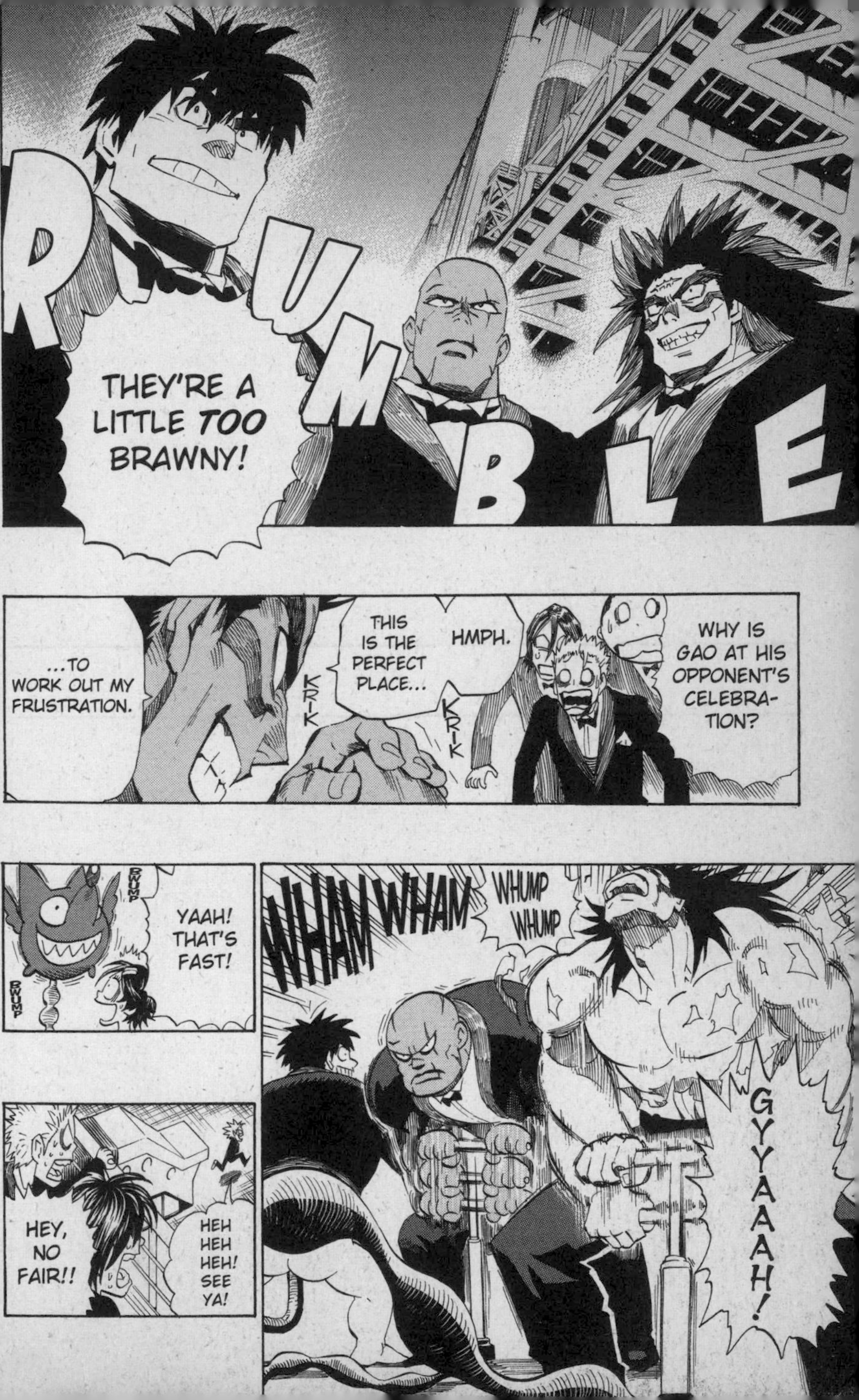
RUMBLE
THEY'RE A LITTLE TOO BRAWNY!
WHY IS GAO AT HIS OPPONENT'S CELEBRATION?
HMPH.
KRIK
THIS IS THE PERFECT PLACE...
KRIK
...TO WORK OUT MY FRUSTRATION.
WHUMP WHUMP
WHAM WHAM
GYAAAH!
BWUMP
BWUMP
YAAH! THAT'S FAST!
HEH HEH HEH! SEE YA!
HEY, NO FAIR!!

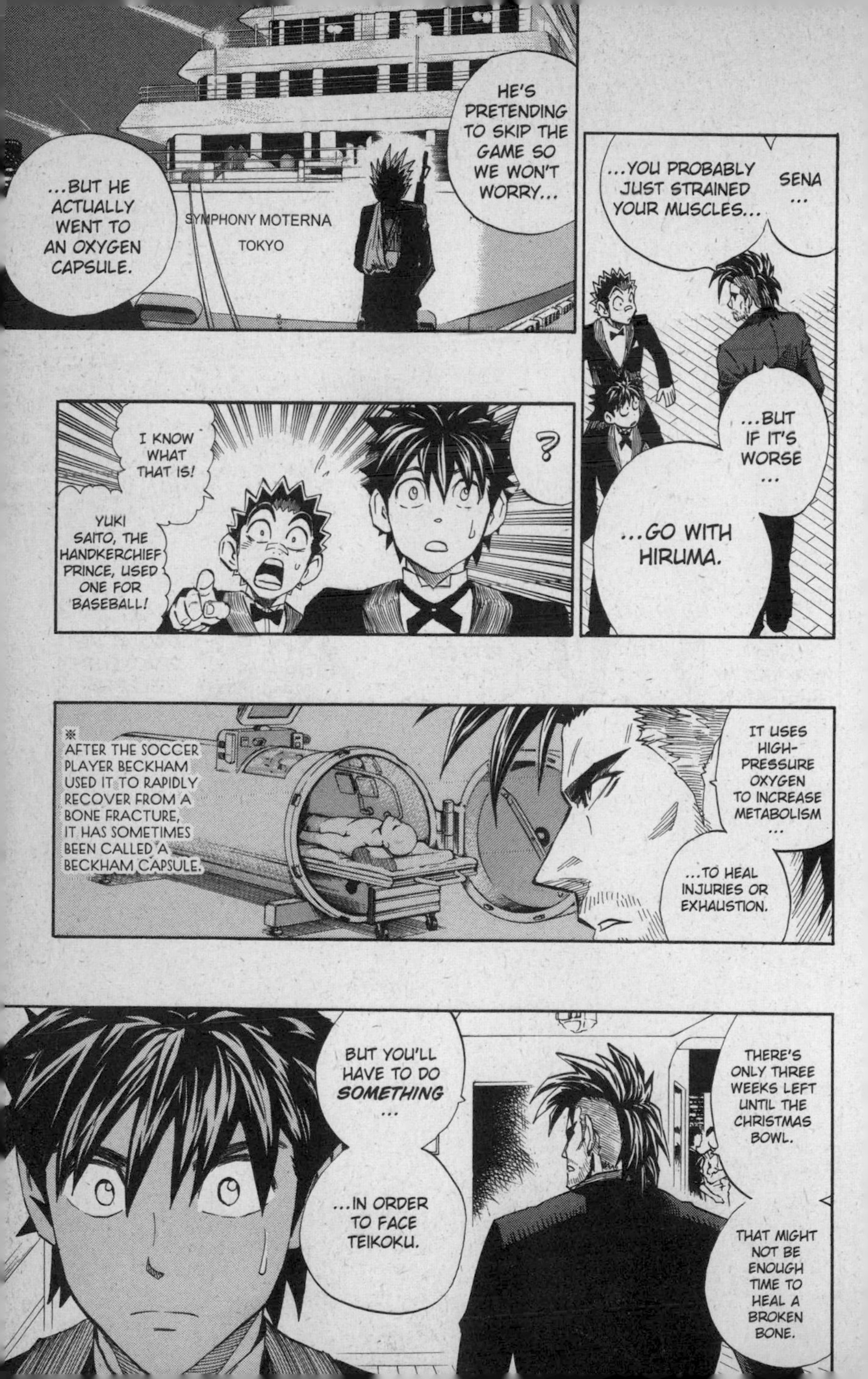
HE'S PRETENDING TO SKIP THE GAME SO WE WON'T WORRY...
...BUT HE ACTUALLY WENT TO AN OXYGEN CAPSULE.
SYMPHONY MOTERNA
TOKYO
SENA...
...YOU PROBABLY JUST STRAINED YOUR MUSCLES...
...BUT IF IT'S WORSE...
...GO WITH HIRUMA.
?
I KNOW WHAT THAT IS!
YUKI SAITO, THE HANDKERCHIEF PRINCE, USED ONE FOR BASEBALL!
IT USES HIGH-PRESSURE OXYGEN TO INCREASE METABOLISM...
...TO HEAL INJURIES OR EXHAUSTION.
※ AFTER THE SOCCER PLAYER BECKHAM USED IT TO RAPIDLY RECOVER FROM A BONE FRACTURE, IT HAS SOMETIMES BEEN CALLED A BECKHAM CAPSULE.
THERE'S ONLY THREE WEEKS LEFT UNTIL THE CHRISTMAS BOWL.
THAT MIGHT NOT BE ENOUGH TIME TO HEAL A BROKEN BONE.
BUT YOU'LL HAVE TO DO *SOMETHING*...
...IN ORDER TO FACE TEIKOKU.

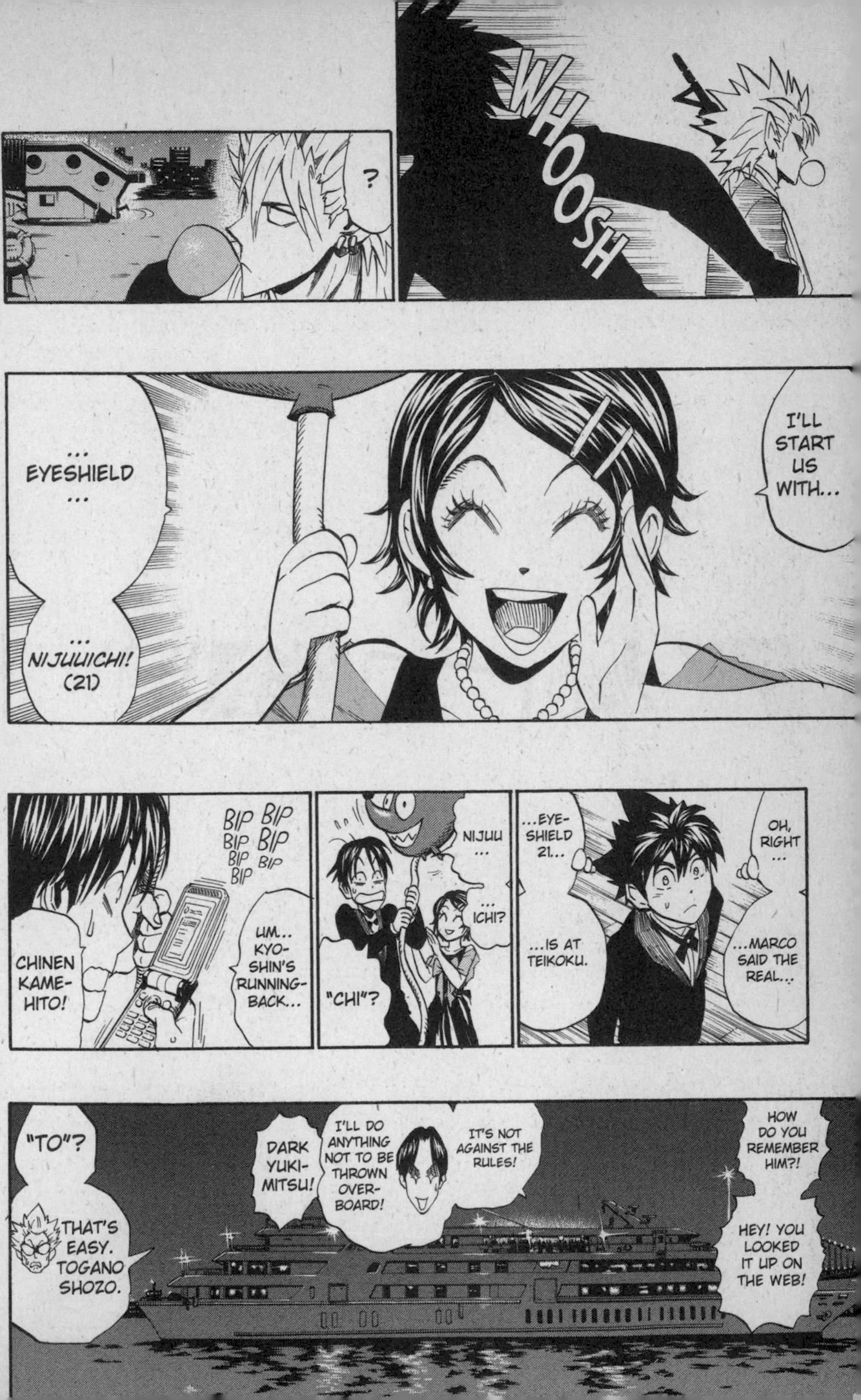
WHOOSH
?
I'LL START US WITH...
...EYESHIELD...
...NIJUUICHI! (21)
OH, RIGHT...
...MARCO SAID THE REAL...
...EYE-SHIELD 21...
...IS AT TEIKOKU.
NIJUU...
...ICHI?
"CHI"?
BIP BIP BIP BIP BIP BIP BIP BIP
UM... KYO-SHIN'S RUNNING-BACK...
CHINEN KAME-HITO!
HOW DO YOU REMEMBER HIM?!
HEY! YOU LOOKED IT UP ON THE WEB!
IT'S NOT AGAINST THE RULES!
I'LL DO ANYTHING NOT TO BE THROWN OVER-BOARD!
DARK YUKI-MITSU!
"TO"?
THAT'S EASY. TOGANO SHOZO.

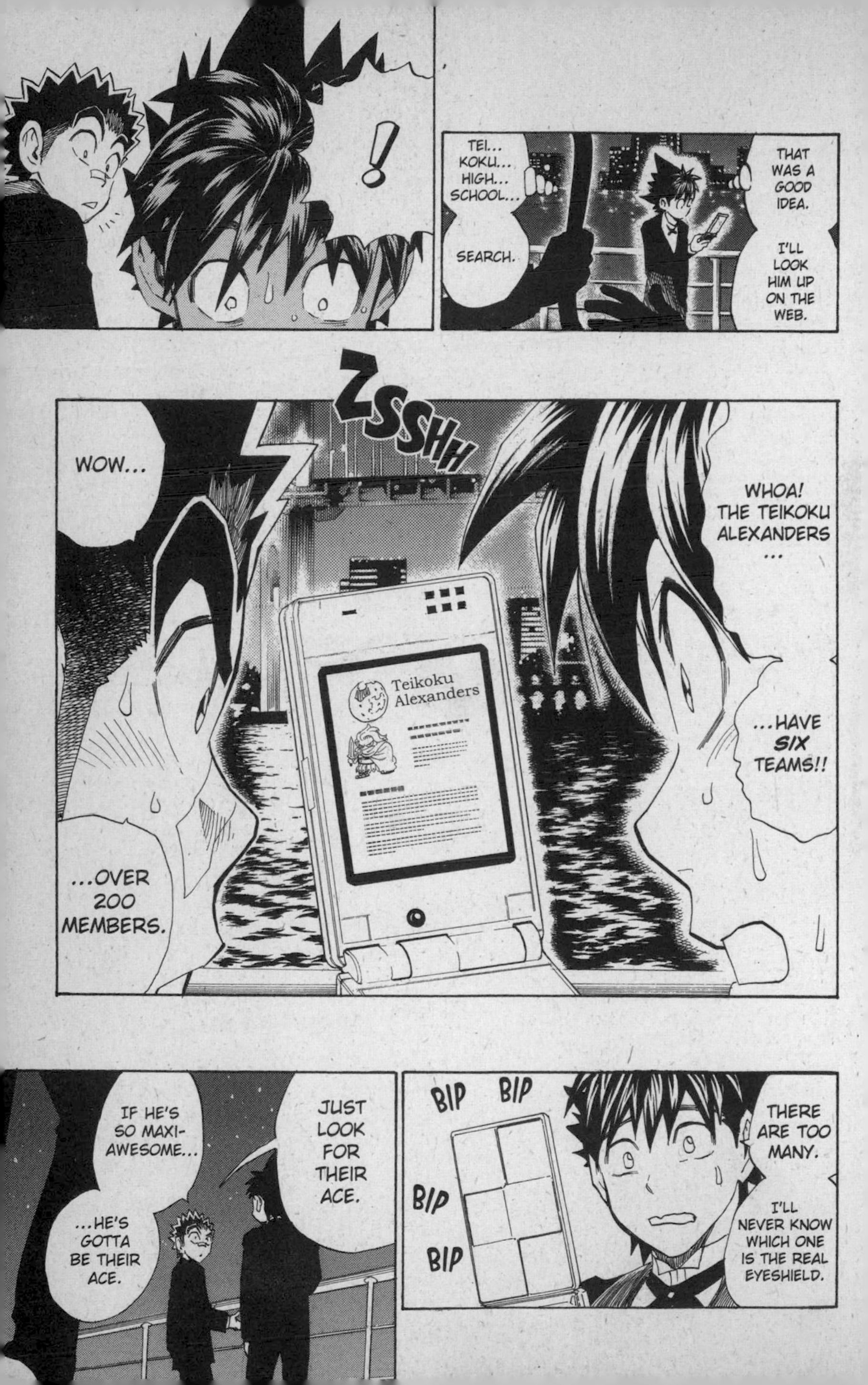
THAT WAS A GOOD IDEA.
I'LL LOOK HIM UP ON THE WEB.
TEI... KOKU... HIGH... SCHOOL...
SEARCH.
ZSSHH
WHOA! THE TEIKOKU ALEXANDERS ...
...HAVE SIX TEAMS!!
WOW...
...OVER 200 MEMBERS.
Teikoku Alexanders
BIP BIP
BIP
BIP
THERE ARE TOO MANY.
I'LL NEVER KNOW WHICH ONE IS THE REAL EYESHIELD.
JUST LOOK FOR THEIR ACE.
IF HE'S SO MAXI-AWESOME...
...HE'S GOTTA BE THEIR ACE.

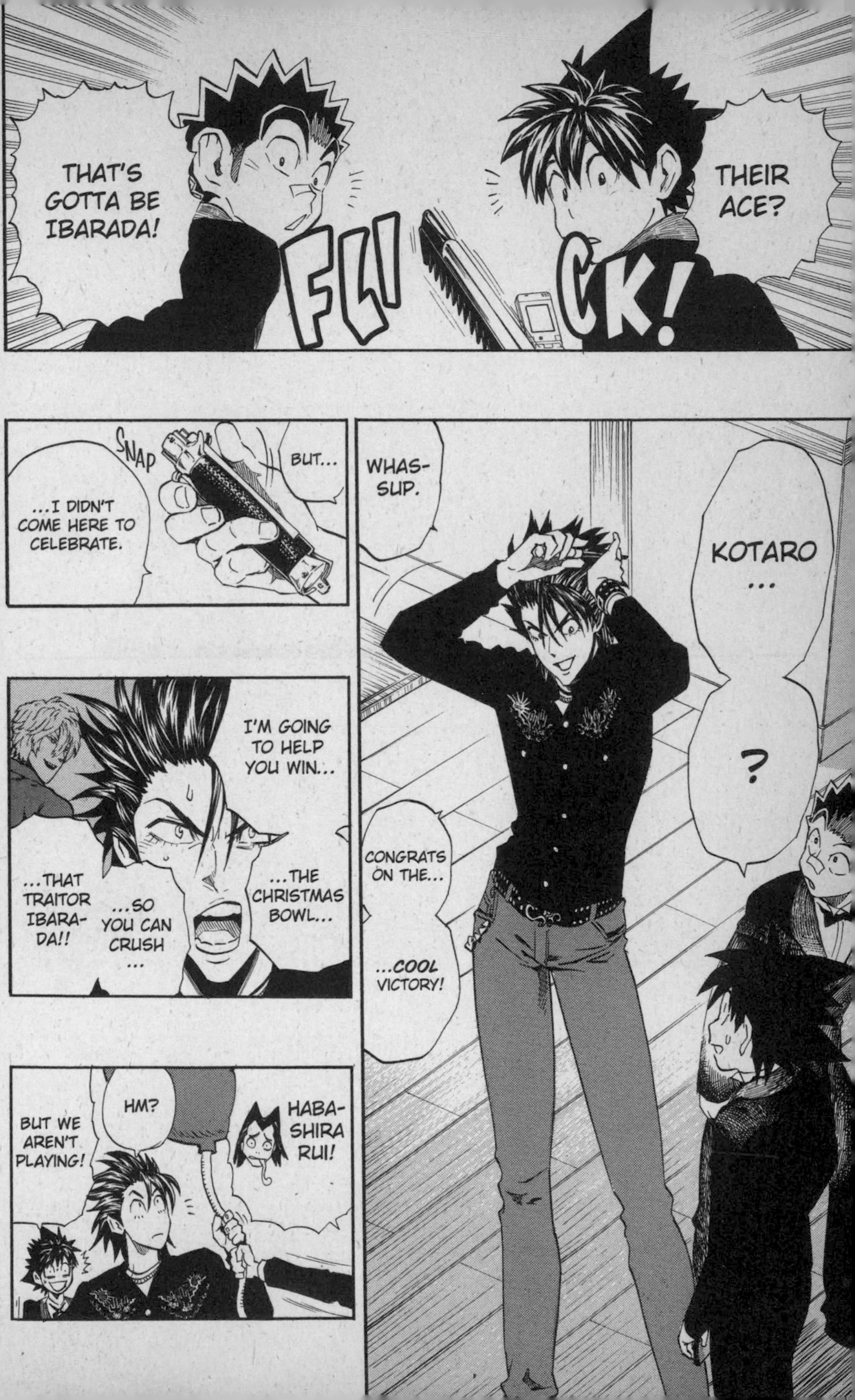
THEIR ACE?
THAT'S GOTTA BE IBARADA!
FLICK!
KOTARO ...
?
WHAS-SUP.
CONGRATS ON THE...
...COOL VICTORY!
BUT...
SNAP
...I DIDN'T COME HERE TO CELEBRATE.
I'M GOING TO HELP YOU WIN...
...THE CHRISTMAS BOWL...
...SO YOU CAN CRUSH ...
...THAT TRAITOR IBARA-DA!!
HABA-SHIRA RUI!
HM?
BUT WE AREN'T PLAYING!

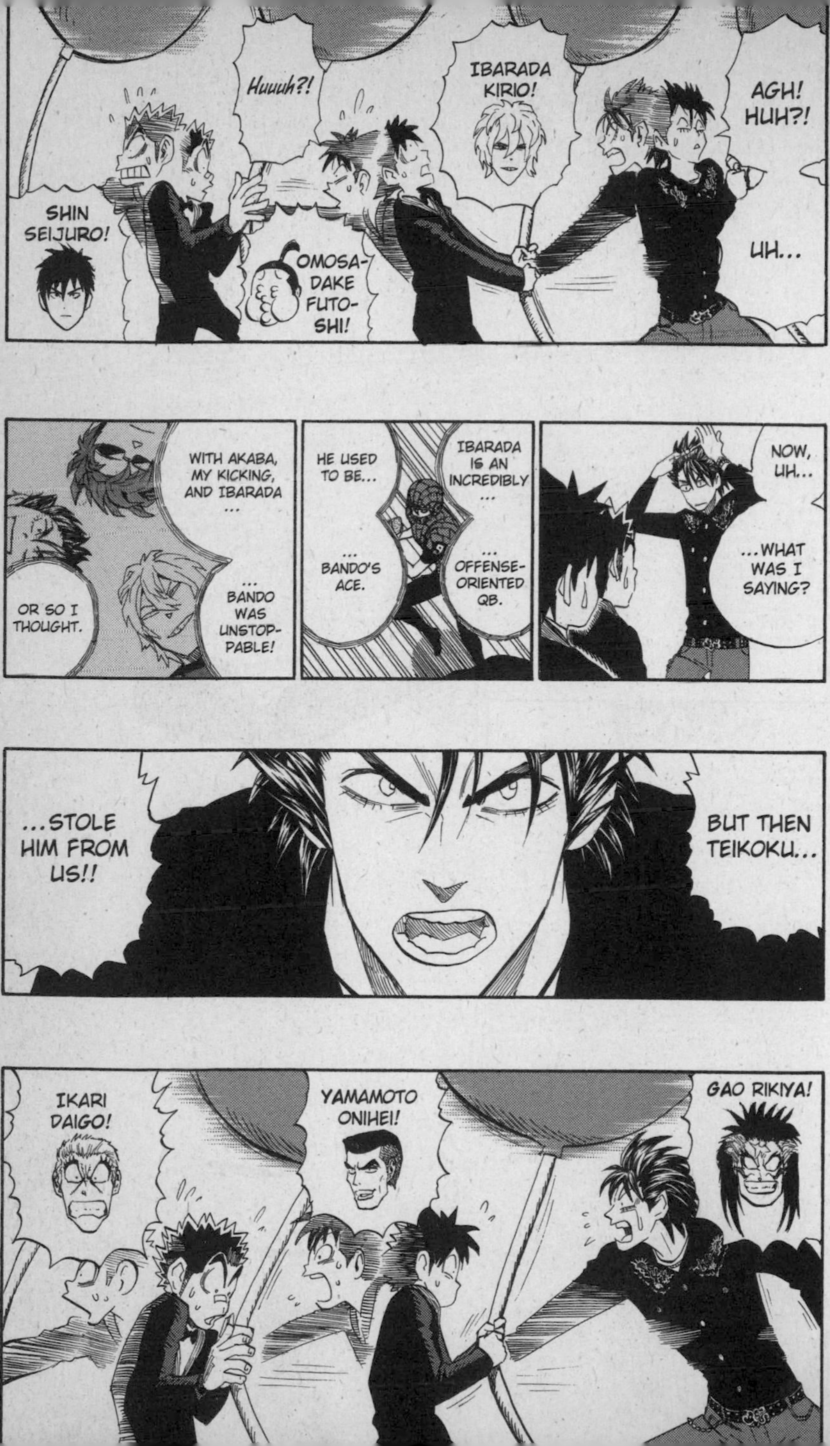
AGH! HUH?!
IBARADA KIRIO!
UH...
Huuuh?!
OMOSA- DAKE FUTO- SHI!
SHIN SEIJURO!
NOW, UH...
...WHAT WAS I SAYING?
IBARADA IS AN INCREDIBLY ...
... OFFENSE- ORIENTED QB.
HE USED TO BE...
... BANDO'S ACE.
WITH AKABA, MY KICKING, AND IBARADA ...
... BANDO WAS UNSTOP- PABLE!
OR SO I THOUGHT.
BUT THEN TEIKOKU...
...STOLE HIM FROM US!!
GAO RIKIYA!
YAMAMOTO ONIHEI!
IKARI DAIGO!

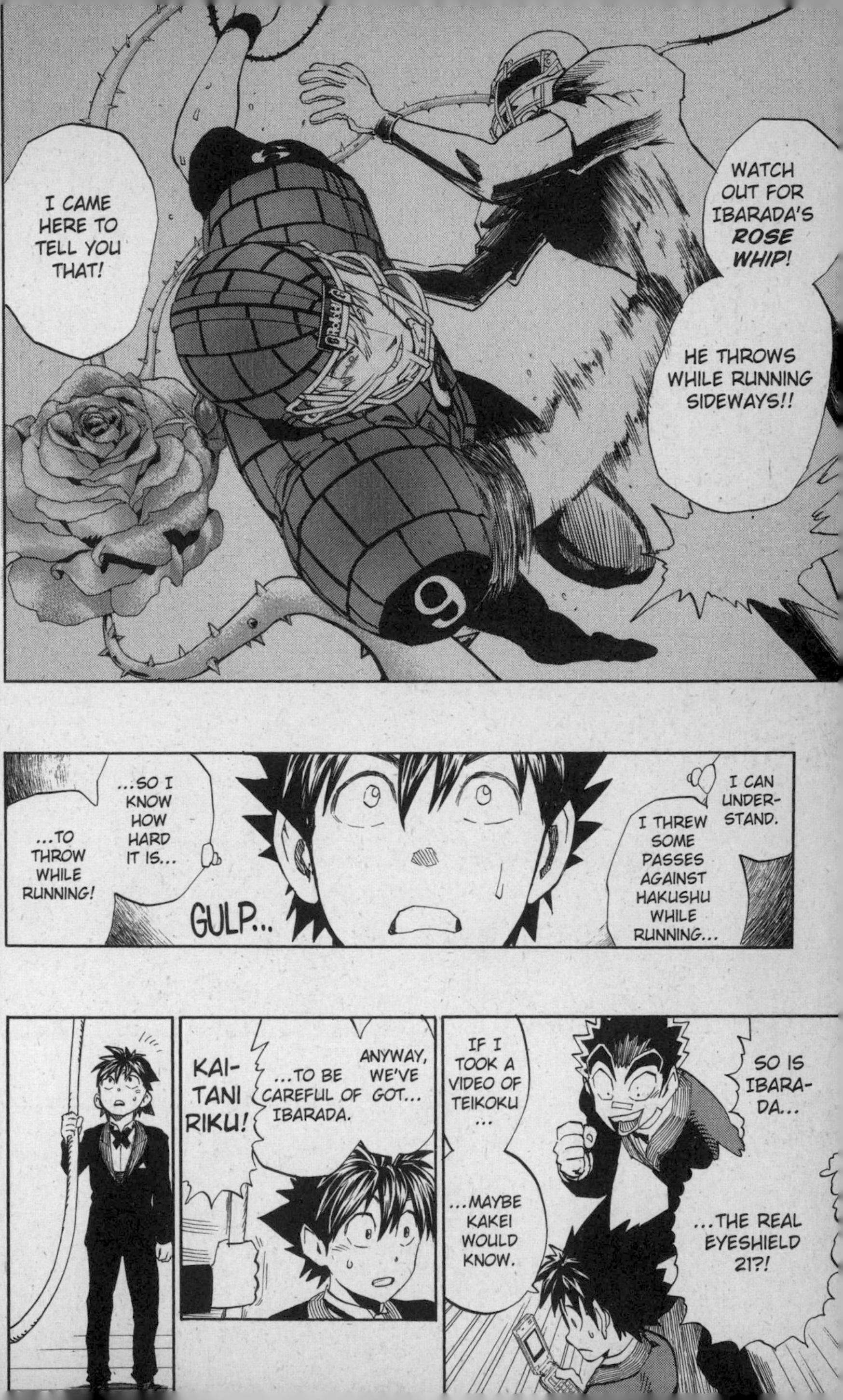
WATCH OUT FOR IBARADA'S ROSE WHIP!
HE THROWS WHILE RUNNING SIDEWAYS!!
I CAME HERE TO TELL YOU THAT!
I CAN UNDERSTAND.
I THREW SOME PASSES AGAINST HAKUSHU WHILE RUNNING...
...SO I KNOW HOW HARD IT IS...
...TO THROW WHILE RUNNING!
GULP...
SO IS IBARADA...
...THE REAL EYESHIELD 21?!
IF I TOOK A VIDEO OF TEIKOKU...
...MAYBE KAKEI WOULD KNOW.
ANYWAY, WE'VE GOT...
...TO BE CAREFUL OF IBARADA.
KAITANI RIKU!

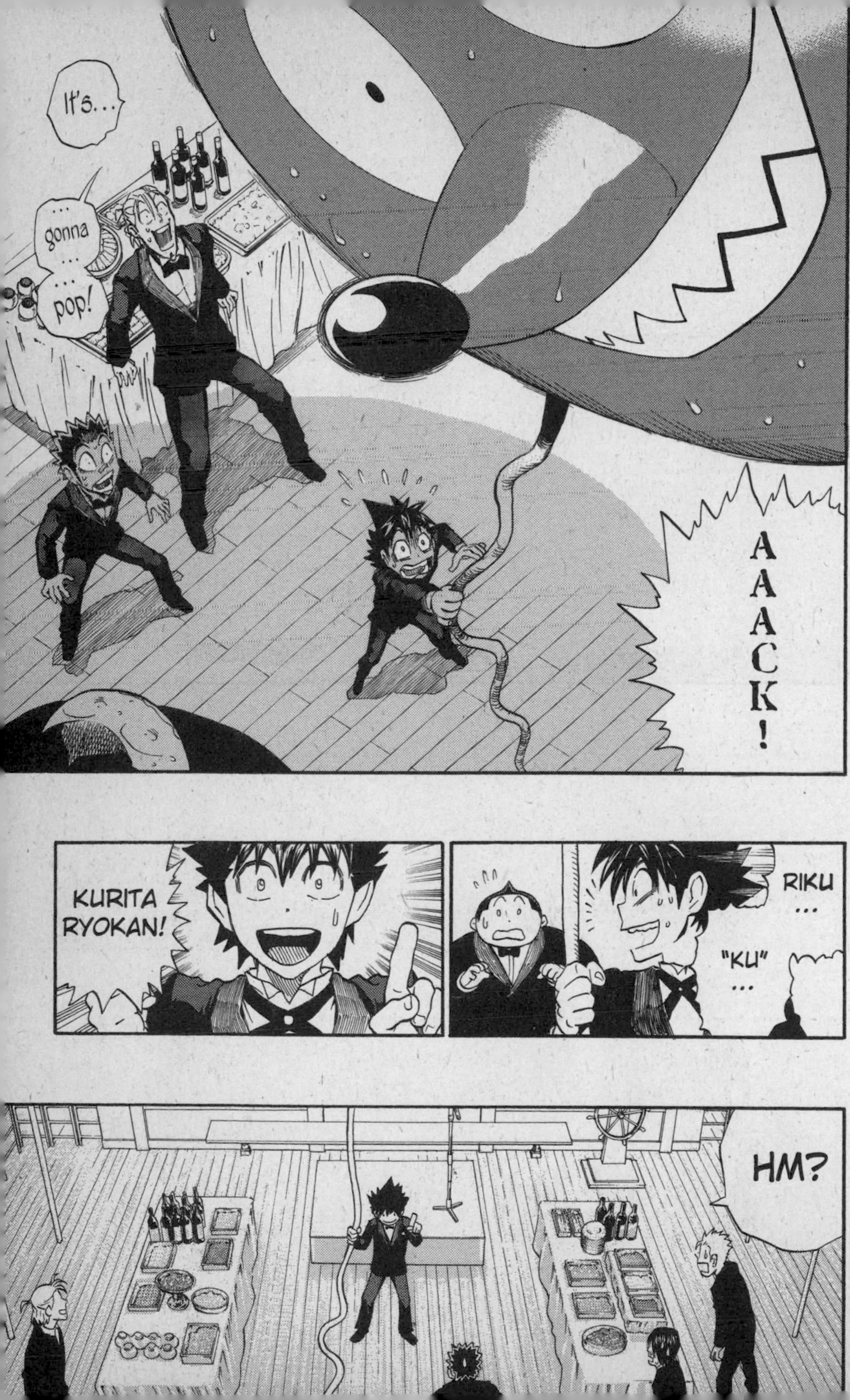
It's...
... gonna ... ... pop!
AAACK!
RIKU ... "KU" ...
KURITA RYOKAN!
HM?

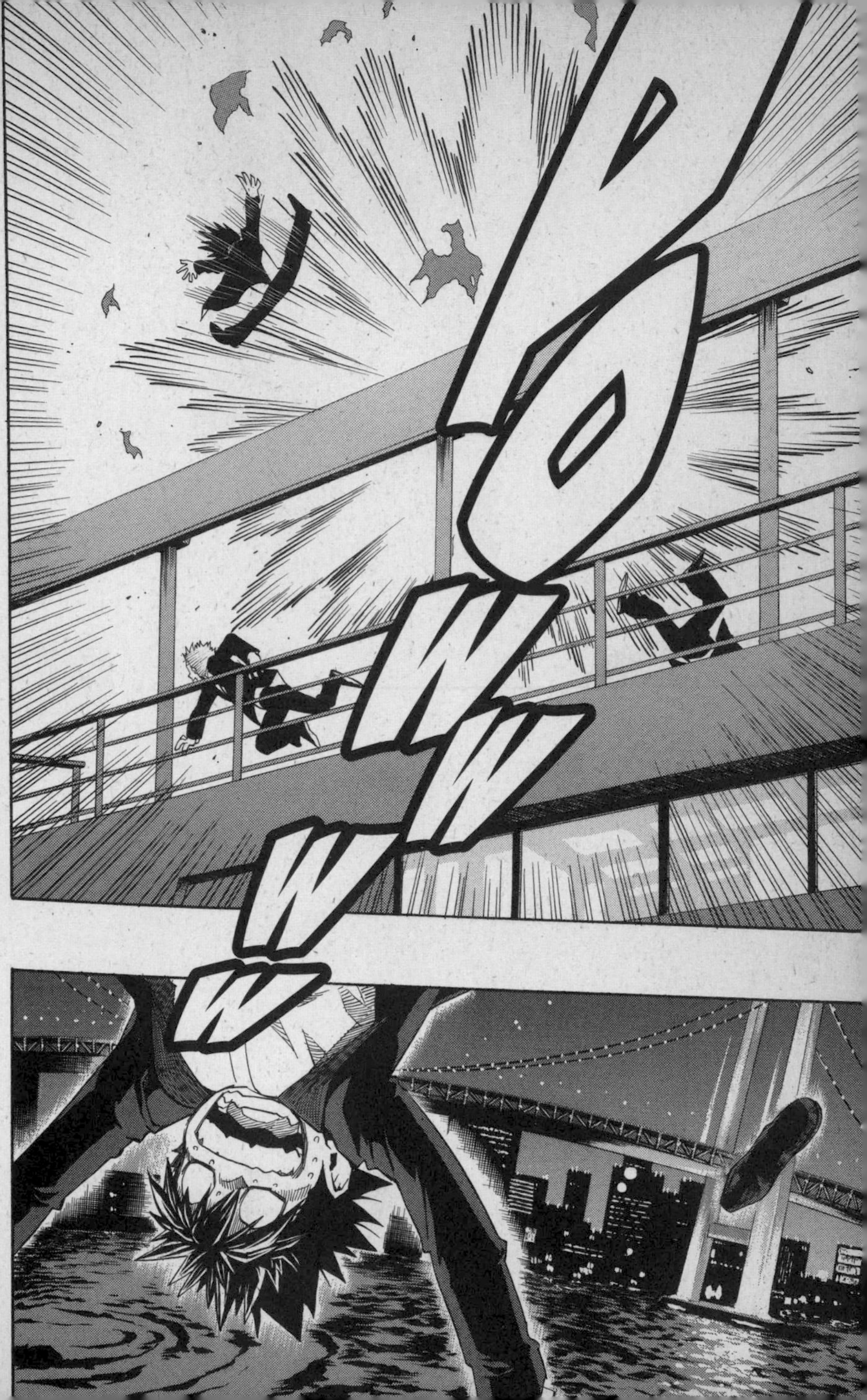

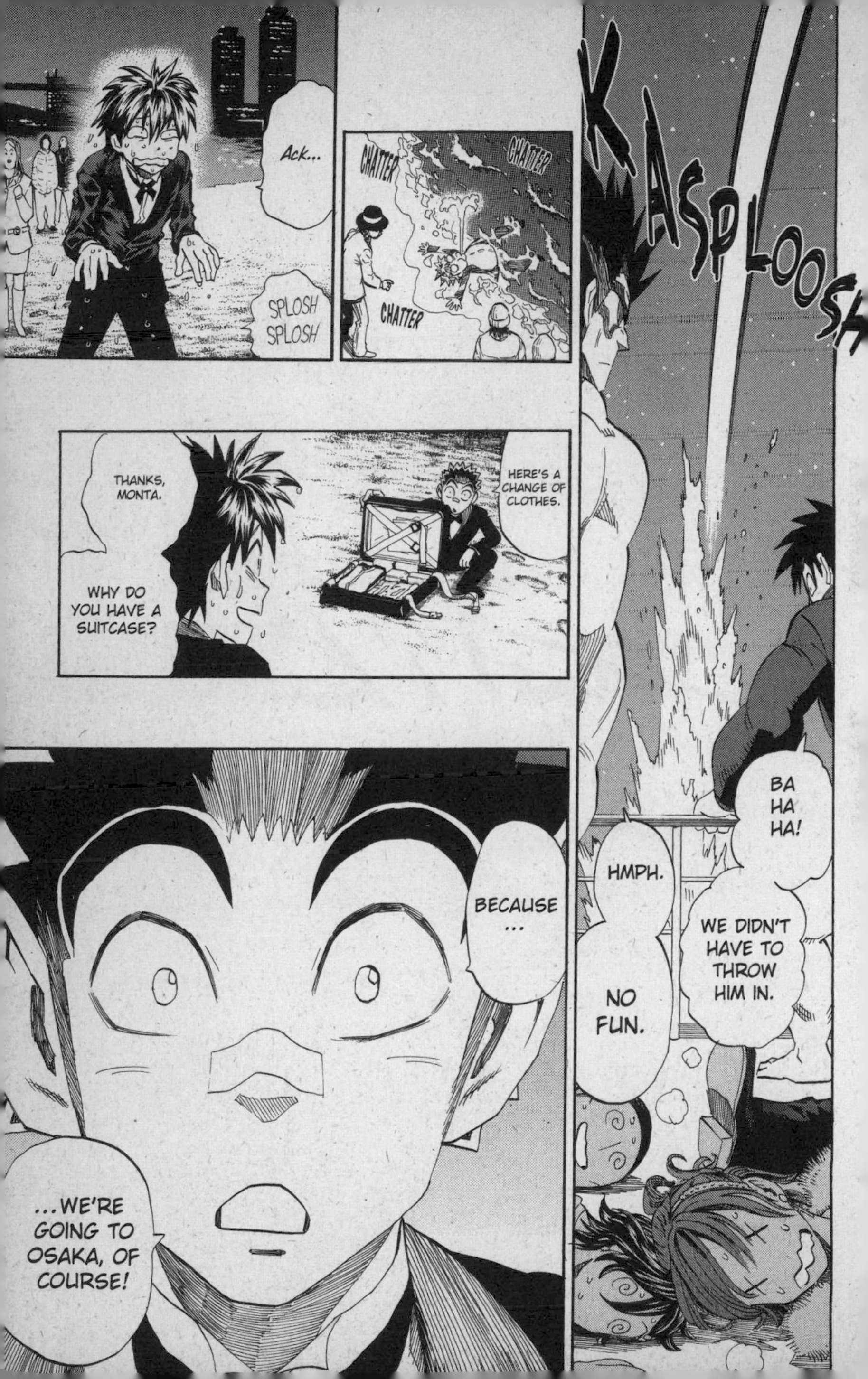
KASPLOOSH
BA HA HA!
WE DIDN'T HAVE TO THROW HIM IN.
HMPH.
NO FUN.
CHATTER
CHATTER
CHATTER
Ack...
SPLOSH SPLOSH
HERE'S A CHANGE OF CLOTHES.
THANKS, MONTA.
WHY DO YOU HAVE A SUITCASE?
BECAUSE...
...WE'RE GOING TO OSAKA, OF COURSE!

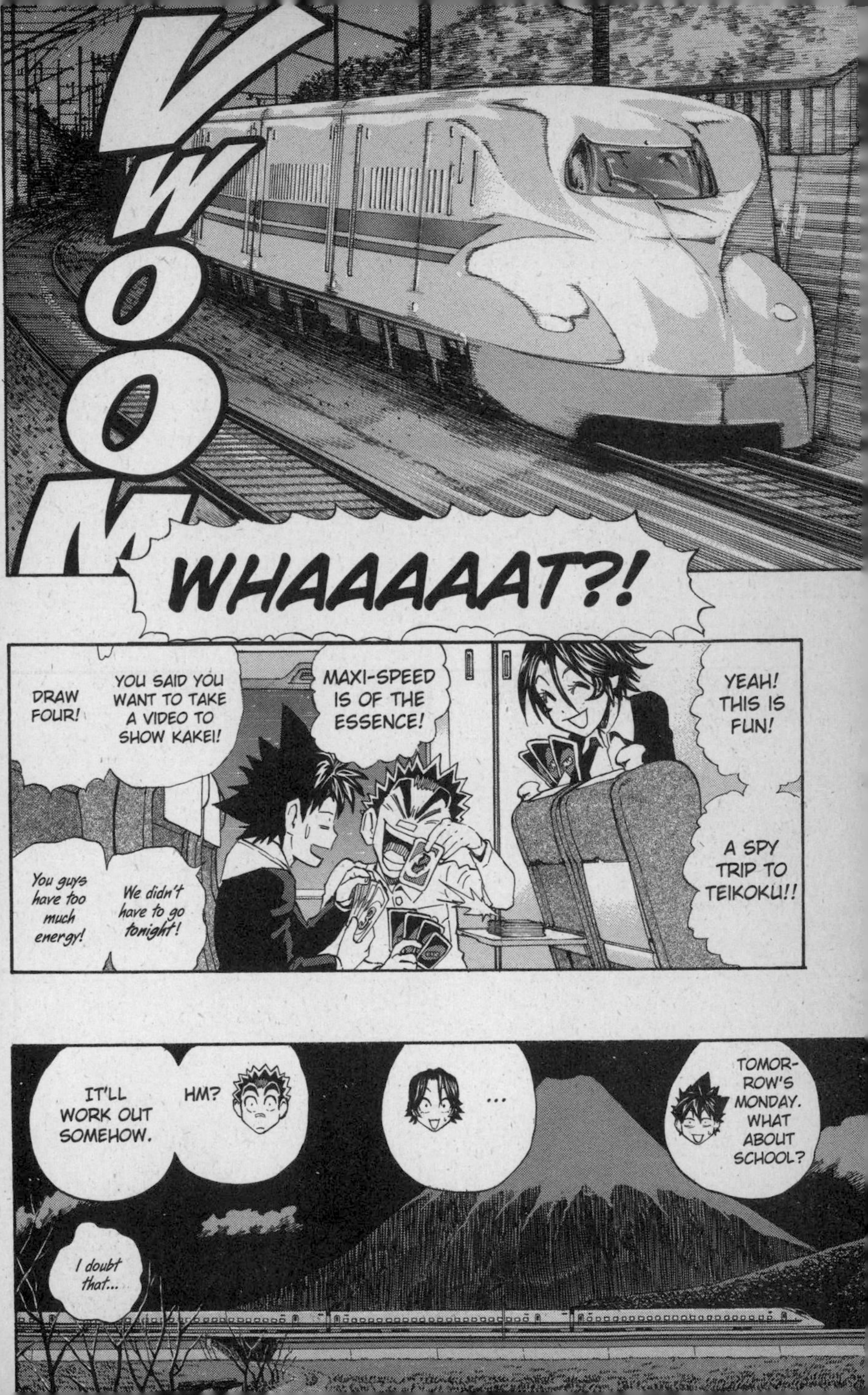
VWOOOM
WHAAAAAT?!
YEAH! THIS IS FUN!
A SPY TRIP TO TEIKOKU!!
MAXI-SPEED IS OF THE ESSENCE!
YOU SAID YOU WANT TO TAKE A VIDEO TO SHOW KAKEI!
DRAW FOUR!
We didn't have to go tonight!
You guys have too much energy!
TOMOR-ROW'S MONDAY. WHAT ABOUT SCHOOL?
...
HM?
IT'LL WORK OUT SOMEHOW.
I doubt that...

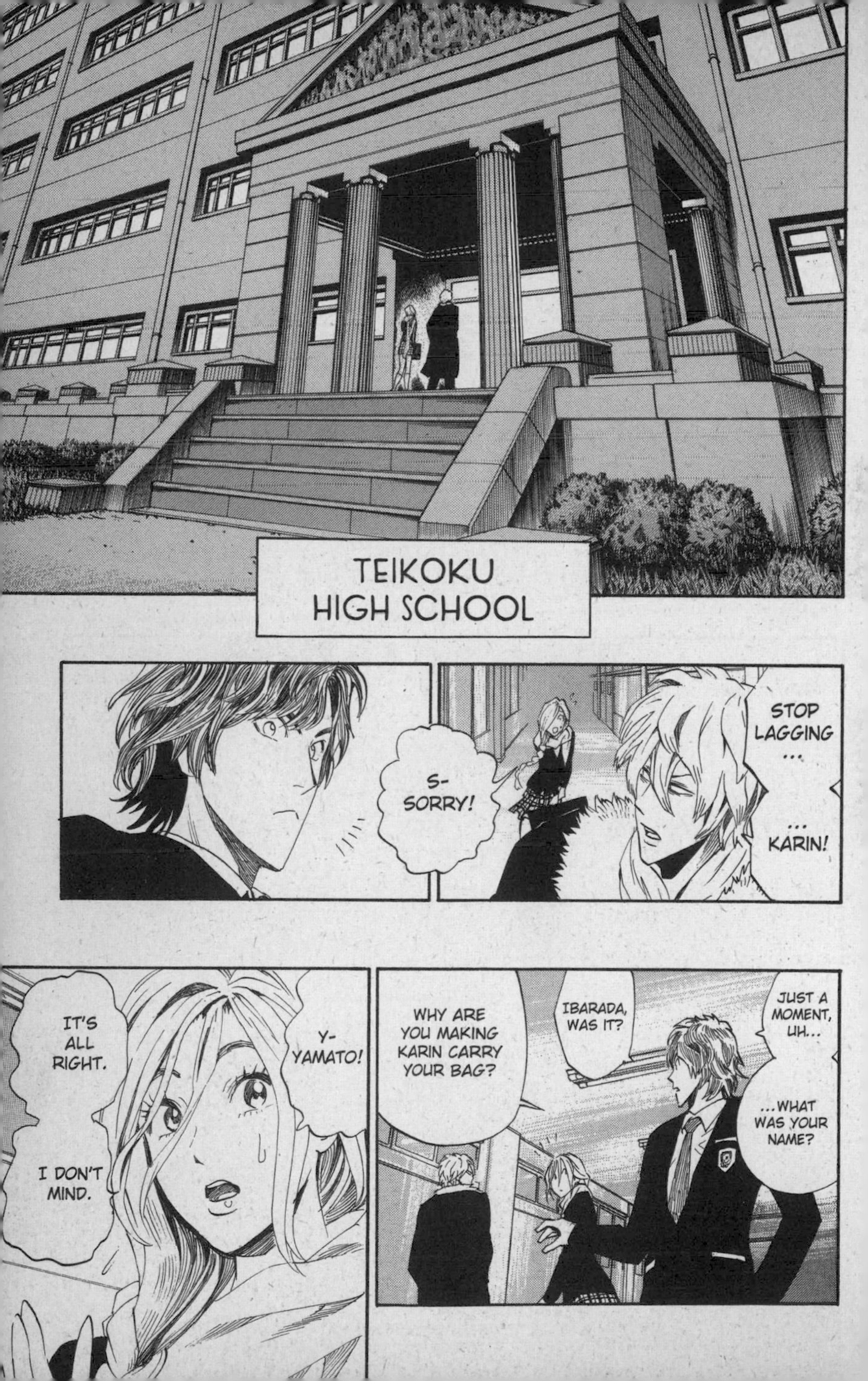
TEIKOKU HIGH SCHOOL
STOP LAGGING ... ... KARIN!
S-SORRY!
JUST A MOMENT, UH...
...WHAT WAS YOUR NAME?
IBARADA, WAS IT?
WHY ARE YOU MAKING KARIN CARRY YOUR BAG?
Y-YAMATO!
IT'S ALL RIGHT.
I DON'T MIND.

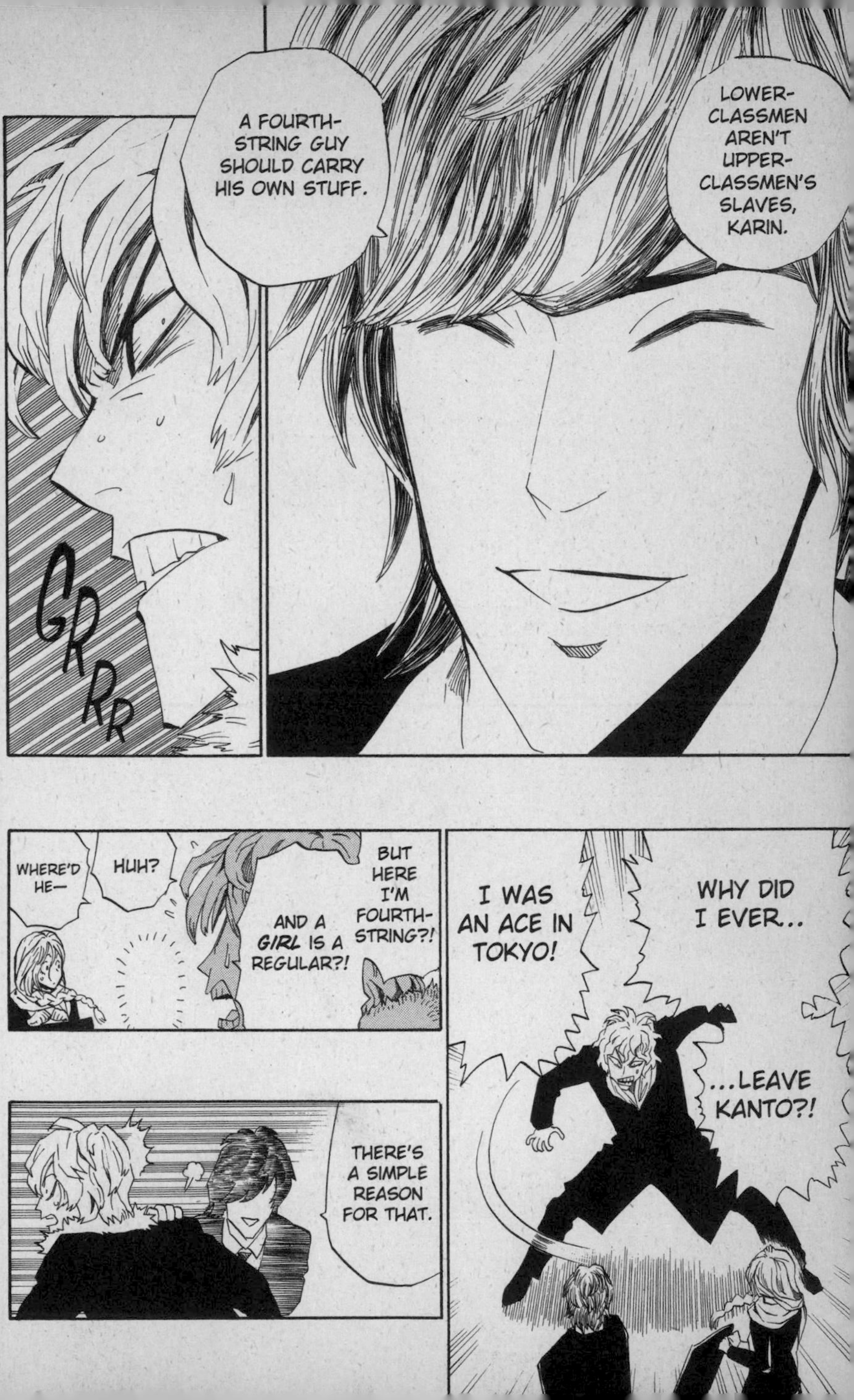
LOWER-CLASSMEN AREN'T UPPER-CLASSMEN'S SLAVES, KARIN.
A FOURTH-STRING GUY SHOULD CARRY HIS OWN STUFF.
GRRR
WHY DID I EVER...
I WAS AN ACE IN TOKYO!
...LEAVE KANTO?!
BUT HERE I'M FOURTH-STRING?!
AND A *GIRL* IS A REGULAR?!
HUH?
WHERE'D HE—
THERE'S A SIMPLE REASON FOR THAT.

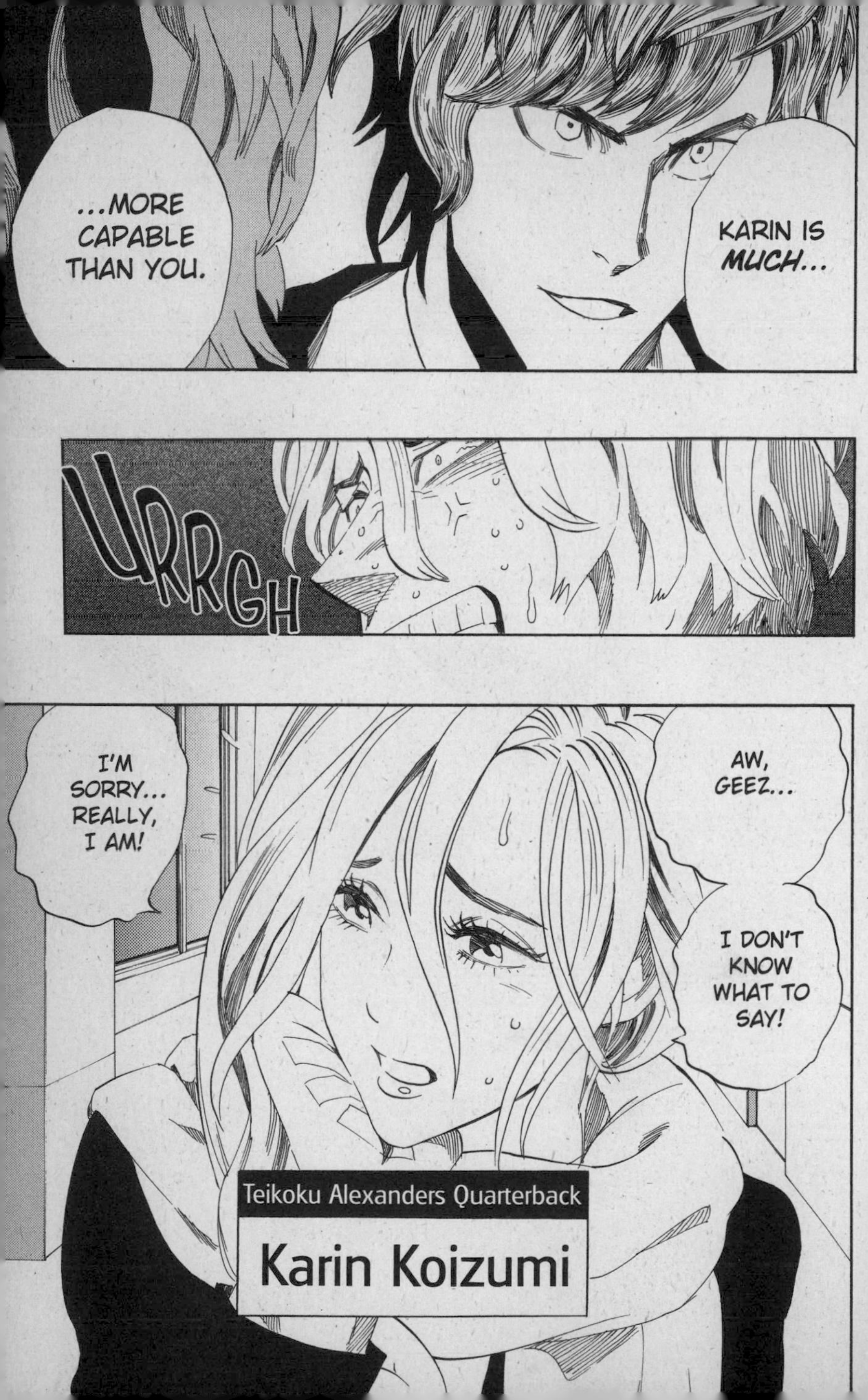
KARIN IS MUCH...
...MORE CAPABLE THAN YOU.
URRGH
AW, GEEZ...
I DON'T KNOW WHAT TO SAY!
I'M SORRY... REALLY, I AM!
Teikoku Alexanders Quarterback
Karin Koizumi

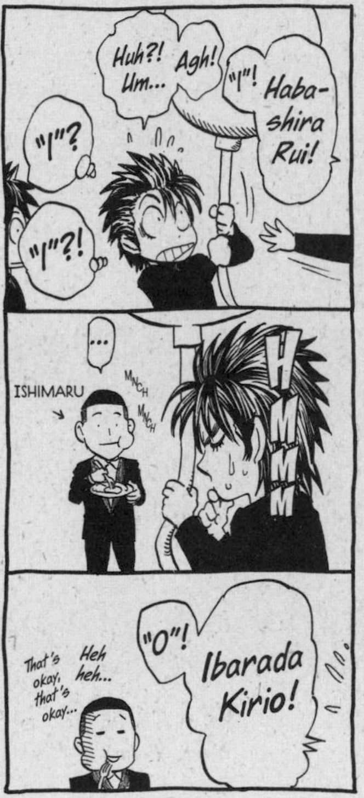
"I"! Haba-shira Rui!
Agh!
Huh?! Um...
"I"?
"I"?!
HMMMM
MNCH MNCH
...
ISHIMARU
"O"! Ibarada Kirio!
Heh heh...
That's okay, that's okay...

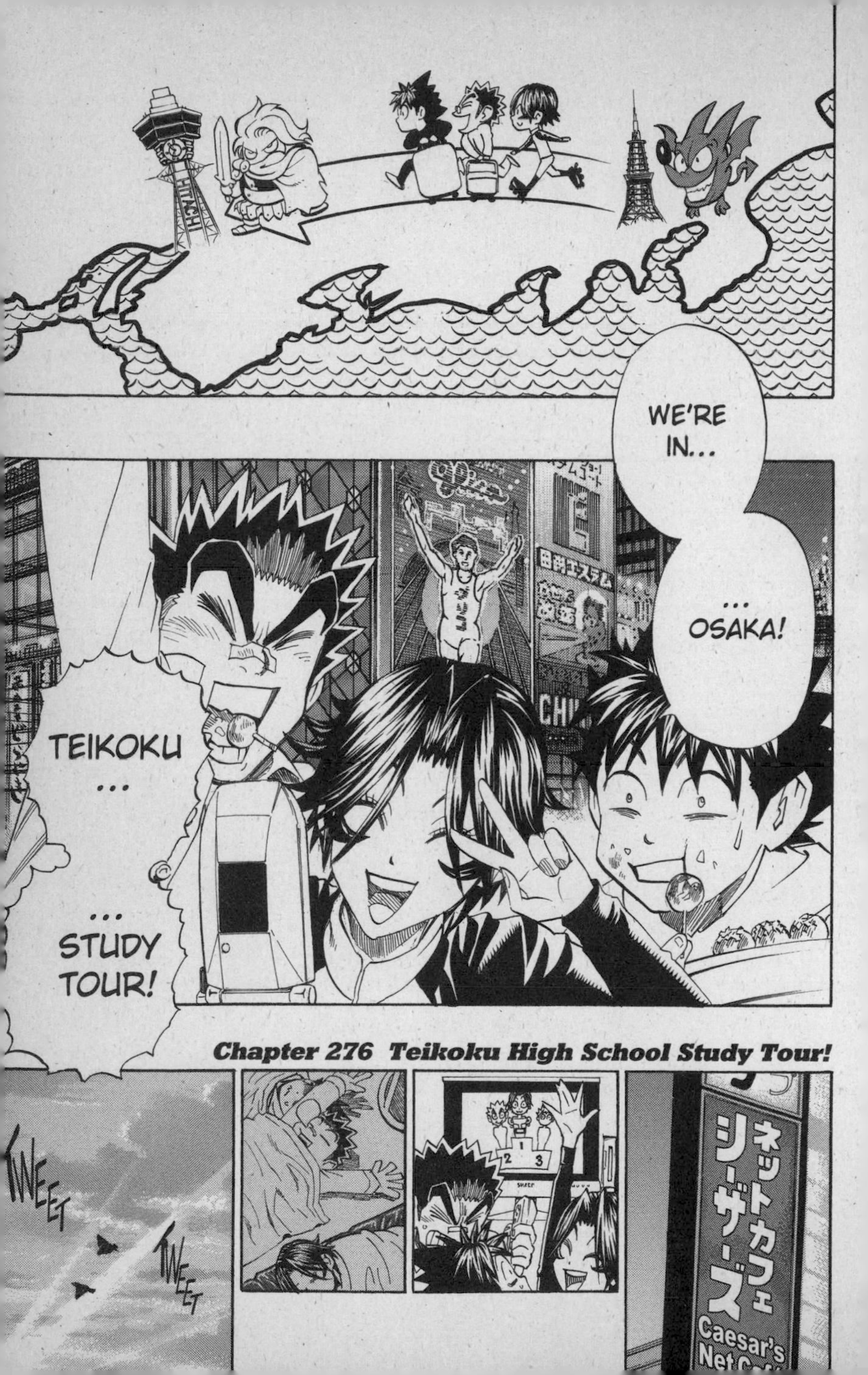
WE'RE IN...
...OSAKA!
TEIKOKU ...
... STUDY TOUR!
Chapter 276 Teikoku High School Study Tour!
ネットカフェ
シーザーズ
Caesar's
TWEET
TWEET

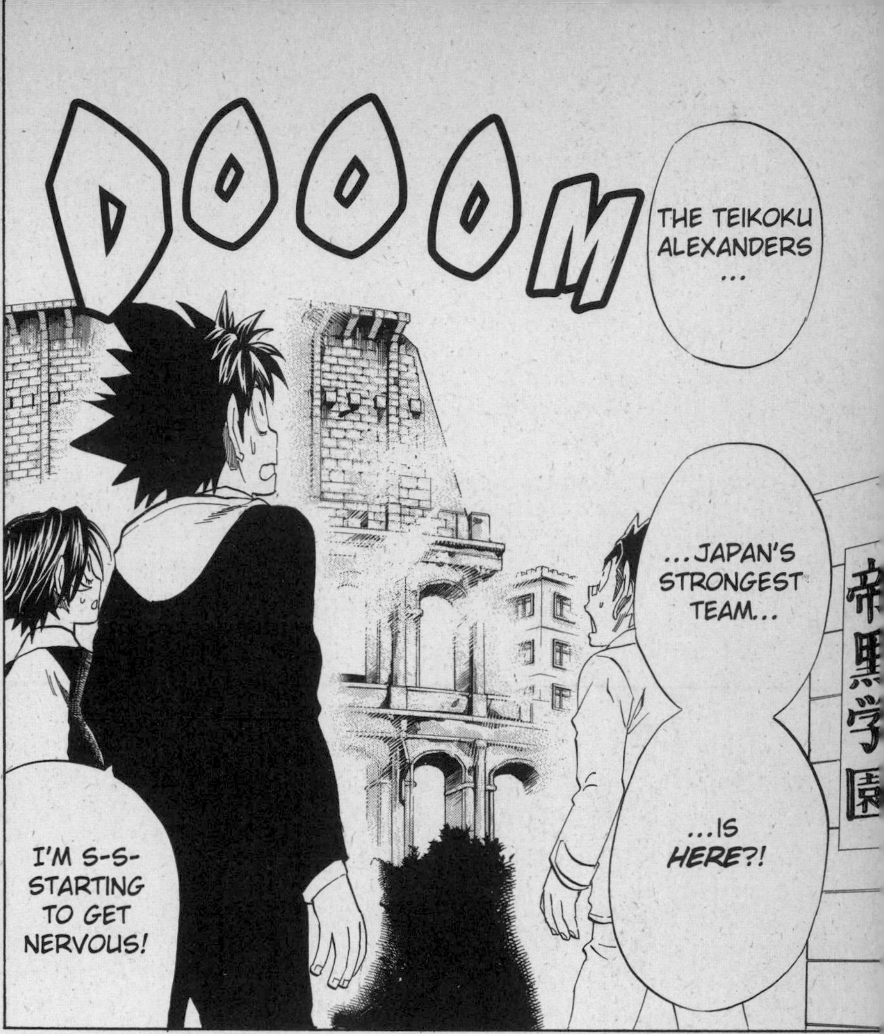
DOOOM
THE TEIKOKU ALEXANDERS ...
...JAPAN'S STRONGEST TEAM...
...IS *HERE?!*
帝黒学園
I'M S-S-STARTING TO GET NERVOUS!

SIGN: TEIKOKU HIGH SCHOOL

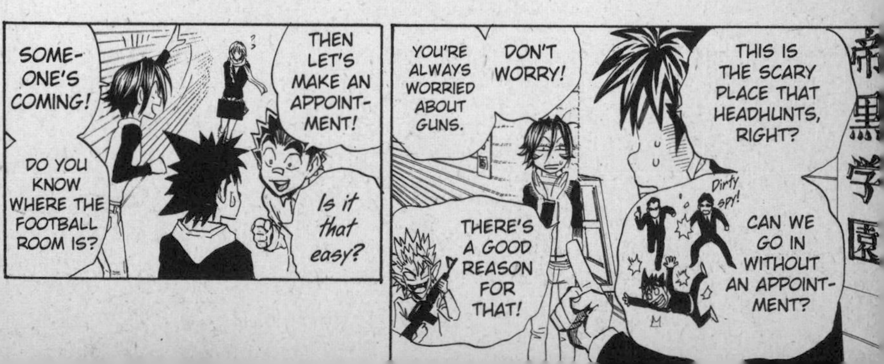
帝黒学園
THIS IS THE SCARY PLACE THAT HEADHUNTS, RIGHT?
CAN WE GO IN WITHOUT AN APPOINTMENT?
Dirty spy!
DON'T WORRY!
YOU'RE ALWAYS WORRIED ABOUT GUNS.
THERE'S A GOOD REASON FOR THAT!
THEN LET'S MAKE AN APPOINTMENT!
Is it that easy?
SOME-ONE'S COMING!
DO YOU KNOW WHERE THE FOOTBALL ROOM IS?

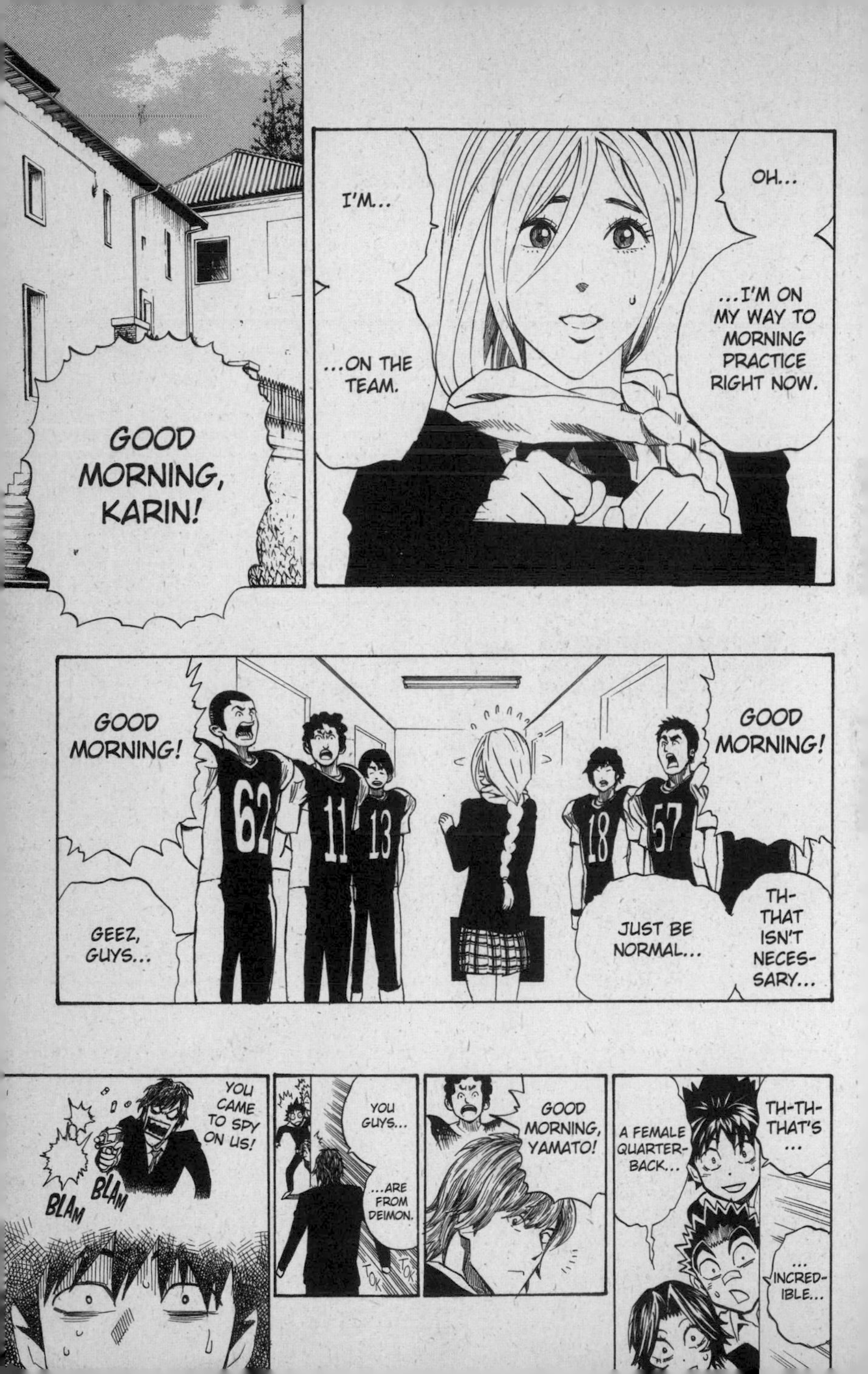
OH...
...I'M ON MY WAY TO MORNING PRACTICE RIGHT NOW.
I'M...
...ON THE TEAM.
GOOD MORNING, KARIN!
GOOD MORNING!
TH-THAT ISN'T NECES-SARY...
JUST BE NORMAL...
GOOD MORNING!
GEEZ, GUYS...
TH-TH-THAT'S ...
A FEMALE QUARTER-BACK...
... INCRED-IBLE...
GOOD MORNING, YAMATO!
YOU GUYS...
...ARE FROM DEIMON.
TOK
TOK
YOU CAME TO SPY ON US!
BLAM
BLAM

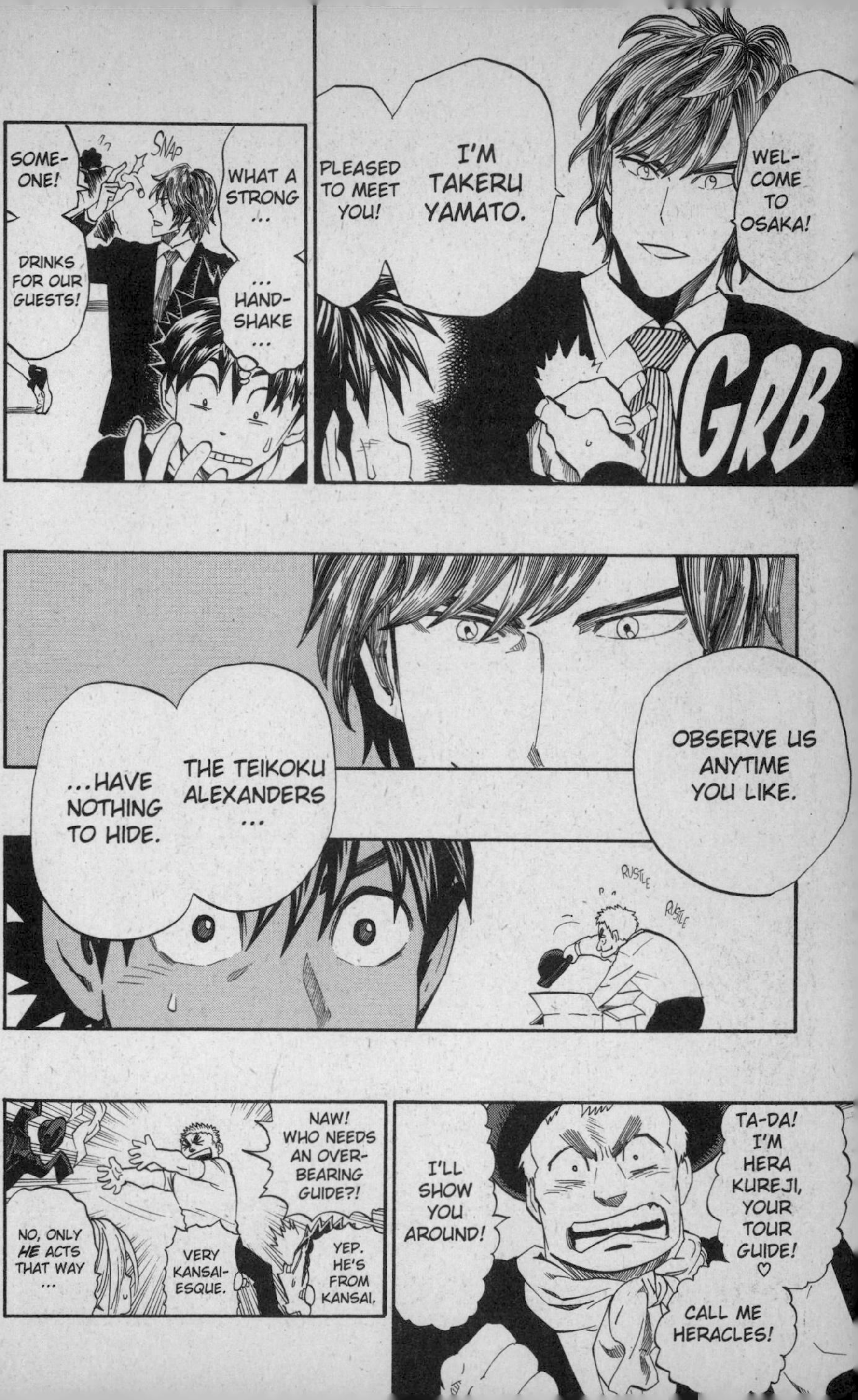
WEL-COME TO OSAKA!
I'M TAKERU YAMATO.
PLEASED TO MEET YOU!
GRB
WHAT A STRONG ...
... HAND-SHAKE ...
SNAP
SOME-ONE!
DRINKS FOR OUR GUESTS!
OBSERVE US ANYTIME YOU LIKE.
THE TEIKOKU ALEXANDERS ...
...HAVE NOTHING TO HIDE.
RUSTLE
RUSTLE
TA-DA! I'M HERA KUREJI, YOUR TOUR GUIDE! ♡
I'LL SHOW YOU AROUND!
CALL ME HERACLES!
NAW! WHO NEEDS AN OVER-BEARING GUIDE?!
YEP. HE'S FROM KANSAI.
VERY KANSAI-ESQUE.
NO, ONLY *HE* ACTS THAT WAY ...

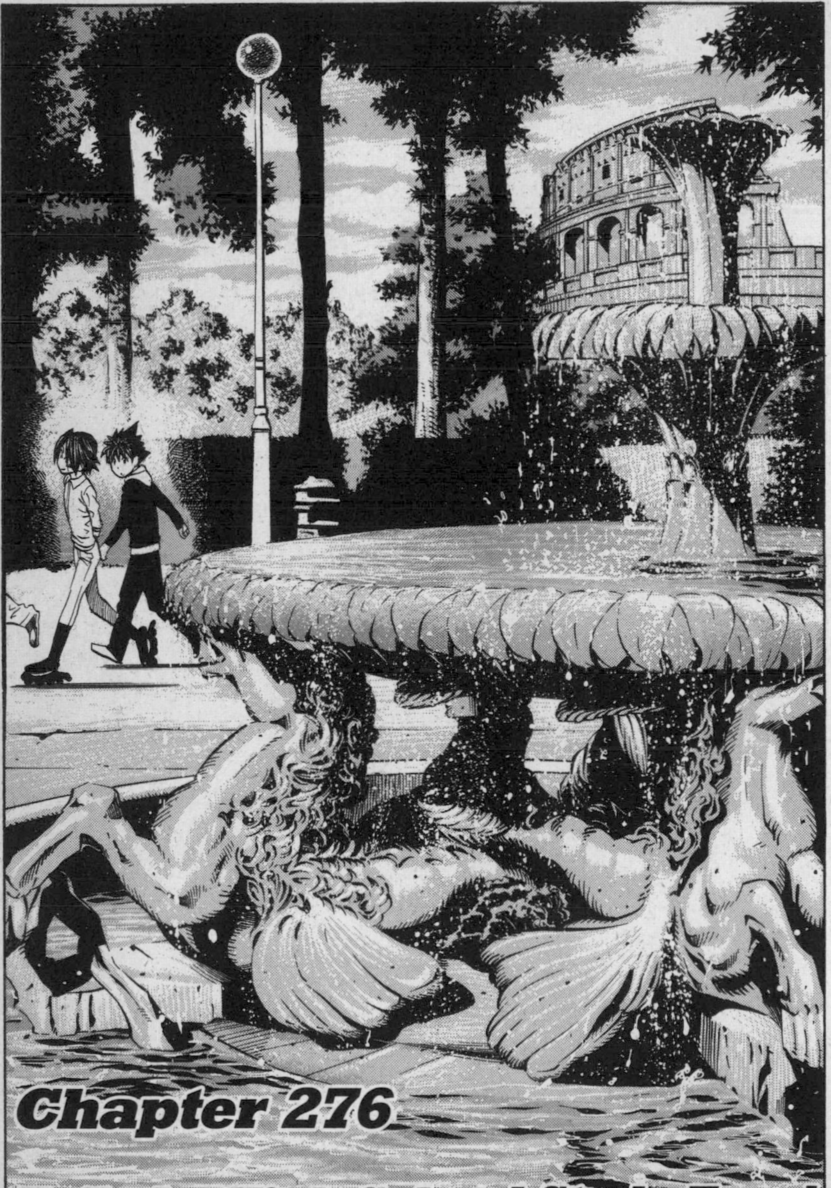
Chapter 276
Teikoku High School Study Tour!

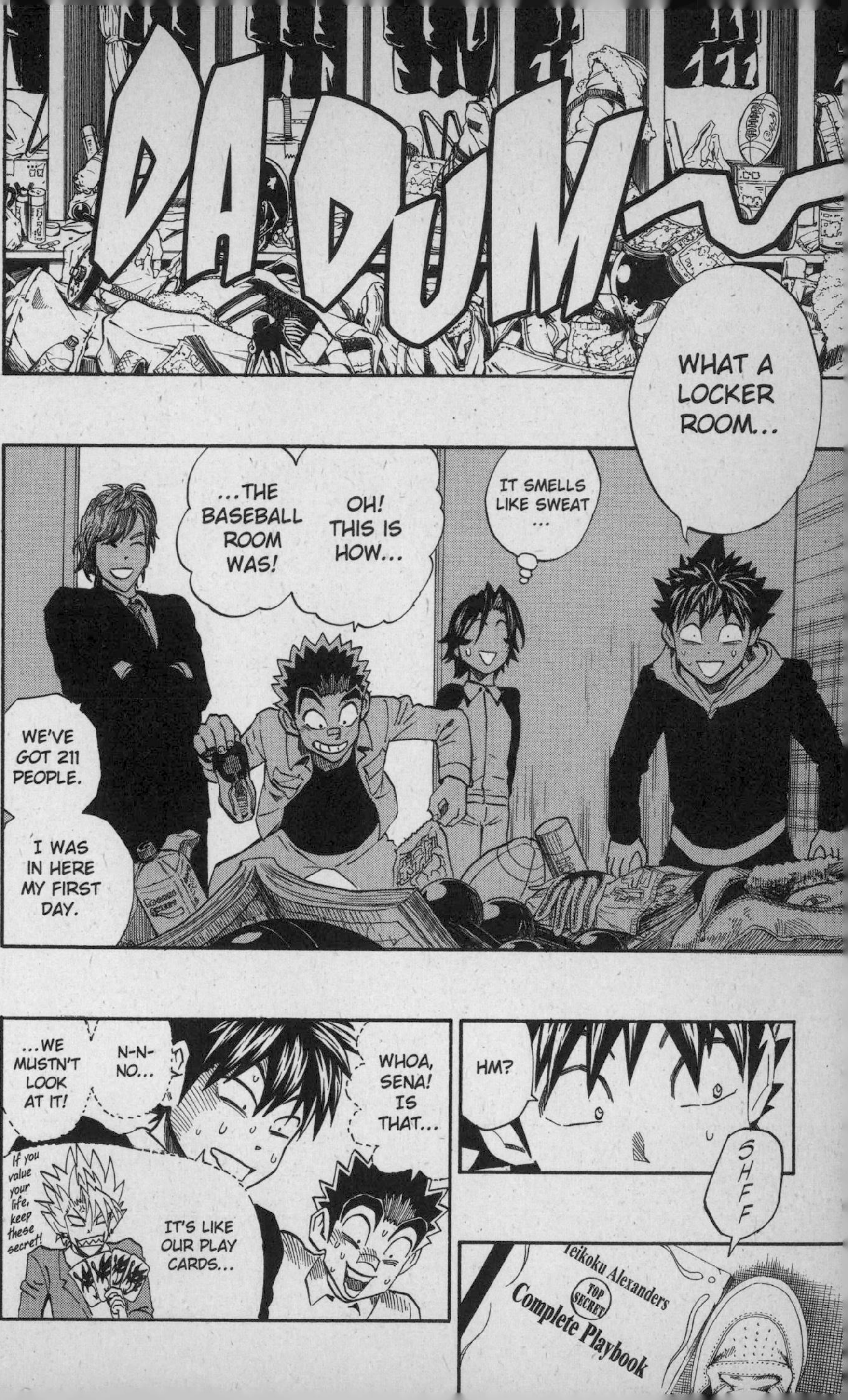
DADUM~
WHAT A LOCKER ROOM...
IT SMELLS LIKE SWEAT...
OH! THIS IS HOW...
...THE BASEBALL ROOM WAS!
WE'VE GOT 211 PEOPLE.
I WAS IN HERE MY FIRST DAY.
HM?
SHFF
Teikoku Alexanders
TOP SECRET
Complete Playbook
WHOA, SENA! IS THAT...
N-N-NO...
...WE MUSTN'T LOOK AT IT!
IT'S LIKE OUR PLAY CARDS...
If you value your life, keep these secret!

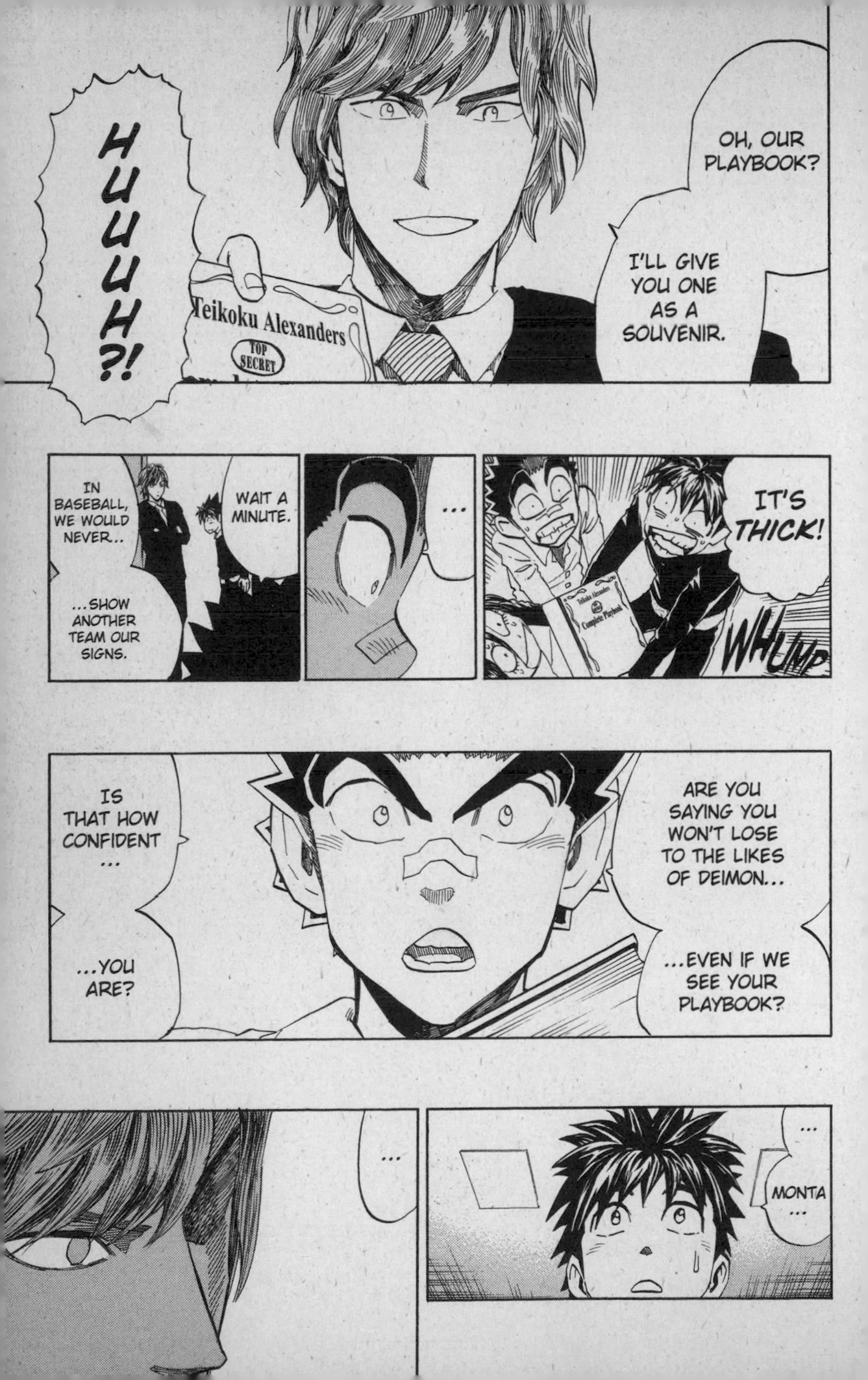
OH, OUR PLAYBOOK?
I'LL GIVE YOU ONE AS A SOUVENIR.
Teikoku Alexanders
TOP SECRET
HUUUH?!
IT'S THICK!
Teikoku Alexanders
Complete Playbook
WHUMP
...
WAIT A MINUTE.
IN BASEBALL, WE WOULD NEVER...
...SHOW ANOTHER TEAM OUR SIGNS.
ARE YOU SAYING YOU WON'T LOSE TO THE LIKES OF DEIMON...
...EVEN IF WE SEE YOUR PLAYBOOK?
IS THAT HOW CONFIDENT...
...YOU ARE?
...
MONTA...
...

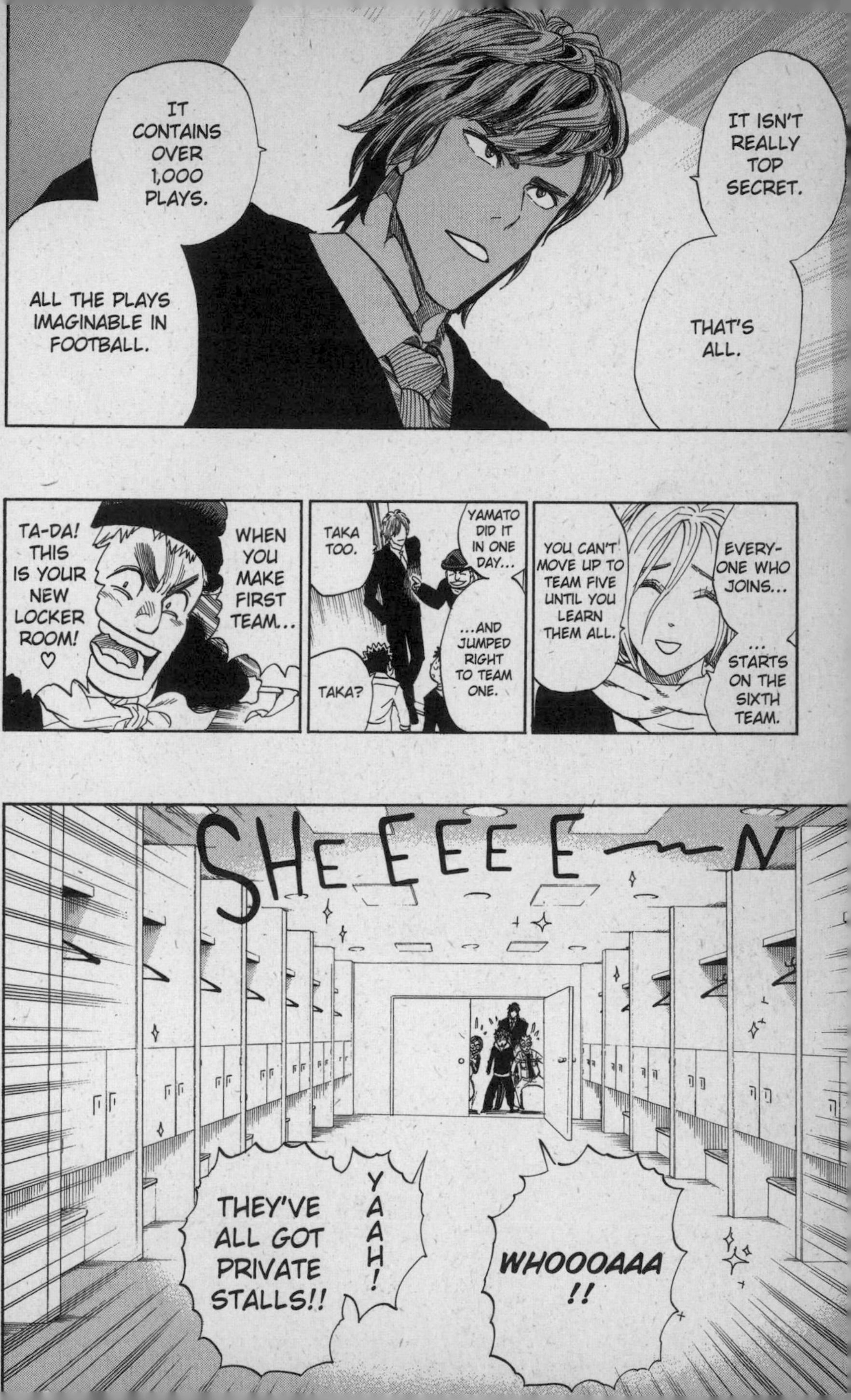
IT ISN'T REALLY TOP SECRET.
THAT'S ALL.
IT CONTAINS OVER 1,000 PLAYS.
ALL THE PLAYS IMAGINABLE IN FOOTBALL.
EVERY-ONE WHO JOINS...
...STARTS ON THE SIXTH TEAM.
YOU CAN'T MOVE UP TO TEAM FIVE UNTIL YOU LEARN THEM ALL.
YAMATO DID IT IN ONE DAY...
...AND JUMPED RIGHT TO TEAM ONE.
TAKA TOO.
TAKA?
WHEN YOU MAKE FIRST TEAM...
TA-DA! THIS IS YOUR NEW LOCKER ROOM! ♡
SHEEEEE—N
WHOOOAAA!!
YAAH!
THEY'VE ALL GOT PRIVATE STALLS!!

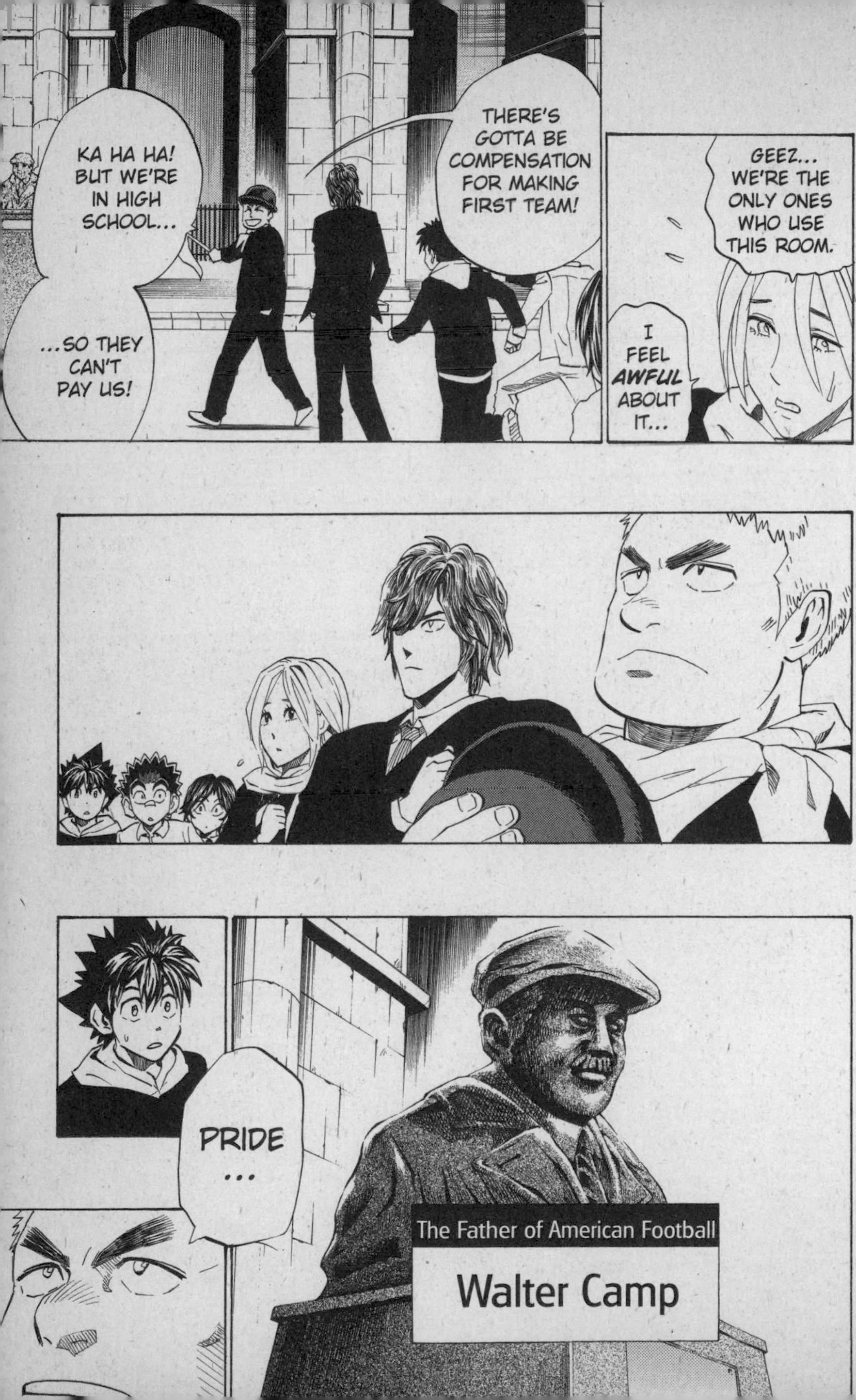
GEEZ... WE'RE THE ONLY ONES WHO USE THIS ROOM.
I FEEL AWFUL ABOUT IT...
THERE'S GOTTA BE COMPENSATION FOR MAKING FIRST TEAM!
KA HA HA! BUT WE'RE IN HIGH SCHOOL...
...SO THEY CAN'T PAY US!
PRIDE ...
The Father of American Football
Walter Camp

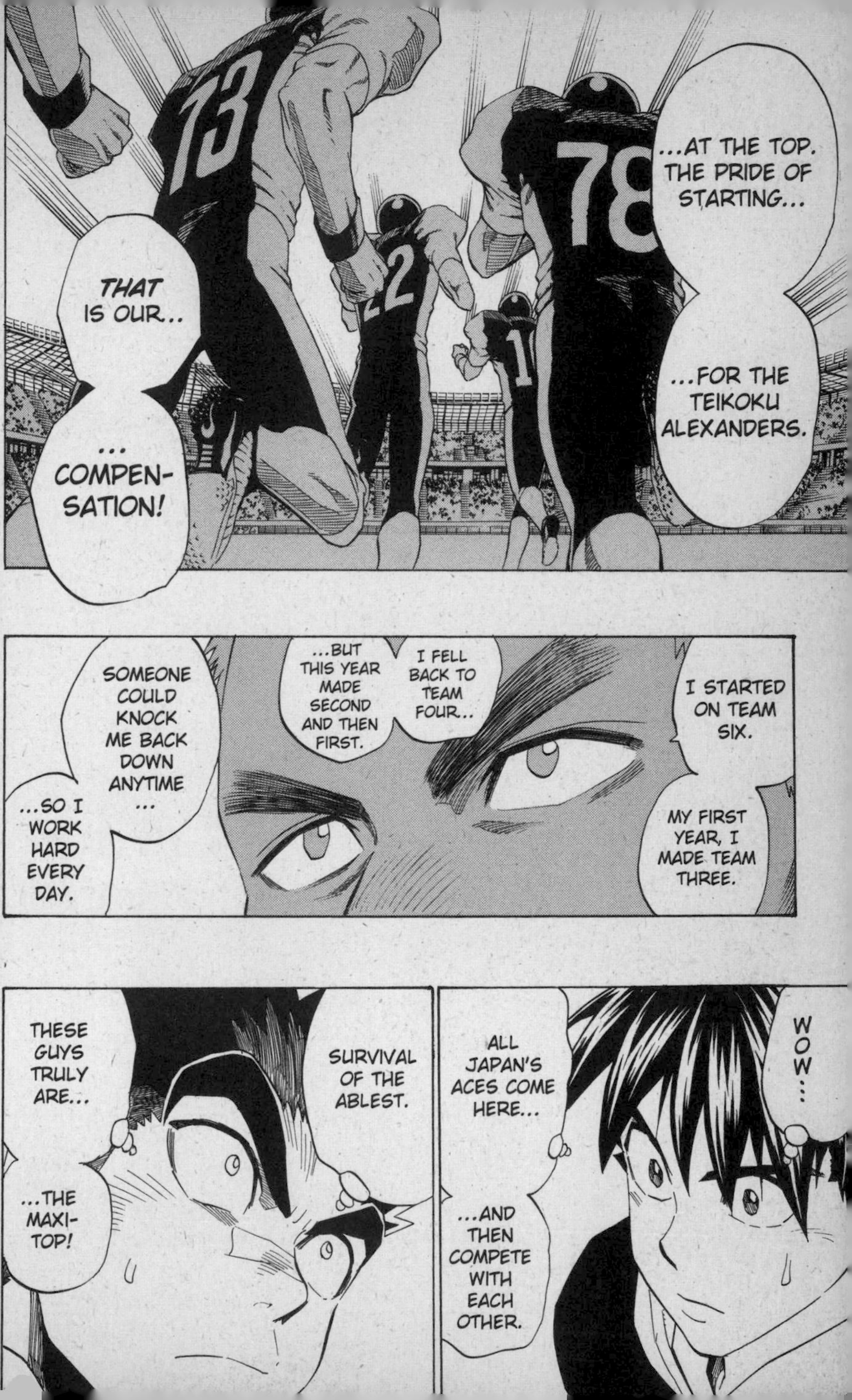
...AT THE TOP. THE PRIDE OF STARTING...
...FOR THE TEIKOKU ALEXANDERS.
THAT IS OUR...
...COMPEN-SATION!
I STARTED ON TEAM SIX.
MY FIRST YEAR, I MADE TEAM THREE.
I FELL BACK TO TEAM FOUR...
...BUT THIS YEAR MADE SECOND AND THEN FIRST.
SOMEONE COULD KNOCK ME BACK DOWN ANYTIME...
...SO I WORK HARD EVERY DAY.
WOW...
ALL JAPAN'S ACES COME HERE...
...AND THEN COMPETE WITH EACH OTHER.
SURVIVAL OF THE ABLEST.
THESE GUYS TRULY ARE...
...THE MAXI-TOP!

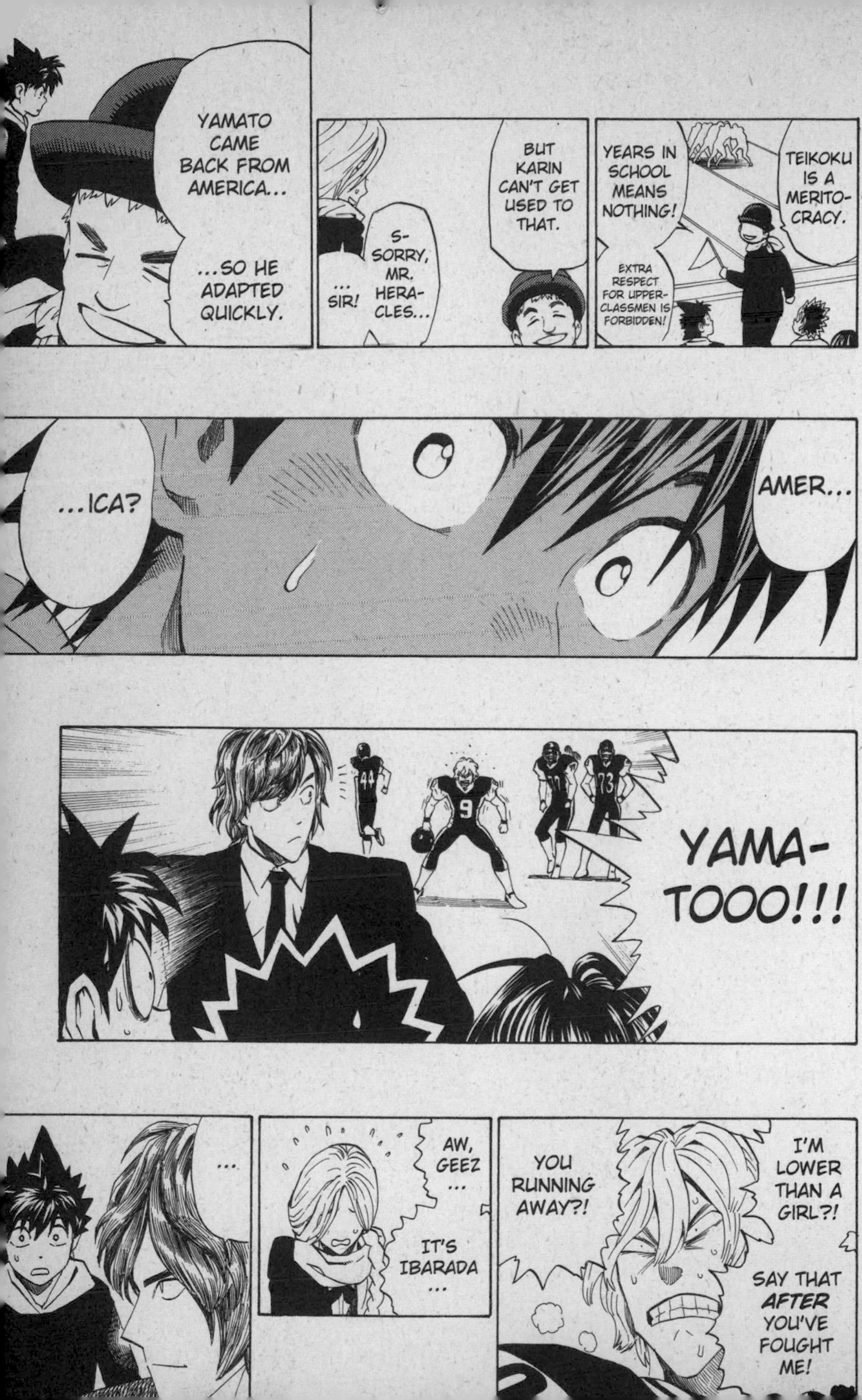
TEIKOKU IS A MERITOCRACY.
YEARS IN SCHOOL MEANS NOTHING!
EXTRA RESPECT FOR UPPERCLASSMEN IS FORBIDDEN!
BUT KARIN CAN'T GET USED TO THAT.
S-SORRY, MR. HERACLES...
...SIR!
YAMATO CAME BACK FROM AMERICA...
...SO HE ADAPTED QUICKLY.
AMER...
...ICA?
YAMATOOO!!!
I'M LOWER THAN A GIRL?!
YOU RUNNING AWAY?!
SAY THAT AFTER YOU'VE FOUGHT ME!
AW, GEEZ...
IT'S IBARADA...
...

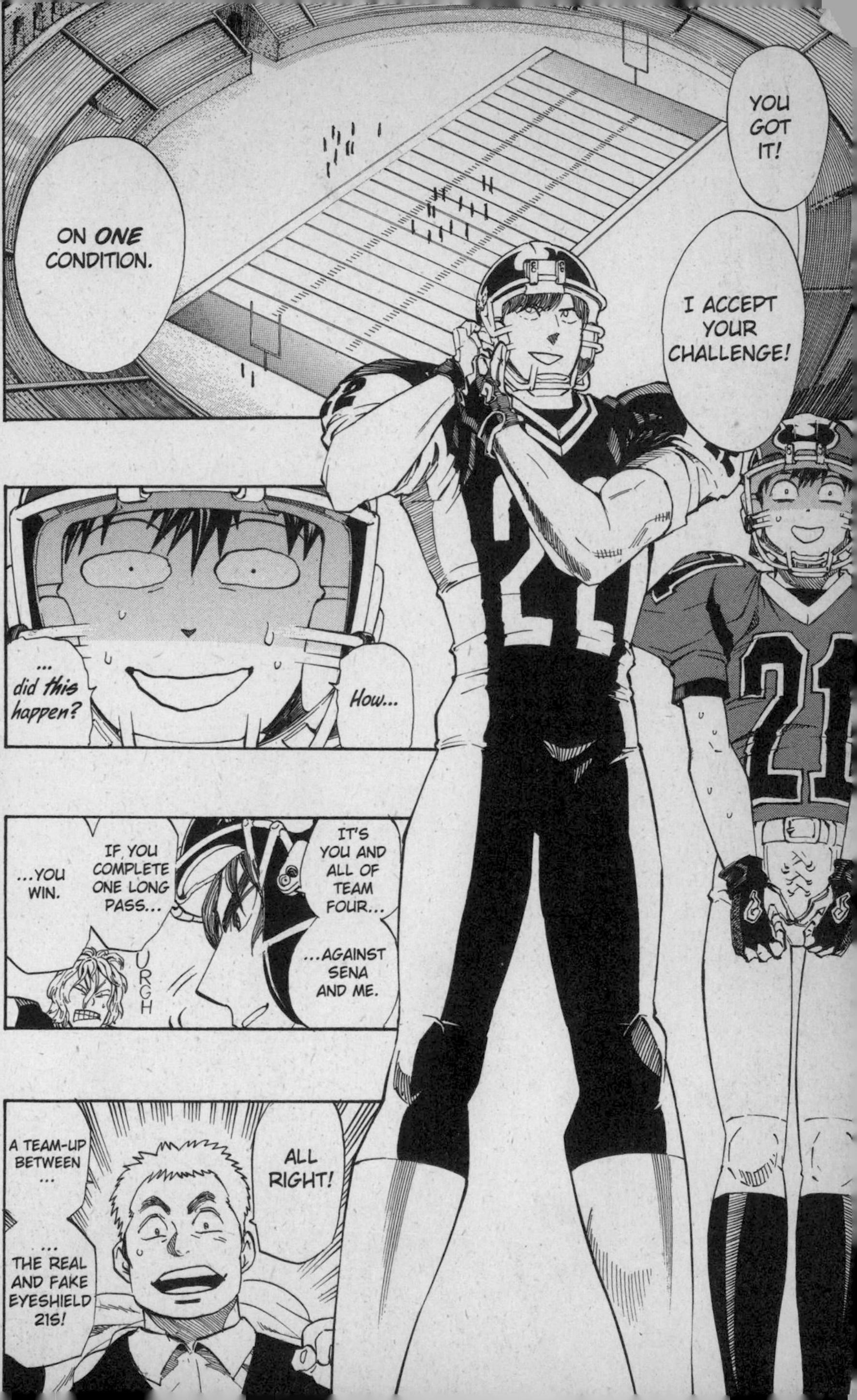
YOU GOT IT!
I ACCEPT YOUR CHALLENGE!
ON ONE CONDITION.
How...
... did this happen?
IT'S YOU AND ALL OF TEAM FOUR...
...AGAINST SENA AND ME.
IF YOU COMPLETE ONE LONG PASS...
...YOU WIN.
URGH
ALL RIGHT!
A TEAM-UP BETWEEN ...
... THE REAL AND FAKE EYESHIELD 21S!

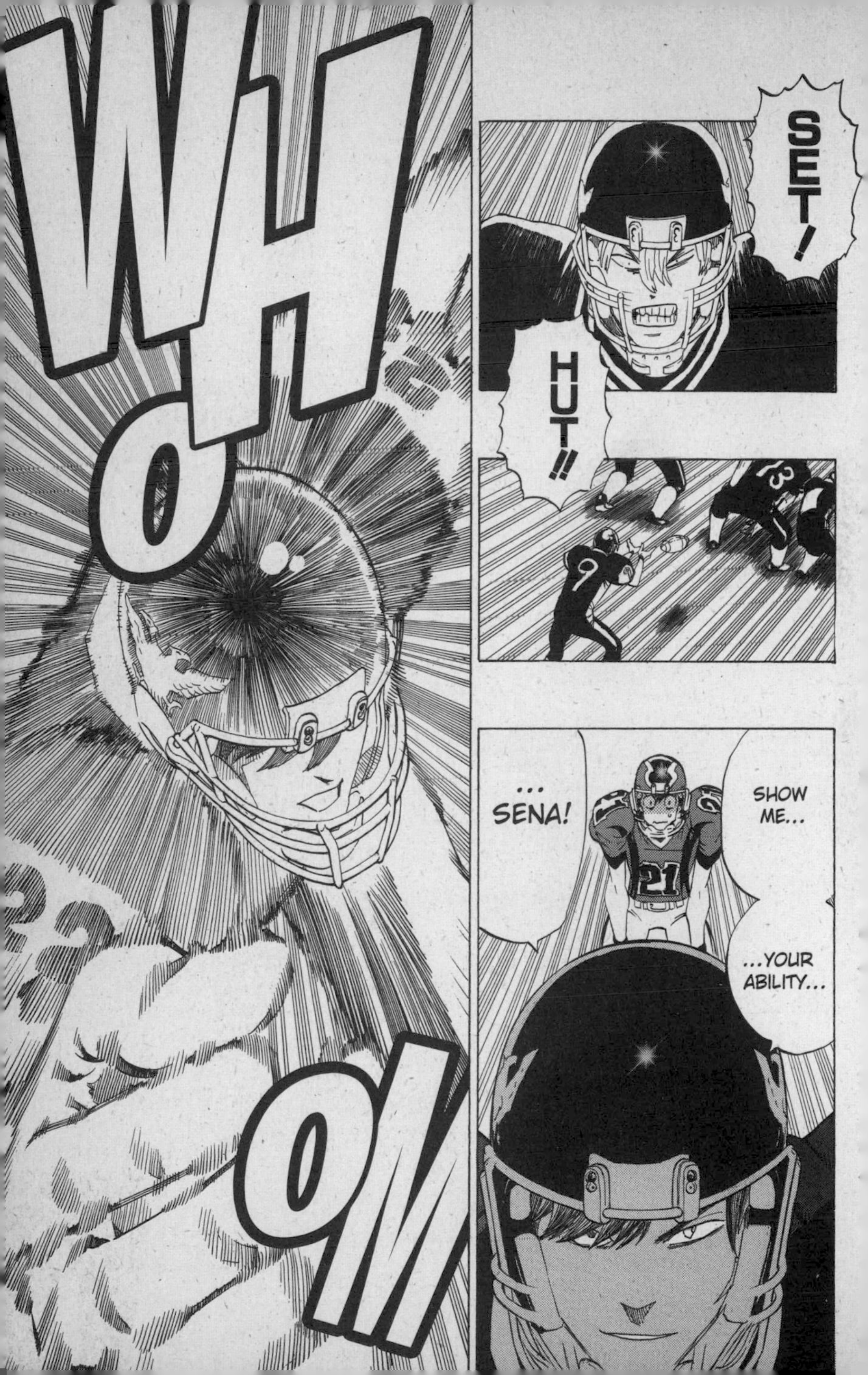
SET!
HUT!!
SHOW ME...
...SENA!
...YOUR ABILITY...
WHOA!!

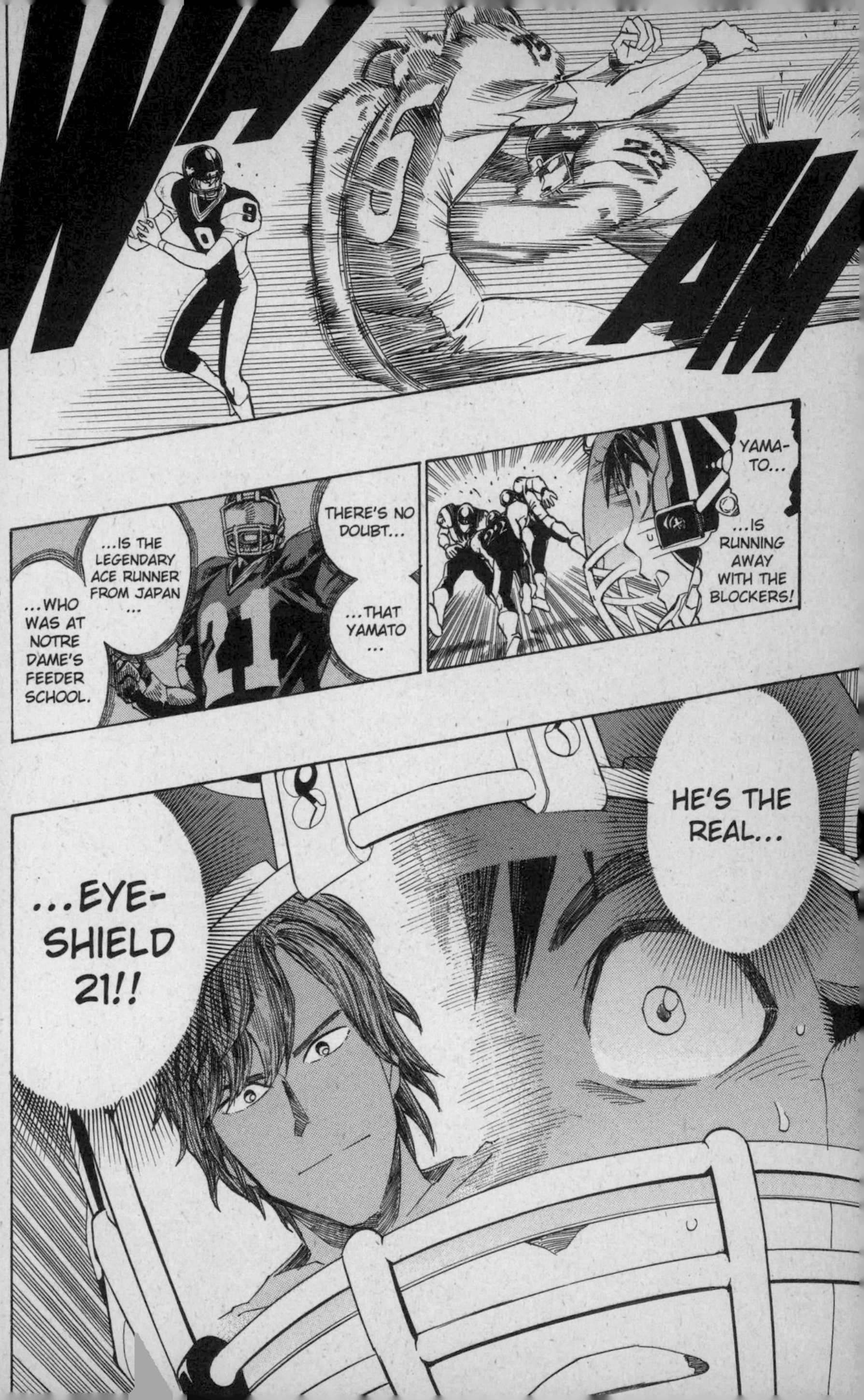
WHAM
YAMA-TO...
...IS RUNNING AWAY WITH THE BLOCKERS!
THERE'S NO DOUBT...
...THAT YAMATO...
...IS THE LEGENDARY ACE RUNNER FROM JAPAN...
...WHO WAS AT NOTRE DAME'S FEEDER SCHOOL.
HE'S THE REAL...
...EYE-SHIELD 21!!

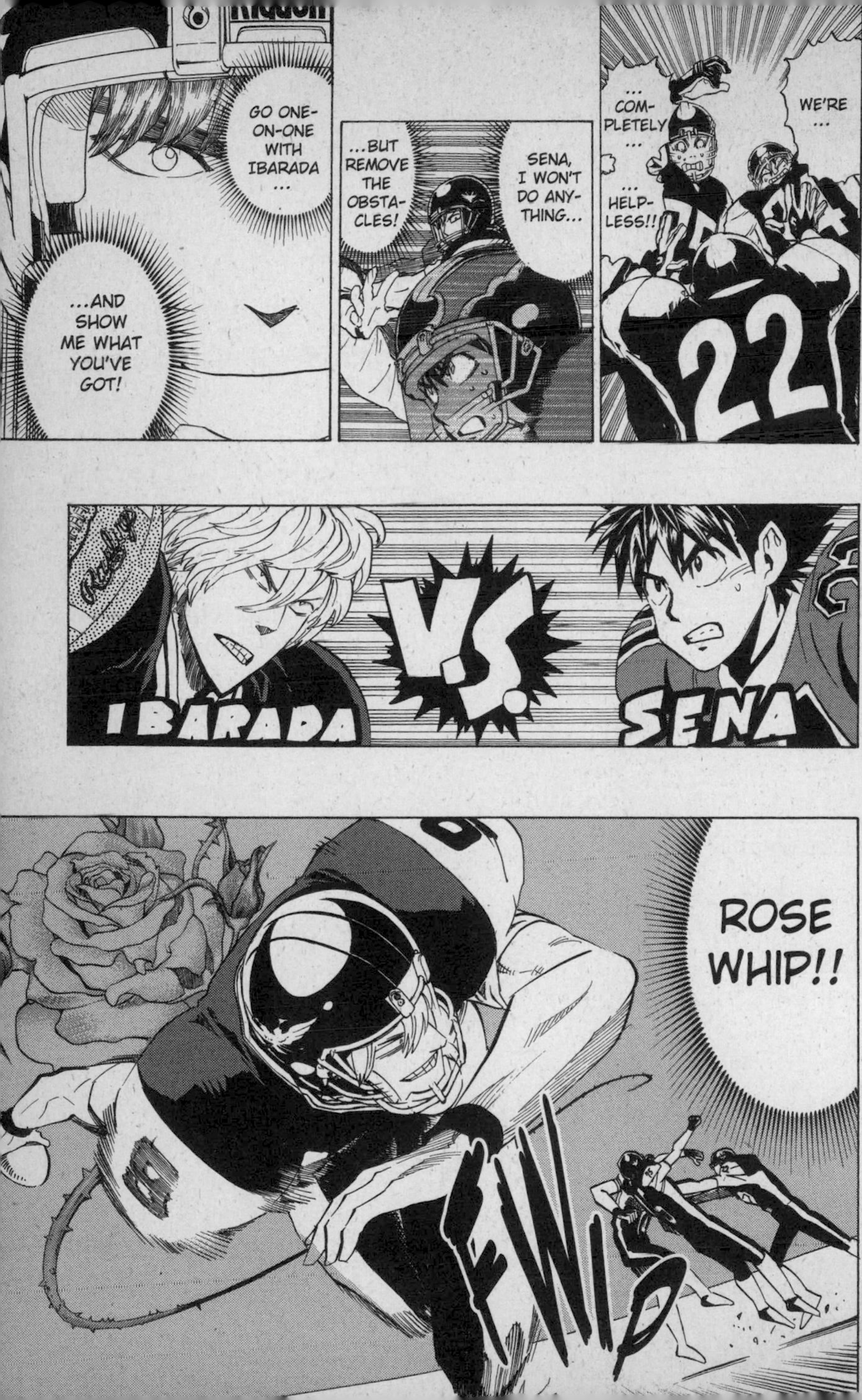
WE'RE ...
... COMPLETELY ...
... HELPLESS!!
SENA, I WON'T DO ANYTHING...
...BUT REMOVE THE OBSTACLES!
GO ONE-ON-ONE WITH IBARADA ...
...AND SHOW ME WHAT YOU'VE GOT!
IBARADA V.S. SENA
ROSE WHIP!!
FWISH

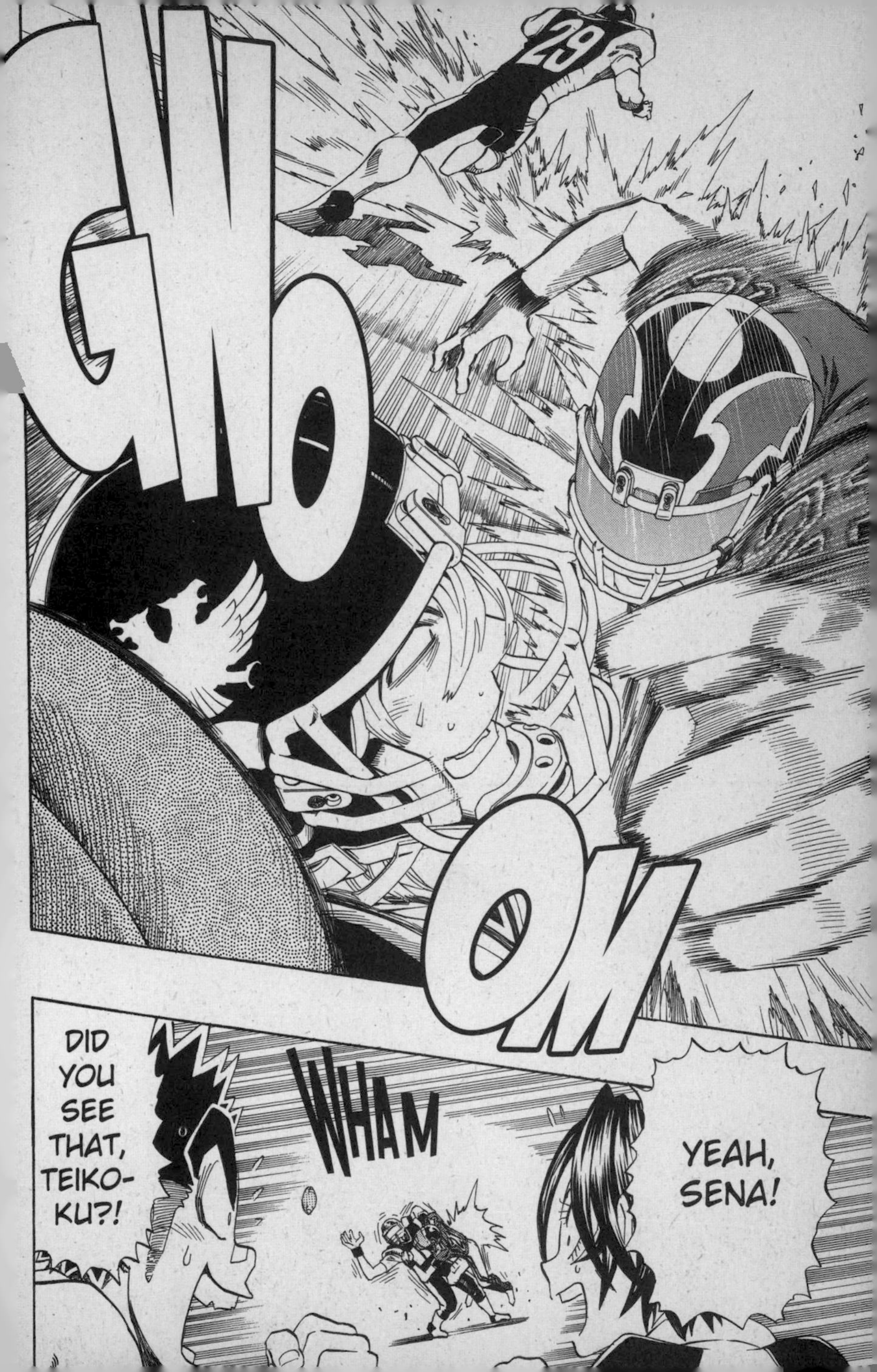
YEAH, SENA!
WHAM
DID YOU SEE THAT, TEIKOKU?!

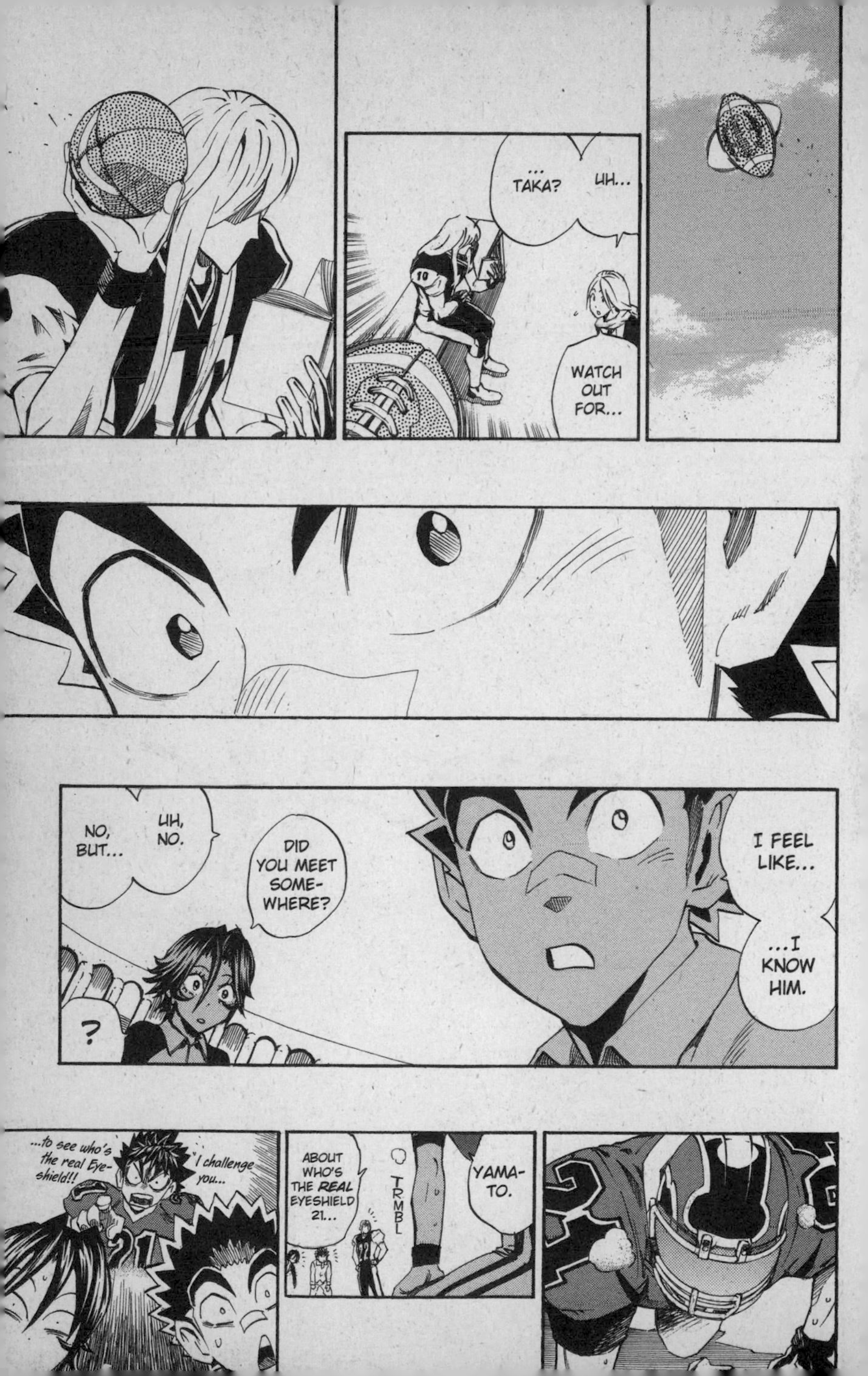
UH...
...TAKA?
WATCH OUT FOR...
I FEEL LIKE...
...I KNOW HIM.
DID YOU MEET SOME-WHERE?
UH, NO.
NO, BUT...
?
YAMA-TO.
TRMBL
ABOUT WHO'S THE *REAL* EYESHIELD 21...
I challenge you...
...to see who's the real Eye-shield!!

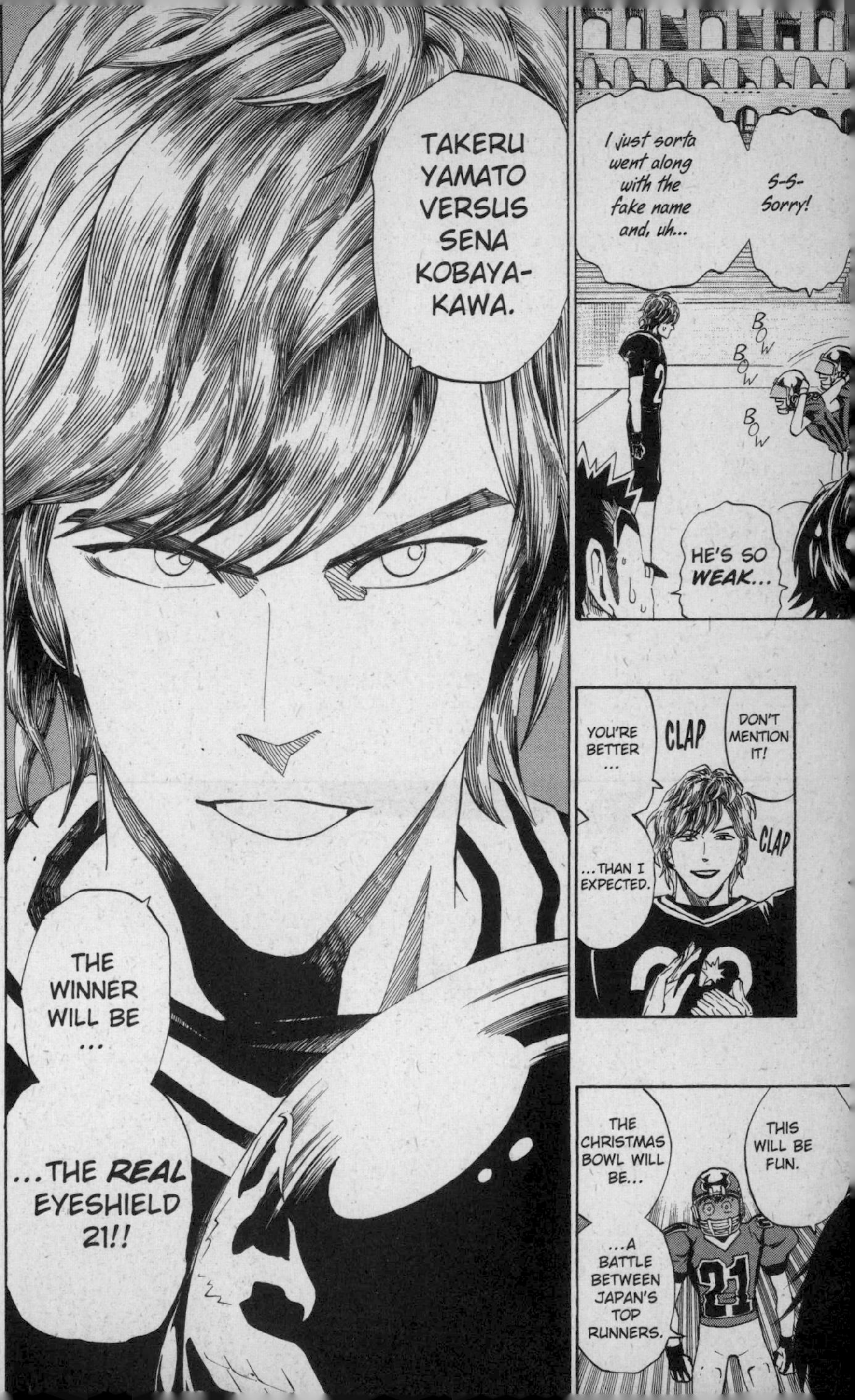
S-S-Sorry!
I just sorta went along with the fake name and, uh...
BOW
BOW
BOW
HE'S SO WEAK...
DON'T MENTION IT!
CLAP
YOU'RE BETTER ...
CLAP
...THAN I EXPECTED.
THIS WILL BE FUN.
THE CHRISTMAS BOWL WILL BE...
...A BATTLE BETWEEN JAPAN'S TOP RUNNERS.
TAKERU YAMATO VERSUS SENA KOBAYAKAWA.
THE WINNER WILL BE ...
...THE REAL EYESHIELD 21!!

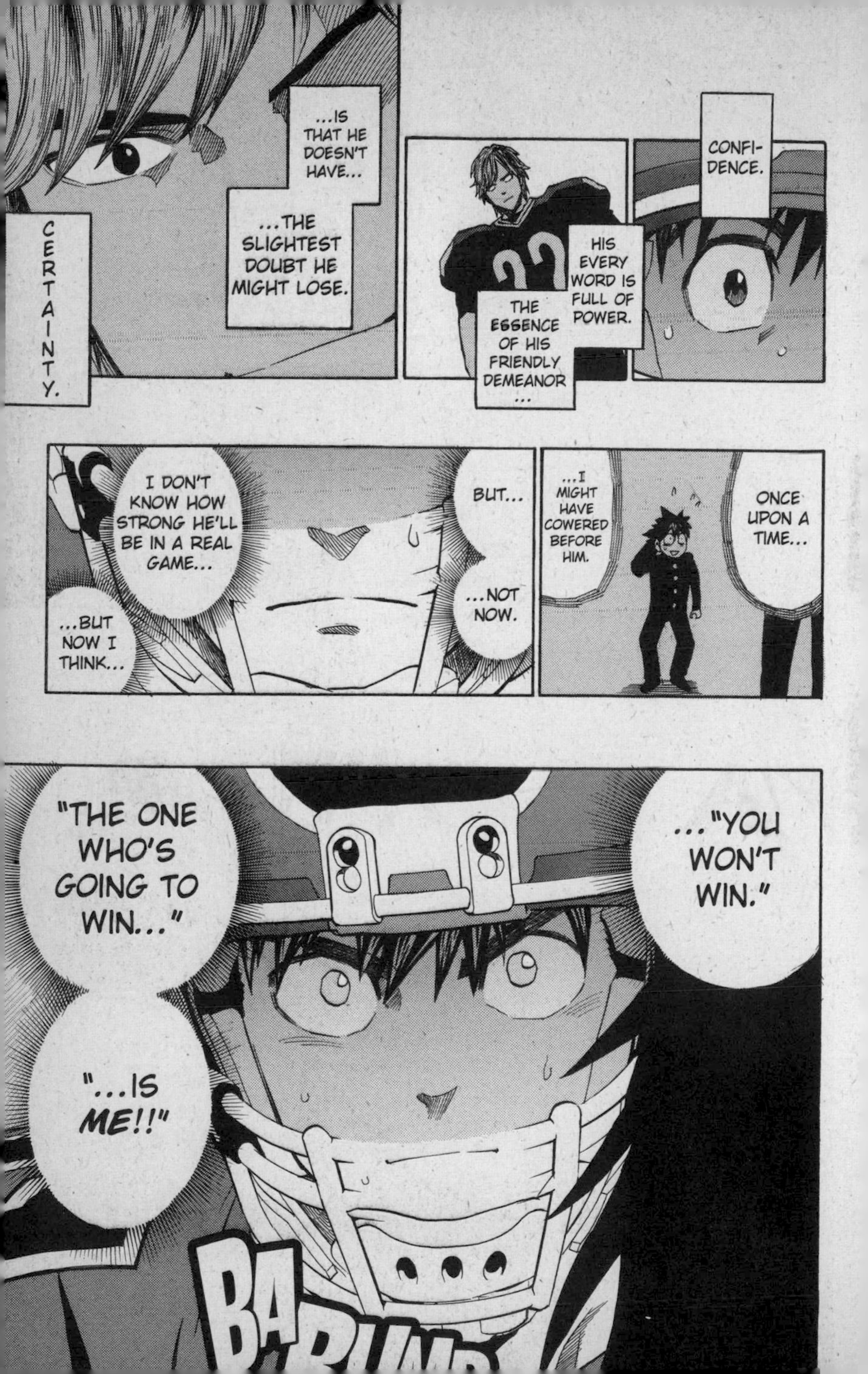
CONFI-DENCE.
HIS EVERY WORD IS FULL OF POWER.
THE ESSENCE OF HIS FRIENDLY DEMEANOR...
...IS THAT HE DOESN'T HAVE...
...THE SLIGHTEST DOUBT HE MIGHT LOSE.
CERTAINTY.
ONCE UPON A TIME...
...I MIGHT HAVE COWERED BEFORE HIM.
BUT...
...NOT NOW.
I DON'T KNOW HOW STRONG HE'LL BE IN A REAL GAME...
...BUT NOW I THINK...
..."YOU WON'T WIN."
"THE ONE WHO'S GOING TO WIN..."
"...IS *ME!!*"
BA

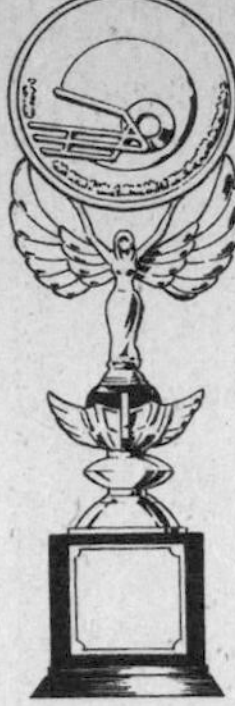

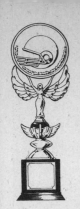

KANTO REGION,
KANTO TOURNAMENT

SHINE ON!! MORE MVPS!

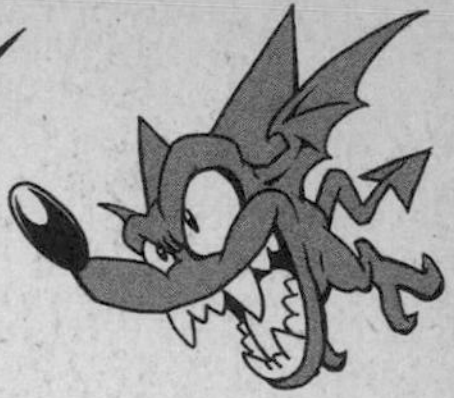

BACKGROUND DATA

MOST OUTSTANDING CHEERING

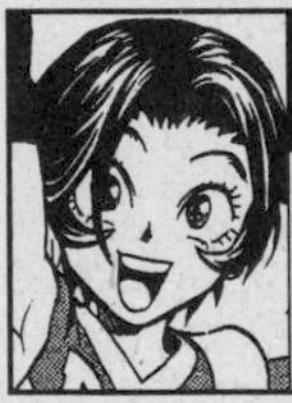

SUZUNA TAKI

RUNNER UP:
KENGO MIZUMACHI

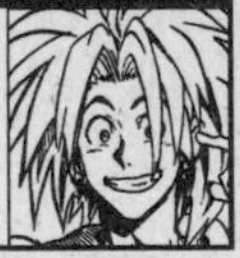

MOST SUPERSTITIOUS

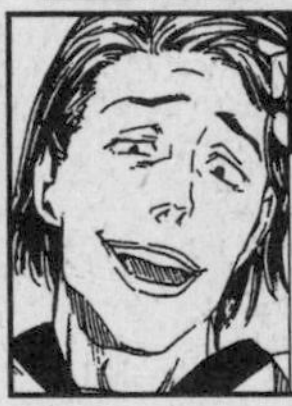

KAORU HATSUJO

RUNNER UP:
GONDAYU YAMABUSHI

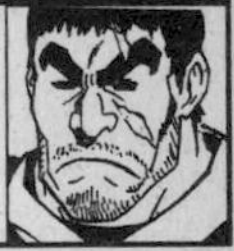

MOST FANS

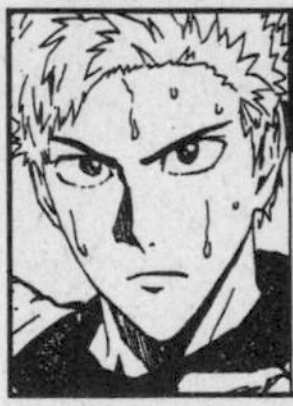

HARUTO SAKURABA

RUNNER UP:
EYESHIELD 21

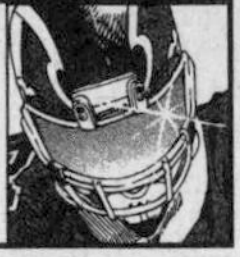

TALKED THE MOST

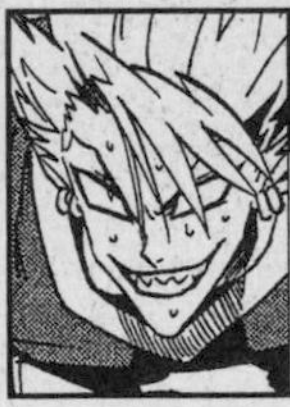

YOICHI HIRUMA

RUNNER UP:
KOTARO SASAKI

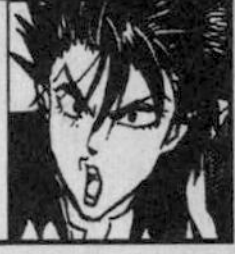

MOST FAMILY MEMBERS PRESENT

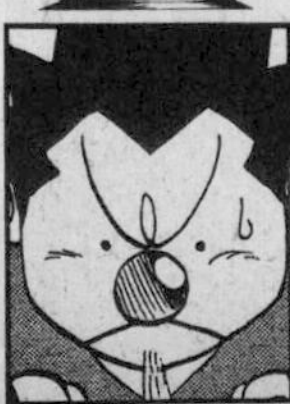

DAIKICHI KOMUSUBI

RUNNER UP:
DAISUKE ATSUMI

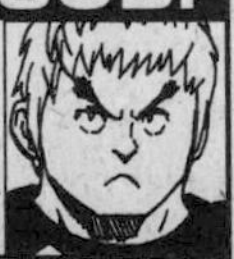

MOST FOOD EATEN

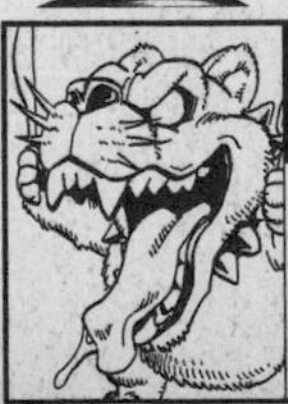

CERBERUS

RUNNER UP:
MAKOTO OTAWARA

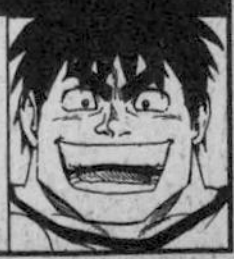

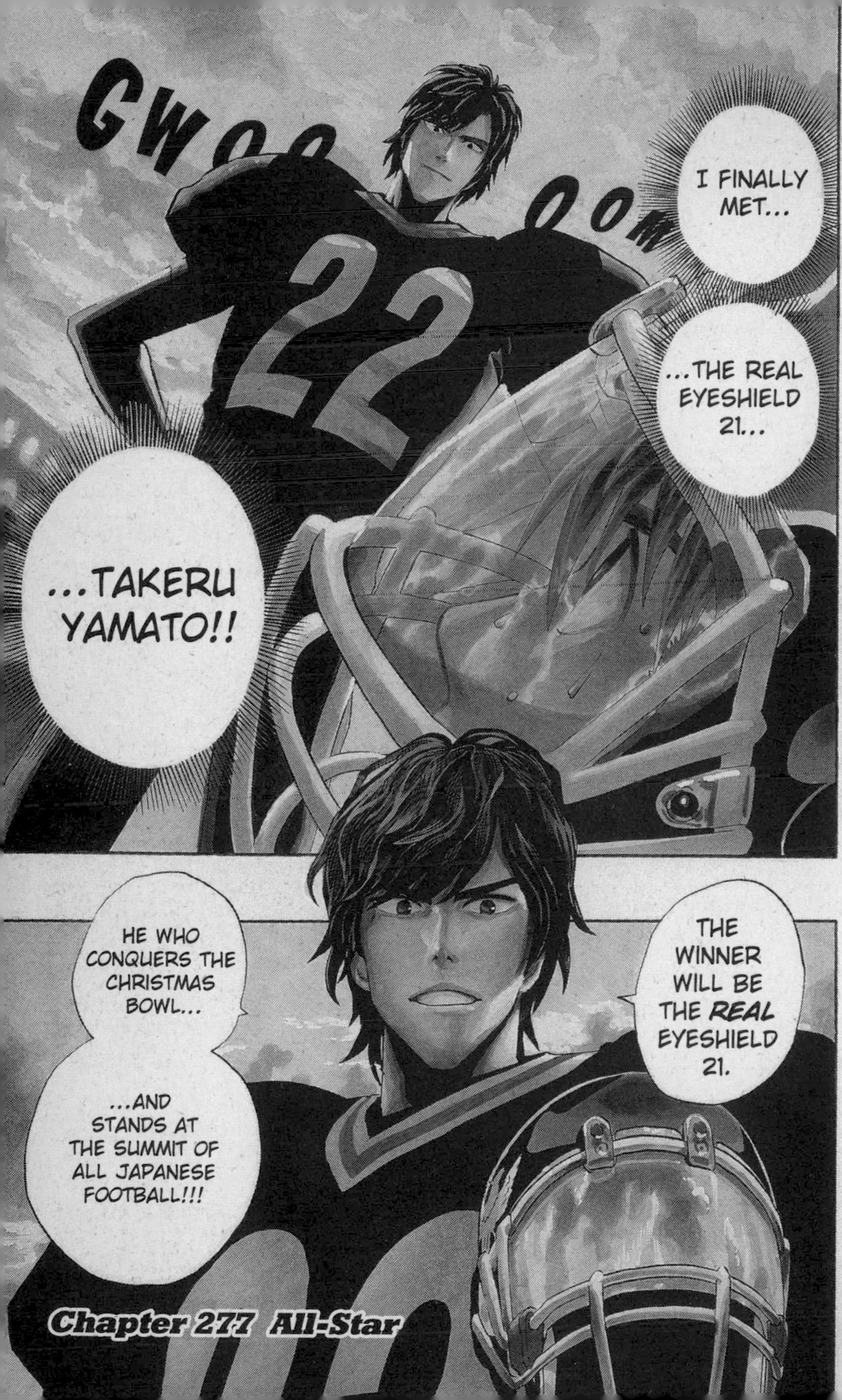
GWOOOOOOM
I FINALLY MET...
...THE REAL EYESHIELD 21...
...TAKERU YAMATO!!
THE WINNER WILL BE THE REAL EYESHIELD 21.
HE WHO CONQUERS THE CHRISTMAS BOWL...
...AND STANDS AT THE SUMMIT OF ALL JAPANESE FOOTBALL!!!
Chapter 277 All-Star

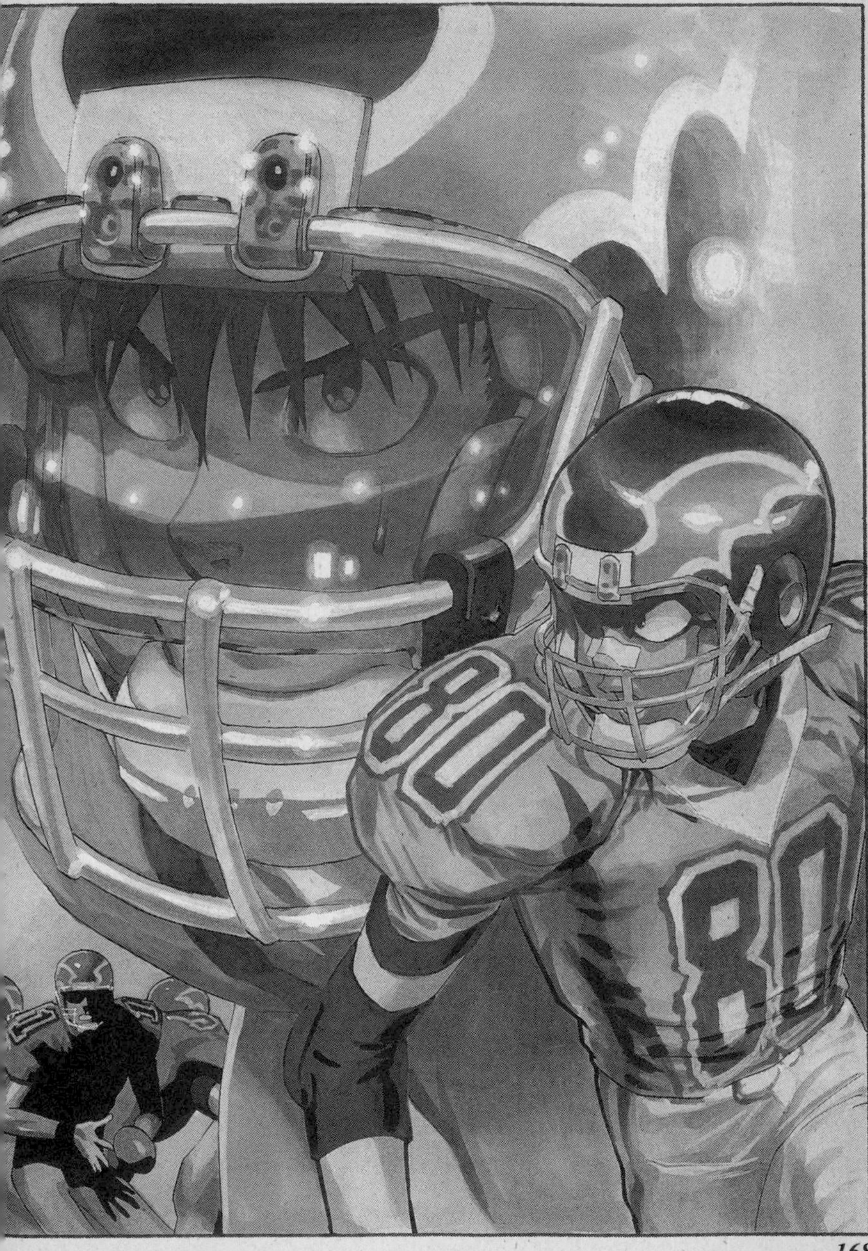

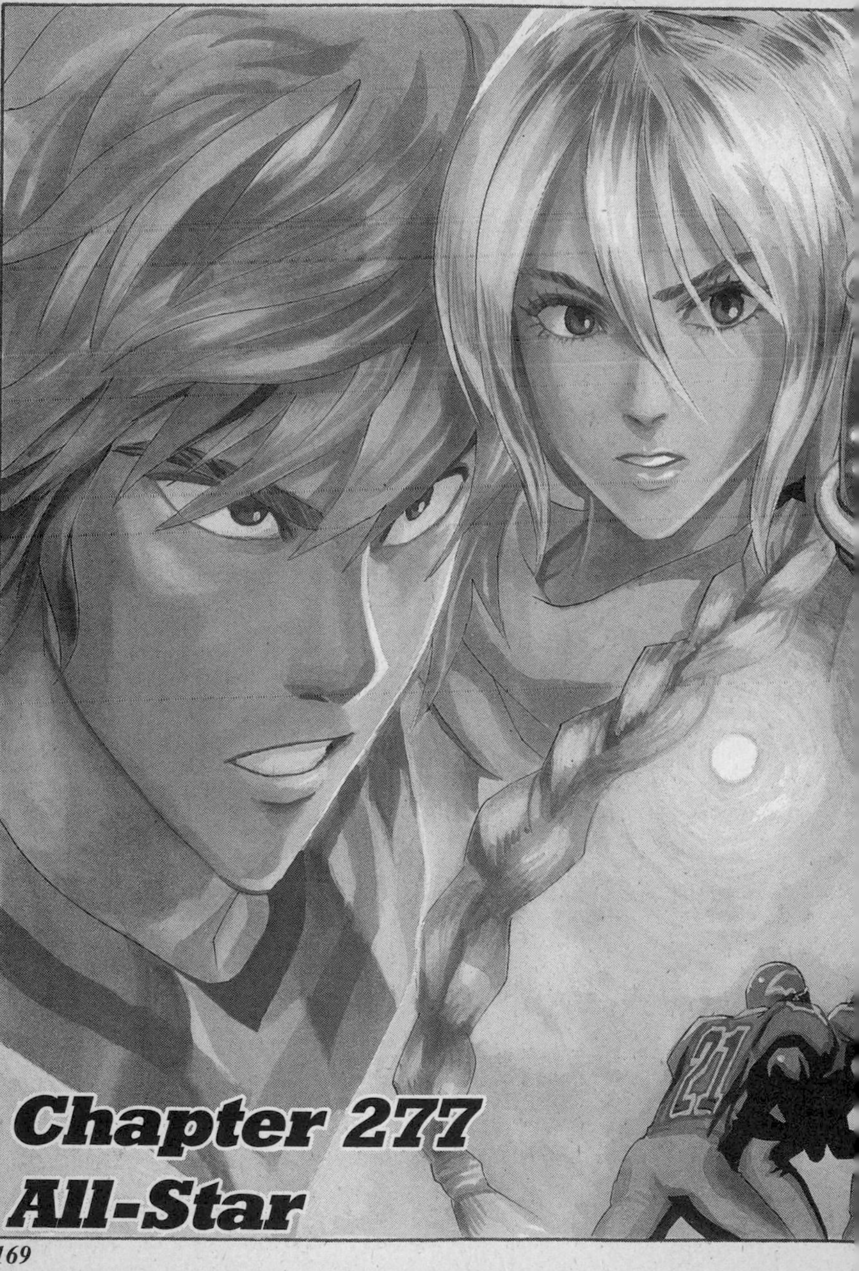
Chapter 277
All-Star

Deluxe Biographies of the Supporting Cast

Taki & Suzuna's Father

He's good at playing the guitar and singing. He proposed through a romantic song he wrote himself and dedicated to his future wife called "The Greatest Person in the World."

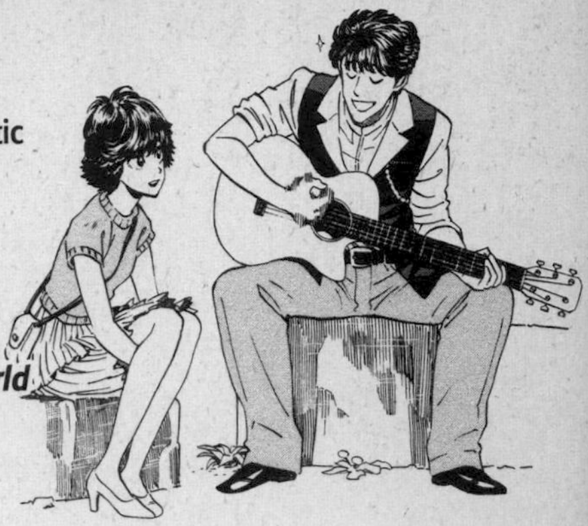

Later it became clear that he meant ***"I am the greatest person in the world*** so you should marry me." Ever since, his wife has looked at him with eyes so cool they could kill.

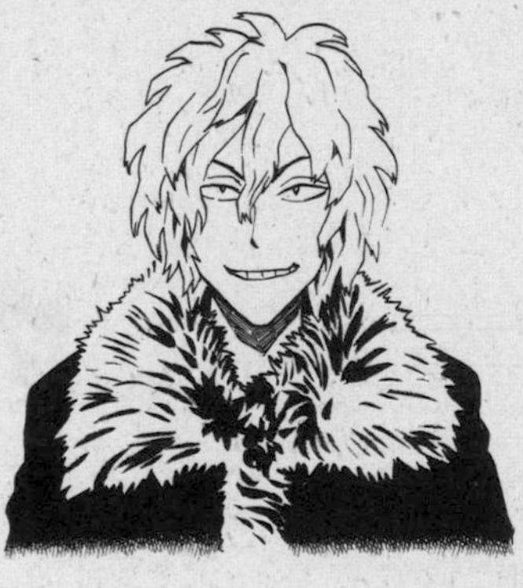

Kirio Ibarada

His special moves are the Rose Whip and picking on lower-classmen! When he heard there was no hierarchy at Teikoku based on grade at school, he decided to bully each of his junior teammates individually. There were ***200***, though, so he gave up.

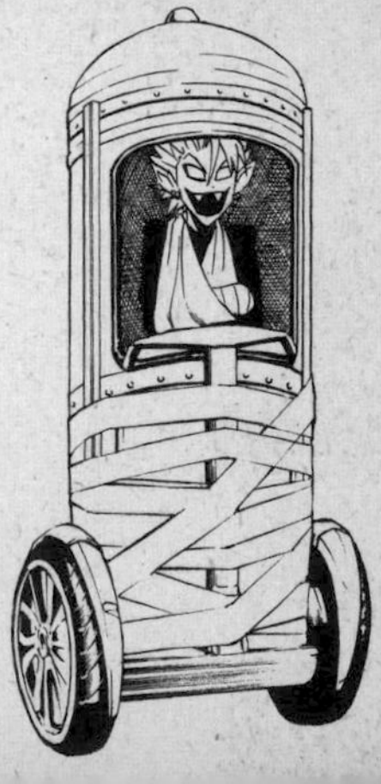

The Moving Oxygen Capsule

It cost five million yen for the oxygen capsule, 800 thousand yen for the Segway, and 100 yen for the duct tape. He got the money by (of course) ***threatening the principal***.

In Japan, it's against traffic laws. But then again, Hiruma has driven around in military tanks before, so...

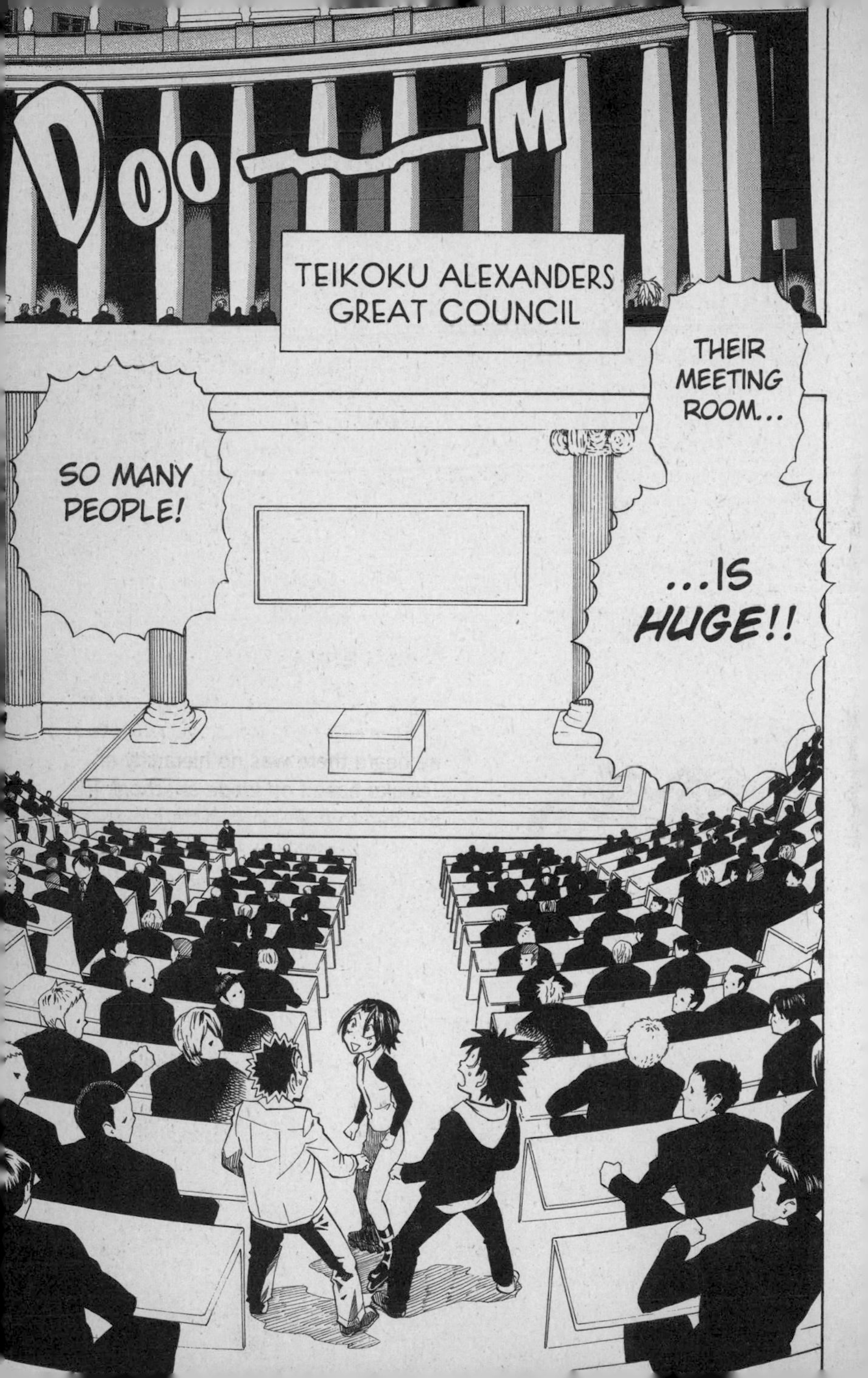
DOO——M
TEIKOKU ALEXANDERS GREAT COUNCIL
THEIR MEETING ROOM...
...IS HUGE!!
SO MANY PEOPLE!

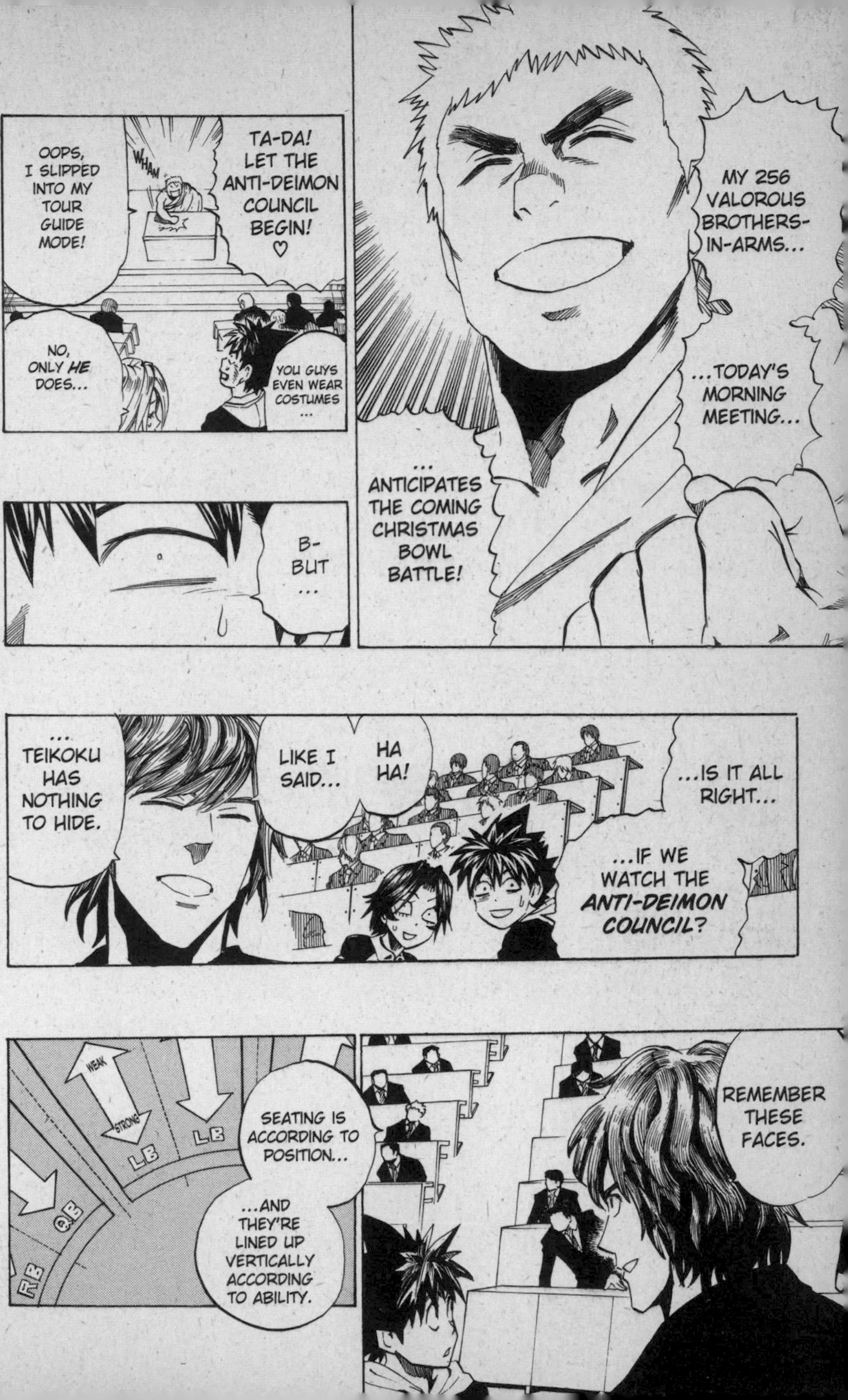
MY 256 VALOROUS BROTHERS-IN-ARMS...
...TODAY'S MORNING MEETING...
... ANTICIPATES THE COMING CHRISTMAS BOWL BATTLE!
TA-DA! LET THE ANTI-DEIMON COUNCIL BEGIN! ♡
WHAM
OOPS, I SLIPPED INTO MY TOUR GUIDE MODE!
YOU GUYS EVEN WEAR COSTUMES ...
NO, ONLY **HE** DOES...
B-BUT ...
...IS IT ALL RIGHT...
...IF WE WATCH THE **ANTI-DEIMON COUNCIL**?
HA HA!
LIKE I SAID...
... TEIKOKU HAS NOTHING TO HIDE.
REMEMBER THESE FACES.
SEATING IS ACCORDING TO POSITION...
...AND THEY'RE LINED UP VERTICALLY ACCORDING TO ABILITY.
WEAK
STRONG
LB
LB
QB
RB

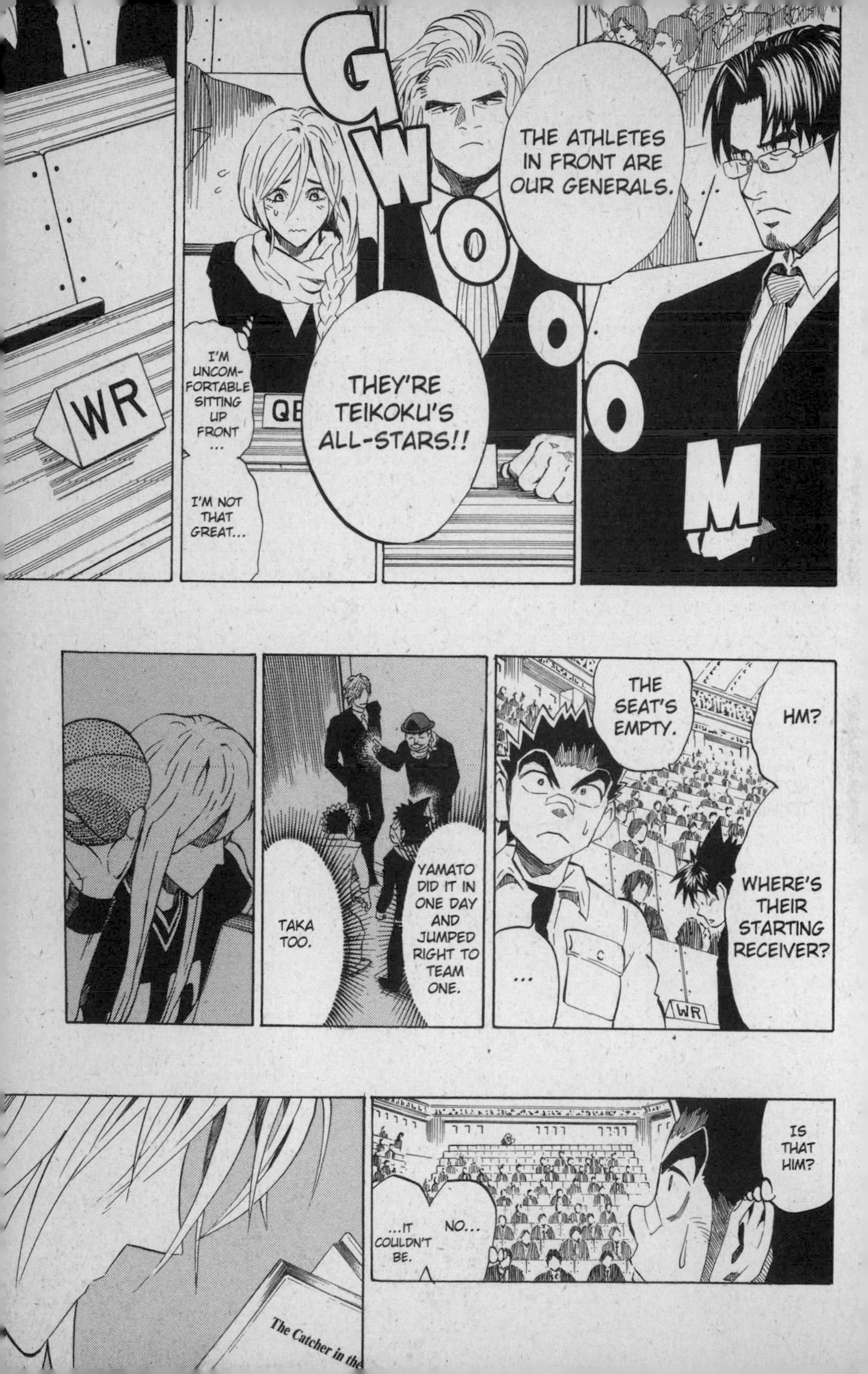
THE ATHLETES IN FRONT ARE OUR GENERALS.
GWOOOOM
THEY'RE TEIKOKU'S ALL-STARS!!
QB
I'M UNCOMFORTABLE SITTING UP FRONT...
I'M NOT THAT GREAT...
WR
THE SEAT'S EMPTY.
HM?
WHERE'S THEIR STARTING RECEIVER?
...
WR
YAMATO DID IT IN ONE DAY AND JUMPED RIGHT TO TEAM ONE.
TAKA TOO.
IS THAT HIM?
NO...
...IT COULDN'T BE.
The Catcher in the

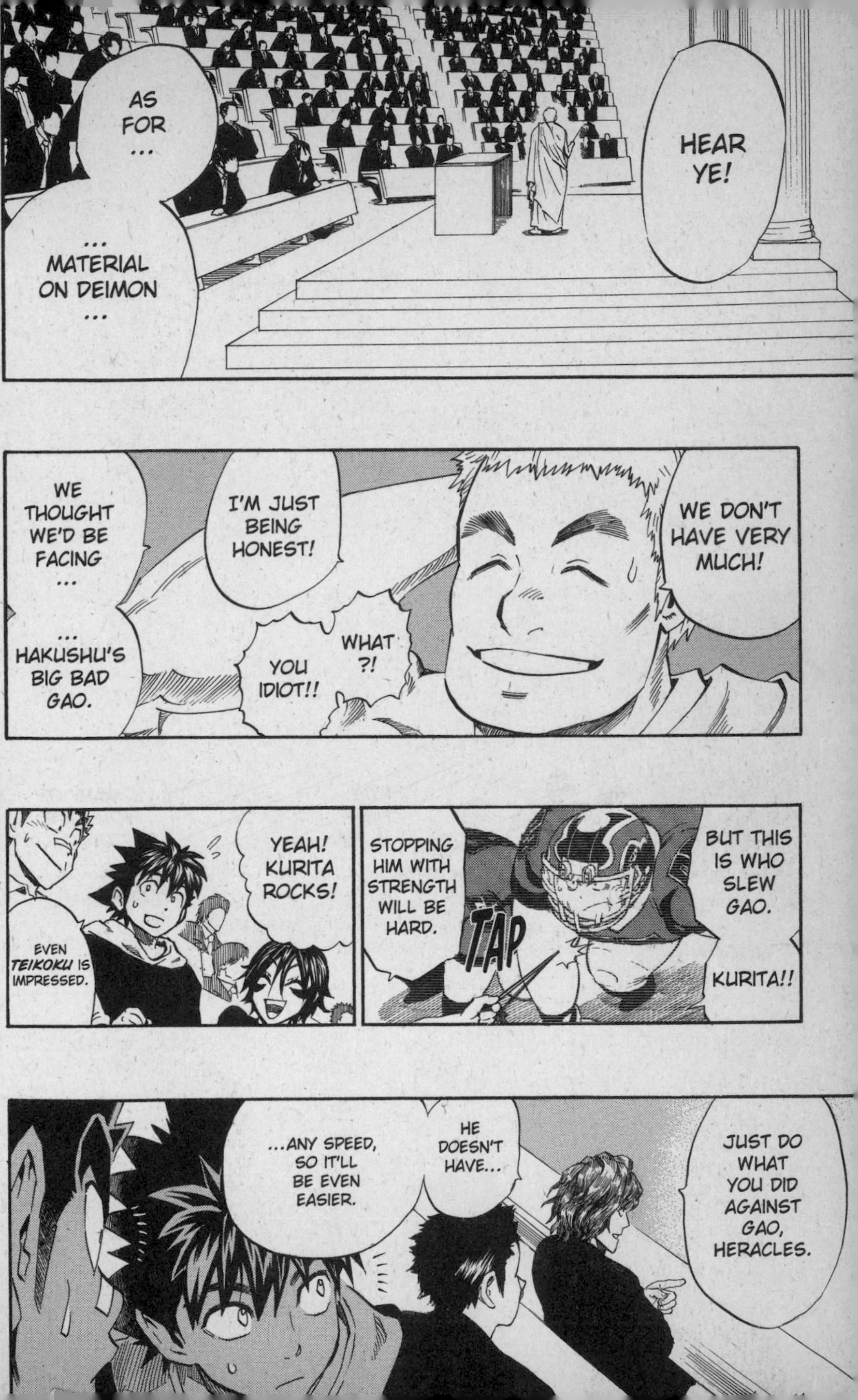
HEAR YE!
AS FOR ...
... MATERIAL ON DEIMON ...
WE DON'T HAVE VERY MUCH!
WHAT?!
YOU IDIOT!!
I'M JUST BEING HONEST!
WE THOUGHT WE'D BE FACING ...
... HAKUSHU'S BIG BAD GAO.
BUT THIS IS WHO SLEW GAO.
KURITA!!
TAP
STOPPING HIM WITH STRENGTH WILL BE HARD.
YEAH! KURITA ROCKS!
EVEN TEIKOKU IS IMPRESSED.
JUST DO WHAT YOU DID AGAINST GAO, HERACLES.
HE DOESN'T HAVE...
...ANY SPEED, SO IT'LL BE EVEN EASIER.

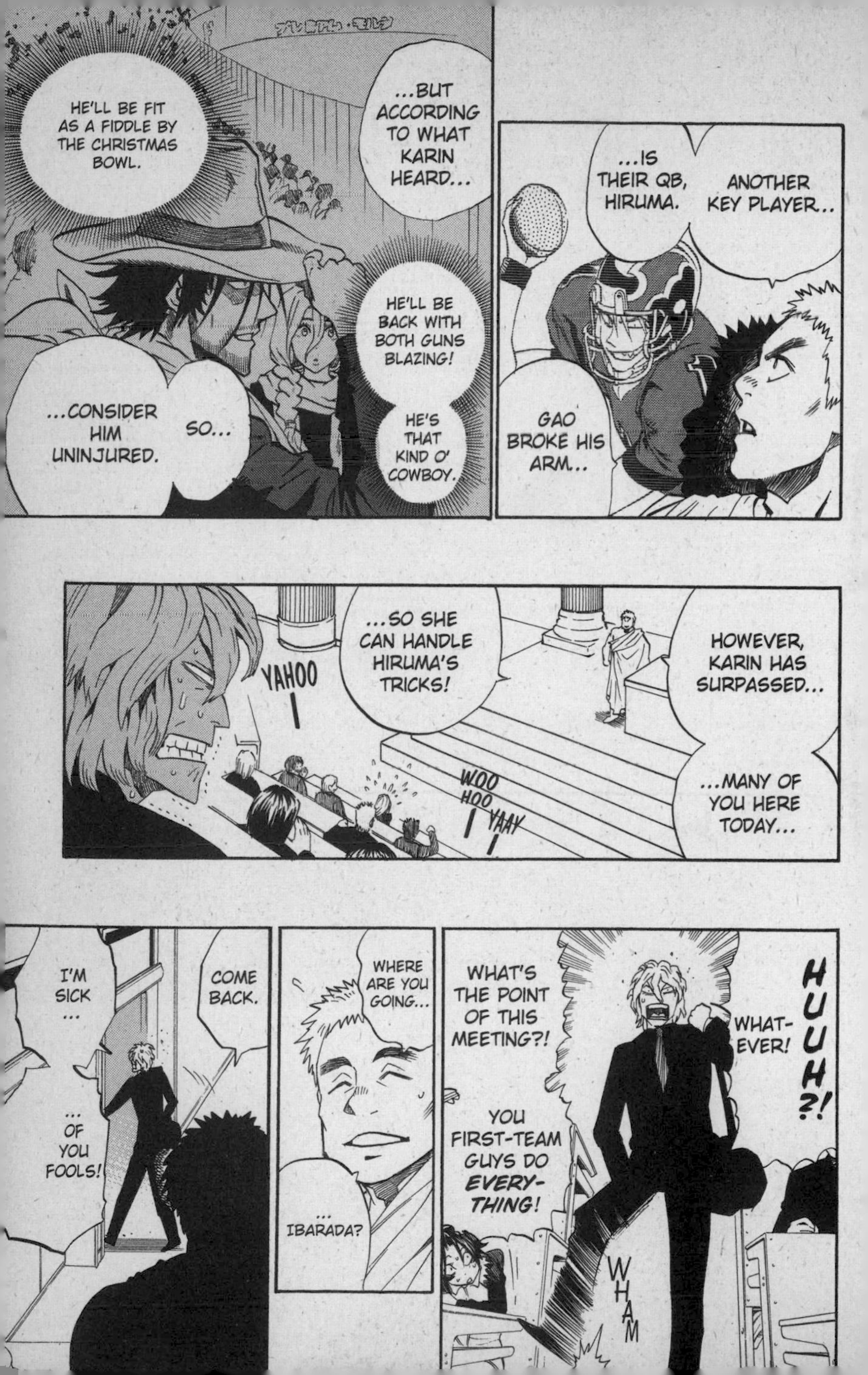
ANOTHER KEY PLAYER...
...IS THEIR QB, HIRUMA.
GAO BROKE HIS ARM...
...BUT ACCORDING TO WHAT KARIN HEARD...
HE'LL BE FIT AS A FIDDLE BY THE CHRISTMAS BOWL.
HE'LL BE BACK WITH BOTH GUNS BLAZING!
HE'S THAT KIND O' COWBOY.
SO...
...CONSIDER HIM UNINJURED.
HOWEVER, KARIN HAS SURPASSED...
...MANY OF YOU HERE TODAY...
...SO SHE CAN HANDLE HIRUMA'S TRICKS!
WOO HOO
YAAY
YAHOO
HUUH?!
WHAT-EVER!
WHAT'S THE POINT OF THIS MEETING?!
YOU FIRST-TEAM GUYS DO *EVERY-THING!*
WHAM
WHERE ARE YOU GOING...
...IBARADA?
COME BACK.
I'M SICK...
...OF YOU FOOLS!

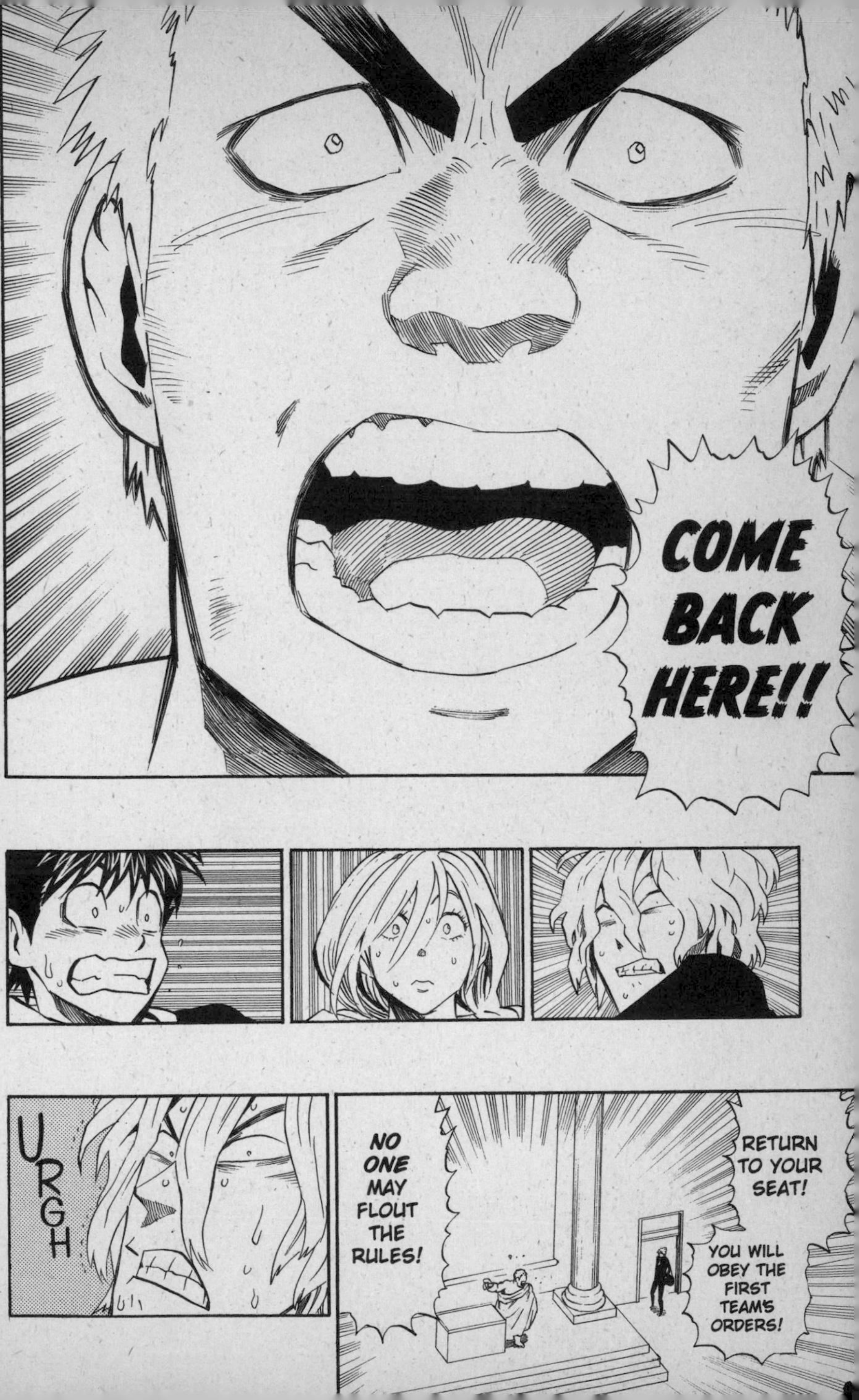
COME BACK HERE!!
RETURN TO YOUR SEAT!
YOU WILL OBEY THE FIRST TEAM'S ORDERS!
NO ONE MAY FLOUT THE RULES!
...
URGH

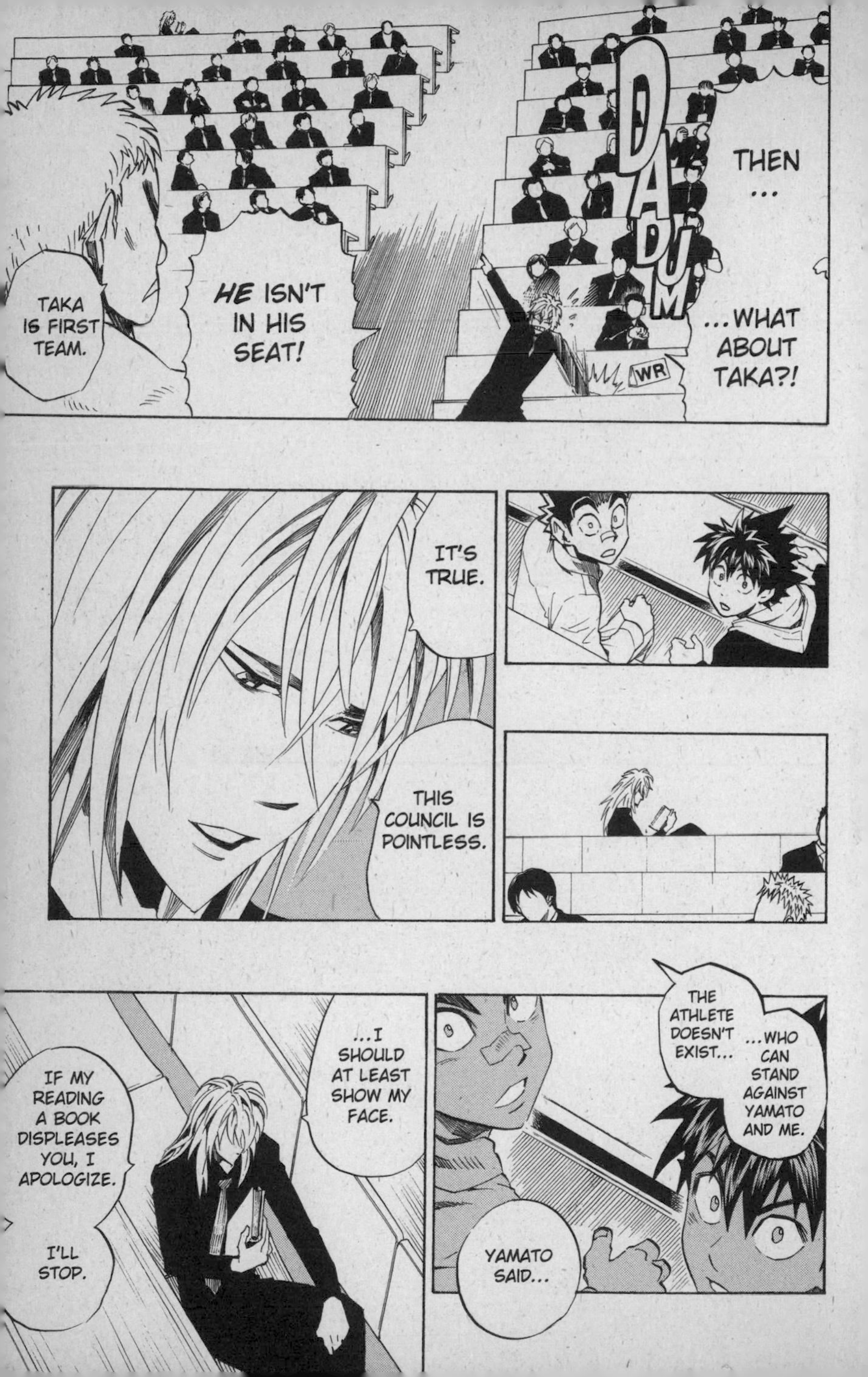
THEN ...
DADUM
WR
...WHAT ABOUT TAKA?!
TAKA IS FIRST TEAM.
HE ISN'T IN HIS SEAT!
IT'S TRUE.
THIS COUNCIL IS POINTLESS.
THE ATHLETE DOESN'T EXIST...
...WHO CAN STAND AGAINST YAMATO AND ME.
YAMATO SAID...
...I SHOULD AT LEAST SHOW MY FACE.
IF MY READING A BOOK DISPLEASES YOU, I APOLOGIZE.
I'LL STOP.

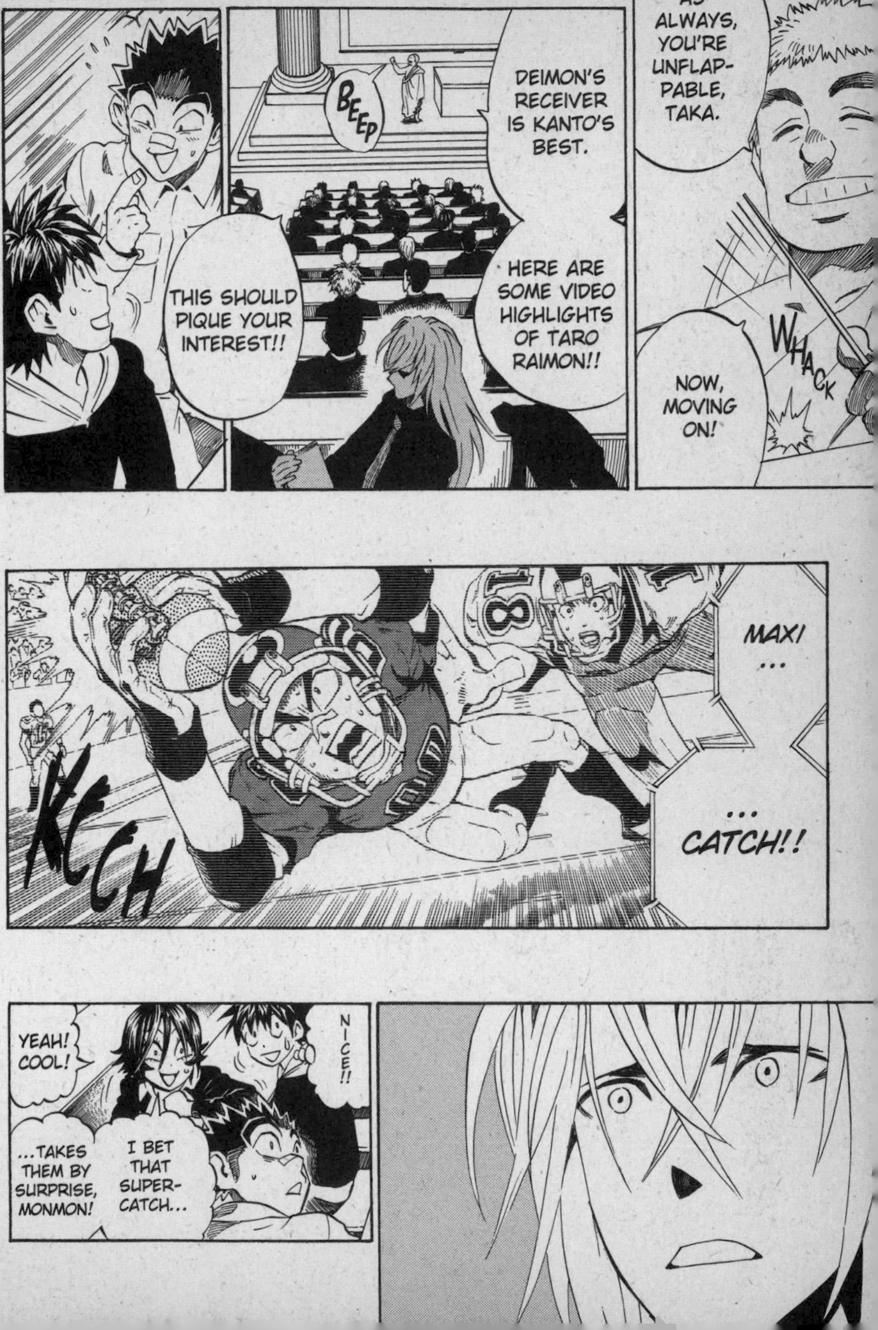
AS ALWAYS, YOU'RE UNFLAP-PABLE, TAKA.
WHACK
NOW, MOVING ON!
DEIMON'S RECEIVER IS KANTO'S BEST.
BEEP
HERE ARE SOME VIDEO HIGHLIGHTS OF TARO RAIMON!!
THIS SHOULD PIQUE YOUR INTEREST!!
MAXI ...
... CATCH!!
KCCH
NICE!!
YEAH! COOL!
I BET THAT SUPER-CATCH...
...TAKES THEM BY SURPRISE, MONMON!

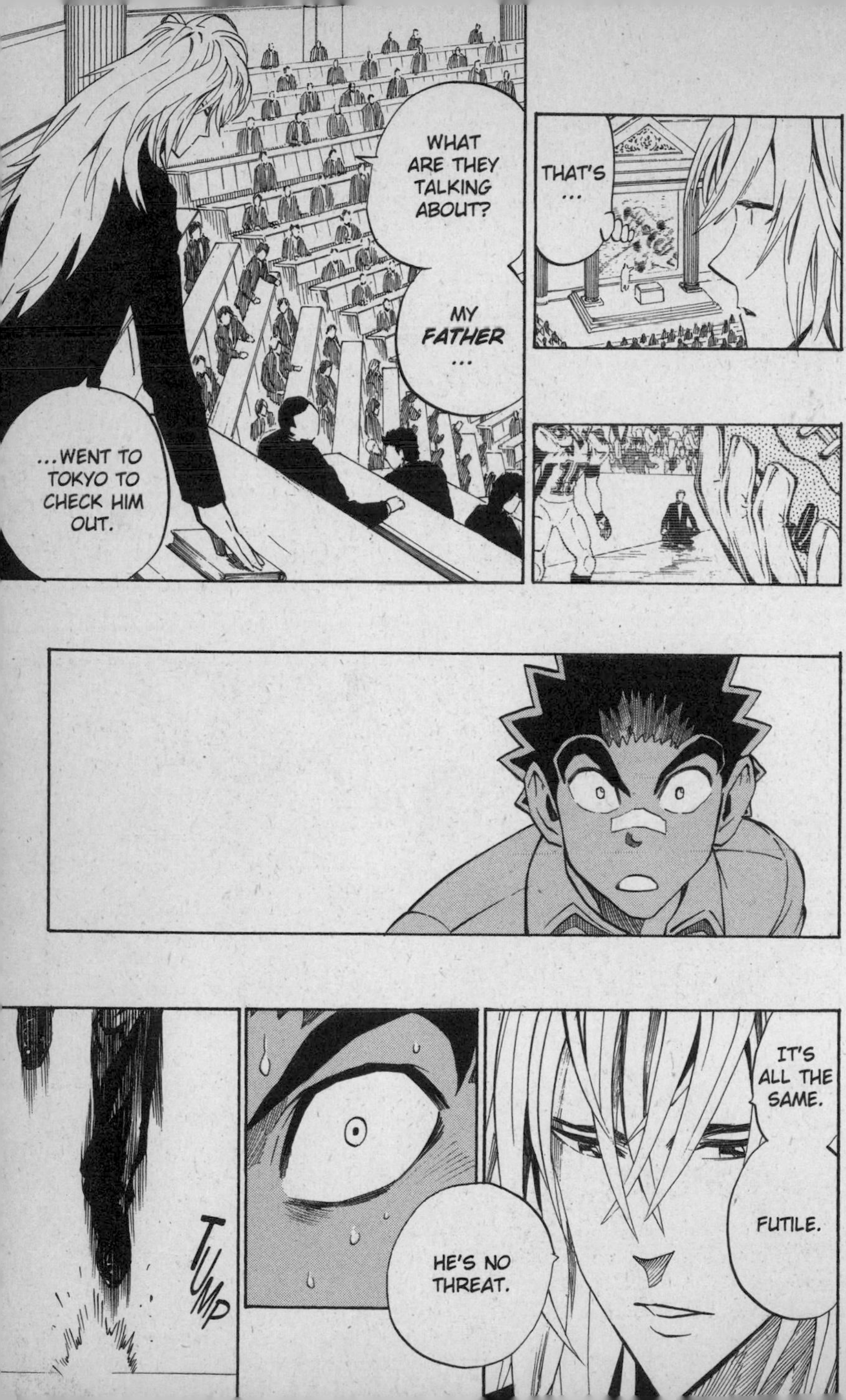
THAT'S ...
WHAT ARE THEY TALKING ABOUT?
MY FATHER ...
...WENT TO TOKYO TO CHECK HIM OUT.
IT'S ALL THE SAME.
FUTILE.
HE'S NO THREAT.
TUMP

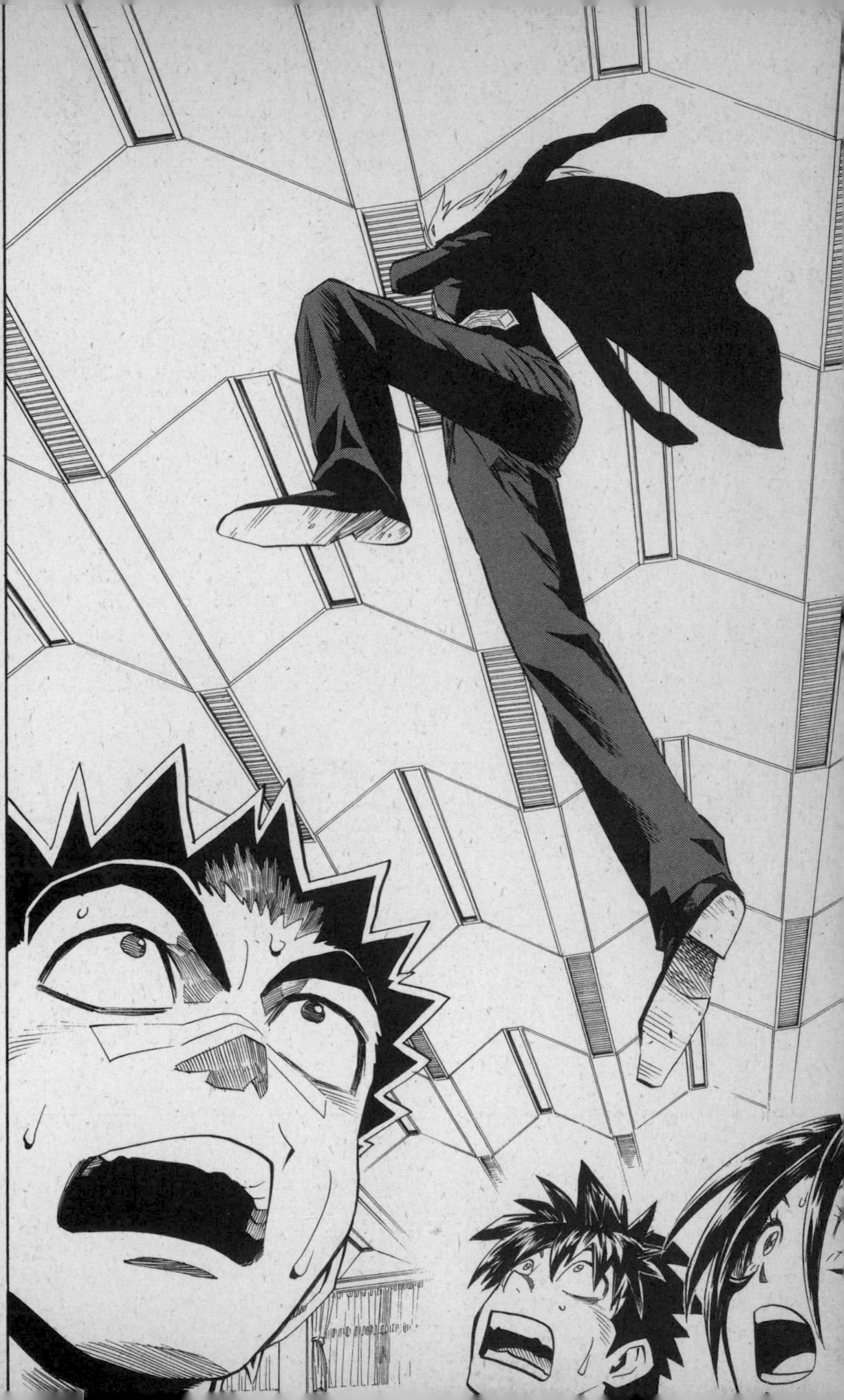

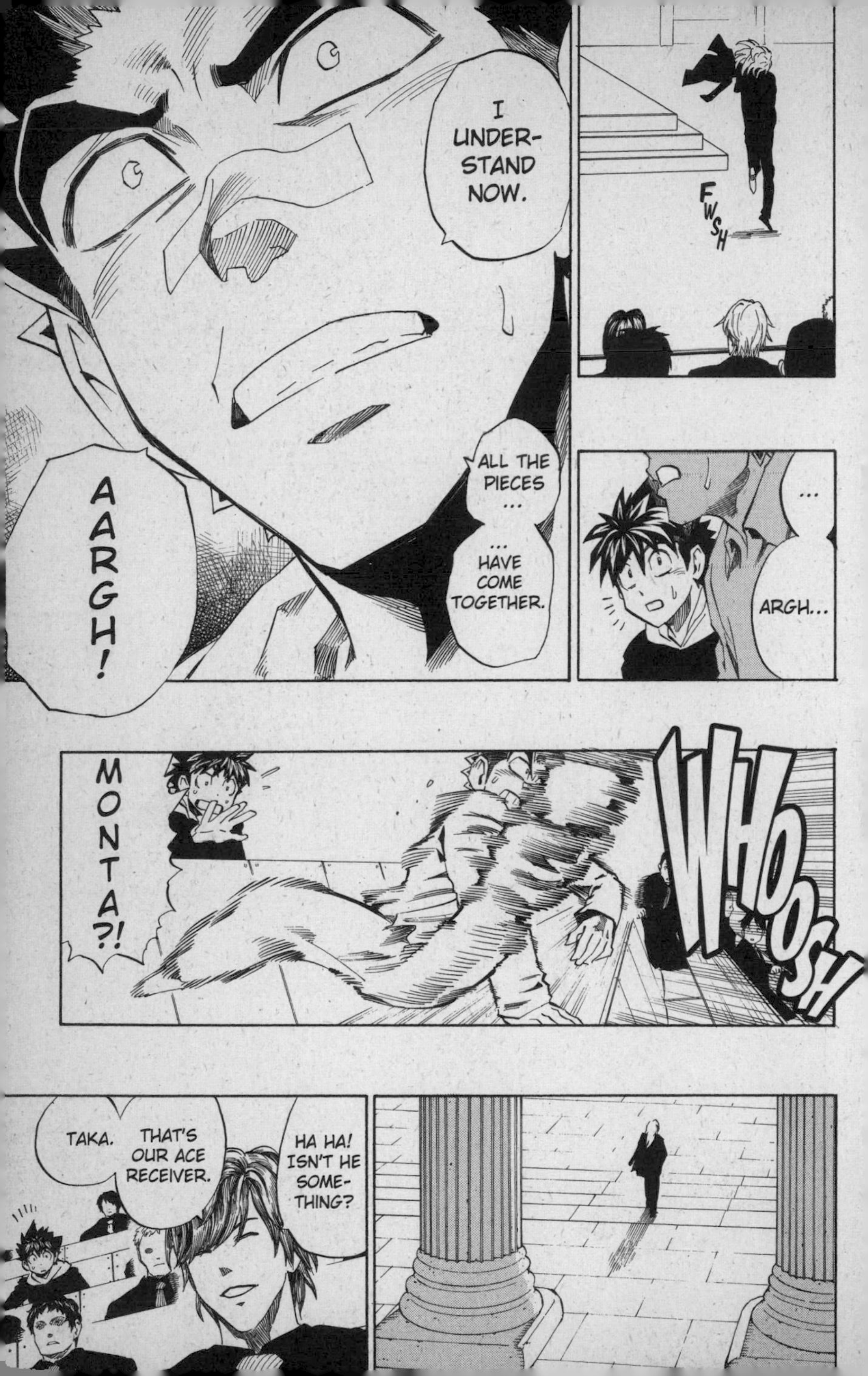
FWSH
...
ARGH...
I UNDER-STAND NOW.
ALL THE PIECES ...
... HAVE COME TOGETHER.
AARGH!
WHOOSH
MONTA?!
HA HA! ISN'T HE SOME-THING?
THAT'S OUR ACE RECEIVER.
TAKA.

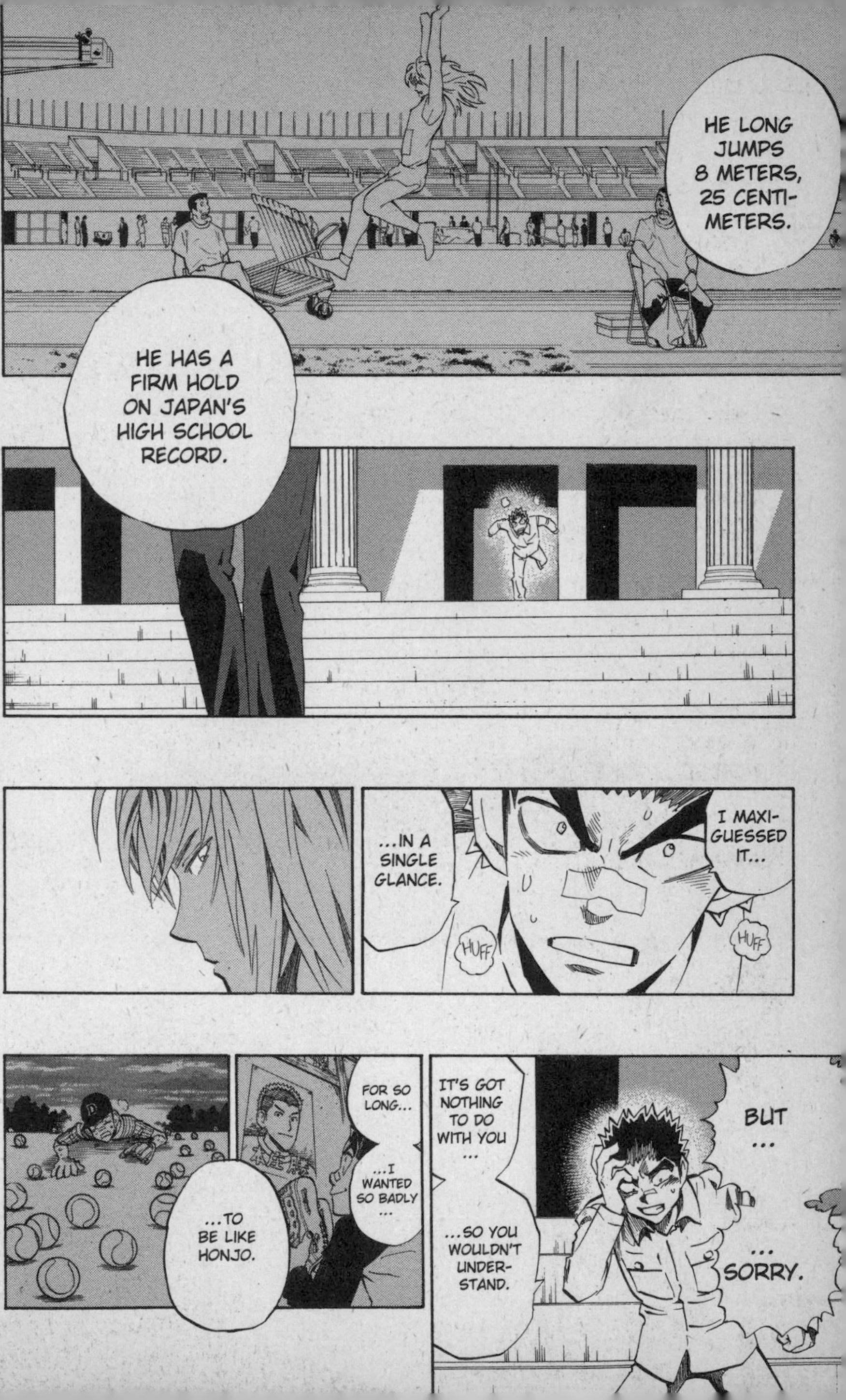
HE LONG JUMPS 8 METERS, 25 CENTI-METERS.
HE HAS A FIRM HOLD ON JAPAN'S HIGH SCHOOL RECORD.
I MAXI-GUESSED IT...
...IN A SINGLE GLANCE.
HUFF
HUFF
BUT ...
... SORRY.
IT'S GOT NOTHING TO DO WITH YOU ...
...SO YOU WOULDN'T UNDER-STAND.
FOR SO LONG...
...I WANTED SO BADLY ...
...TO BE LIKE HONJO.

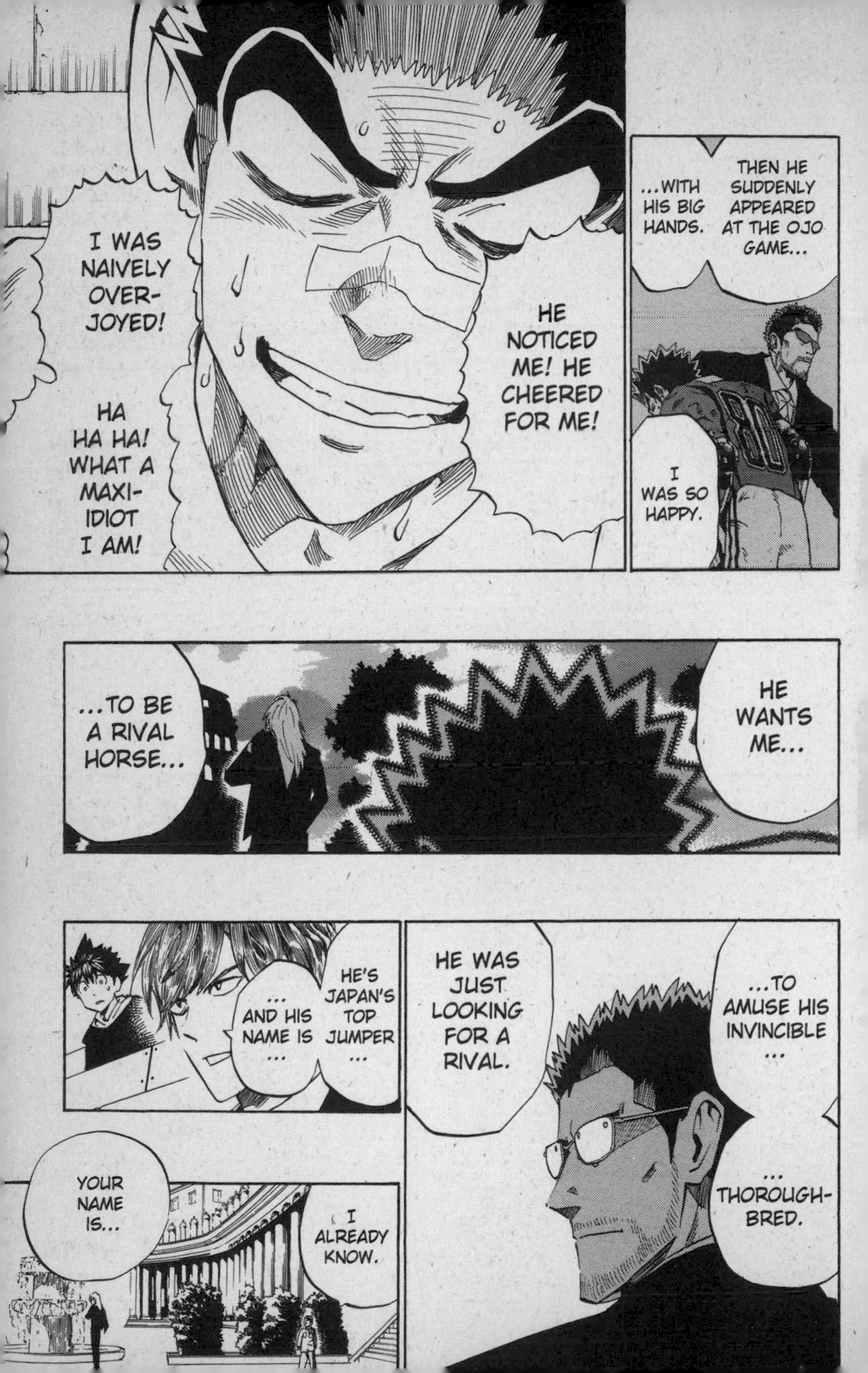
THEN HE SUDDENLY APPEARED AT THE OJO GAME...
...WITH HIS BIG HANDS.
I WAS SO HAPPY.
HE NOTICED ME! HE CHEERED FOR ME!
I WAS NAIVELY OVER-JOYED!
HA HA HA! WHAT A MAXI-IDIOT I AM!
HE WANTS ME...
...TO BE A RIVAL HORSE...
HE WAS JUST LOOKING FOR A RIVAL.
...TO AMUSE HIS INVINCIBLE...
...THOROUGH-BRED.
HE'S JAPAN'S TOP JUMPER...
...AND HIS NAME IS...
YOUR NAME IS...
I ALREADY KNOW.

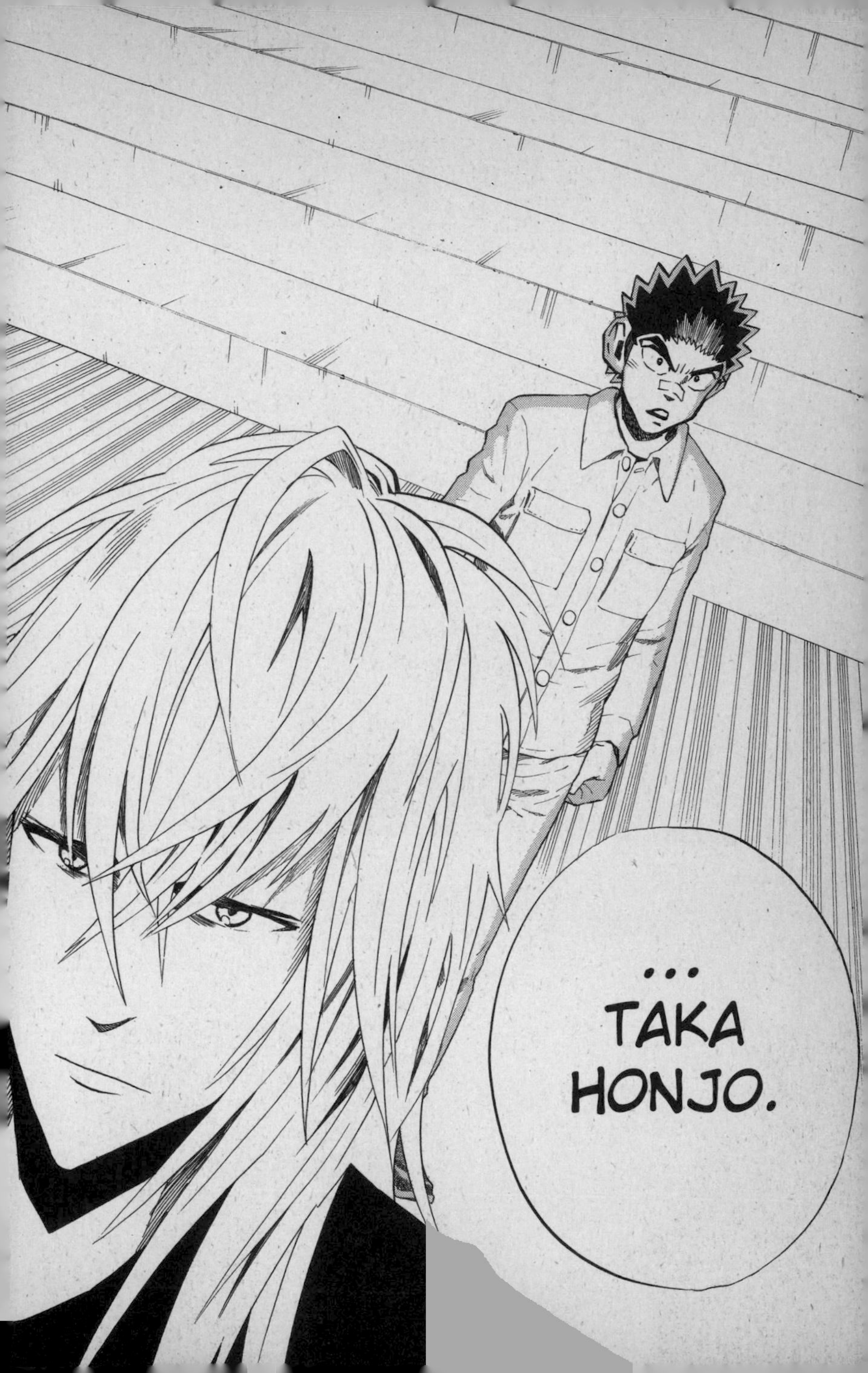
... TAKA HONJO.

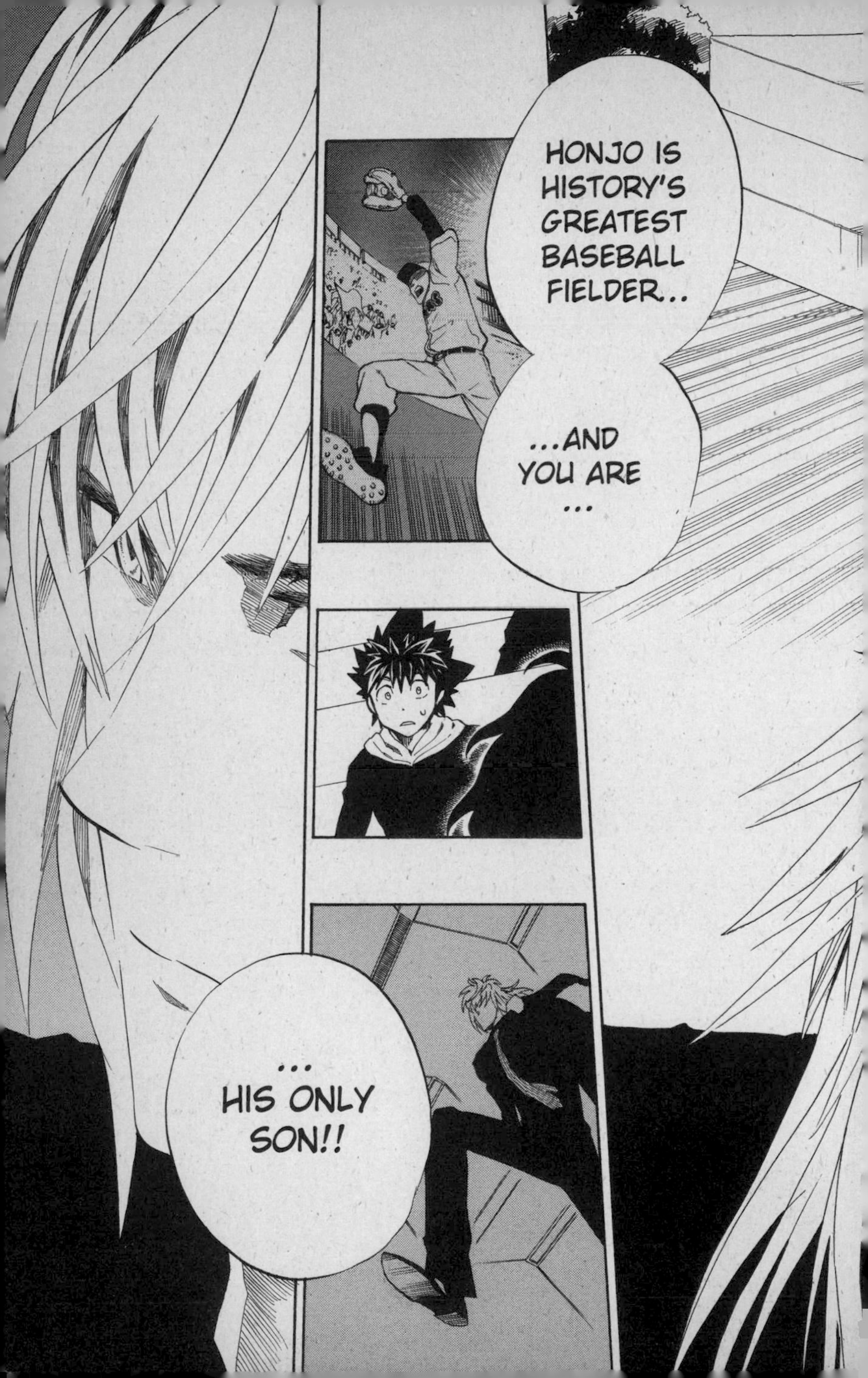
HONJO IS HISTORY'S GREATEST BASEBALL FIELDER...
...AND YOU ARE ...
... HIS ONLY SON!!

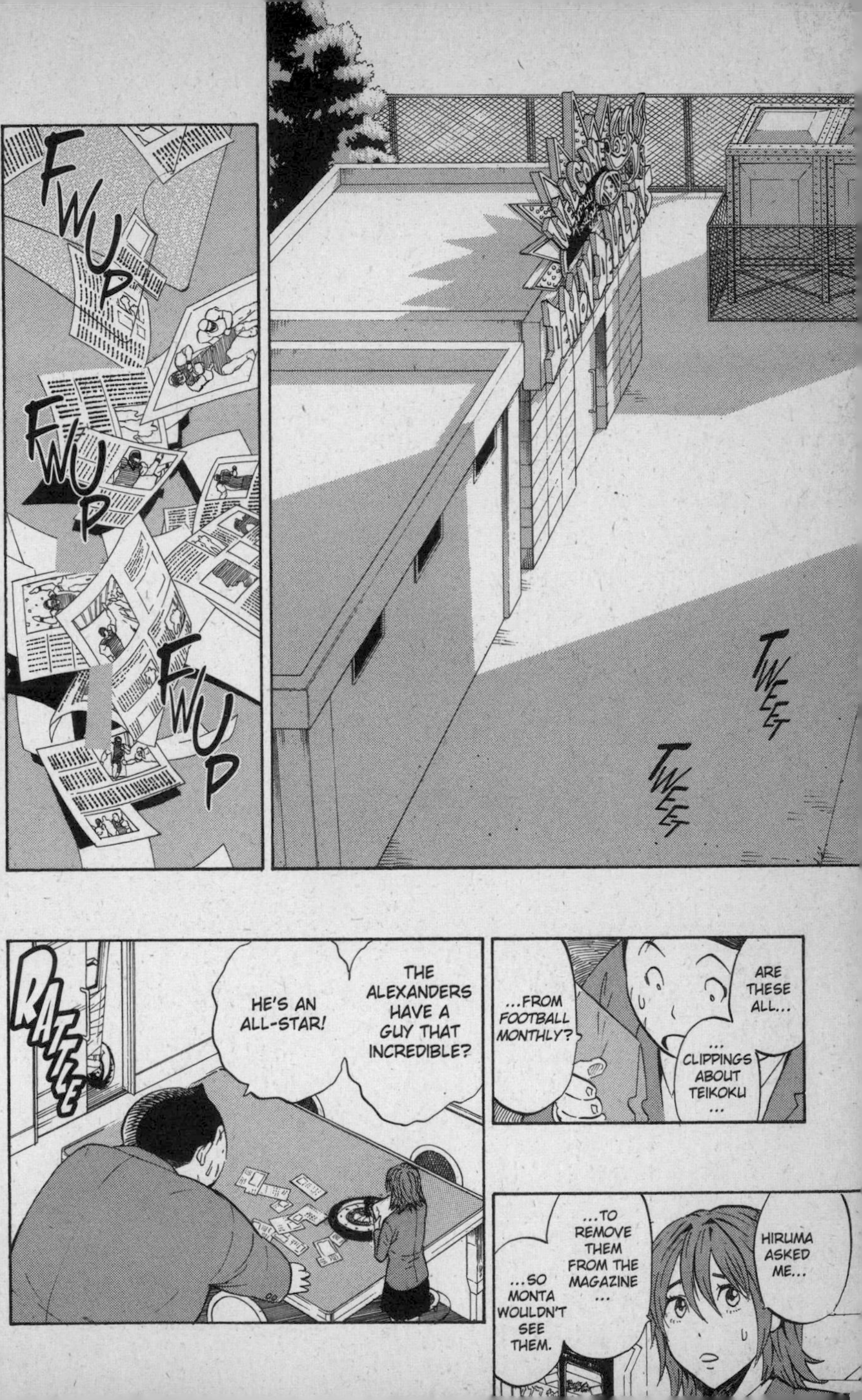
TWEET
TWEET
FWUP
FWUP
FWUP
ARE THESE ALL...
...CLIPPINGS ABOUT TEIKOKU...
...FROM FOOTBALL MONTHLY?
HIRUMA ASKED ME...
...TO REMOVE THEM FROM THE MAGAZINE...
...SO MONTA WOULDN'T SEE THEM.
THE ALEXANDERS HAVE A GUY THAT INCREDIBLE?
HE'S AN ALL-STAR!
RATTLE

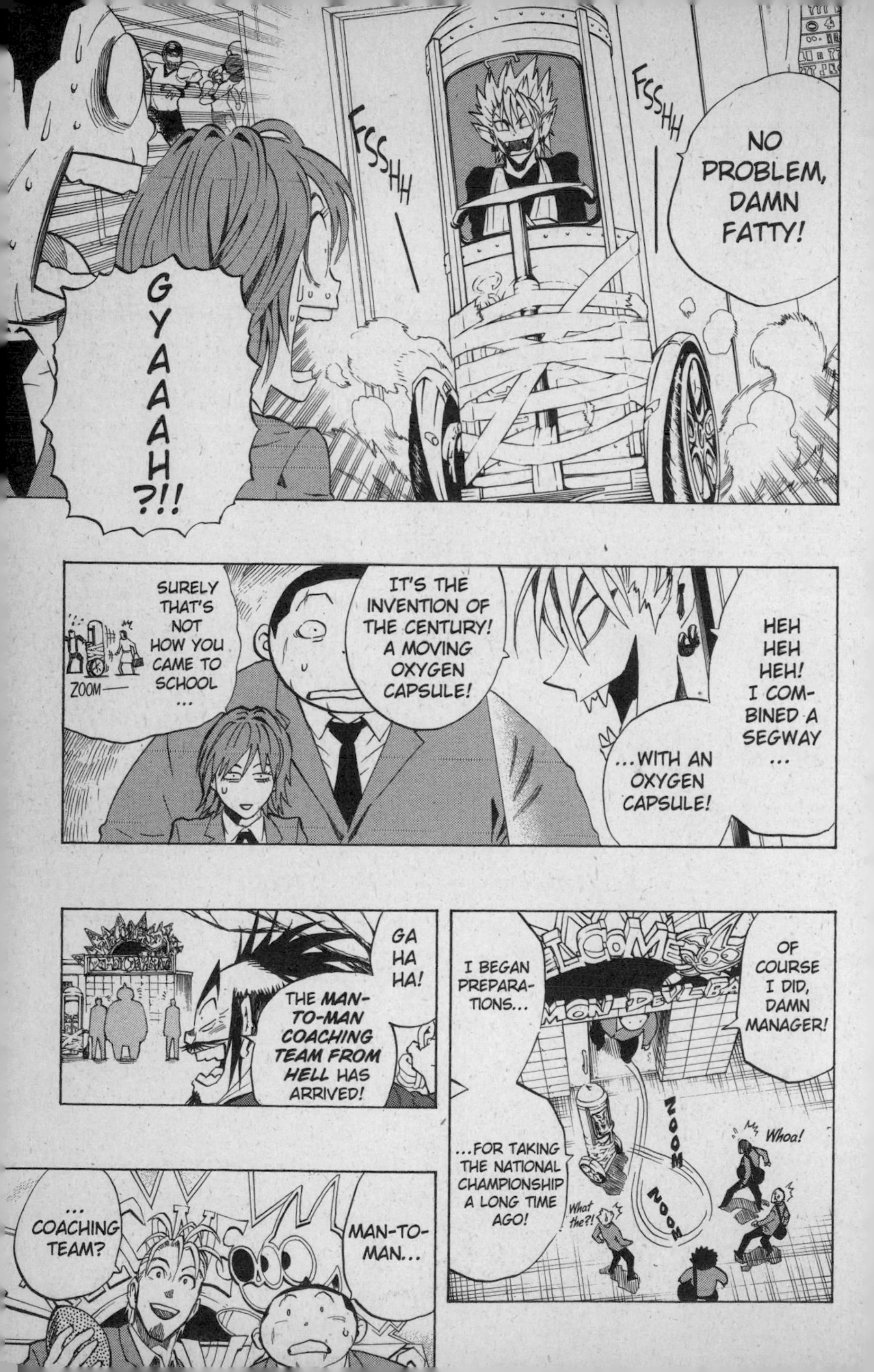
NO PROBLEM, DAMN FATTY!
FSSHH
FSSHH
GYAAAAH?!!
HEH HEH HEH! I COMBINED A SEGWAY...
...WITH AN OXYGEN CAPSULE!
IT'S THE INVENTION OF THE CENTURY! A MOVING OXYGEN CAPSULE!
SURELY THAT'S NOT HOW YOU CAME TO SCHOOL...
ZOOM
OF COURSE I DID, DAMN MANAGER!
I BEGAN PREPARATIONS...
ZOOM
Whoa!
ZOOM
...FOR TAKING THE NATIONAL CHAMPIONSHIP A LONG TIME AGO!
What the?!
GA HA HA!
THE *MAN-TO-MAN COACHING TEAM FROM HELL* HAS ARRIVED!
MAN-TO-MAN...
...COACHING TEAM?

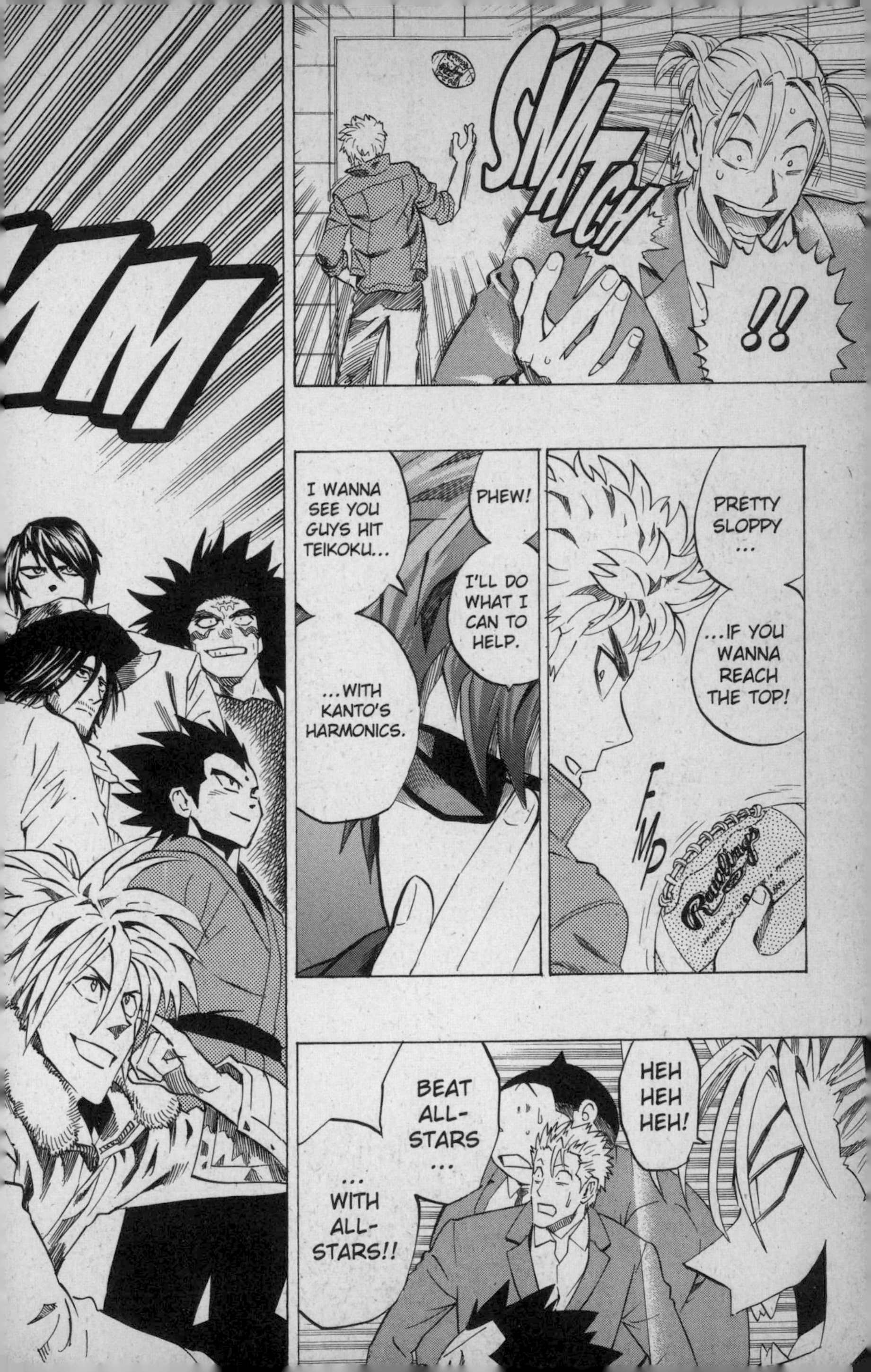
SMATCH
!!
PRETTY SLOPPY ...
...IF YOU WANNA REACH THE TOP!
FMP
PHEW!
I'LL DO WHAT I CAN TO HELP.
I WANNA SEE YOU GUYS HIT TEIKOKU...
...WITH KANTO'S HARMONICS.
HEH HEH HEH!
BEAT ALL-STARS ...
... WITH ALL-STARS!!
MM

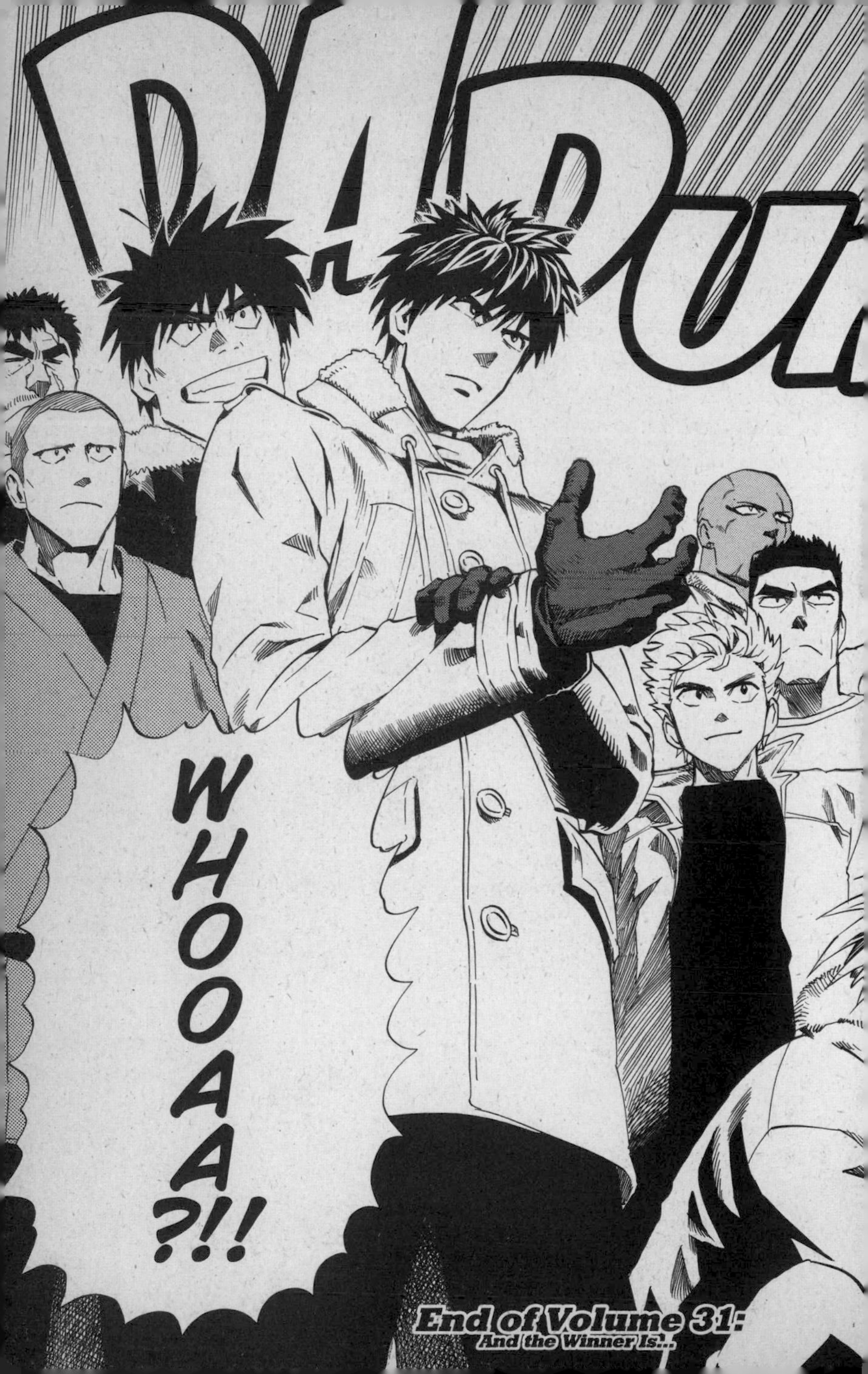
BADUM
WHOOAA?!!
End of Volume 31:
And the Winner Is...

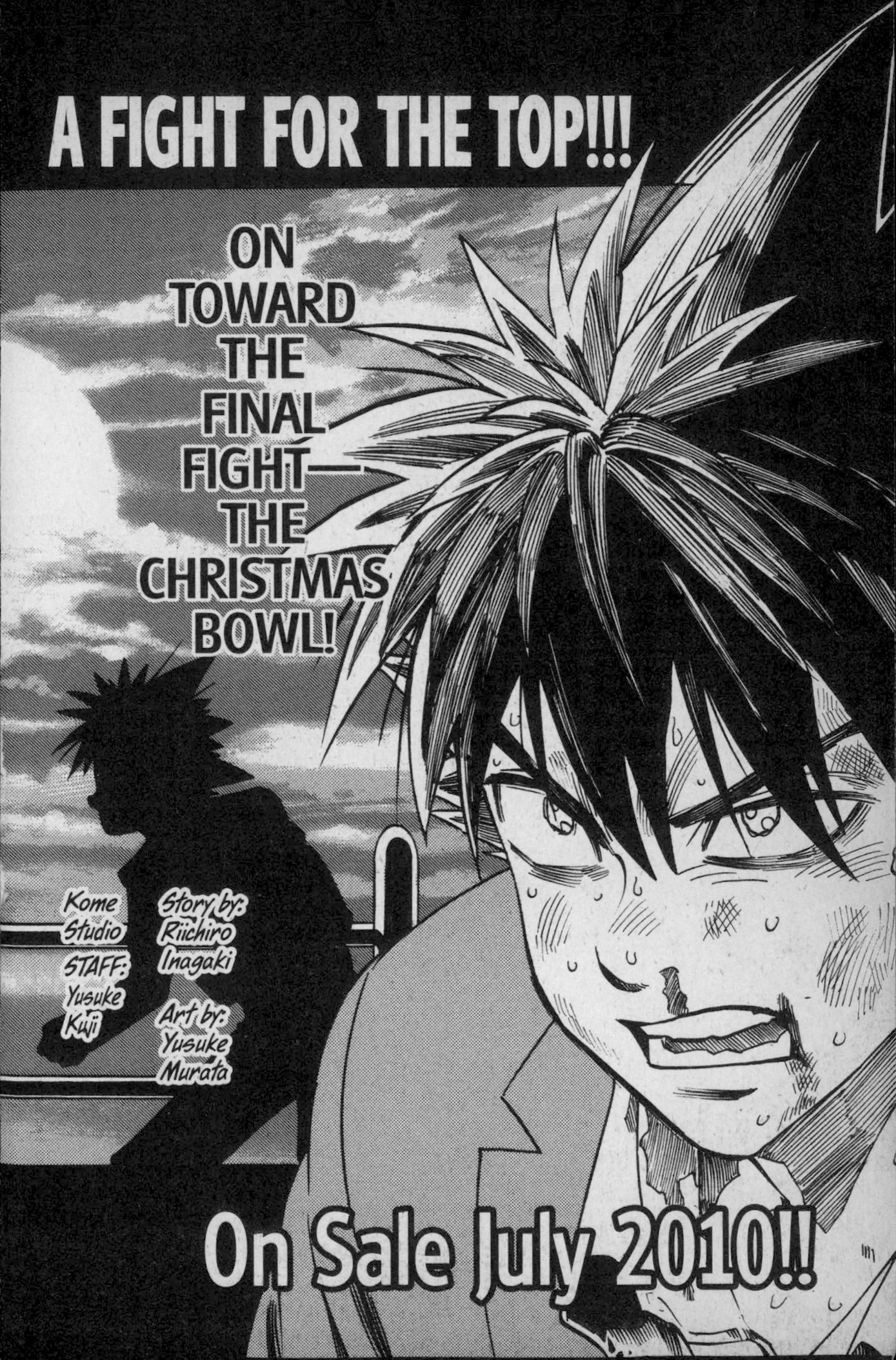
A FIGHT FOR THE TOP!!!
ON TOWARD THE FINAL FIGHT— THE CHRISTMAS BOWL!
Story by: Riichiro Inagaki
Art by: Yusuke Murata
Kome Studio STAFF: Yusuke Kuji
On Sale July 2010!!

PUPIL BATTLES MASTER IN

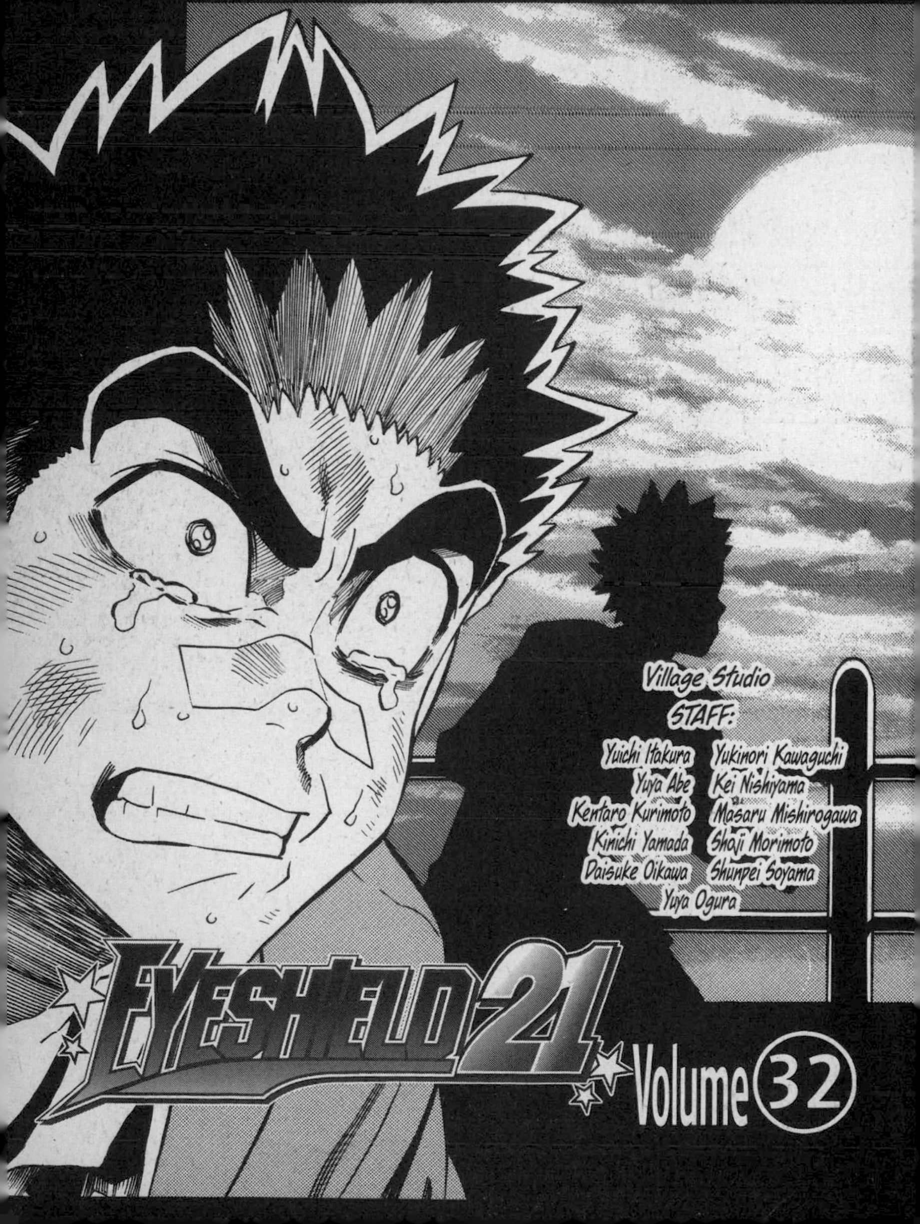
Village Studio
STAFF:
Yuichi Itakura
Yukinori Kawaguchi
Yuya Abe
Kei Nishiyama
Kentaro Kurimoto
Masaru Mishirogawa
Kinichi Yamada
Shoji Morimoto
Daisuke Oikawa
Shunpei Soyama
Yuya Ogura
EYESHIELD 21
Volume 32

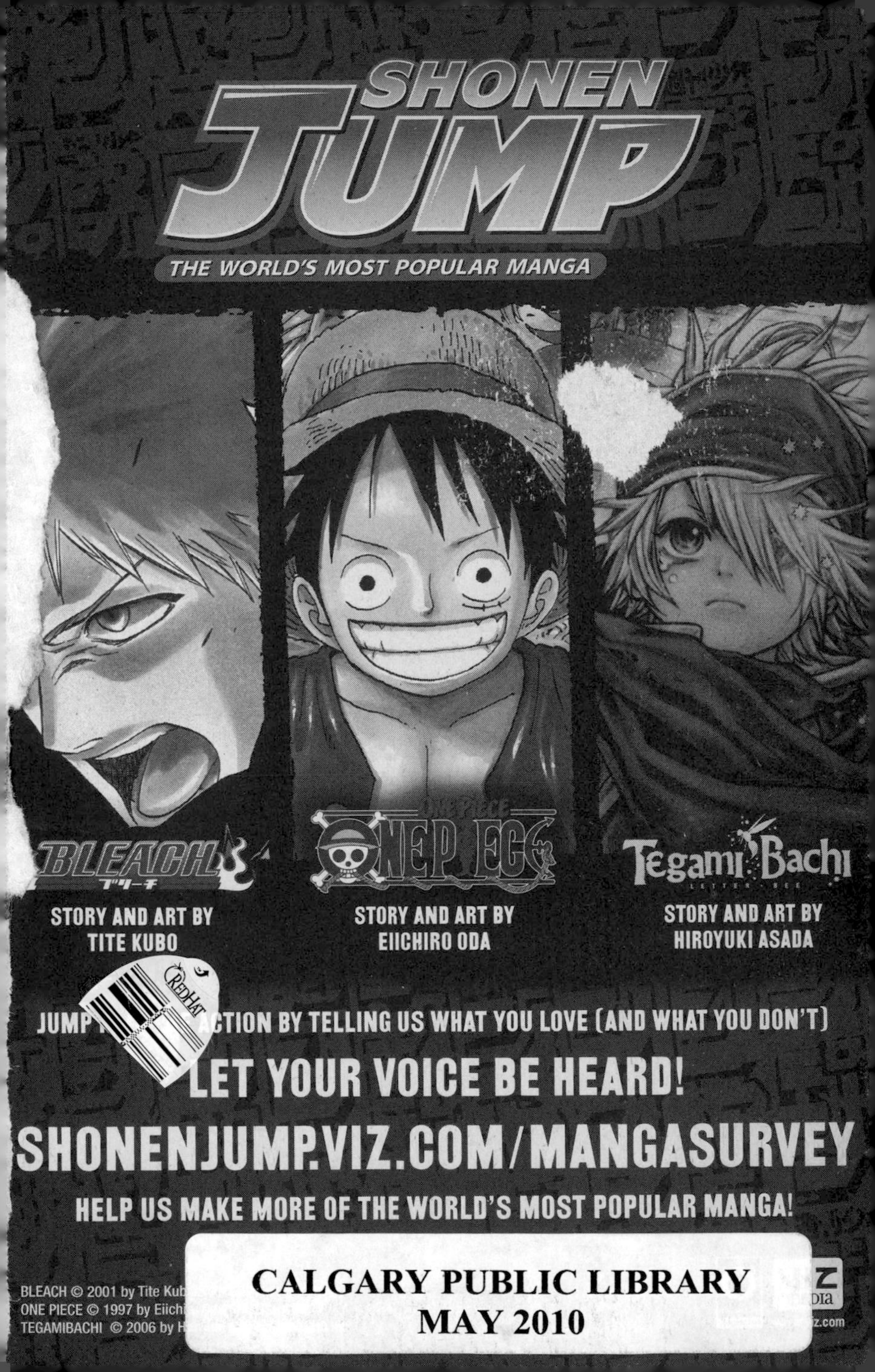
SHONEN JUMP
THE WORLD'S MOST POPULAR MANGA
BLEACH
ブリーチ
STORY AND ART BY
TITE KUBO
ONE PIECE
STORY AND ART BY
EIICHIRO ODA
Tegami Bachi
LETTER BEE
STORY AND ART BY
HIROYUKI ASADA
JUMP
ACTION BY TELLING US WHAT YOU LOVE (AND WHAT YOU DON'T)
LET YOUR VOICE BE HEARD!
SHONENJUMP.VIZ.COM/MANGASURVEY
HELP US MAKE MORE OF THE WORLD'S MOST POPULAR MANGA!
BLEACH © 2001 by Tite Kub
ONE PIECE © 1997 by Eiichi
TEGAMIBACHI © 2006 by H
iz.com